Using QuickBooks 2009

... With High Speed

College Edition-Revised

Emmanuel Ike, MBA

SOW Publishing

Using QuickBooks with High Speed *College Edition*

PO Box 702063
Dallas, TX 75370
Website: www.sowpublishing.com
E-mail: publisher@sowpublishing.com

TRADEMARKS

Intuit, the Intuit logo, Quicken, QuickBooks, TurboTax, Quicken Loan, and QuickBase, among others, are registered trademarks and/or registered service marks of Intuit Inc., in the United States and other countries. Quicken.com, Quicken Brokerage, and QuickPayroll, among others are trademarks and/or service marks of Intuit in the United States and other countries.

Microsoft office products and Microsoft Internet Explorer are registered trademarks of Microsoft Corporation in the United Sates and other countries.

ISBN 978-09770693-6-1
Library of Congress Control Number 2008908554
Printed in the United States of America.

Using QuickBooks with High Speed 2009 College Edition
SOW Publishing
Dallas, TX 75370

10 9 8 7 6 5 4 3 2 1

SOW Publishing
P.O. Box 702063, Dallas, TX 75370, USA. www.sowpublishing.com

ABOUT THE AUTHOR

Emmanuel Ike is an expert in accounting software, database management, and spreadsheet programming. He has been an accountant for more than 12 years, specializing in the areas of cash flow, asset management, and financial reporting. He consults on corporate finance, accounting, database, and credit management. As a hobby, he enjoys aggressive legal research. Mr. Ike has a Bachelor of Science degree in accounting and a master's degree in finance with honors. He also has a certificate in private investigation and holds a diploma in the legal assistant program, specializing in medical and legal research, from a prestigious law school. Mr. Ike is an author, publisher, and entrepreneur.

ACKNOWLEDGEMENTS

My un-ending whole-hearted gratitude goes to God for the incredible passion, energy, and determination to publish this book. I wish to extend a special thank-you and profound gratitude to the people at Intuit, especially the technical staff at QuickBooks for their hard work and cooperation in being market-driven and customer-focused. Over the years, QuickBooks has dominated the personal finance software market because of its unwavering determination to respond to ever-changing and ongoing customer demands for product improvements. I wish Intuit and QuickBooks strong and fruitful years ahead.

Also, a special thank-you goes to the staff, associates and consultants at SOW Publishing, including designers and editors, for the tremendous task of putting this project together. I also extend my sincere gratitude to all the professors, assistant professors, teachers, and tutors of various schools, colleges, and universities who participated in testing and fine-tuning this book.

NOTICE

Dedication

This book is dedicated to my family, especially my father who taught me wisdom, understanding, power, and concentration are the keys to success. And to my mother who taught me love, beauty, kindness, peace, and integrity are the keys to life.

After all, genius is simple!
Emmanuel Ike

Mastery is the ability to perform a task with confidence and precision acquired by training and practice. I will provide the training, you will provide the practice—and the rest is history!
Emmanuel Ike

TABLE OF CONTENTS

Introduction......1

- Free Trial QuickBooks Software
- Helpful Hints
- Navigating Tips
- QuickBooks Window Parts
- Navigating Registers and Calendars
- Installation: Welcome Appears
- Installation: No Welcome Appears

Sample Quick Company......14

- Create New Company
- Create Bank Account
- Create Liability Account
- Create Customers
- Create Vendors
- Financial Results: Profit & Loss
- Financial Results: Balance Sheet
- Chapter Summary

Chapter 1. File......23

- Review File Submenus
- Back Up
- Restore
- New Company
- New Customer
- Open Company
- Export IIF File
- Import IIF File
- Verify Data
- Save Report as PDF
- Export Report to Excel
- Delete Company
- Financial Results: Profit & Loss
- Financial Results: Balance Sheet
- Chapter Summary
- Exercise 1

Chapter 2. Edit......41

- Review Edit Submenus
- Make Entry
- Create New Check
- Void Check
- Memorize Check
- Use Notepad
- Use Calculator
- Simple Find
- Advanced Find
- Delete Check
- Accounting Preferences
- Bill, Items & Inventory
- Checking Preferences
- Finance Charge Preferences
- General Preferences
- Integrated Application & Service Connection
- Jobs & Estimates, Sales & Customers
- Payroll & Employees
- Reminders
- Reports & Graphs
- Sales Tax Preferences
- Tax: 1099, Time & Expenses
- Financial Results: Profit & Loss
- Financial Results: Balance Sheet
- Chapter Summary
- Exercise 2

Chapter 3. View......71

- Review View Submenus
- Customize Icon Bar
- Add window to Icon Bar
- Financial Results: Profit & Loss
- Financial Results: Balance Sheet
- Tax Guidelines: Starting a Business
- Tax Guidelines: Business Structures
- Tax Guidelines: Employer Identification Number
- Tax Guidelines: Business Taxes
- Tax Guidelines: Record Keeping
- Tax Guidelines: Employer Tax Record Keeping
- Chapter Summary
- Exercise 3

Chapter 4. Lists..82

- Review Lists Submenus
- Review Chart of Accounts & Item List
- Money Market Account
- Truck Accounts
- Credit Card Account
- Equity Accounts
- Income: Main Accounts
- Income: Sub Accounts
- Cost of Goods Sold: Inventory
- Operating Expense: Job Expense
- Operating Expense: Other Expense Accounts
- Merging Accounts
- Merging: Sub Accounts
- Merging: Main Accounts
- Designing Financial Statements Report
- Inventory Items
- Non Inventory Items
- Service Items: Labor
- Service Items: Subcontractor
- Fixed Asset Item List
- Price Level List
- Sales Tax Code List
- Class List
- Other Names List
- Sales Rep List
- Customer Type List
- Vendor Type List
- Job Type List
- Payment Method List
- Vehicle List
- Memorized Transaction List
- Review Basics of Account Numbers
- Financial Results: Profit & Loss
- Financial Results: Balance Sheet
- Chapter Summary
- Exercise 4

Chapter 5. Company..124

- Review Company Submenus
- Review Home Page
- Company Snapshot
- Company Information

❖ Set Up Passwords
❖ Edit User's Password
❖ Edit Admin's Password
❖ Set Closing Date
❖ Remove Closing Date
❖ Planning & Budgeting
❖ Budget Report
❖ To Do List
❖ Reminders & Alert Manager
❖ General Journal Entries
❖ Vehicle Mileage
❖ Review Principles of Journal Entries
❖ Review Month-End Journal Entries
❖ Financial Results: Profit & Loss
❖ Financial Results: Balance Sheet
❖ Chapter Summary
❖ Exercise 5

Chapter 6. Customers..156

❖ Review Customers Submenus
❖ Review Customer Center
❖ Customer Information: Adams Address
❖ Customer Information: Adams Additional Info
❖ Customer Information: Allen
❖ Customer Information: Brown
❖ Customer Information: US Machines
❖ Customer Information: Johnson
❖ Johnson's Information: Job Auto Sales
❖ Johnson's Information: Job Auto Parts
❖ Estimates
❖ Invoices
❖ Sales Receipts: Allen
❖ Sales Receipts: Brown
❖ Credit Memos/Refunds
❖ Statement Charges
❖ Finance Charges
❖ Customer Statements
❖ Customer Payments
❖ Deposit Payments
❖ Weekly Timesheet
❖ Time/Enter Single Activity
❖ Change Item Prices
❖ Delete Invoice without Payment

- Invoice with Payment
- Delete Invoice with Payment
- Accounts Receivable Graph
- Sales Graph
- Customer Balance on PDF
- Financial Results: Profit & Loss
- Financial Results: Balance Sheet
- Chapter Summary
- Exercise 6

Chapter 7. Vendors..........199

- Review Vendors Submenus
- Review Vendor Center
- Vendor Information: Telephone America
- Vendor Information: US Supplies
- Vendor Information: Payroll Services
- Purchase Order
- Inventory with Bill
- Inventory without Bill
- Enter Bill for Received Inventory
- Pay Inventory Bill
- Enter Operating Expense Bill
- Pay Operating Expense Bill
- Pay Sales Tax
- Run Sales Tax Liability Report
- Run Sales Tax Revenue Summary Report
- Physical Inventory Worksheet
- Inventory Adjustment Accounts
- Inventory Adjustment
- Tax Form 1099 & 1096 Reports
- Delete Bill without Payment
- Bill with Payment
- Delete Bill with Payment
- Accounts Payable Graph
- Vendor Balance on PDF
- Financial Results: Profit & Loss
- Financial Results: Balance Sheet
- Chapter Summary
- Exercise 7

Chapter 8. Employees..........231

- Review Employees Submenus
- Review Employee Center

- Free Trial Payroll Subscription
- Hourly
- Overtime & Sick Hourly
- Vacation Hourly
- Salary
- Commission & Bonus
- Job & Mileage Reimbursement
- Insurance
- Taxes
- Sick Leave
- Fate's Information
- Fate's Taxes, Sick & Vacation
- Jerry's Information
- Jerry's Taxes, Sick & Vacation
- Time Tracking
- Pay Fate Acres
- Pay Jerry Jordan
- Print Pay Stubs
- Fate's Pay Stub
- Jerry's Pay Stub
- Manage Payroll Items
- Pay Payroll Liabilities
- Financial Results: Profit & Loss
- Financial Results: Balance Sheet
- Chapter Summary
- Exercise 8

Chapter 9. Banking..266

- Review Banking Submenus
- Write Checks
- Enter Credit Card Charges
- Print Single Checks
- Print Batch Checks
- Go To Register
- Register Reports
- Edit Check Register
- Register QuickReport
- Sort Register
- Split Entry
- Make Deposits
- Transfer Funds
- Loan Manager: Accounts
- Loan Manager: Lender

- ❖ Loan Calculator
- ❖ Loan Manager: Loan
- ❖ Bank Statement
- ❖ General Journal Entry
- ❖ Bank Reconciliation
- ❖ Financial Results: Profit & Loss
- ❖ Financial Results: Balance Sheet
- ❖ Review Bank Reconciliation Steps
- ❖ Review Bank Reconciliation Journal Entries
- ❖ Chapter Summary
- ❖ Exercise 9

Chapter 10. Reports..304

- ❖ Review Reports Submenus
- ❖ Review Report Center
- ❖ Process Multiple Reports
- ❖ Company & Financial
- ❖ Income & Expense Graph
- ❖ Customers & Receivables
- ❖ Sales
- ❖ Jobs, Time & Mileage
- ❖ Vendors & Payables
- ❖ Purchases
- ❖ Inventory
- ❖ Employees & Payroll
- ❖ Banking
- ❖ Accountant & Taxes
- ❖ Budgets
- ❖ List
- ❖ Transaction History
- ❖ Transaction Journal
- ❖ Print Forms
- ❖ Send Forms
- ❖ Financial Results: Profit & Loss
- ❖ Financial Results: Balance Sheet
- ❖ Chapter Summary

Chapter 11. Window..331

- ❖ Review Window Submenus
- ❖ Close All

Chapter 12. Help..334

- Review QuickBooks Help Submenus
- Review Learning Center Tutorials
- QuickBooks Help
- Year-End Guides
- Financial Results: Profit & Loss
- Financial Results: Balance Sheet
- Chapter Summary

Index..343

Please Note! This book was written on QuickBooks Pro 2009 and may be used on the QuickBooks 2007 and 2008 with no adverse effects on financial results.

PREFACE

Time and again, evaluation after evaluation, students like to practice what they are learning. It is in answer to this need for a hands-on training manual that we introduce the *Using QuickBooks with High Speed 2009 College Edition.* It is not enough to read text after text without really feeling the confidence of learning by doing. We could have easily stretched this book to 750 pages; instead, we gave each student a practical tool of how to use QuickBooks. This text book was written on QuickBooks Pro 2009 software; however, it may be used on the QuickBooks 2008 software version with no adverse effects on the financial results generated.

OBJECTIVE

The primary stated objective and goal of this textbook is to remove any fear a student might have in using accounting software. To this end, the textbook will avoid any situation that defeats this purpose. The textbook is responding to a growing market of students who want to learn accounting software but cannot, because most learning tools are too complex, sophisticated, and downright scary for them. By using real numbers we hope to bridge the gap of timidity and increase the confidence of everyone who is drawn to the study of accounting by computer.

By providing user-friendly material, this text can increase the student's learning curve. In the end, a student will be familiar with the fundamentals of accounting and can become acclimated easily to any other accounting software.

UNIQUE FEATURES

The chapter materials are arranged according to the QuickBooks software menus to make it easier for a student to follow. By arranging the chapters in sequential order according to the software, the textbook focuses on implementing as many submenus as possible.

Each chapter starts with a review of all the submenus under each menu, and under each title page there is an explanation of **why** certain tasks react the way they do. This is followed by instructions of **how** to perform the task, and lastly there are financial statements that test students on **what** happened. Additionally, this text uses real numbers and names that students can relate to. So in the future, an individual is able to re-create accounting data and information presented in the book. The pinnacle of every chapter is the end-of-chapter financial results and summary, which focus on the activities of the respective chapter. The self-confidence generated when a student completes a chapter with accurate financial results is overwhelming.

INSTRUCTOR'S SUPPORT

The textbook is strict about financial results and has done everything to encourage students and teachers within that framework. The instructor's manual is a comprehensive material of financial results, exercises, questions—true and false, as well as multiple choices—and examinations, all with answer keys.

Using QuickBooks with High Speed 2009 College Edition is an integrated hands-on manual that is oriented toward accurate results; therefore, an instructor's support is of utmost importance.

CREDIT COURSES

Using QuickBooks with High Speed 2009 College Edition is a featured textbook in accounting by computer, computerized accounting, microcomputer accounting, and practical accounting courses and labs. The text is used for one to three credit-hour courses and can be completed within one semester. If a student can point and click, he or she will be able to use the textbook with speed and confidence.

INTRODUCTION

I was teaching a group of students, and I asked them if they would like to learn the theory in class, and then go home to practice the book, or if they would like to review each chapter and then practice the book in class. Practicing in class would allow me to watch and make sure they do everything right. Overwhelmingly they answered that they wanted to practice the book in class. Generally, students like more practice and less reading.

If you want to learn how to drive, you don't go to a classroom and sit for months reading volumes of books on how to start the engine and press the gas. The best way to learn how to drive is to review the fundamentals of driving and then go outside and drive. You learn by just driving! What about swimming? You don't sit in a classroom listening to tapes, watching videos, and analyzing charts and graphs about successful swimming. You learn how to swim by just swimming, not by reading a bunch of technical manuals on swimming.

This book teaches you how to use QuickBooks. It takes a different approach from other books by reviewing each software menu and allowing users to practice with real numbers. In so doing, students will become proficient with QuickBooks. What you will be doing in QuickBooks are keying in numbers, completing windows, running reports, and analyzing results. This is a result-driven textbook, an experiential learning tool that leads individuals to a predictable, accurate outcome.

The two driving forces of this book are speed and accuracy. You probably don't have time to flip through accounting manuals that are too complex to understand, that leaves you empty not knowing where to start or what to do next. I've arranged this book according to the menus and submenus in the QuickBooks software to increase your speed of mastery. I've written this book with real examples so you can understand what is going on and be able to follow accordingly.

In no time you will be creating files, accounts, customers, vendors, and writing checks—all with real numbers! Not only that, you will be reconciling bank statements, doing journal entries, and printing reports—easily and effortlessly, guaranteed! If you can click your mouse, you can use this book—that's how easy it is! My goal is to get you up and running with QuickBooks in a matter of minutes. QuickBooks is one the most powerful pieces of financial software in the market today, and my job is to show you how to use it to control the accounting traffic. I've worked with small, medium, and large companies, and the single thread that runs through the most successful ones, without exception, is absolute financial control.

I've made the process easy to increase your confidence. When you start printing your financial reports, you will be amazed how clearly your financial picture will become, and when you start managing your finances with ease and confidence, I will have succeeded!

— Emmanuel Ike

Free Trial QuickBooks Software

If you want QuickBooks Pro, it is better to buy the full version from the store or from the Internet by going to www.quickbooks.com. However, if you are in a hurry and want to practice at home immediately, you can download the Simple Start trial version, by going the Internet. When you open the download window, under the Simple Start image, click the Learn More… link to read what features the Simple Start can or cannot do. You need enough computer space to download the software. It is faster to use the high speed internet (DSL) for this process.

Intuit, the makers of Quicken, QuickBooks and Online Payroll will like students to try their products, and see how easy, fast, flexible and yet comprehensive they are; I have confident that you will make Intuit products your number one choice.

- Open the Internet
- Address: Type **www.quickbooks.com**. Press **Enter**
- In the **Select** box (left of the window): Type **trial version**. Press **Enter**
- Click **QuickBooks Trial Products**
- Click **Download** under **Simple Start** image
- Email: Type your email address
- Click **Start Download**
- Click **Save** on File Download window
- Click **Save** on Save As window
- As soon as the Save As window disappears, go to the desktop
- Double click **Setup QuickBooks** Icon on your desktop
- QuickBooks Simple Start Direct.exe will start to download
- When download is completed
- Click **Finish**

Helpful Hints

- You may skip the review pages and go directly to the activity pages, and it is not necessary for you to read the explanations at the top of the activity pages before practicing the instructions. It's easier to run your left finger through the practice activities (if you're right-handed) while you click in the QuickBooks window, to make sure you don't skip a line.

- When you see a phrase followed by a colon, you have to look for that phrase in the window currently in front of you. The colon will be followed by activities of what you're required to do such as type, click, select, accept, or checkmark.

- When an instruction says to checkmark a box, click an option or select a word or phrase. If the box is already checkmarked, or the option is already clicked, or the word or phrase is already selected, just go to the next instruction, and not remove the checkmark, the click or the selection in the window. Keep your eyes open and not mix Save & Close with Save & New

- When an instruction says to type a word or phrase in a text box, if the word is already typed, just skip the activity and go to the next instruction. Just make sure the word or phrase is entirely what is required. For example, if the instruction says, "Type Quick Company 2009." If you see only "Quick Company," make sure you add the "2009" to complete the instruction.

- For best results, the year on this book and the year of the QuickBooks software you're using must be the same. You must use the names, numbers, and especially the dates in this book.

- From time to time you will see "Very Important" at the end of an instruction. It's absolutely necessary that you perform the instruction exactly as shown and not skip it to receive the intended results.

- Only essential and relevant activities you need are included. Do not worry about empty boxes or defaulted statements not included in the activities.

- Be sure to complete all the activities in each section, irrespective of screen shots, charts, and other inserts in the middle of the activities.

Navigation Tips

I urge you to read this entire section before using this book. The section is included to enable you navigate through your QuickBooks software with ease. Every effort has been made to ensure your journey with QuickBooks is exciting and rewarding. Some helpful hints are repeated in this section for a purpose. Like a new automobile, you'll need to get used to the features and know where they are located. As soon as this is taken care of, the rest is history! Relax and enjoy the ride!

- **Common Sense:** As you go through these windows, you will see a lot of default information. When in doubt, accept the default QuickBooks is suggesting. You can override it only if you know a better option. The more you practice, the more your speed, comprehension, and expertise will increase. Remember: Practice makes perfect!

- **Colon:** You will see many phrases that are followed by a colon (:). The statement before the colon is found in the window you've just opened, whether a small or big window! The statement after the colon is the activity you have to perform such as: Type, Select, Read, or Accept. For example, as in the image above, you will see, "Company name**:** Type Quick Payroll" Look for "Company name" in the window, and then type "Quick Payroll."
- **Accept:** Sometimes, QuickBooks will default words or information in a box

or a field for you, and the instruction will be to accept what is given. In that case, I will include the word "Accept." For example, as in the image above, "Country: Accept U.S." For Country, the instruction is asking you to accept U.S. All you need to do is make sure the information in the box or field is U.S. If QuickBooks defaults another word other than U.S., you must change it to U.S. before you leave the area. I have included only the activities you need, and have ignored irrelevant empty boxes and defaulted statements. Hence, do not worry about empty boxes or defaulted statements not in the activities.

- **Checkmark:** When the instruction is to checkmark an option, a box, or phrase, be sure there is a checkmark in the option or box before you leave that window. If you see a checkmark already in the option or box, go to the next instruction, and do not remove the checkmark already on the option, box, or the phrase. Sometimes, there will be an option or a check box beside a phrase and if you're told to click the option of the phrase, checkmark the box, not just the phrase itself.

- **Type:** An instruction may require you to type information in a field or box. If the information is already in that box or field, just make sure it says exactly what you're told to type, and then go the next instruction. For example, if the instruction is to "Type Quick Payroll," if Quick Payroll is already in the field or box, confirm that it says "Quick Payroll." As soon as you've confirmed the information is correct, go on to the next instruction.

- **Select:** Sometimes, the instruction will tell you to select a word or a number from a drop-down window, if you know the first letter of the first word, it is recommended that you press it on the keyboard to pull up the entire word. For example, as in the image above, you can press "T" twice to select Texas. Also, if the word you are told to select is already in the box or window, just make sure it's the right word or number, then keep going.

- **Click:** When the instruction is to click a word or phrase in a drop-down window, if that word or phrase has a checkmark already on it, do not click it again for that will remove the checkmark and as a result, nullifies the instruction. When you see the checkmark, just press the Esc key on your keyboard or click on a blank space on the window to make the drop-down window disappear. Keep an eye on Save & Close and Save & New. Do not click Save & Close when you want to click Save & New.

- **Menus and Submenus**: This book is arranged according to the QuickBooks menus. There are 13 menus located at the top of your computer, and every time I refer to these menus, I'll use the word "Menu." If you did not see "Menu" after a word, then I'm not referring to one of 13 menus. The word I'm referring to is located in the window or subwindow you've just opened. Titles within this book are also arranged according to the QuickBooks' submenus for easy reading and location.

- **Window Directions:** I have used phrases such as: top right, top left, bottom right, and bottom left, to give you directions on where to find information on the window, thereby increasing your speed. Every instruction is directed to the current window you've just opened. If, for instance, you opened a small or subwindow, any instruction given at that moment is for that small or subwindow. Do not look at the big window.

- **Tab and Enter key:** Use the Tab key, especially in a window where you have to provide information for several boxes or fields. Sometimes, you have to press Enter on your keyboard for QuickBooks to accept your action. You can choose between pressing the Enter key on your keyboard and clicking Enter in the window, but it's a good idea to stay consistent to increase your speed. The resolution or the size of your monitor will determine how much information is displayed on the screen. If you have a small monitor, you may have to scroll down to find information. However, rest assured, the information is there; you just have to look for it. It is essential to repeat this: When an instruction says click Print or click Report, it is talking about the report or print in the smaller window and not the Report or Print menus located at the top of the window; otherwise, it would be followed by the word "Menu." When you are in a text box or a field, you may press the Home key to go the beginning of the text box or field, and you may press the End key to go the end of the text box or field.

- **Review:** Most of the time, an instruction will ask you to review a window, report, register, etc. All you have to do is read or browse through the information on the report or the window. The purpose is to allow you to gain a visual experience of the information, which helps you to gain in-depth knowledge of the subject matter as you work through the software.

- **Exit:** Some instructions will require you to click X to exit or close the window. The X is referring to the submenu not the QuickBooks' main window X located at the top right corner of the window. The submenu X is located below the main window X. You will not be asked to click the QuickBooks' main window X. QuickBooks has many "doors" to different windows, and the purpose of this book is to show you as many doors as possible. Later on, as you continue to use the software, you will choose where to go and which doors to open.

QuickBooks Window Parts

If you have a working knowledge of Microsoft Windows, you might find this section redundant. That's OK; I recommend you scan through it anyway. If you are not experienced in using Microsoft Windows, that's alright. I have taken nothing for granted. You will notice QuickBooks has many parts when you open its window. In all Microsoft Windows, the top part is called the "TMT," which stands for Title, Menus, and Tools. Following the TMT is the Workspace. Any instruction without the words "Menus" or "Tool" (such as "Report Menu and "Print Tool") is talking about the information in the Workspace. Navigation tips are arranged according to the QuickBooks image below.

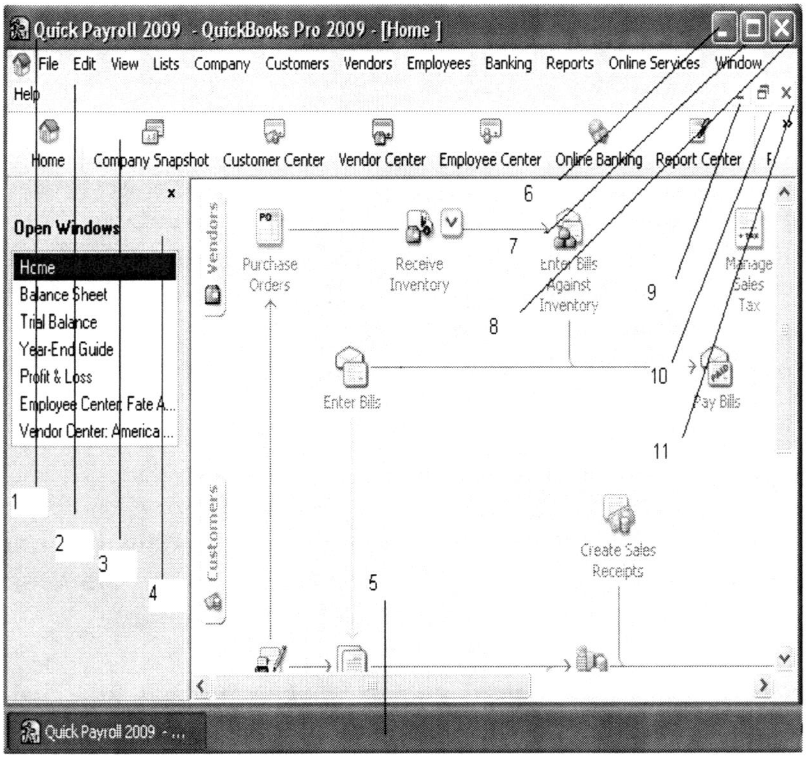

1. Title bar
2. Menu bar
3. Tool bar (or Icon bar)
4. Open window
5. Taskbar
6. Minimize (Main window)
7. Maximize (Main window)
8. Exit (Main window)
9. Minimize (Sub window)
10. Maximize (Sub window)
11. Exit (Sub window

- **Title bar:** Every time you open a QuickBooks window, you should immediately look at the title bar to make sure you're in the right Company or File window. It is imperative to be in the right file, because if you spent hours working on the wrong file, it will take more time to fix the problems.

- **Menu bar:** Below the Title bar is the menu bar. QuickBooks has 13 menus, and they are arranged in this book according to how they are arranged when you open the QuickBooks window. It is vital to recognize the 13 QuickBooks menus. In your free time, click on these menus and submenus to see where they are located. As you build your confidence using QuickBooks with this book, you will remember where most of the submenus are located.

- **Tool bar or Icon Bar:** Below the menu bar is the Icon bar. It's recommended to display your most-used Icons on the Icon bar. Reports and check registers should be placed on the Icon bar for easy access. It is professional to access the windows by going through the Icon bar rather than going through the menus. However, most instructions will take you through the menus for consistency's sake during your training period.

- **Open Window List:** If you want to have instant access to the most-used windows, always see if they have already been open and are now on the Open Window List. To display the Open Window List, click the View menu and Open Windows List. Then, you should be able to see all open windows and access them instead of going through the menus and submenus.

- **Taskbar:** From time to time, you would like to minimize windows for easy access at a later time. When you minimize a window it goes to the taskbar, where you can click it again to maximize it. And if you click minimize on the QuickBooks main window, it takes QuickBooks to the taskbar where you can click it again to maximize it.

- **Minimize main window:** After you have launched QuickBooks, the default main window will be in the Maximum mode. If you want to see other programs on the desktop, you should minimize QuickBooks to the Task Master. From time to time, you will be instructed to minimize QuickBooks to review information that has been saved to the desktop, or to minimize QuickBooks to open other programs such as Excel or Word.

- **Maximize main window:** This is the square button located at the top right of the computer. You will maximize a window when it is too small to view all the window data or after it was minimized to the Task Master. Subwindow's Exit, Maximize, and Minimize buttons will be under those of the main windows. From time to time, you will be required to minimize, maximize, or exit a subwindow to perform certain activities.
- **Exit main window:** Most Exit or X instructions will be referring to the subwindows. The subwindow X is located below the main window X. While you're still working with QuickBooks, you will only be clicking the smaller X for the subwindow. Any time you click the big X or the main window exit, be sure you really want to shut down your QuickBooks program.

- **Minimize sub window:** At other times when you click a menu and a submenu, the window that opens will cover the workspace and will not allow you to drag it around. The best action is to minimize it, so you are able to move it around from one side of the window to another. If you click the View menu and One Window, you will not see the Minimize button, only the Exit.

- **Maximize sub window:** After you've opened the main window, other windows are subwindows. Most of the time, when you click a menu and submenu, the subwindow that opens will be too small to see all the content of that subwindow. The next thing to do is maximize the subwindow. If you click Multiple Windows from the View menu, you can minimize and move the subwindows around; otherwise, you will not see the Maximize button.

- **Exit sub window:** This button is important when you want to exit a subwindow. Many times, I've seen clients who exit the main window and shut down QuickBooks, when in fact they wanted to exit the subwindow. Every time I say exit a window, I'm referring to the subwindow, not the main window.

Navigating Registers & Calendars

1	Open Register	Ctrl and R
2	Go to Next field	Press Tab
3	Go to Previous field	Shift and Tab
4	Go to beginning of the field	Press Home
5	Go to end of the field	Press End
6	Go to Next transaction	Page down
7	Go to Previous transaction	Page up
8	Go to first field column	Press Home twice
9	Go to last field column	Press End twice
10	Go to first transaction (top)	Press Home three times
11	Go to last transaction (bottom)	Press End three times
12	Increase check number	Press +
13	Decrease check number	Press -
14	Open Calendar	Ctrl and K
15	Go to Current date	Press T
16	Go to First of the Month	Press M
17	Go to Last of the Month	Press H
18	Go to First of the Year	Press Y
19	Go to Last of the Year	Press R
20	Go to First of last Month	Press -
21	Go to Previous Month	Alt and P
22	Go to Next Month	Alt and D
23	Go to Specific date	Alt and G
24	Go to a new Note	Alt and N

Installation Tips: Window Appears

If you order the QuickBooks software through the mail, you will receive a CD. When you put the CD into the drive, the welcome window will appear after a few seconds. Read each window carefully to determine exactly what you should do. Your QuickBooks software will default options it thinks you need. Unless you know exactly the result of another option, you should accept the suggested defaults. The instructions below might be different if this is the first time you're installing QuickBooks on your computer. However, the instructions will get you started. You should note the location of your QuickBooks folder during the installation process.

Activities:

- Load **CD in the drive**
- In seconds installation window will open.
- **Welcome to QuickBooks Installations wizard!** Click **Next**
- Read **Software License Agreement?**
- Click **Accept.** Click **Next**
- Click **One user** or **More than one user**. Click **Next**
- License Number: Type number from yellow sticker
- Product Number: Type product number from yellow sticker
- Click **Next**
- Accept the click on **Install QuickBooks Pro 2009**. Click **Next**
- In Copy previous QuickBooks settings window
- Please select...Click **down arrow**
- Select **QuickBooks Pro 2008**. Click **Next**
- Ready to Install QuickBooks window
- Click **Install**
- When Installation is completed
- Click **Finish**

Installation Tips: No Window Appears

When you put the CD into the drive and wait for few minutes, if nothing happens, click Start, Settings, and Control Panel. If you have Windows XP, you might not see Settings, so click Control Panel and proceed as shown below. QuickBooks is user-friendly. Here are a few instructions to get you started.

Activities:

- Load **CD in the drive**
- If after a few seconds Welcome does not appear
- Click **Start. (**Click **Setting** if available**)**
- Click **Control Panel**
- Double click **Add/Remove Programs**
- Click **Add New Programs** (left)
- Click **CD or Floppy.** Click **Next**
- Click **Finish**
- Welcome to QuickBooks Installation Wizard. Click **Next**
- Continue as in the previous page
- When Installation is completed
- Click **Finish**

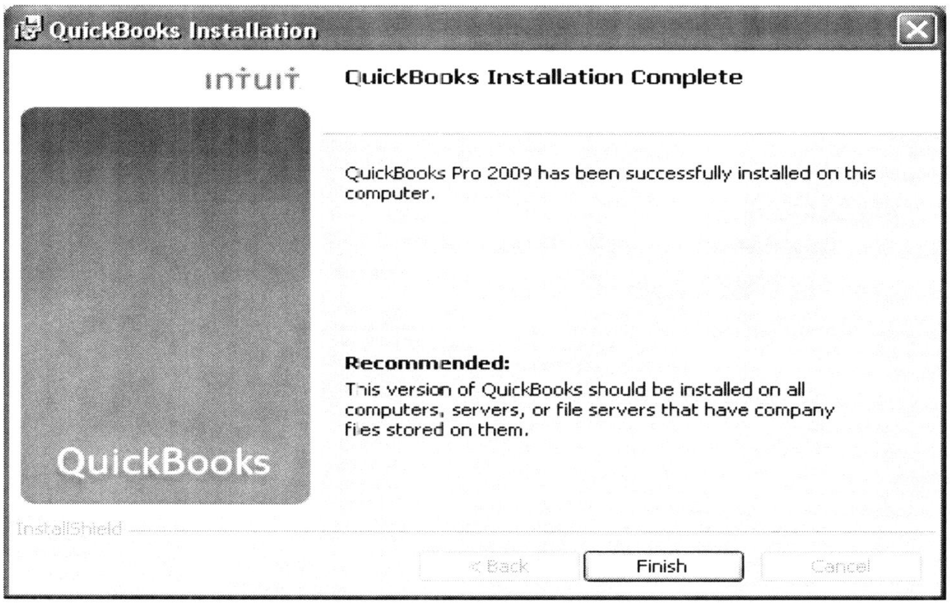

$

Sample

Quick Company

Objectives: After you've completed this chapter, you will be able to:

- ✓ Create a new file
- ✓ Create a bank account
- ✓ Create a liability account
- ✓ Create customers with opening balances
- ✓ Create vendors with opening balances
- ✓ Process financial reports and compare your results

Create New Company

Note: You do not need to read this explanation to practice the instructions below. The same goes with other pages in this book. You will be creating a new file, and the name should reflect the year of creation or the ownership of the file. For example, you may call your file John Doe & Associates or John Doe (this year). The name you give the file here is what you see on the window title, and you must change the name here to change the window title also.

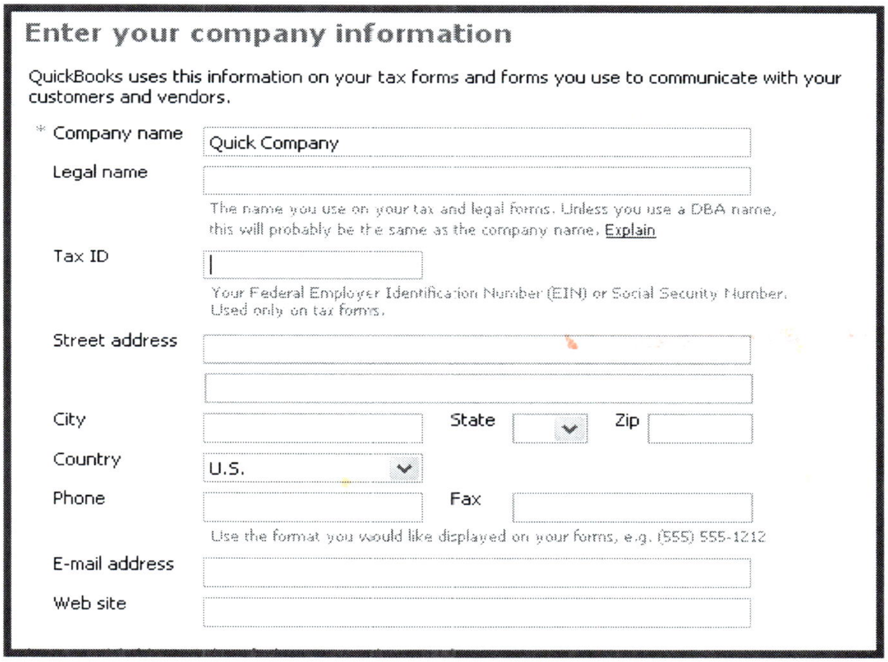

Activities:

- Double click **QuickBooks** shortcut on desktop
- Click **Create New Company** (if this is your first time)
- Click **File menu.** Click **New Company…**
- Click **Skip Interview** (bottom right of window)
- Company name: Type **Quick Company**. Click **Next**
- Click **Sole Proprietorship.** Click **Next**
- My fiscal year start in: Accept **January**. Click **Next**
- In the left window. Scroll to the bottom
- Click **General Service-based Business**. Click **Next**
- Create your company file. Click **Next**
- Click **Save**

- You're almost done. Click **Remind me later**
- Click **Edit menu**
- Click **Preferences**
- Click **Accounting** (left of the window)
- Click **Company Preferences** tab
- Uncheck **Warn if transactions are 90 day(s) in the past**
- Uncheck **Warn if transactions are 30 day(s) in the future**
- Click **Desktop View**
- Click **Yes** to "You have made changes…"
- Click **My Preferences** tab
- Uncheck **Show Live Community**
- Click **Multiple Currencies** (left of the window)
- Click **Company Preferences** tab
- Click **No, I use only one currency**
- Click **OK** to close Preferences window
- Click **X** to close Live Community, if open (top right of the window)

Create Bank Accounts

You will be creating new accounts from the Chart of Accounts window. After you right click in the window and click new, you will be taken to a window where you will create the new accounts. The bank option allows you to create accounts such as checking, savings, payroll, petty cash and other accounts that are banking-related. You will be allowed to enter the opening balance and the date of the account in the "Enter Opening Balance" window.

Activities:

- Click **View menu**
- Click **Open Window List**
- Click **Lists menu**
- Click **Chart of Accounts**. **Maximize window**
- Right click in the window. Click **New**
- Click **Bank**
- Click **Continue**
- Account Name: Type **USA Checking**
- Click **Enter Opening Balance**
- Statement Ending Balance: Type **800,000**
- Statement Ending Date: Type **1/1/09.** Click **OK**

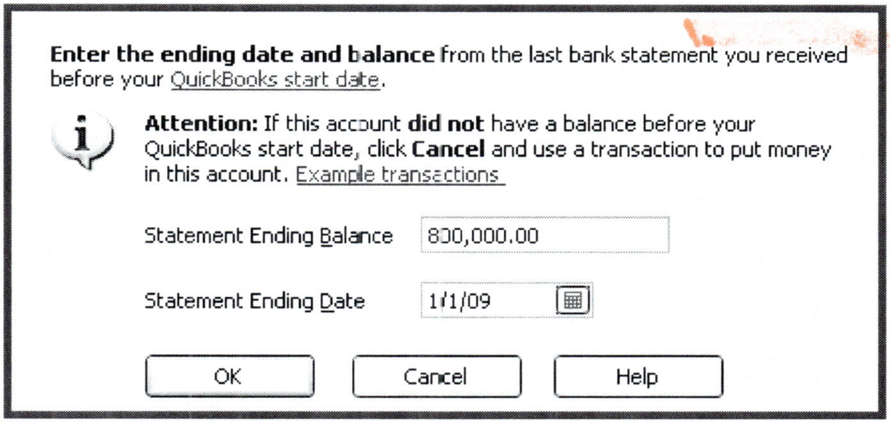

- Click **Save & New**
- Account Name: Type **USA Savings**
- Click **Enter Opening Balance**
- Statement Ending Balance: Type **250,000**
- Statement Ending Date: Type **1/1/09.** Click **OK**
- Click **Save & Close**
- Click **No** to "Set up online services…"

Create Liability Account

Chart of Accounts window is also used to create a liability account. This account is used for the debt you owe other companies, including accounts payable, credit cards, payroll, and sales tax liabilities. After you right click in the Chart of Accounts window, and click new, the next window is where you will create the liability account. You must click the "Other Account Types" option and click the down arrow to see a list of liability accounts to choose from.

Activities:

- Right click in the Chart of Accounts window
- Click **New**
- Click **Other Account Types** (bottom of window)
- Click **Long Term Liability**
- Click **Continue**
- Account Name: Type **Office Building Loan**
- Click **Enter Opening Balance**
- Opening Balance: Type **50,000** as of: Type **1/1/09.** Click **OK**
- Click **Save & Close**

Create Customers

Before you can sell goods and services you must have customers, therefore, creating customers is one your first tasks. In this exercise, you will be creating new customers with opening balances for John Allen and Tommy Brown. QuickBooks will not allow you delete customers. You may edit amount in the Accounts Receivable register. You do not have to exit the Customer List window to create the next customer; all you do is click the Next button and continue with the next customer. You will skip a lot of boxes, but don't worry; you'll still get a good financial result.

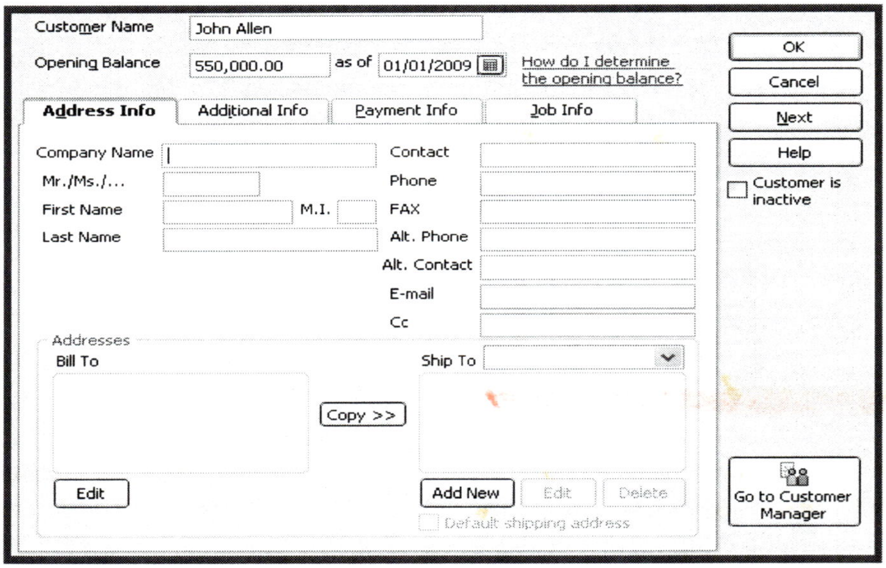

Activities:

- Click **Customers menu**
- Click **Customer Center**
- Right click in the left window
- Click **New Customer**
- Customer Name: Type **John Allen**
- Opening Balance: Type **550,000** as of: Type **1/1/09**
- Click **Next** (right of window)
- Customer Name: Type **Tommy Brown**
- Opening Balance: Type **455,000** as of: Type **1/1/09.** Click **OK**

Create Vendors

Like Customers, you must create vendors before you can receive merchandise and supplies. You will be creating new vendors with opening balances for Telephone America and Electric America. Also, QuickBooks will not allow you to delete vendors, but you can edit amount in the Accounts Payable register. You do not have to leave the Vendor List window to enter another vendor; all you do is click the Next button and continue with the next vendor. The opening balance is the closing balance you have on your books as of the date you are creating the new vendor.

Activities:

- Click **Vendors menu**
- Click **Vendor Center**
- Right click in the left window
- Click **New Vendor**
- Vendor Name: Type **Telephone America**
- Opening Balance: Type **3,500** as of: Type **1/1/09**
- Click **Next** (right of window)
- Vendor Name: Type **Electric America**
- Opening Balance: Type **1,500** as of: Type **1/1/09.** Click **OK**

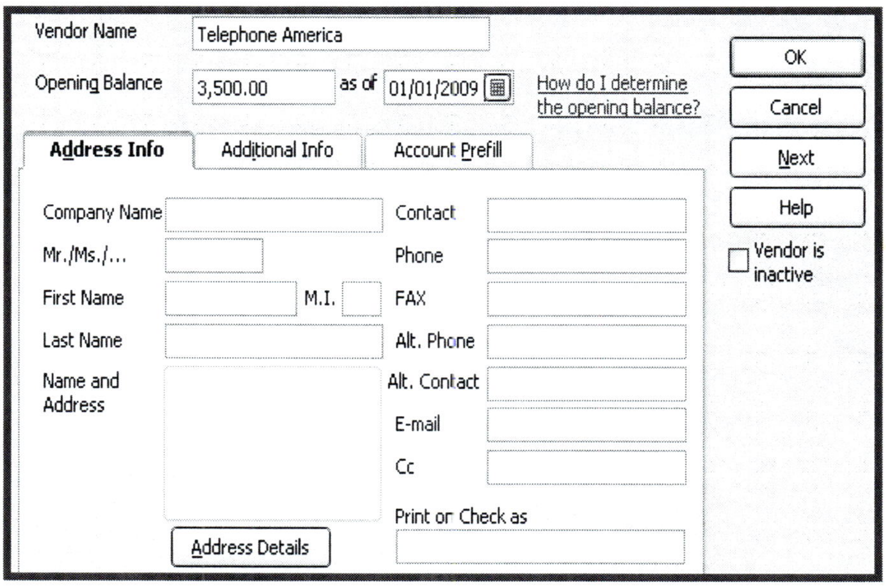

Financial Results: Profit & Loss

I expect you to get the end-of-chapter report numbers to the penny. However, if you do not get the exact figures, that's OK! The intent is to make sure you are following accordingly and to help you figure out where you made an error. Mistakes are inevitable in accounting, and it happens to everyone. As you continue to practice, you will build an extraordinary confidence with numbers. The first report is Profit & Loss statement, which includes income and expenses. Net Income is $1,000,000.

Quick Company
Profit & Loss
January through December 2009

	Jan - Dec 09
Ordinary Income/Expense	
Income	
Uncategorized Income	1,005,000.00
Total Income	1,005,000.00
Expense	
Uncategorized Expenses	5,000.00
Total Expense	5,000.00
Net Ordinary Income	1,000,000.00
Net Income	**1,000,000.00**

Activities:

- Click **Reports menu**
- Click **Company & Financial**
- Click **Profit & Loss Standard**
- Dates (top left of window): Select **This Fiscal Year**
- From: Accept **1/1/09.** To: Accept **12/31/09**
- **Look! Net Income is 1,000,000**
- Click **X** under red X (top right) to close Profit & Loss report window
- Checkmark **"Do not display this message in the future"**
- Click **No** to close the Memorize Report window

Financial Results: Balance Sheet

After you run the Profit & Loss statement, your next financial report is the Balance Sheet. Unlike the Profit & Loss statement, the Balance Sheet report is made up of Assets, Liabilities, and Owner's Equity. Make sure you select the right date from the top left side of the window; otherwise, your results will be different from the ones stated in this book. After the date, make sure you are in the right company. Hence, the company and the date are two vital pieces of information on your financial reports.

Activities:

- Click **Reports menu**
- Click **Company & Financial**
- Click **Balance Sheet Standard**
- Dates (top left of window): Select **This Fiscal Year**
- As of: Accept **12/31/09**
- **Look! Total Assets is $2,055,000**
- Click **X** to close Balance Sheet Standard

Quick Company
Balance Sheet
As of December 31, 2009

	Dec 31, 09
ASSETS	
Current Assets	
Checking/Savings	
USA Checking	800,000.00
USA Savings	250,000.00
Total Checking/Savings	1,050,000.00
Accounts Receivable	
Accounts Receivable	1,005,000.00
Total Accounts Receivable	1,005,000.00
Total Current Assets	2,055,000.00
TOTAL ASSETS	**2,055,000.00**

Chapter Summary

The purpose of this chapter is to show you how fast QuickBooks can be in creating a new company, accounts, customers, vendors and in running reports. What you see in this section is a real life example of how companies are using this powerful yet, flexible system to report their monthly and annual financial status. They may use other systems at the store locations but at the corporate level, they use QuickBooks to summarize their financial activities.

What we accomplished:

- Reviewed the File submenus
- Created a new company called Quick Company
- Opened bank accounts with opening balances
- Opened a liability account with opening balance
- Created new customers with opening balances
- Created new vendors with opening balances
- Processed financial statements

Additional financial activities:

- Created USA Checking account for 800,000
- Created USA Savings account for 250,000
- Created Office Building Loan account for 50,000
- Opened John Allen's account opening balance at 550,000
- Opened Tommy Brown's account opening balance at 455,000
- Created Telephone America's account opening balance at 3,500
- Created Electric America's account opening balance at 1,500

$

Chapter 1

File Menu

Objectives: After you've completed this chapter you will be able to:

- ✓ Review File submenus
- ✓ Perform the backup process
- ✓ Perform the restore process
- ✓ Create a new company file
- ✓ Create a new customer without details
- ✓ Open a company using different strategies
- ✓ Export IIF files
- ✓ Import IIF files
- ✓ Verify Data
- ✓ Save financial reports as PDFs
- ✓ Export reports to Excel
- ✓ Delete a QuickBooks company
- ✓ Process financial reports and compare results

Review File Submenus

When you start practicing with this book, you should skip all pages with the word "Review" in their titles. After you have finished practicing the pages, you may come back and read the "Review" pages; they are theoretical in nature and will not prevent you from successfully completing this book. The File menu is one of the key menus in QuickBooks, and understanding its submenus is also essential for using QuickBooks. The File menu has activities that are not specific to a QuickBooks window, but are global in nature. For example, when you are using the backup, restore, or password windows, it is for the entire company not just for one window. When logging off, click the File menu and then Exit, the last item in the File menu drop down window or click the X at the top right corner of your computer.

- Click **File menu**

The following submenus are found under the File menu:

- **New Company:** The New Company function will help you create a complete set of files that are needed to operate a company. You may choose to skip the detailed process of creating a company by clicking the Skip Interview button. If you choose to skip the interview, you must select your form of business window. QuickBooks will use your company type information to provide you with a set of accounts appropriate for your company. The name you give your company is what is reflected on the window title. If you copy a file, your title will reflect the name of the original company. To change the title of the new file, you must click the Company menu and then Company Information, only then will the window title be changed.

- **Open or Restore Company :** By clicking on this submenu, you will be taken to a window that lists all the files you've just created and other default QuickBooks files that are associated with your work. You must come to this window anytime you want to see all the files available to you. Restore allows you to load your backup or your portable files.

- **Open Previous Company:** This is one of the most used handy tools in your QuickBooks financials. Anytime you want to open a previous window, it is quicker to use the Open Previous Company. Do this instead of clicking the File menu and then Open Company submenu, because you're not looking for all the files you have created. Rather, you are looking for the one file you've recently closed. QuickBooks will keep only 10 files you've previously closed in the drop-down window. You may increase that number by clicking the "Set number of previous companies…" located at the end of the drop-down list A small window will open to allow you to change the number to a maximum of 20.

- **Save Copy or Back up:** You should save or back up your files at the end of every month. This way, you can re-create a month of activities if you happen to lose your computer to virus or fire. Don't forget to store your backed-up files somewhere outside your current QuickBooks work location.

- **Close Company:** As the name implies, when you choose this submenu, QuickBooks will close the current window and open the "Select a Company" window. You do not click Close Company when you mean to logoff from the QuickBooks program, where the best action is to click the File menu and then Exit. Another option you may use to close a company is to click the X button located at the top right corner of your computer.

- **Switch to Multi-user Mode:** If you you're your QuickBooks database be accessible to more than one person, you click this submenu. Every time you keep getting a message window, "Create New User immediately," you should know you are in the Multiuser mode, unless you disable the message window. You have previously clicked the Switch to Multiuser mode.

- **Utilities:** This is one submenu you want to pay much attention to. To start with, you must remember QuickBooks activities that are hidden under this submenu. They include the following: Import, Export, Synchronize Contacts, Convert, Verify Data, Rebuild Data, Clean Up Company Data. When you back up, it is for the entire company file not just an account such as the bank account. If you've had a computer problem like virus attack and your files are corrupt, this is the time to run the Verify Data function. If QuickBooks find any damaged files, it will go ahead and rebuild it. If you started with Quicken Home and Business, and with rapid business growth, you may have decided to change to QuickBooks. The Convert tool allows you to move your files from Quicken to QuickBooks.

- **Accountant's Copy:** This is one of the most complex submenus in entire QuickBooks program. If you have an accountant and you want him or her to review you files for mistakes, one of the ways to do that is to send your files to your accountant. When you use the Accountant's Copy tools, QuickBooks restricts the accountant from changing certain files such as the Chart of Accounts.

- **Print:** Different Print functions will be activated depending on which window you are in. For example, if you are in the Chart of Accounts or Item List windows, and you click the File menu, you can only see Print List, and if you go to a report window, Print Report will only come up or be activated.

- **Save as PDF:** With the information age, document security is becoming absolutely necessary. If you send your financial files on programs like Excel, someone can change that file and make it seem like the original. To restrict someone from tampering with a file, it is becoming a universal practice to send financial information as a PDF. This way, originality of data is assured, and tampering is made difficult.

- **Print Form:** QuickBooks has several reports you can print or preview, including payment stubs, checks, credit memos, invoices, labels, paychecks, pay stubs, purchase orders, sales receipts, timeshares, and 1099s/1096. An significant use of these forms is to preview for availability of data, before you go to other windows. For example, if you want to find out if you have checks to be printed, the quickest way is to click File menu, Print Forms, and then click Checks. Any checks you have to be printed will be listed in this window.

- **Printer Setup:** When it comes to the layout of reports, people have different tastes. One person might like to have a report in Portrait while another person likes to see the same report in a Landscape format. It is pertinent to come to the Print Setup submenu and choose the options you like. When you have reports displayed in a way you don't like, remember to come to Print Setup window for changes.

- **Send Forms:** If you communicate with your customers and vendors by internet, this is one submenu you will want to know how it works. After you've completed an invoice, simply click the "To be e-mailed" box located at the bottom left of the invoice window. Then when you are ready to send your invoice by e-mail, you come to this submenu. Just select the invoice and click the Send button. My favorite is to send a batch of invoices at one time.

- **Shipping:** This submenu allows you to send packages by FedEx or UPS. It allows you to find a drop off location, schedule pickup, track or cancel shipment, print Ground End-of-Day manifest.

- **Exit:** Generally, you will have two X buttons, one for the main window and the other is the subwindow. Both are located at the top right corner of subwindow and main window. If you want to exit the subwindow you will use the small X, but if you want to log off and shut down QuickBooks, you will need to click the big X at the top right corner of your computer. Another way of logging off from QuickBooks without clicking the big X is to click File menu and then Exit.

Back Up

You are going to backup the Quick Company file to the desktop. From time to time you should backup your files and store them away for security reasons. **If you are practicing backup the second time with the same file, after you click "Local backup" and Next, QuickBooks will skip to "Save it now" because it memorized what you did the last time.** Therefore, if you have to backup the same file before, be ready to skip to "Save right now" after you've clicked the "Local backup" and the Next button.

Activities:

- Open the Quick Company file
- Click **File menu**
- Click **Save Copy or Backup**
- Click **Backup copy**. Click **Next**
- Click **Local backup**. Click **Next**
- Tell us where to save your backup copies
- Click **Browse…**
- Scroll up. Click **Desktop.** Click **OK**
- Tell us where to save your backup copies
- Accept **C:\...Desktop.** Click **OK**
- Click **Use this Location**
- Click **Save it now**. Click **Next**
- Save in: Select **Desktop**
- File name (bottom left): Type **Quick Company**
- Click **Save**
- Click **OK** to "QuickBooks has saved this…"

> The "Use this Location" button will not appear if you've saved to the desktop before or you're using Floppy, CD, USB, or any other external destinations.

Restore

There are two ways of restoring your file. You can restore a file to create another file or restore a file to replace the original file. Your objective here is to create a second file not to replace the old file. You should back up each chapter to a CD for security reason, should anything happen to the computer. If you lost the Quick Company file for instance, you will restore it from your CD and still call it Quick Company or whatever file name you lost.

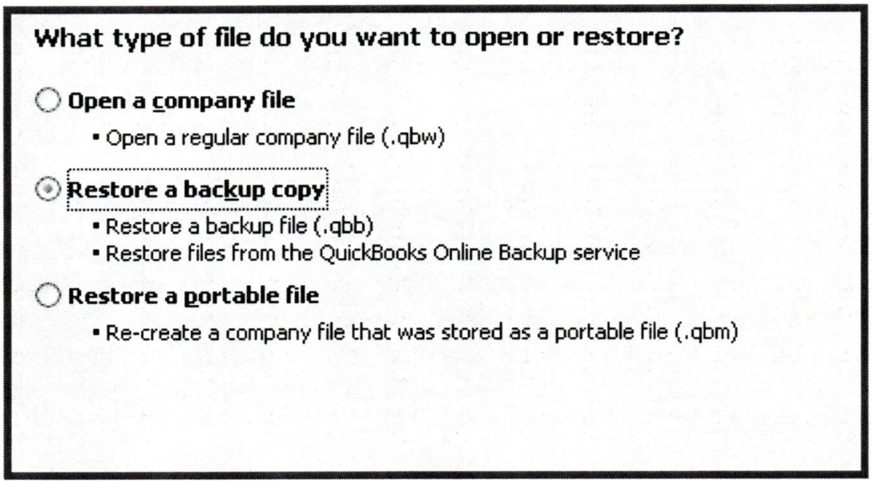

Activities:

- You're still in Quick Company window
- Click **File**
- Click **Open or Restore Company…**
- Click **Restore a backup copy.** Click **Next**
- Click **Local backup**. Click **Next**
- Look in: Select **Desktop**
- Click **Quick Company**
- Click **Open**
- Where do you want to restore the file? Click **Next**
- Save in: Accept **Company File**
- File name: Type **Quick Company 2009.** Click **Save**
- Click **OK** to "Your data has been restored successfully."
- Click **X** to close Overview & Setup window
- Click **Company menu**
- Click **Company Information…**
- Company Name: Type **Quick Company 2009**
- **Students add your first name initial and your last name after 2009**
- Click **OK.** Congratulations! You have created the 2009 file.
- Click **View menu**. Click **Open Window List**

New Company

Creating a new company is an essential task you would have to perform before using a QuickBooks file. Generally, you would want to fill in as much information as possible in the new company windows. You will create a file called Testing Company, which is used as a practicing file for this chapter **alone**. In the next chapter, you will create another file for the rest of the book. You will be selecting Service Business, which is used to preload your company's Chart of Accounts.

Activities:

- You're still in **Quick Company 2009**
- Click **File menu**
- Click **New Company**
- Click **Skip Interview**
- Company Name: Type **Testing Company.** Click **Next**
- Click **Sole Proprietorship.** Click **Next**
- My fiscal year starts in: Accept **January**. Click **Next**
- In the left window. **Scroll to the bottom**
- Click **General Service-based Business**. Click **Next**
- Create your company file. Click **Next**
- Click **Save**
- You're almost done! Click **Remind me later**

New Customer

When creating a new customer, you must decide ahead of time if you're going to add an opening balance or not. You get this information from the Customer Balance report. If you entered a customer's invoice, you can delete that invoice using the Edit menu, Delete Invoice, but if you want to delete a customer's opening balance, you must open the Accounts Receivable register from the Chart of Accounts window and edit or delete the opening balance using the Edit menu and Delete function.

Activities:

- You're now in Testing Company file
- Click **View menu**
- Click **Open Window List**
- Click **Customers menu**
- Click **Customer Center**

- Right click in the left window
- Click **New Customer**
- Customer Name: Type **Tony Jones**
- Opening Balance: Type **2,500** as of: Type **1/1/09**
- Click **OK**

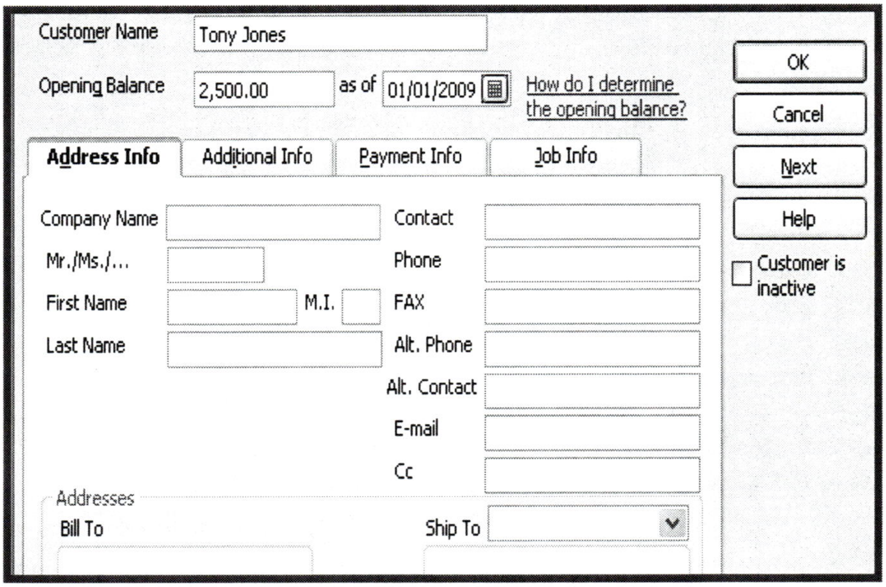

Open Company

Opening a company is easy in Microsoft windows. However, with QuickBooks there is an added twist to opening a company. Normally, you open a new company by clicking File menu and clicking Open. With QuickBooks you can open previous windows by clicking File menu, Open Previous Company. As the name implies, you must have previously opened the window, and now you are going back into it. You can choose the number of files you would like to display in this window.

Activities:

- Click **File menu**
- Click **Open or Restore Company**
- Click **Open a company file.** Click **Next**
- Click **Quick Company** in the window
- Click **Open**

- **Look! You are now in Quick Company window**
- Click **File menu**
- Click **Open Previous Company**
- Click **Set number of previous**... (bottom of list)
- How many companies...?: Type **20**
- Click **OK**
- Click **File menu**
- Click **Open Previous Company**
- Click **...Testing Company**
- **Look! The window title must say "Testing Company"**

Export IIF Files

When you want to import information into your current company file, you first export the file and then complete the process by importing it into your current company file. During the process, you will first go to the Item List window to see that you have no items in the window. It is totally blank. When you're finished, the Item List window will be filled with items you imported from the original file. Some files will not allow you to import numbers only the names of the items or accounts.

Activities:

- Click **Lists menu**
- Click **Item List**
- **Look! You have no entries in the window**
- Click **X** to close window
- Click **File menu**
- Click **Open or Restore Company**
- Click **Open a company file.** Click **Next**
- Click **Cancel**
- Click **Open a sample file down arrow** (bottom right
- Click **Sample service-based business**
- Click **OK to** "This is the QuickBooks sample file."
- You're now in **Sample Larry's Landscaping**… file
- Click **File menu**
- Click **Utilities**
- Click **Export**
- Click **Lists to IIF Files**
- Click **Item List**. (bottom left) Click **OK**

- Save In: Select **Desktop**
- File name (bottom of window): Type **Item List**
- Click **Save**
- Click **OK** to "Your data has been exported successfully."

Import IIF Files

After you've completed the export process, the next step is to import the IIF file into your current company file. This is essential if you want to import Chart of Accounts or other lists from other files or from your accountant. In this process, you will use your desktop as the intermediary warehouse. This is where you export the original file to and then export it from the desktop to the destination file. Hence, during the export and import process, you will choose the desktop in each case.

.

Activities:

- You're still in Sample Larry's Landscaping…file
- Click **File menu**
- Click **Open Previous Company**
- Click **...Testing Company**
- You're now in Testing Company file
- Click **File menu**
- Click **Utilities**
- Click **Import**
- Click **IIF Files**
- Look In: Select **Desktop**
- Click **Item List** in the window

- Click **Open**
- Click **OK** to "Your data has been imported."
- Click **Lists menu**
- Click **Item List**.
- **Look! Your Item window is filled with new items**
- Click **X**
- **Look! Window title says Testing Company**

Verify Data

What if you have a virus attack, or you suspect that your computer may have been infected? You want to sweep your files for damages. For QuickBooks users, there is a better way of checking your files: by running the Verify Data process. If you have more than one file, you have to run the process on each file. In other words, you will be verifying each file one at a time. Your screen will be gray after the process is completed. You'll have to click Company menu and then Home Page.

Activities:

- You normally should open the file you want to verify
- You're still in Testing Company file
- Click **File menu**
- Click **Utilities**
- Click **Verify Data**
- Click **OK** to "Before verifying your data
- Click **OK** to "QuickBooks detected no problems with your data."

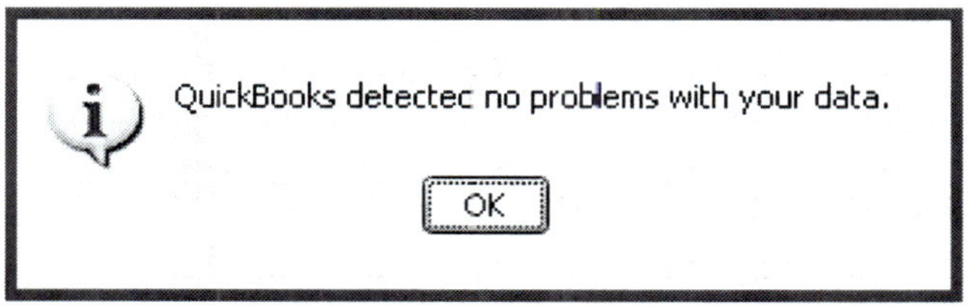

- Window is grey
- Click **Company menu**
- Click **Home Page** to open the window

Save Report as PDF

It is essential to distribute financial information, but before you do so, make sure it is not easy for anyone to change your records. It used to be easy for other's to alter your financial records until PDFs came along. Now you can send information protected from dubious tampering. You will have the opportunity to create a financial statement and then save it in a PDF format, which is exported to your desktop. Your file extension will be pdf; be sure to open the file to make sure you have converted the right file.

Activities:

- Click **Reports menu**
- Click **Company & Financial**
- Click **Profit & Loss Standard**
- Date (top left): Select **This Fiscal Year**
- Click **File menu**
- Click **Save as PDF**
- Save in: Select **Desktop**
- File name: Type **Profit & Loss**. Click **Save**
- Click **X** to close Profit & Loss report window
- Checkmark **Do not display this message.** Click **No**
- **Minimize QuickBooks and other programs to see desktop**
- Double click **Profit & Loss** on desktop to open
- Click red **X** to close PDF
- **Maximize QuickBooks**

Testing Company
Profit & Loss
January through December 2009

	Jan - Dec 09
Ordinary Income/Expense	
Income	
Uncategorized Income	2,500.00
Total Income	2,500.00
Gross Profit	2,500.00
Net Ordinary Income	2,500.00
Net Income	2,500.00

Export Reports to Excel

In this section, you will be practicing how to export financial report into Excel. Sometimes, you want to perform calculations in Excel that was not provided in QuickBooks such as financial ratios. The most significant point to remember is that you must open the particular report you want to export first, and then click the Export button located at the top of the Report window. You must have Excel on your computer to complete this process.

Activities:

- ❖ You're still in Testing Company file
- ❖ Click **Reports menu**
- ❖ Click **Company & Financial**
- ❖ Date (top left): Select **This Fiscal Year**

	A	B	C	D	E	F	G
1					Dec 31, 09		
2	ASSETS						
3		Current Assets					
4			Accounts Receivable				
5				Accounts Receivable	2,500.00		
6			Total Accounts Receivable		2,500.00		
7		Total Current Assets			2,500.00		
8	TOTAL ASSETS				2,500.00		
9	LIABILITIES & EQUITY						
10		Equity					
11			Net Income		2,500.00		
12		Total Equity			2,500.00		
13	TOTAL LIABILITIES & EQUITY				2,500.00		

- ❖ Click **Export**…(top of Balance Sheet window)
- ❖ Click **"a new Excel workbook"**
- ❖ Checkmark **"Include a new worksheet in the workbook…"**
- ❖ Click **Export**
- ❖ **Look! You're now in Excel**
- ❖ Click red **X** to close Excel. Click **No**
- ❖ **You're back to QuickBooks**
- ❖ Click **Window menu.** Click **Close All**
- ❖ Window is grey
- ❖ Click **Company menu.** Click **Home Page**

Delete Company

Before you start this process, you must make sure you have created the company file named "Testing Company," because this is the company you will be deleting. From time to time you may have too many dummy companies you created to test QuickBooks processes and results. There is no Delete Company function in QuickBooks. Because it is risky, you must be sure you want to delete a particular company before you initiate the process.

Activities:

- ❖ You must be still in the Testing Company
- ❖ Click **File menu**
- ❖ Click **Open Previous Company**
- ❖ Click **...Quick Company**
- ❖ You're now in Quick Company file
- ❖ Click **File menu**
- ❖ Click **Open or Restore Company…**
- ❖ Click **Open a company file**
- ❖ Click **Next**
- ❖ Right click **Testing Company** in the window
- ❖ Click **Delete**
- ❖ Click **Yes**. "Are you sure…"
- ❖ Click **Quick Company 2009** in the window
- ❖ Click **Open**
- ❖ **Look! Window title must say Quick Company 2009**

Financial Results: Profit & Loss

Most of the activities we completed in this chapter were administrative in nature. We set up a new company called Testing Company and created a new customer named Tony Jones with an opening balance of $2,500. There were no income and expenses for this chapter and therefore we ended up with the same Net Income. However, we practiced how to delete a company which is very important in managing your QuickBooks files and then switched back to our previous Quick Company.

Quick Company 2009
Profit & Loss
January through December 2009

	Jan - Dec 09
Ordinary Income/Expense	
Income	
Uncategorized Income	1,005,000.00
Total Income	1,005,000.00
Expense	
Uncategorized Expenses	5,000.00
Total Expense	5,000.00
Net Ordinary Income	1,000,000.00
Net Income	**1,000,000.00**

Activities

- You're still in Quick Company 2009 file
- Click **Reports menu**
- Click **Company & Financial**
- Click **Profit & Loss Standard**
- Date: Select **This Fiscal Year**
- From: Accept **1/1/09**. To: Accept **12/31/09**
- **Net Income is 1,000,000**
- Click **X** to close window

Financial Results: Balance Sheet

Because we switched back to Quick Company, our previous financial report is still in tact. It is absolutely essential to run your Balance Sheet report each time you complete a chapter to keep abreast of how you're doing. You want to make sure you are matching the textbook's total. If there are no activities it's still essential to get the right numbers, as this will build a profound confidence in you at this early stage. Very soon, as you face more financial activities, you will ride on your earlier success.

Activities:

- Click **Reports menu**
- Click **Company & Financial**
- Click **Balance Sheet Standard**
- Date (top left): Select **This Fiscal Year**
- As of: Accept **12/31/09**

- ❖ **Total Assets is 2,055,000**
- ❖ Click **X** to close window

Quick Company 2009
Balance Sheet
As of December 31, 2009

	Dec 31, 09
ASSETS	
Current Assets	
Checking/Savings	
USA Checking	800,000.00
USA Savings	250,000.00
Total Checking/Savings	1,050,000.00
Accounts Receivable	
Accounts Receivable	1,005,000.00
Total Accounts Receivable	1,005,000.00
Total Current Assets	2,055,000.00
TOTAL ASSETS	**2,055,000.00**

Chapter Summary

Our main objective is to create a new company called Testing Company and use it to learn about the File menu. There are several submenus under the File menu, and their actions and reactions affect the entire QuickBooks company. For example, when you are using the Save Copy or the Verify Data functions, their process results are for the entire company not just the File menu. You deleted a company, which is not a part of QuickBooks functions but a vital process to learn.

What we accomplished:

- Reviewed the File submenu
- Performed the backup process
- Performed the restore process
- Created a new company called Testing
- Created a new customer without details
- Learned different ways of opening a company
- Exported IIF file
- Imported IIF file
- Verified Data
- Saved QuickBooks report as PDF

- Exported reports into Excel
- Deleted a company
- Processed financial statements

Additional Financial activities:

- Customer Tony Jones for 2,500 was deleted with company

Exercise 1

Complete Exercise 1 by using the following information:

1. Create new company.
   Company name: Excellent Company (add your 1st name initial and last name)
   Company organization: Corporation (Aka Regular or C Corporation)
   Fiscal year starting: January
   Industry: Manufacturing

2. Set up preferences
   Accounting as on page 16
   Desktop View as on page 16
   Multiple Currencies as on page 16

3. Customize home page
   Bring up the Open Window List as on page 16

4. Create new bank account.
   Checking account opening balance 950,000 date 1/1/09
   Savings account opening balance 100,000 date 1/1/09

5. Create new fixed asset account.
   Equipment loan opening balance 170,000 as of 1/1/09

6. Create new customers.
   Jenny Lane LLC opening balance 500,000 as of 1/1/09
   Luke Walsh Company opening balance 250,000 as of 1/1/09

7. Create new vendors.
   National Electric Inc opening balance 14,000 as of 1/1/09
   World Telecom opening balance 25,000 as of 1/1/09

6. Process the following reports
   Profit & Loss Statement ending 12/31/09
   Balance Sheet Standard ending 12/31/09

   Statement of Cash Flow ending 12/31/09
   AR Aging Summary as of 1/31/09
   Customer Balance Details as of 1/31/09
   Collection Report as of 1/31/09
   AP Aging Summary as of 1/31/09
   Vendor Balance Details as of 1/31/09
   Account Listing as of today

$

Chapter 2

Edit Menu

Objectives: After you've completed this chapter you will be able to:

- ✓ Explain Edit submenus
- ✓ Make an entry in the check register
- ✓ Create a new check
- ✓ Void a check
- ✓ Memorize a check
- ✓ Use the Notepad
- ✓ Use the Calculator
- ✓ Use the Simple Find
- ✓ Use the Advanced Find
- ✓ Delete a check
- ✓ Set up the preferences windows
- ✓ Process financial reports and compare results

Review Edit Submenus

You have more submenus under the Edit menu than under any other menu. Always remember, if you just open the Home Page, you will not activate a lot of Edit submenus, therefore, any time you don't see more submenus, it could be you have not opened the right windows that could force the submenus to be activated. For example, if you open the Chart of Accounts window, you will get more submenus you have never seen before. Preference is one of the most important submenus under the Edit menu—easy to set up, learn and use. Edit menu works best when a check register or a report window is open, since more submenus are activated.

- Click **Lists menu**
- Click **Chart of Accounts**
- Double click **USA Checking**
- Click **Check #1001** for Telephone America
- Click **Edit menu**

The following submenus are found under the Edit menu when you click in the check register:

- **Undo:** When you highlight an amount and press the Delete key, the amount will disappear. If you want the amount you've just deleted to re-appear because it is the right amount, just click the Edit menu, and choose Undo. The deleted amount will return back in the amount field. You must delete the amount and not do anything else for the Undo function to come up. If you press Tab or Enter key, Undo will not be activated.

- **Revert:** This tool works much like the Undo function. After typing an amount you may decide to change to the original amount you had earlier, all you have to do before you press Tab is to click Edit and then Revert.

- **Cut:** Cut will allow you to cut a field or an entry to another location, most probably, the last blank line. Cut will not come up unless that field is highlighted. If you cut a field by mistake, remember to restore it by using Revert, Paste or by clicking Restore located at the bottom right of the register.

- **Copy:** Like the Cut function, the Copy works best when the check register is opened and a field is highlighted. You can copy any part of the entry as long as it is highlighted.

- **Paste:** When you cut or copy a field, paste will allow you to paste that field to another location. Make sure you're pasting the right information in the right field. If you're pasting an entry, remember to change the basic information of that entry, otherwise you will have two identical entries, which is not good. At the least, you should be changing the number of the new entry.

- **Edit Check:** After writing a check, you may find out there is a problem with it. For example, you may find out that you typed 456 Adam Lane instead of 465 Adam Lane. Edit Check will allow you to make changes to the check. Be sure to click the Save & Close button, otherwise a message window will come up and ask you if you want to accept the changes you've just made.

- **New Check:** The window allows you to go to the check window. You must click an entry in the check register with the letters CHK, then click Edit menu and the New Check submenu is activated.

- **Delete Check:** It is highly recommended to void a check rather than deleting it. If a check has been reconciled, QuickBooks still allows you to delete that check though it has been used behind the scenes to debit and credit different accounts and the check also has hit several reports. Before you delete a check make sure you really want to do so. You can also delete the amount of the check and preserve the information about the check for future reference.

- **Memorize Check:** This is one the best features in QuickBooks. If you have a need to write the same check to same vendor for the same amount every month many times in the future, it's best to go ahead and memorize it. This way next month, your check register will automatically be populated with the check's information. Automating or memorizing a check is more efficient than manually writing the same check month after month.

- **Void Check:** Void will not show up because the check was voided. It is better to void a check than delete it, unless it's the last check you've just written and, therefore, not yet reconciled. If you want to avoid wasting checks and keep your work clean, it is better to re-write a voided check to another vendor. There is nothing like having all your check numbers all lined up. Be sure when you are re-writing a check to another vendor that you re-write every field or box. It will be a bad check if you left the old address that belonged to the previous vendor.

- **Copy Check:** This is one of the tools you can use to speed up your transaction entry. If you are in the check register and you have a check with similar in characteristics to the one you want to write like the amount and payee. You can just copy the check and change date and other information to match your current need, instead of creating a new check from scratch.

- **Go To Transfer:** To use this feature, you must transfer some money to another account and the account field must be other accounts except Income and Expense accounts such as a Savings Account or a Payroll Account. The Go To Transfer lets you jump over to the other register account where the amount was transferred to, so you can see the account balance after the transfer.

- **Transaction History:** This submenu does not come up unless you are in a check register and a transaction is clicked. If you click a transaction in the check register and click QuickReport located at the top of the window; Transaction History will also be activated.

- **Notepad:** This feature will not come up unless you click on an entry in the check register. You must open a check register and click on an entry, and then the Edit menu before Notepad is listed.

- **Change Account Color:** What if you don't like the color of the check register; QuickBooks has given you an option to change it. Just click on this submenu and a window opens where you can select your favorite color.

- **Use Register:** This submenu will allow you to select the exact bank account you want to open. It is absolutely necessary to choose the right account from this window; otherwise you could be entering data in an incorrect account. It will cost you time and effort to correct an error because you chose a wrong account.

- **Use Calculator:** From time to time you will want to do some additions and subtractions in the check register. Always remember that there is a calculator handy in your QuickBooks software. I've seen many people reaching for their calculators when they can easily switch to their QuickBooks calculator.

- **Search:** If you're working on a project and you want search for some information online, this is the submenu to come to. It will take you to the Internet where you can conduct your online search. Be sure to read how your financial information is protected from being transmitted through the Internet.

- **Find:** You cannot truly enjoy using your QuickBooks software until you know how to use the Find window. Any time you want to find information about a vendor, the Find is your best ally. You have two tabs in the Find window, the basic Find—called Simple and a more detailed Find window—called Advanced.

- **Preferences:** This is one of the most important submenus under the Edit menu. Preferences will help you to set up the following areas: Accounting, Checking, Desktop View, Finance Charge, General Information, Integrated Application, Job & Estimate, Payroll & Employees, Purchase & Vendors, Reminders, Reports & Graphs, Sales & Customers, Sales Tax, Send Forms, Service Connections, Spelling, Tax: 1099, and Time Tracking. Selecting your Preferences is paramount to using QuickBooks correctly. Most windows and submenus will not be activated if the right Preferences are not selected. In fact, if you did not see any windows described in this book, it may be because you have not selected the right Preferences to activate that window or the window is not a part of your QuickBooks software due to version differences.

Make Entry

Recording an entry in QuickBooks is very easy. You start with the date box, then tab over to the number box. The fist number you choose is very essential, because QuickBooks will default the next number each time you make an entry. You may choose number 1, 100 or 1000 for the entry. Don't forget to always press the first letters of a word in the drop-down window, so that all the words with identical letter are pulled up for you to select the right information, instead of scrolling the window.

Activities:

- You're still in Quick Company 2009 file
- Click **Edit menu**
- Click **Use Register**
- Select Account: Select **USA Checking.** Click **OK**
- Date: Type **1/1/09**. Press **Tab each time**
- Number: Type **1001**
- Payee: Select **Telephone America**
- Payment: Type **150.00**
- Account: Select **Telephone Expense**. Press **Tab**
- Click **Record** (Bottom right)

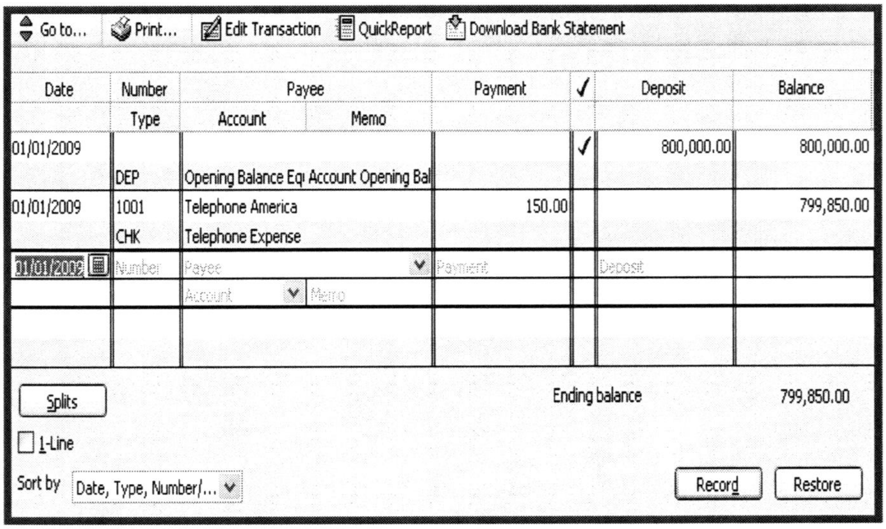

Create New Check

Writing a new check is necessary to pay your bills. As we continue to move toward being a cashless society, electronic transactions will ultimately replace the current paper checks. Until then, we must continue to write new checks. Be sure you are using the right bank account. This is imperative, otherwise your check will be returned to you even if you have money in the right account. You'll open the USA Checking account register to write a new check.

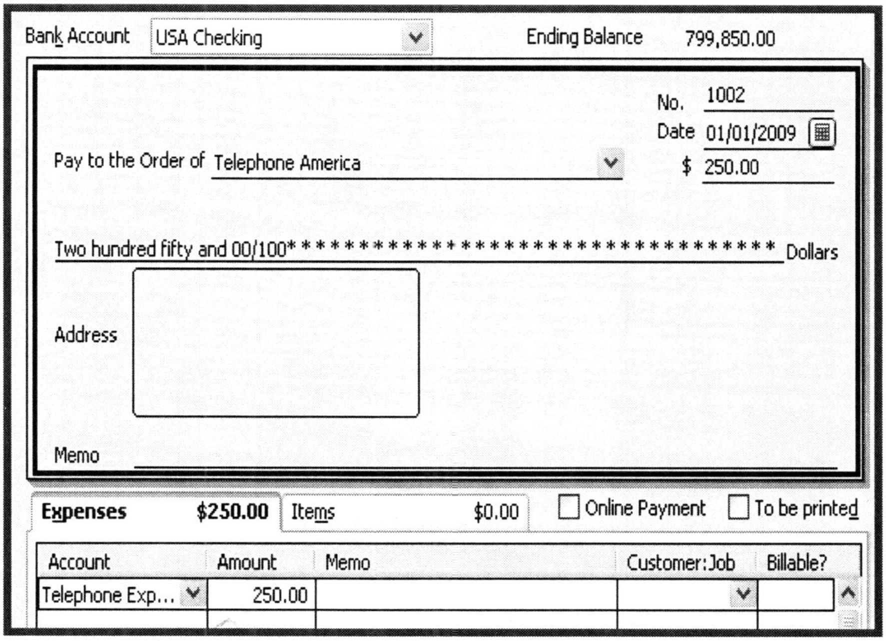

Activities:

- Click **Edit menu**
- Click **New Check**
- Bank Account: Accept **USA Checking**
- No.: Accept **1002** (top right of window)
- Date: Accept **1/1/09**
- Pay to the Order of: Select **Telephone America**
- Click **Continue Writing Check.**
- For amount. Type **250.00**
- Under Account (bottom left): Accept **Telephone Expense.** Press **Tab**
- Under Amount: Accept **250.00**
- Click **Save & Close**

Void Check

For one reason or the other, you may decide to get rid of a check. What you do next depends on when you wrote the check. If you've just written the check, QuickBooks will let you delete the check using the Edit menu, instead of just voiding, unless you want to keep the check's information in your database. When you void a check, the word "Void" is placed on the entry line. A checkmark is placed on the row to show the check has cleared and will not show up during reconciliation.

Activities:

- Click on **Telephone America check #1001**
- Click **Edit menu**
- Click **Void Check**
- Click **Record**
- Click **Yes** to "You have changed…"
- **Look! Amount is 0.00**
- **A checkmark is placed on the entry**
- **VOID is placed on the Memo field**

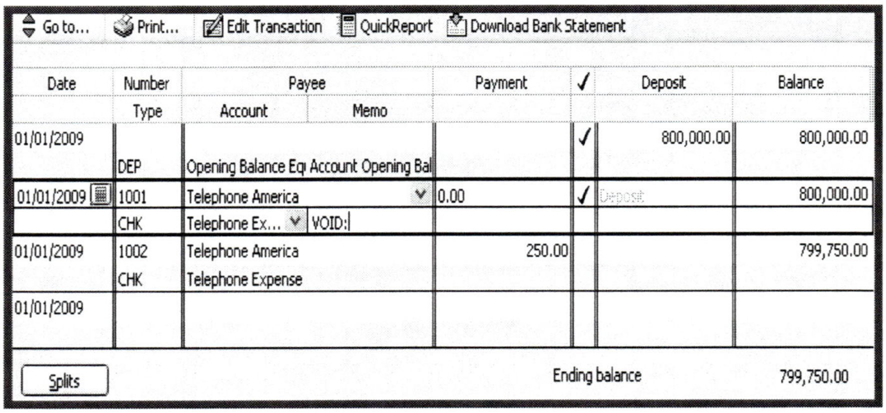

Memorize Check

If you have to write a same check at the same time every month, it is recommended to memorize the check. Then it will always go straight into the check register. Checks for loans, insurance, rents, etc., should be memorized. In this section you will practice memorizing a Telephone American check. In this exercise for the How Often box, you will accept Never. However, when using QuickBooks for your business, you should select Monthly.

Activities:

- Click on **Telephone America check # 1002 for 250.00**
- Click **Edit menu**
- Click **Memorize Check**
- Name: Accept **Telephone America**
- Click **Automatically Enter**
- How Often: Accept **Never**
- Next Date: Type **2/1/09**.
- Click **OK**

> Normally, you should select Daily, Weekly, or Monthly for "How Often."

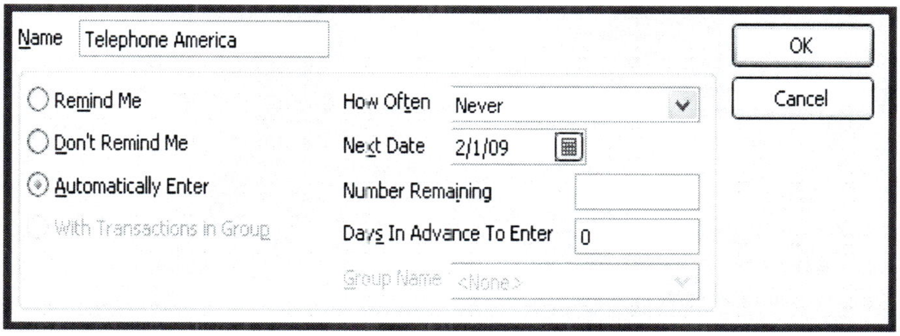

- Click **Lists menu**.
- Click **Memorized Transaction List**
- **Look! Telephone America for 250.00 is listed**
- Click on **Telephone America** in the window
- Click **Edit menu**
- Click **Delete Memorized Transaction**
- Click **OK** to "Are you sure…?"
- Click **X** to close Memorize window

Use Notepad

Notepad is one of my favorite tools in QuickBooks. In bookkeeping, the worst thing you can do is let entries or activities fall through the cracks. It can cost you hundreds, if not thousands, of dollars. You make notes to yourself about calling or sending e-mails to your banker for a refund on an overpayment on your check. You can also make a note to back up your QuickBooks software at the end of the month, which is highly recommended. You must click Edit menu, Preference, Reminders, My Preferences tab, and check the "Show Reminder List when opening a Company file."

Activities:

- Click **on Telephone America for Check # 1002**
- Click **Edit menu**
- Click **Notepad**
- Click **in the white window**
- Click **Date Stamp** (right). Today's date is stamped
- Type **Call bank to research overpayment**
- Click **New To Do...** (Right of window)
- Click **in white window**
- Type **Email vendor to deduct $8 from the next bill.** Press **Tab**
- Remind me: Type **2/1/09.** Click **OK**
- Click **OK** again to close Notepad window

You must select a transaction in the check register for the Notepad to be activated as a submenu.

Use Calculator

It's a good practice to display your QuickBooks calculator and then minimize to the Task Master. This will increase your speed and prevent you from looking for another calculator. As long as your keyboard Num Lock is on, you can use the keyboard numbers and functions instead of clicking the calculator itself with your mouse, unless you want to clear the calculator by clicking the C on the QuickBooks calculator. Do not click the plus sign followed by the equal sign; you'll get a wrong result, and do not click = twice, otherwise you will get a wrong answer. QuickMath is activated when you press the Equal to or Plus sign (= or +) in most amount boxes.

Activities:

- Click **Edit menu**
- Click **Use Calculator**
- On your keyboard perform the following:
- Type **1234**
- Press **Backspace** on keyboard **to delete 4**
- Type **+ 1000.** Press **Enter.**
- Answer is 1123
- Press **Delete** on keyboard to clear calculator
- Type **251 + 863 + 741 + 145.** Press **Enter**.
- Answer is 2000
- Press **Delete** on keyboard to clear calculator
- Type **100,000** * .25 (25%). Press **Enter.**
- Answer is 25000
- Click **View** (top of Calculator)
- Click **Scientific**
- Click **View**
- Click **Standard**
- **Minimize Calculator** to the Taskbar for later use

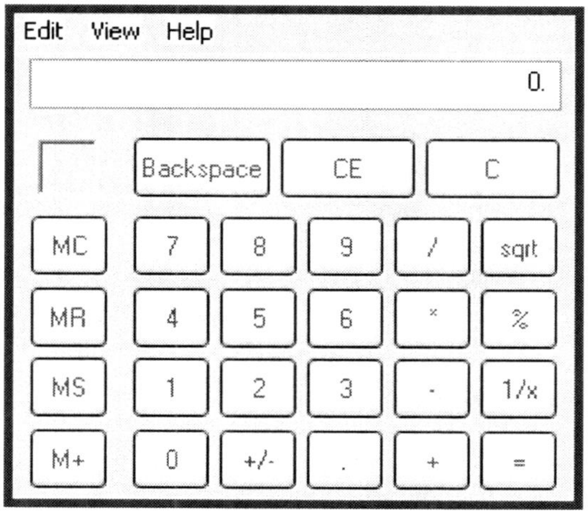

Simple Find

Using the Find function is worth every penny you spent on this software. You can find information in your database using a lot of criteria including invoices, estimates, sales receipts, credit memos, bills, checks, credit cards, purchase orders, sales orders, and journals. What if a company calls or you receive mail that says you have not paid your old bill? All you have to do is go to the Find window and search for the name of the company with Check as the Transaction Type. Click the Find button, and voila!

Activities

- Click **Edit menu**
- Click **Find...**
- Accept **Simple** tab (top left of Find window)
- Transaction Type: Select **Check**
- Payee: Select **Telephone America**
- Click **Find** (top right of window)
- **Look! Two entries are displayed**
- Click **Reset** (right of window)

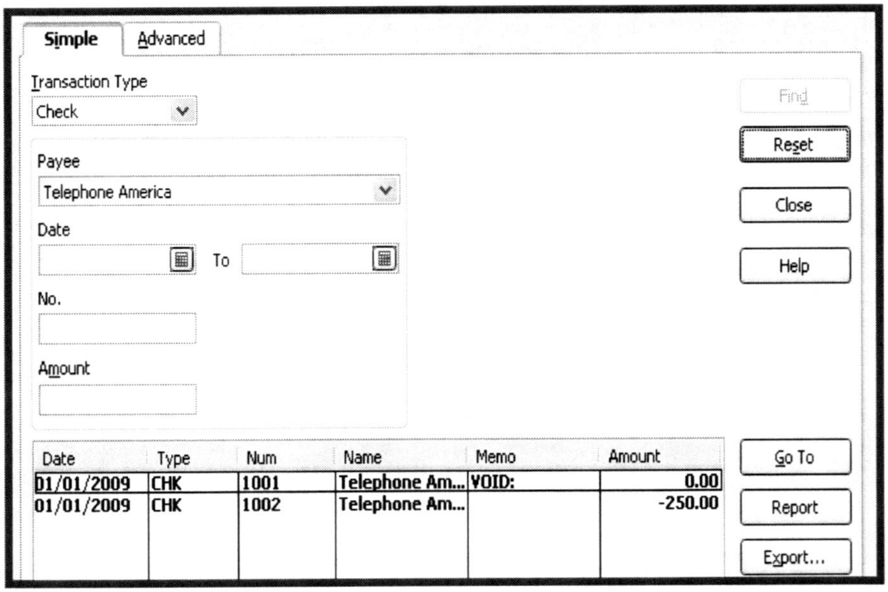

Advanced Find

We've talked about the Simple Find tab. Wait until you see what you can do with the Advanced Find. You have more options to find the financial information you're looking for. I call this speed! If this is the only reason you want to switch from Quicken to QuickBooks, it's worth it. In Quicken, when you find a list of information, you will not have the total at the bottom of the list. This is not a problem in QuickBooks. The Find Report will have total at the bottom of the list.

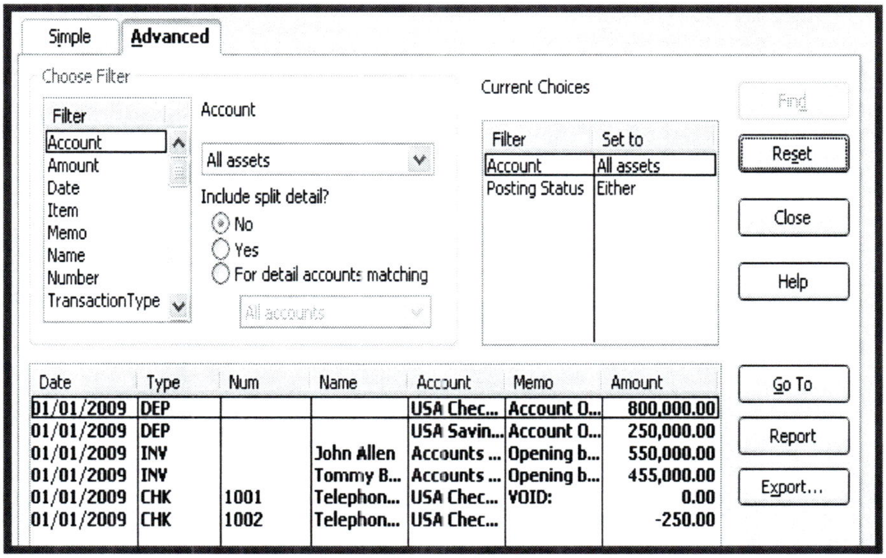

Activities:

- Click **Advanced tab**
- In Choose Filter box. Accept **Account**
- Account (right of Filter): Select **All balance sheet accounts**
- Click **Find**. (right of window)
- Balance sheet accounts are displayed
- Account (right of Filter): Select **All assets**
- Click **Find**
- Six entries are displayed
- Click **X** to close Find window

Delete Check

Sometimes, you may be forced to void a check, especially if a vendor calls to ask for a check that never reached the company. Lost-in-transit checks should be voided from the file, and your bank should be alerted. If the amount is large, it is recommended that you put a stop payment on that check. Deleting a check is done when it is just written, not cleared or reconciled. If other checks are written after the check, it is better to void than to delete it. QuickBooks will allow you to delete a check if it has not been reconciled and checks are deleted in check register.

Activities:

- Before you delete a check make sure it's the right check
- Click on **Telephone America check #1002 for 250.00**
- Click **Edit menu**
- Click **Delete Check**
- Click **OK** to "Are you sure...?"
- **Look! In the register check #1002 is gone**

You can almost delete any thing from the Edit menu, just open the window, click Edit menu and look for Delete.

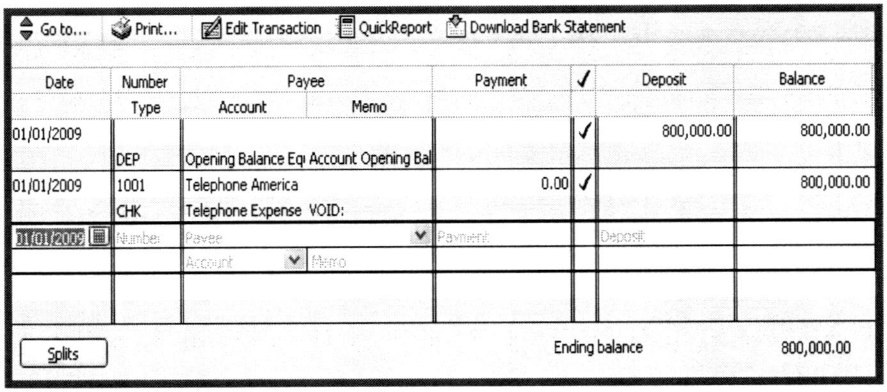

Accounting Preferences

If you plan on using account numbers, class tracking, or setting a password, you need to pay a particular attention to this section. Many account numbers will be defaulted for you; but you'll need to provide account numbers to the new accounts you created yourself. QuickBooks will allow you set a password to edit transactions on or before the closing date. The reason is that you don't want an intruder to change your financial information for last year; with a closing date and password, all is safe!

Activities:

- Click **Edit menu**
- Click **Preferences**
- Click **Accounting** (1st Item left column window)
- Click **Company Preferences** tab
- Checkmark **Use class tracking**
- Uncheck **Prompt to assign classes**
- Uncheck **Warn if Transaction are 90 days in the past**
- Uncheck **Warn if Transaction are 30 days in the future**
- Click **OK** to close Preferences window

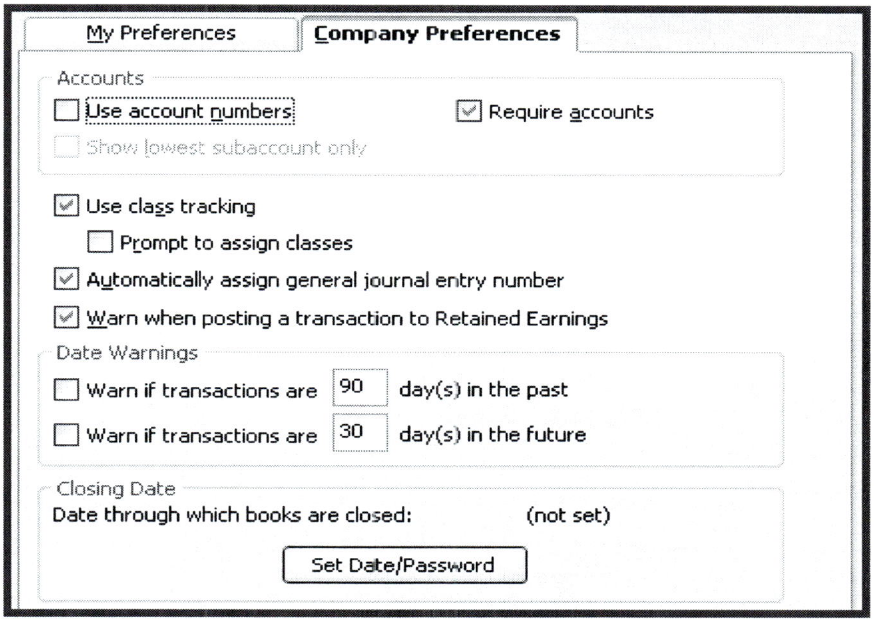

Bills, Items & Inventory

You should double check your work after completing the Inventory windows. I cannot tell you the number of times I have seen clients pay duplicate purchase orders and bills. For some companies, it is an honest mistake. But for others, it's just a game of testing your accounting systems. You must key in Vendor Purchase and Bill numbers on your checks and other documents. This allows QuickBooks to track duplicates for you. If you skip this process, you're doing so at your own risk. **If you purchased goods and received a discount, it becomes a reduction of the cost of purchasing the goods, not an income. And if you sale goods and give a discount, it becomes a reduction of income of selling the goods, not an expense.**

Activities:

- Click **Edit menu**
- Click **Preferences**
- Click **Bills** (left of window)
- Click **Company Preferences** tab
- Bills are due: Accept **10** days after receipt
- Checkmark **Warn about duplicate bill numbers…**
- Checkmark **Automatically use discounts and credits**
- Default Discount Account: Click **Down arrow**

Make sure you always checkmark this box. This is one of the most important boxes in the preferences setup process.

- **Scroll up.** Click **Add New**
- Account **Type**: Select **Cost of Goods Sold** (Very Important)
- Account Name: Type **Discount Received**
- Click **Save & Close**
- Click **Items & Inventory.** (left of window)
- Click **Yes** to "You made changes…"
- Click **Company Preferences** tab
- Checkmark **Inventory and Purchases orders are active**
- Checkmark **Warn about duplicate purchase order numbers**
- Checkmark **Warn if not enough inventory quantity on hand(QOH) to sell**
- Click **OK** to close Preferences window
- Click **OK** to "QuickBooks must close all…"
- Click **Company menu**
- Click **Home Page**

Discount Given is a reduction of income and Discount Received is a reduction of cost of goods.

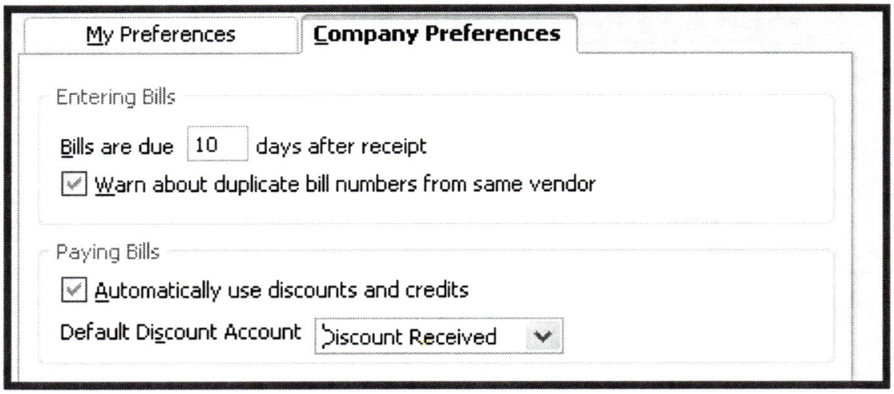

Checking Preferences

By now you know that your QuickBooks will act and react in a certain way due to the ways you set your Preferences. It is pertinent to set your Preferences correctly. One of the most important Preferences you will be setting is the Payroll default account. In the payroll liabilities box, you want to select the payroll account. Anytime you want to write a payroll related check, you want that check to come from the payroll account. Another setting is to make deposits go to your checking account.

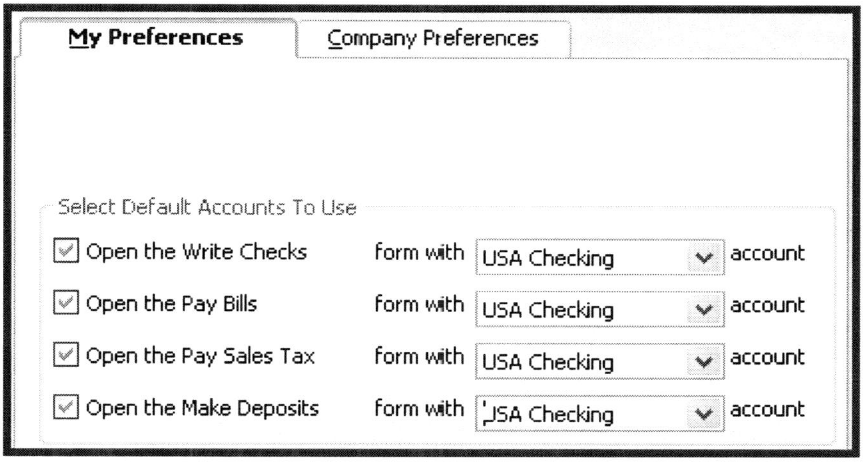

Activities:

- Click **Edit menu**.
- Click **Preferences**
- Click **Checking** (left column window)
- Click **My Preferences** tab
- Checkmark **Open the Write Checks** form with: Select **USA Checking**
- Checkmark **Open the Pay Bills** form with: Select **USA Checking**
- Checkmark **Open the Pay Sales Tax** form with: Select **USA Checking**
- Checkmark **Open the Make Deposits** form with: Select **USA Checking**
- Click **Company Preferences** tab
- Checkmark **Warn about duplicate check numbers**
- Checkmark **Open the Create Paychecks** form with: Select **Add New**
- Account Name: Type **USA Payroll Checking**
- Click **Enter Opening Balance**
- Statement Ending Balance: Type **100,000**
- Statement Ending Date: Type **1/1/2009.** Click **OK**
- Click **Save & Close**
- Checkmark **Open the Pay Payroll Liabilities**
- form with: Select **USA Payroll Checking**
- Click **OK** to close Preferences window

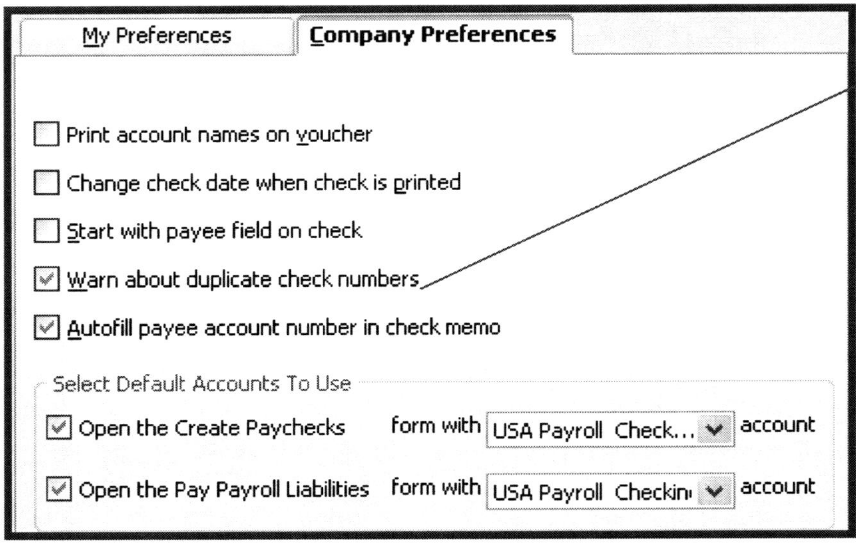

Warning about duplicate check numbers is a setup process you must never forget.

Finance Charge Preferences

Finance charges can be a legal issue and, therefore, must be set with the help of the tax staff or your accountant. You have to find out the industry standard in the business you are operating in; what Finance Charges customers are suppose to pay. Annual interest rate and the grace period must be provided. You may also set a minimum Finance Charge, and when a customer does not pay a bill by a certain date, your QuickBooks software will enter the charges as you run the process.

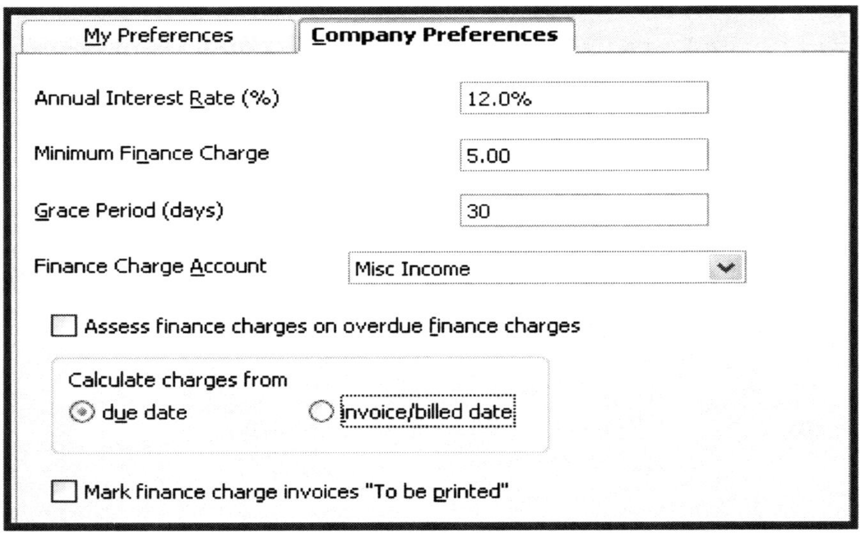

Activities:

- Click **Edit menu**
- Click **Preferences**
- Click **Finance Charge** (left of window)
- Click **Company Preferences** tab
- Annual Interest Rate (%): Type **12**. Press **Tab**
- Minimum Finance Charge: Type **5**. Press **Tab**
- Grace Period (days): Type **30**. Press **Tab**
- Finance Charge Account: Click **Add New**
- Account Name: Type **Misc Income**
- Click **Save & Close.**
- Click **OK** to close Preferences window

General Preferences

There are many Preferences you can set on your QuickBooks software. You have the more specific ones that relate to a particular window or task, and the general Preferences available every time you perform certain tasks in all the windows. A general one is for QuickBooks to beep every time you record an entry. You must understand where this preference is located. I've seen a lot of customers who allow the beep to go on, just because they don't know where to go and turn it off.

Activities:

- Click **Edit menu**
- Click **Preferences**
- Click **General** (left column of window)
- Click **My Preferences** tab
- Checkmark **Automatically open drop-down lists…**
- Uncheck **Beep when recording a transaction**
- Click **OK** to close Preferences window

Integrated App & Service Connection

For security reasons, you have to a pay particular attention to this exercise. Because QuickBooks respects your privacy, it gives you the option to accept or reject other applications' access to your database. If you don't want other applications to access your QuickBooks files behind your back, checkmark the "Don't allow any application to access this company" box. Also, QuickBooks gives you the option of being required to enter your password before connecting to the Internet.

Activities:

- Click **Edit menu**
- Click **Preferences**
- Click **Integrated Applications** (left of window)
- Click **Company Preferences** tab
- Checkmark **Don't allow any application to access this company**

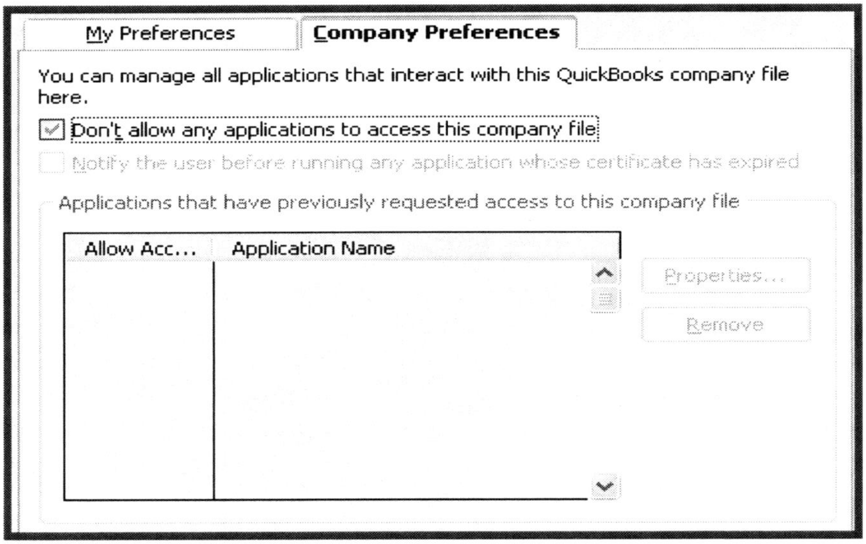

- Click **Service Connection** (left of window)
- Click **Yes** to "You have made changes to Interpreted Application…"
- Click **My Preferences** tab
- Checkmark **Give me the option of saving a file whenever…**
- Checkmark **If QuickBooks is run by my browser**
- Click **Company Preferences** tab
- Click **Always ask for a password before connecting**
- Uncheck **Allow background downloading of service messages**.
- Click **OK** to close Preferences window

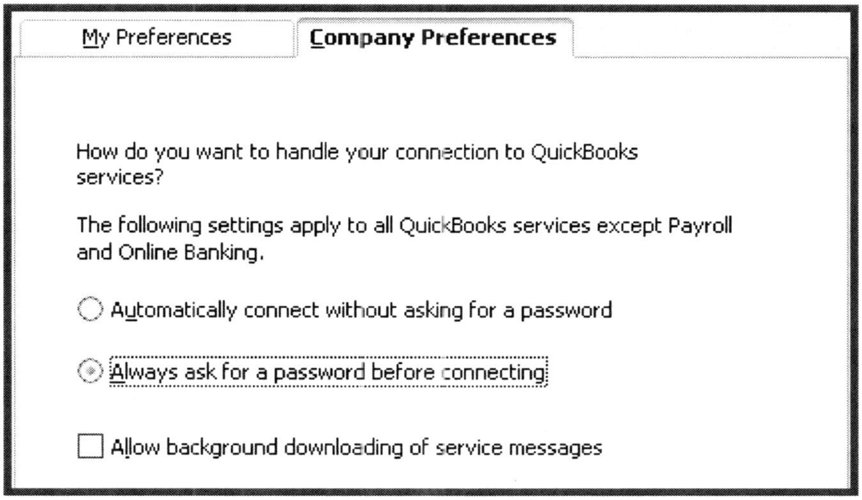

Jobs & Estimates, Sales & Customers

In the Jobs & Estimate preferences windows, there is one check box that is of utmost importance to every QuickBooks user the: "Warn about duplicate estimate numbers." You should click a checkmark on this box; it's for your protection. You don't want to accept two estimates; most likely the same company will send you two invoices. So, the earlier you deal with duplicate estimates, the better. In the Sales & Customer Preferences windows, you should check "Warn about duplicate invoice numbers."

> Multiple Currencies is the next setup after Jobs and Estimates. But it has been completed in the Quick Company chapter before you started using the QuickBooks files.

Activities:

- Click **Edit menu**
- Click **Preferences**
- Click **Jobs & Estimates** (left)
- Click **Company Preferences** tab
- Click **Yes** to "Do You Create Estimates?"
- Click **Yes** to "Do You Do Progress Invoice?"
- Checkmark **Warn about duplicate estimate numbers**
- Checkmark **Don't print items that have zero amount**
- Click **Sales & Customers** (left of window)
- Click **Yes** to "You have made changes to Job & Estimates…"
- Click **OK** to "QuickBooks must close…"
- Click **Company Preferences** tab
- Checkmark **Warn about duplicate…**
- Click **OK** to close Preferences window

- Click **Company menu.**
- Click **Home Page**

Payroll & Employees

As always, it is advisable to set up your Preferences windows before you embark on practicing with the rest of the QuickBooks submenus. It is much more significant to set up the Payroll & Employee Preferences first before attempting to work with the submenus. This way the necessary submenus are activated after the Preferences are setup. More submenus will be displayed after you registered for the Quick Company, without which you may have fewer Payroll & Employees submenus available.

Activities:

- Click **Edit menu**
- Click **Preferences**
- Click **Payroll & Employees** (left of window)
- Click **Company Preferences** tab
- Click **Full Payroll**
- Uncheck **Copy earnings details from previous paycheck**
- Click **OK** to close Preferences window

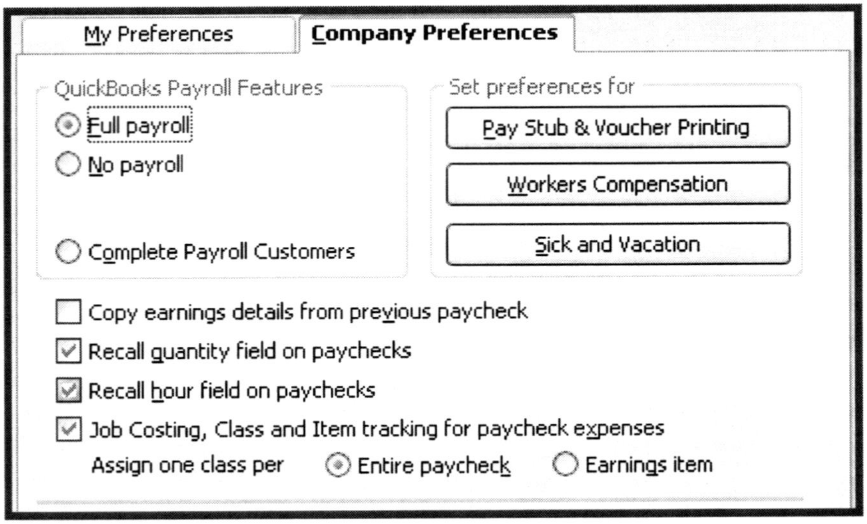

Reminders

Whatever you do be sure to set up your Reminder Preferences. I will not tell you the cost of missing payments to your vendors, including government regulators—you already know! You should complete the Reminder windows. Do not forget to put a checkmark on "Always check spelling before printing." With this preference, your financial reports will have little or no spelling errors. You will uncheck Show Reminder List, but in your business, check this box for Reminder come up each time.

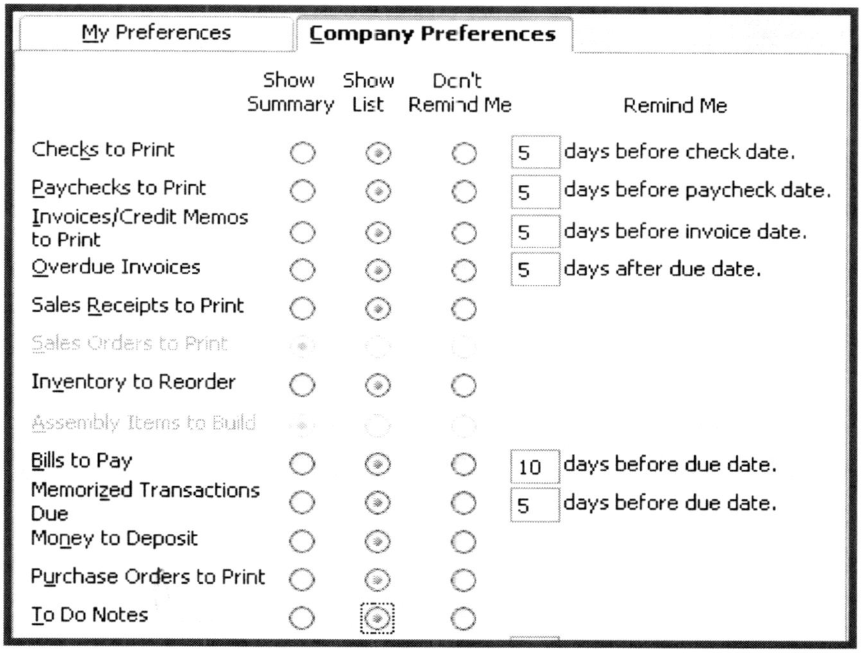

Activities:

Normally, you checkmark this box because you want to see the Reminder list when you open QuickBooks.

- Click **Edit menu**
- Click **Preferences**
- Click **Reminders** (left of window)
- Click **My Preference** tab
- Uncheck **Show Reminders List when opening a Company file**
- Click **Company Preferences** tab
- Click **all middle options under Show List column**
- **See image above**
- Click **OK** to close Preferences window

Reports & Graphs

How the report appears when you run the Reports menu will depend on how you set up your Report & Graph Preferences window. You should click the "Refresh automatically," so you don't have to confront the message window that asks you if you want to refresh your Report window. Also, make sure the "Draw Graph in 2D" box is **unchecked.** Most companies are using the Accrual basis of accounting, but if for any reason you're using the Cash basis, you must click the Cash option.

Activities:

- Click **Edit menu**
- Click **Preferences**
- Click **Reports & Graphs** (left of window)
- Click **My Preference** tab
- Click **Refresh automatically…"**
- Click **OK** to close Preferences window

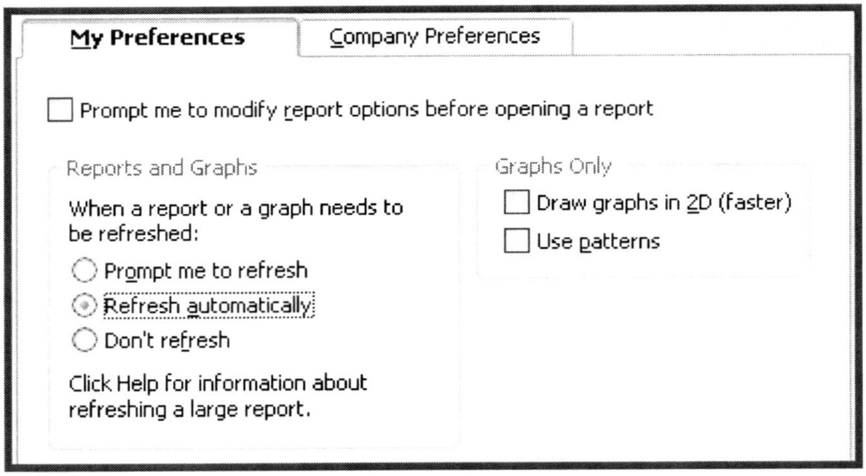

Sales Tax Preferences

Setting your sales tax Preferences is very essential, because you must understand which items on the Item List window are taxable and which ones are non taxable. You don't want to be collecting taxes from the public and not remitting them to the government. If you don't know which items are taxable or nontaxable, you should consult with your local tax agency or a tax accountant. You should also set up the Tax Preferences, if you want to pay your Sales Tax monthly or quarterly.

Activities:

- Click **Edit menu**
- Click **Preferences**
- Click **Sales Tax**
- Click **Company Preferences tab**
- Do you charge tax? Click **Yes**
- Your most common sales tax item: Click **Add New**
- Type: Accept **Sales Tax Item**. Press **Tab**
- Sales Tax Name: Type **TX Sales Tax**
- Description: Type **Taxable Sales**
- Tax Rate (%): Type **7.5%.** Press **Tab**
- Tax Agency: Click **Add New**
- Vendor Name: Type **Texas Comptroller**. Click **OK**

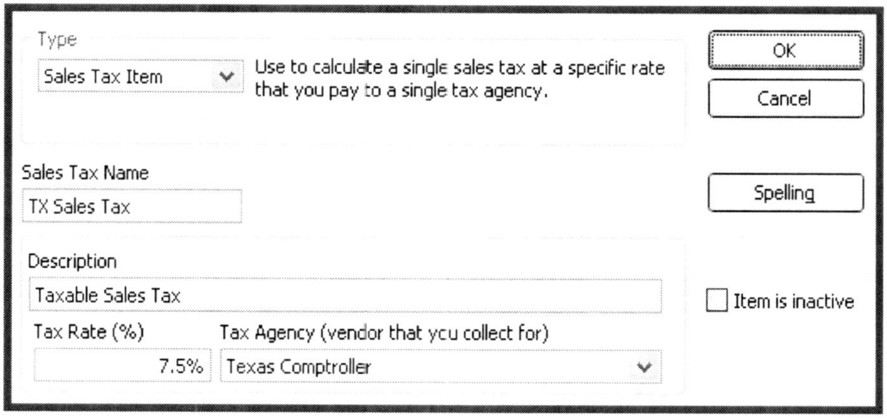

- Click **OK** to close New Item window
- Your most common sales tax item: Again Click **Add New**
- Type: Accept **Sales Tax Item**. Press **Tab**
- Sales Tax Name: Type **Out of State TX**
- Description: Type **Non Taxable Sales**
- Tax Rate(%): Accept **0.0%**
- Tax Agency: **(Leave blank)**. Click **OK**
- Taxable item code: Accept **Tax**
- Non-Taxable item code: Accept **Non**
- Click **OK** to close Preference window
- Click **OK** to Updating Sales Tax
- Click **OK** to "QuickBooks must close…"
- Click **Company menu.** Click **Home Page**

Tax: 1099, Time & Expenses

If you have vendors, some of them may qualify for the Form 1099, especially your subcontractors. When setting up the New Vendor windows, be sure to click the Additional Info tab and click the "Vendor eligible for 1099" box. Before you create a New Vendor, you must come to the Preference window and click the Yes to "Do you file 1099_MISC forms?" If you fail to click yes, most Form 1099 related windows will not be activated. You will also be setting the Time Tracking preferences here.

Activities:

- Click **Edit menu**
- Click **Preferences**
- Click **Tax: 1099** (bottom left of window)
- Click **Company Preferences**
- Click **Yes** on **"Do you file 1099-MISC forms?"**
- Click **Time & Expenses** (bottom left of window
- Click **Company Preferences**
- Click **Yes** on "Do You Track Time?"
- First Day of Work Week: Select **Monday**.
- Uncheck **Track reimbursed expense as income**
- Click **OK** to close Preferences window

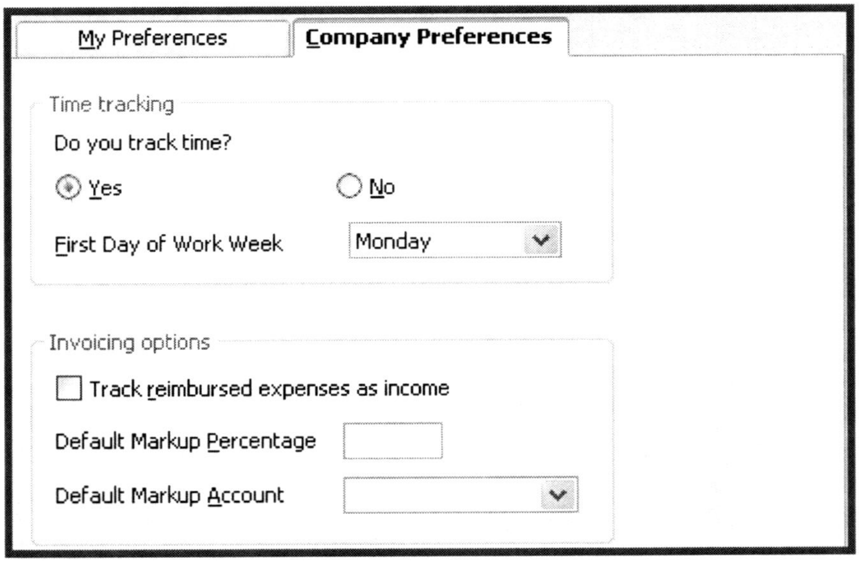

Financial Results: Profit & Loss

In this chapter we accomplished a lot of things including creating, deleting, and restoring entries. But in the final analysis nothing we did or accomplished had anything to do with the Profit & Loss statement. We started with $1,000,000 when we copied Quick Company, and we ended up with the same amount. When you open any financial statements remember to click the Dates down arrow to select This Fiscal Year, otherwise, your results will match the results in this book.

Quick Company 2009

Profit & Loss

January through December 2009

	Jan - Dec 09
Ordinary Income/Expense	
Income	
Uncategorized Income	1,005,000.00
Total Income	1,005,000.00
Gross Profit	1,005,000.00
Expense	
Telephone Expense	0.00
Uncategorized Expenses	5,000.00
Total Expense	5,000.00
Net Ordinary Income	1,000,000.00
Net Income	**1,000,000.00**

Activities:

- Click **Reports menu**
- Click **Company & Financial**
- Click **Profit & Loss Standard**
- Date: Select **This Fiscal Year**
- From: Accept **1/1/09.** To: Accept **12/31/09**
- **Net Income is 1,000,000**
- Click **X** to close window

Financial Results: Balance Sheet

Like the Profit & Loss statement, most activities did not affect the Balance Sheet. However, we created two checks for a total amount of $400, which affected the Checking Account and therefore the Balance Sheet report. Since, we voided and deleted those entries; the Balance Sheet report remains unchanged. It's essential to remind yourself to click the Date down arrow any time you open the financial report and select This Fiscal Year, otherwise, your figures will be different.

Activities:

- Click **Reports menu**
- Click **Company & Financial**
- Click **Balance Sheet Standard**
- Date (top left): Select **This Fiscal Year**
- As of: Accept **12/31/09**
- **Total Assets is 2,155,000.00**
- Click **X** to close window

Quick Company 2009

Balance Sheet

As of December 31, 2009

	Dec 31, 09
ASSETS	
Current Assets	
Checking/Savings	
USA Checking	800,000.00
USA Payroll Checking	100,000.00
USA Savings	250,000.00
Total Checking/Savings	1,150,000.00
Accounts Receivable	
Accounts Receivable	1,005,000.00
Total Accounts Receivable	1,005,000.00
Total Current Assets	2,155,000.00
TOTAL ASSETS	**2,155,000.00**

Chapter Summary

The Edit menu is one the most important menus, because you cannot perform your work efficiently without setting up your Preferences correctly. Going forward, after completing this chapter, you should be able to set up your Preferences with speed and confidence. The Edit menu will also allow you edit or delete a lot of windows in QuickBooks. Any time you want to get rid of any window in QuickBooks, just open that window and click the Edit menu to see if QuickBooks allows you to edit or delete the window. This is a very important point to remember.

What we accomplished:

- Reviewed the Edit submenus
- Made entries in the check register
- Created a new check
- Voided a check
- Memorized a check
- Used the Notepad
- Practiced the Calculator
- Practiced the Simple Find
- Practiced the Advanced Find
- Deleted a check
- Set up the preferences windows
- Processed financial statements

Additional Financial activities:

Created Payroll Checking for $100,000 in the Checking preferences window

Exercise 2

Complete Exercise 2 by using the following information:

1. Set up preferences.
   Set up all preferences as on pages 54 to 66 (Accounting to Time & Expense)
   Set up Payroll opening balance 250,000(Very Imp) date 1/1/09 as on page 57

2. Create new customer.
   John Arlington Inc. opening balance 225,000 at 1/1/09

3. Create new vendors.
   World Insurance opening balance 12,500 at 1/1/09
   Auto Services Inc. opening balance 0.00 at 1/1/09
   First Realty LLC opening balance 0.00 at 1/1/09
   Great Cell Phones opening balance 0.00 at 1/1/09
   Town & Country Insurance opening balance 0.00 at 1/1/09

4. Enter the following transactions in the checking register.
   1/1/09 Check #1001 Auto Services for 2,500 Automobile Expense
   1/2/09 Check #1002 First Realty for 10,500 Rent Expense
   1/2/09 Check #1003 Great Cell Phones for 3,400 Telephone Expense

5. Process the following reports
   Profit & Loss Statement ending 12/31/09
   Balance Sheet Standard ending 12/31/09
   Statement of Cash Flow ending 12/31/09
   Customer Balance Details as of 1/31/09
   Vendor Balance Details as of 1/31/09
   Use Simple and Advanced Find to preview and print these reports:
   Auto Services Inc. check #1001
   All current assets for January
   All current liabilities for January
   Checking account all transactions
   All A/R and A/P

$

Chapter 3

View Menu

Objectives: After you've completed this chapter you will be able to:

- ✓ Identify the View submenus
- ✓ Customize icon bar
- ✓ Add window to icon bar
- ✓ Processed financial reports and compare results
- ✓ Reviewed the tax guidelines

Review View Submenus

When you think about the View menu, you think about what you can see on your Desktop. Most icons on your desktop are defaults. In other words, they have been pre-set by QuickBooks. For example, if you want to change what you see on the Tool and Icon Bar, click the Customize Icon Bar to add or subtract the Icon on the bar. The easy access to these Icons is worth every second you spend in setting it up.

- Click **View menu**

The following submenus are located under the View menu:

- **Open Window List:** Most of the time you want to have the window lists displayed on the left side of the window and other times you want the list to go away so you can have enough space to display the main window. When you click View menu and uncheck the Open Window list, the list will go away. But it is pertinent to display the Open Window List so you can always reach for it instead of first clicking the menus and then the submenus.

- **Icon Bar:** Tool bar or the Icon Bar as QuickBooks calls it, is where you will place the most frequently used tools. Check Registers, Customers, Vendors, and Reports should be placed on the Icon bar for easy access.

- **Customize Icon Bar:** Not only are you able to place tools on the Tool bar, you can also customize the Tool bar the way you see fit. Customization, for example, allows you to rearrange the position of the tools and allows you add, edit and delete tools.

- **Add "USA Checking" to Icon Bar:** After you've opened a favorite window, the USA Checking register window for example, you can decide to place the window on the Tool bar for easy access. This is one of the most popular functions under the View menu.

- **One/Multiple Windows:** These two functions work in reverse to one another, that is, if your window is on the One Window default, you can switch to the Multiple Windows by clicking on the function. When you click Multiple Windows function, you will be able to move multiple windows you've opened to the left or to the right, up or down the screen as you see fit.

Customize Icon Bar

You can customize your Icon Bar by adding, removing, or editing icons. Reordering the Icon Bar is also one of the easiest tasks you can perform in this window. It is recommended that you place the most frequently used windows on the Icon bar for easy access, instead of going through the menus each time. Remember you cannot add, remove, or edit a menu icon, such as Customers and Vendors. These are permanently placed on the Icon bar by QuickBooks and cannot be changed.

Activities:

- Click **View menu**
- Click **Customize Icon Bar**
- Click **Add…**
- In the left window. Scroll to the bottom
- Click **Use Register**. Click **OK**
- Click **Reg**
- Click **Edit...**
- Label: Type **Register**. Click **OK**
- Click **Add**…
- Click **Adjust Sales Tax**.(left window) Click **OK**
- Click **Adjust Tax**
- Adjust Sale Tax is gone
- Click **OK** (bottom) to close Customize Icon bar window

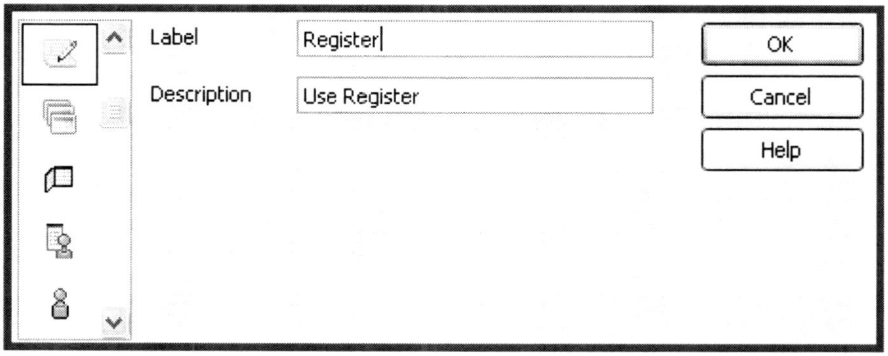

Add Window to Icon Bar

Adding windows to the Icon Bar, I think, is one of the best features on your QuickBooks software. Can you imagine adding your favorite windows like reports to the Icon Bar list? Yes, it is now possible. All you have to do is open that hard to reach window, click the View menu and then Add Window to the Icon Bar. In less than a second you have your favorite window listed with other Icons. Bank accounts and financial statements reports are the best candidates for the Icon Bar.

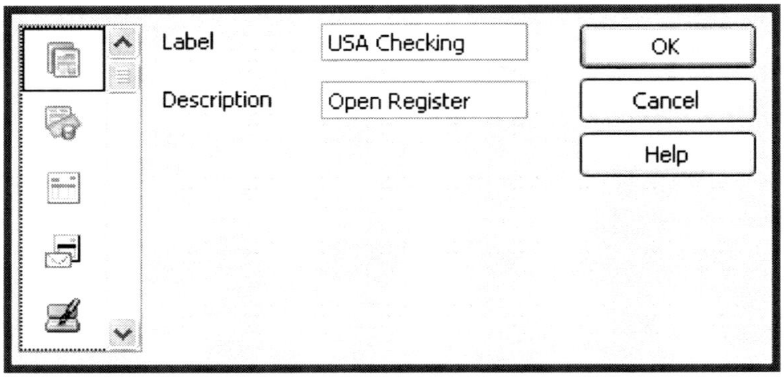

Activities:

- Click **Edit menu**
- Click **Use Register**
- Select Account: Select **USA Checking**. Click **OK**
- Click **View menu**
- Click **Add "USA Checking to Icon Bar**
- Label: Accept **USA Checking**
- Description: Accept **Open Register**. Click **OK**
- Click the **Double arrow** at the end of the toolbar
- **Look! USA Checking is listed**
- Click **X** to close USA Checking check register

Financial Results: Profit & Loss

In the View menu chapter, we concentrated on navigating through QuickBooks. We used One Window and Multiple Windows functions. We did not perform any entries that increased or decreased any account in the Profit & Loss statements. Don't forget to customize your financial by clicking Modify Report located at the top left of the report window, then Header/Footer tab. This window allows you to make changes to the way your reports look, like modifying the report.

Quick Company 2009
Profit & Loss
January through December 2009

	◇ Jan - Dec 09 ◇
Ordinary Income/Expense	
Income	
Uncategorized Income	▶ 1,005,000.00 ◀
Total Income	1,005,000.00
Gross Profit	1,005,000.00
Expense	
Telephone Expense	0.00
Uncategorized Expenses	5,000.00
Total Expense	5,000.00
Net Ordinary Income	1,000,000.00
Net Income	**1,000,000.00**

Activities:

- Click **Reports menu**
- Click **Company & Financial**
- Click **Profit & Loss Standard**
- Date (top left): Select **This Fiscal Year**
- From: Accept **1/1/09.** To: Accept **12/31/09**
- **Net Income is 1,000,000**
- Click **X** to close window

Financial: Balance Sheet

Like the Profit & Loss statement above, the Balance Sheet result is unchanged. We started with Total Assets $2,155,000, and we ended with the same amount. Note that the report below did not include the Total Liabilities & Equity—the bottom half of this report—due to space. However, the Total Assets and Total Liabilities & Equity will always be the same number and in this case, the figure is $2,155,000. Remember to select the right date range to get the right results.

Activities:

- Click **Reports menu**
- Click **Company & Financial**
- Click **Balance Sheet Standard**
- Date (top left): Click **down arrow**
- Select **This Fiscal Year**
- As of: Accept **12/31/09**
- **Total Assets is 2,155,000.00**
- Click **X** to close window

Quick Company 2009

Balance Sheet

As of December 31, 2009

	Dec 31, 09
ASSETS	
Current Assets	
Checking/Savings	
USA Checking	800,000.00
USA Payroll Checking	100,000.00
USA Savings	250,000.00
Total Checking/Savings	1,150,000.00
Accounts Receivable	
Accounts Receivable	1,005,000.00
Total Accounts Receivable	1,005,000.00
Total Current Assets	2,155,000.00
TOTAL ASSETS	**2,155,000.00**

Tax Guidelines

The rest of this chapter is devoted to the IRS guidelines relating to business and payroll taxes. In addition to consulting a tax professional, the IRS would like you to have a basic understanding of these tax rules. You need to login to their website www.irs.gov to review the guidelines. Let's look at a few of theses from the IRS website:

Major tax guidelines relating to payroll are:

Starting a business
Business structures
Employer identification number
Business taxes
Record keeping
Employment tax record keeping

Starting a business

When you're conducting a business you need to know if what you're doing is considered a business for tax purposes. If your activity is not considered a business, it is a called a hobby. Your activity is considered a business if you make profit in at least three of the last five tax years including the current year. If your business consists primarily of breeding, showing, training or racing horses, you are required to show profit in at least two of the last seven years. Other considerations are:

- Does the time and effort put into the activity indicate an intention to make a profit?
- Does the taxpayer depend on the income from the activity?
- If there are losses, are they due to circumstances beyond the taxpayer's control or did they occur in the start-up phase of the business?
- Has the taxpayer changed methods of operation to improve profitability?
- Does the taxpayer or his/her advisors have the knowledge needed to carry on the activity as a successful business?
- Has the taxpayer made a profit in similar activities in the past?
- Does the activity make a profit in some years?
- Can the taxpayer expect to make a profit in the future from the appreciation of assets used in the activity?

Business Structures

QuickBooks gives you options to choose which business structure you are setting up. The name of the structure you chose determines the chart of accounts QuickBooks defaults in the new company. And according to the IRS, there are five major business structures namely:

- Sole Proprietorship
- Partnership
- Corporation
- S Corporation
- Limited Liability Company (LLC)

Employer Identification Number (EIN)

Generally, businesses need the EIN, otherwise know as the Employer Identification Number. You can apply for this number through the IRS and it is a free service. You will need an EIN, if you answer yes to any of the following:

- Do you have employees?
- Do you operate your business as a corporation or a partnership?
- Do you file any of these tax returns: Employment, Excise, or Alcohol, Tobacco and Firearms?
- Do you withhold taxes on income other than wages paid to a non-resident alien?
- Do you have a Keogh plan?
- Are you involved with any of the following types of organizations?
    - ✓ Trusts except certain grantor-owned revocable trusts, IRAs Exempt Organization Business Income Tax Return
    - ✓ Estates
    - ✓ Real estate mortgage investment conduits
    - ✓ Non-profit organization
    - ✓ Farmers cooperatives
    - ✓ Plan administrators

In general, you need a new EIN when you change ownership or business structure. For sole proprietors, you need a new EIN if any of the following are true:

- You are subject to a bankruptcy proceeding
- You incorporate
- You take in partners and operate as a partnership
- You purchase or inherit an existing business that you operate as a sole proprietorship.

You will not be required to obtain a new EIN if any of the following statements are true:

- You change the name of your business
- You change your location and/or add other locations
- You operate multiple businesses

Business Taxes

The form of business you operate determines what taxes you pay. There are four general types of business taxes:

- Income Tax
- Self-Employment Tax

- Employment Taxes
- Excise Tax

Self-employment tax or the SE tax is a Social Security and Medicare tax primarily for individuals who work for themselves. Your Social Security coverage provides you with retirement benefits, disability benefits, survivor benefits, and hospital insurance (Medicare) benefits. You must pay SE tax and file Schedule SE (Form 1040) if either of the following applies:

- If your net earnings from self-employment were $400 or more
- If you work for a church or a qualified church-controlled organization (other than as a minister or member of a religious order) that elected an exemption from social security and Medicare taxes, you are subject to SE tax if you receive $108.28 or more in wages from the church or organization.

Employment taxes are required when you have employees and you must file the related forms. The following are the employment taxes:

- Social Security and Medicare taxes
- Federal income tax withholding
- Federal unemployment (FUTA) tax

Record Keeping

Businesses must keep accurate records if they plan to be profitable. You may not keep your records forever and therefore should follow certain guidelines in keeping or destroying records. The length of the time you keep your records depends on the action, expense, or event the document records. These are the general guidelines on how long to keep your records:

- Keep for 3 years: if you owe additional tax and you reported all your income in the previous years and you did not file a fraudulent returns and you filed a return.
- Keep for 6 years: if you did not report all income that you should have been reported and it is more than 25% of the gross income shown on your return
- Keep indefinitely: if you file a fraudulent return.
- Keep indefinitely: if you did not file a return.
- Keep for 3 years from the date you filed your original return: if you file a claim for credit or refund after you file your return or keep for 2 years from the date you paid the tax whichever is later.

- Keep for 7 years: if you file a claim for a loss from worthless securities or bad debt deduction.
- Keep for at least 4 years: for all employment tax records after the tax due date or tax is paid whichever is later.

Employment Tax Record Keeping

Extra care must be given to employment documents especially payroll and tax related documents. You are required to keep employment taxes for at least four years after filing the 4th quarter of the year. The following records should be available for IRS review:

- Your employer identification number
- Amounts and dates of all wages, annuity, and pension payments
- Amounts of tips reported
- The fair market value of in-kind wages paid
- Names, addresses, social security numbers, and occupations of employees and recipients
- Any employee copies of Form W-2 that were returned to you as undeliverable
- Date of employment
- Periods for which employees and recipients were paid while absent due to sickness or injury and the amount and weekly rate of payments you or third-party payers made to them.
- Copies of employees and recipients income tax withholding allowance certificates (Form W-4, W-4P, W-4S, and W-4V)
- Dates and amounts of tax deposits you made
- Copies of returns filed
- Records of allocated tips
- Records of fringe benefits provided including substantiation

Chapter Summary

There is not much to the View menu except the Icon Bar and the Open Window List. With practice, you can understand how to manipulate the One and Multiple Windows functions. Both functions allow you to either view one window at a time or view multiple windows by dragging the windows around. The Open Window List is handy; it allows you instant access to windows already opened rather than going through the menus each time you want to open a window.

What we accomplished:

- Reviewed the View submenus
- Learned how to customize icons on the icon bar
- Learned how to add windows to the icon bar
- Processed financial statements
- Reviewed tax guidelines

Additional Financial activities:

- No financial activities

Exercise 3

Complete Exercise 3 by using the following information:

1. Create new customers.
   Terrence & Company opening balance 154,000 at 1/1/09

2. Create new vendors.
   All Star Transportation opening balance 23,000 at 1/1/09

3. Enter the following transactions in the checking account register.
   1/5/09 Check #1004 Auto Services Inc. for 159 Automobile Expense
   1/5/09 Check #1005 Great Cell Phones for 2,400 Telephone Expense
   1/5/09 Check #1006 Town & Country Insurance 1,590 Insurance Expense

4. Process the following reports
   Profit & Loss Statement ending 12/31/09
   Balance Sheet Standard ending 12/31/09
   Statement of Cash Flow ending 12/31/09
   AR Aging Summary as of 1/31/09
   Customer Balance Details as of 1/31/09
   Collection Report as of 1/31/09
   AP Aging Summary as of 1/31/09
   Vendor Balance Details as of 1/31/09
   QuickReport on Jenny Lane LLC in Customer Center window 12/31/09

$

Chapter 4

Lists Menu

Objectives: After you've completed this chapter you will be able to:

- ✓ Identify Lists submenus
- ✓ Explain chart of accounts and Item list
- ✓ Create main accounts
- ✓ Merge main and subaccounts
- ✓ Create main items and sub items
- ✓ Complete the asset item list
- ✓ Create price level items
- ✓ Create sales tax items
- ✓ Create class items
- ✓ Complete the customer & vendor profile lists
- ✓ Memorize a transaction
- ✓ Process financial reports and compare results

Review Lists Submenus

The List menu is one of the most useful menus, in terms of setting up accounts and items, because this is where the foundation of your ivory tower is laid. If the concrete is not strong and the steel is not properly laid and connected, sooner or later the entire building will come crashing down. I have seen customers spend thousands of dollars trying to correct mistakes that should have never happened in the first place. This is where an "I can do it" attitude can get you into trouble, if you did not set up your Chart of Accounts and Item List window correctly.

- Click **List menu**

The following submenus are located under the List menu:

- **Chart of Accounts:** Any time you think about accounts, you think Chart of Accounts. Whether you are creating a new one or editing an old account, you can't do it without the Chart of Accounts window. It lets you write checks and make deposits. You can access the windows in the Chart of Accounts by right clicking anywhere in the window. If an account is associated with another account or an item it cannot be deleted. Some functions cannot be accessed by right clicking in the window, rather by clicking the account and Edit menu

- **Item List:** By implication if you are using the Chart of Accounts to create accounts, you will be using the Item List to create items. Items can be what you sell to your customers, or what you buy from vendors. The purpose of the Item List is to keep record of all items, sort of a warehouse where every item that pulls into QuickBooks windows is stored.

- **Fixed Asset Item List:** Fixed items are long-lived assets used in the operation of a business. If you are going to pull certain Fixed Assets information into QuickBooks windows, you have to record them in the Item List window. Major assets such as Trucks, Building, Equipments, and Computer are recorded in the Fixed Asset windows. Remember Fixed Assets are also recorded in the Chart of Accounts first. The difference between the Fixed Asset window and the Chart of Accounts window is that Fixed Asset has full details of each asset, while Chart of Accounts has limited information of assets, such as amount. Like other accounts in the Chart of Accounts window, you can change the opening balance when you think the original amount is incorrect.

- **Price Level List:** If you have price levels in your pricing policy, you should let QuickBooks know by completing this window, because sooner or later in one of the windows, you will be required to pull the price level.

- **Sales Tax Code List:** If you collect taxes, you will have to choose the sales tax code to be included anytime you sell merchandise with tax. You are also able to pay and Adjust Sales Tax from this window.

- **Payroll Item List:** If you have employees and plan to use QuickPayroll, it is important to list your Payroll Items. QuickBooks will preload most of the Payroll Items for you. However, you must double check to see if you need additional Payroll Items, which you can create by right clicking in the Payroll Item List window and clicking New to complete the window.

- **Class List:** If you have more than one type of business line, it is recommended to use the Class List. It will help you monitor income and expenses by Class or line of business. When one class is identified as making more money than others, you want to know why. As you find out what you're doing right in that one business, you can leverage that experience to other lines of businesses. You don't have to reinvent the wheel.

- **Other Names List:** You might have other names that are not a good fit with other list windows. The Other Names List window is the place to come anytime you have a name that is not related to other names; for example: Transfer to Checking, Transfer to Saving, Transfer from Checking, and Transfer from Savings. These are names that belong to the Other Names List window.

- **Customer & Vendor Profile Lists:** This is a unique submenu that keeps other lists not included above. The Profile List has many lists including Sales Rep, Customer Type, Vendor Type, Job Type, Term, Customer Message, Payment Method, Ship Via, and Vehicle List.

- **Templates:** It is to your benefit to preview what's available in the Template window. You do not need to waste time duplicating effort by creating forms that are already provided for you. The following are available in the template: Invoice, Credit Memo, Sales Receipt, Purchase Order, and Sales Order

- **Memorized Transaction List:** If you have recurring transactions, it is efficient to memorize that transaction, rather than manually processing the same information on a daily, weekly, or monthly basis. You don't want to process the same transaction every week to a customer or vendor when you can just memorize it. It is also highly recommended to group your transactions according to time—daily, weekly, monthly, quarterly, or annually.

Review Chart of Accounts & Item List

Depending on the type of business you selected at the time you created a company, QuickBooks will default certain accounts for you. Once you understand the principles of creating accounts and items as explained below, you will never have problems creating and managing them. As soon as you determine which group the account or item belongs, the next step is to create it—with ease and confidence. There are six major account types: Assets, Liabilities, Equity, Income, Cost of Goods Sold, and Operating Expenses. Review the summary below especially the difference between service and product company Profit & Loss Statements.

Balance Sheet accounts:

- Assets: these are what the business own. For example, checking, savings, petty cash, money market, employee advancement, prepaid insurance, accounts receivable, inventory, furniture, equipment, cars & trucks.

- Liabilities: these are what the business owes. For example, accounts payable, payroll liability, sales tax liability, mortgage loan, equipment loan, office building loan

- Equities: these are what the owners of the business brought into the business, what they took and what is left. For example opening balance equity, owners equity, owners contribution, owners distribution, owners retained earnings, partners contribution, partners distribution, capital stock, treasury stock.

When you're in the QuickBooks account selection window, you'll see the following:

- Assets: including bank, fixed asset, other account types—accounts receivable, other current asset, and other asset.

- Liability: including loan, credit card, other account types—accounts payable, other current liability, and long term liability.

- Equity.

Profit & Loss Statement accounts:

- Income: these are products you sell to customers or services you render to clients. Each business determines what it sells to customers and how much to charge for the products or services. For example landscaping services

- Cost of Goods Sold: Generally, these are the cost of inventory goods and services you bought from vendors that are used directly to produce goods and services. There are two types of cost of good sold: inventory (you track of cost and quantity) and non inventory. And there are two types of business: service and **product (some call it manufacturing)**. When a business either service or product company has **inventory** items, it **used directly** in producing goods and services, it links the items to cost of goods sold. When a business either service or product company has **inventory** items, it did **not used directly** in producing goods and services, it links the items to cost of goods sold, e.g. retail sales. When a product company has **non inventory** items, it **used directly** in products, it links the items to Job Cost, a part of cost of goods sold. When a service company has a **non inventory** items, it **used directly** in services, it links the item to Job Expense, a part of operating expense (as shown below)

- Operating Expense (Expense): Generally, these are the cost of **non inventory** goods and services you bought from vendors that are **not used directly** to produce goods and services. For example, rent, advertising, insurance (unless the insurance on products which is a cost of goods sold), repairs, automobile expense.

When you're in the QuickBooks account selection window, you'll see the following:

- **Income**: including other account types—other income.
- **Expense**: including other account types—cost of goods sold and other expense.

The difference between Service and Product company Profit & Loss Statements:

Income: Any product or service you sell to customers or clients (applies to both service and product companies)

1. Design
2. Deck & Patio
3. Garden Lighting
4. Drip Systems, and a host of others

Cost of Goods Sold:

1. Cost of Goods Sold: cost and quantity of **inventory** items **used directly** in producing goods and services (applies to **both service and product** company) and cost and quantity of **inventory** items **not used directly** in producing goods and services (applies to **both service and product** company)
2. Job Cost: cost of **non inventory** items **used directly** in producing the goods (applies to **only product company**)

Operating Expense:

1. Job Expense: cost of **non inventory** items **used directly** in producing the services (applies to **only service company**)
2. Payroll
3. Automobile
4. Rent
5. Insurance
6. And a host of others

(Items 2–6:) cost of **non inventory** goods and services **not used directly** in producing goods and services (applies to both service and product companies)

Money Market Account

We need to create a new account in the Chart of Accounts window and the beginning accounts are mainly the banking accounts. Most of the time, you need money in your bank accounts to pay your vendors. In creating a new account, remember to enter the opening balance and the date of the new account. If you have multiple bank accounts, you use the Next button to enter the next account instead of leaving and entering the Chart of Accounts window.

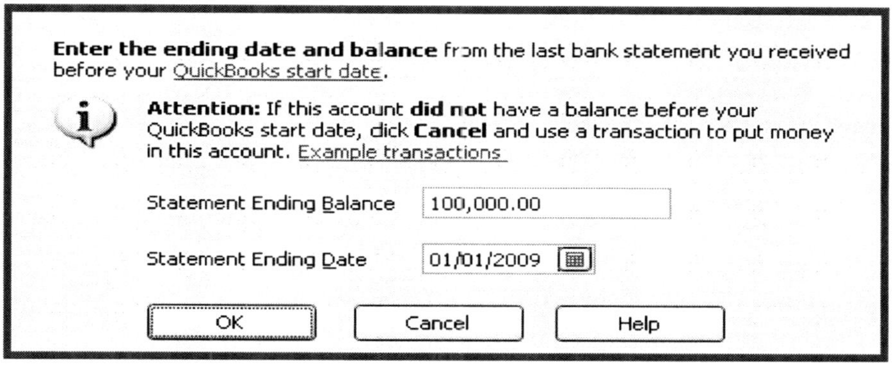

Activities:

- ❖ Click **Lists menu**
- ❖ Click **Chart of Accounts**
- ❖ Maximize window
- ❖ Right click in the window. Click **New**
- ❖ Click **Bank**. Click **Continue**
- ❖ Account Name: Type **Money Market Account**
- ❖ Click **Enter Opening Balance…**
- ❖ Opening Balance: Type **100,000** as of: Type **1/1/09.** Click **OK**
- ❖ Click **Save & Close** to close window
- ❖ Click **No** to "Set up online services…"

Truck Accounts

After creating bank accounts, sometimes you may have assets you need to bring into the Company. Bear in mind that most assets are depreciated over time and therefore, a corresponding Depreciation Expense and Accumulated Depreciation account should be created. As usual, you need to complete the opening balance amount and the opening date you're employing the asset into your business. The opening balance and date are the ending date from your old books.

Activities:

- Right click in the Chart of Accounts window
- Click **New**
- Click **Fixed Asset (major purchases)**
- Click **Continue**
- Account Name: Type **Truck**
- Click **Enter Opening Balance…**
- Opening Balance: Type **0.00** as of: Type **1/1/09.** Click **OK**
- Click **Save & New**
- Account Name: Type **Truck at Cost**
- Click **Sub-account of**: Select **Truck**
- Click **Enter Opening Balance**
- Opening Balance: Type **40,000** as of: Type **1/1/09.** Click **OK**
- Click **Save & Close** to close window
- Right click **Accumulated Depreciation** (towards the top left of the window)
- Click **Edit Account**
- Account Name: Accept **Accumulated Depreciation**
- Click **Sub-account of**: Select **Truck**
- Click **Save & Close**

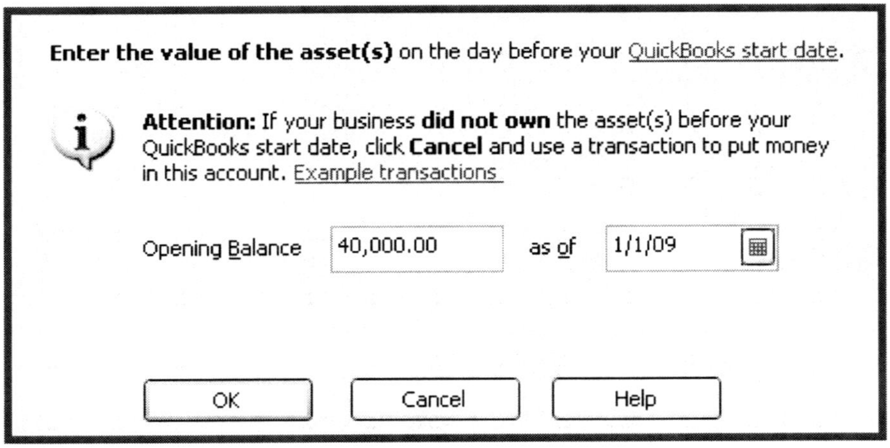

Credit Card Account

Credit Card may be one of the new accounts you would like to create for your business. It is vital to remember that you should select Credit Card in the Account Type window. There may be different credit cards for different purposes. It is essential to complete the description box, so anybody can see for what purpose an account was created. The tax line for credit card is Unassigned because QuickBooks has pre-assigned the right tax line for your business.

Activities:

- Right click in the Chart of Accounts window.
- Click **New**
- Click **Credit Card**
- Click **Continue**
- Account Name: Type **Visa Credit Card**
- Click **Enter Opening Balance**
- Statement Ending Balance: Type **500**
- Statement Ending Date: Type **1/2/09.** Click **OK**
- Click **Save & Close**
- Click **No** to "Set up online services…"

Equity Accounts

Before you start your business you have assets in the form of cash, furniture or equipment you want bring into your business. When you first record these assets they represent Equities to you. Hence, creating Equity accounts is a requirement before you start operating your business. QuickBooks will default few Equities accounts, however, our job is to create additional Equity accounts and organize them as to how we want to see them on the financial reports.

Activities:

- In the Chart of Accounts window
- Right click **Owners Equity**
- Click **Edit Account**
- Account Name: Type **Owners Retained Earnings**
- Click **Save & Close**
- Right click in the window
- Click **New**
- Click **Equity**
- Click **Continue**

- Account Name: Type **Owners Equity**
- Click **Save & New**
- Account Name: Type **Owners Contribution**
- Click **Sub-account of**: Select **Owners Equity**
- Click **Save & Close**
- Right click **Owners Draw**
- Click **Edit Account**
- Account Name: Type **Owners Distribution**
- Click **Sub-account of:** Select **Owners Equity**
- Click **Save & Close**

Income: Main Accounts

After you've created the Equity accounts, the next item is to create the Income accounts. Unless you have money already in the bank, before you can write checks and spend money, you must sell something. This is where the Income accounts come in. In this section, you are going to create accounts that are related to the sales you will make or the services you will render to your customers. On the Tax Line box, you will be selecting the Schedule C: Gross receipts and sales.

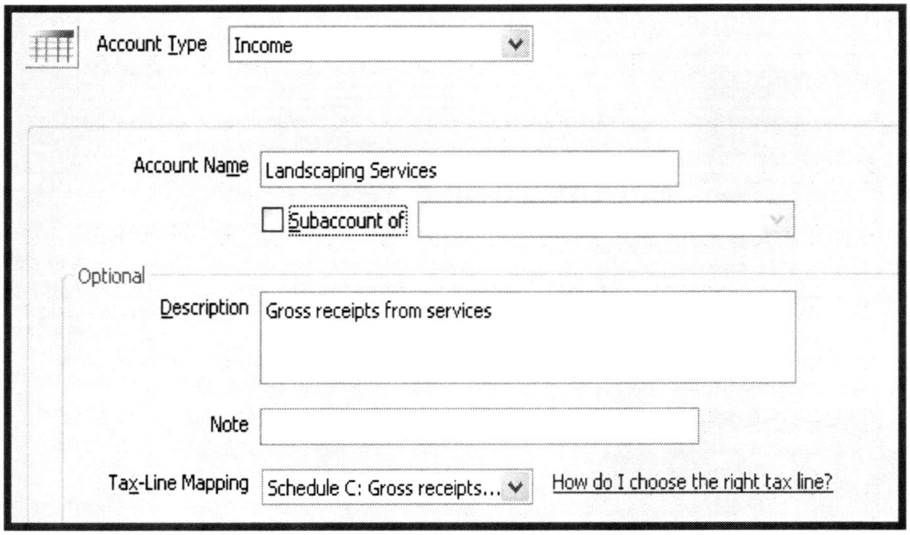

Activities:

- Click **Lists menu**.
- Click **Chart of Accounts**
- Right click **Sales**

- Click **Edit Account**
- Account Name: Type **Landscaping Services**
- Click **Save & Close**
- Scroll to the bottom of window
- Right click **Misc Income** (toward the bottom of the list)
- Click **Edit Account**
- Account Type: Select **Income.** (Very Important)
- Account Name: Accept **Misc Income**
- Click **Sub-account of**: Select **Landscaping Services**
- Click **Save & Close**
- Right click in the window. Click **New**
- Click **Income**. Click **Continue**
- Account Name: Type **Markup Income**
- Click **Sub-account of**: Select **Landscaping Services**
- Click **Save & Close**
- Right click **Uncategorized Income**
- Click **Edit Account**
- Account Name: Type **Opening Balance Income**
- Click **Save & Close**
- Right click **Uncategorized Expense** (toward the bottom of the list)
- Click **Edit Account**
- Account Name: Type **Opening Balance Expense**
- Click **Save & Close**

> The job of these accounts is to group items together. For example an account called office machine will be set up for printers, faxes, telephone items.

Income: Sub Accounts

This time you will be creating sub accounts for the main Income account. You have three options on how to create income sub-accounts. You may use the account names, product names or a combination of accounts and products. Here we are going to use the account names. If you choose the product method, you will be listing the names of the product you will be selling. And if you choose the combination, you will create accounts and products and make the products sub-accounts to the accounts.

Activities:

- Right click in the Chart of Account window
- Click **New**
- Click **Income**
- Click **Continue**
- Account Name: Type **Design Services**

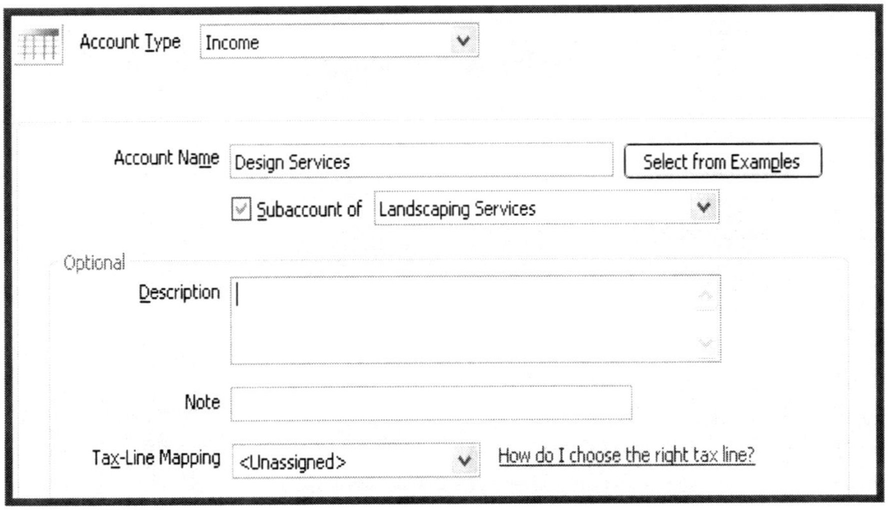

- Click **Sub-account of**: Select **Landscaping Services**
- Click **Save & New**
- Account Name: Type **Equipment Rental**
- Click **Sub-account of**: Select **Landscaping Services**
- Click **Save & New**
- Account Name: Type **Materials**
- Click **Sub-account of:** Select **Landscaping Services**
- Click **Save & New**
- Account Name: Type **Labor**
- Click **Sub-account of:** Select **Landscaping Services**
- Click **Save & New**
- Account Name: Type **Supplies**
- Click **Sub-account of:** Select **Landscaping Services**
- Click **Save & New**
- Account Name: Type **Subcontractors**
- Click **Sub-account of:** Select **Landscaping Services**
- Click **Save & Close**
- **Look! You created income sub accounts**

> In all you do, you must set up Materials, Supplies, Labor and Subcontractors in the income group you never know what will prompt you to use them.

Cost of Goods Sold: Inventory

When you have items in your warehouse you re-sell to your customers, you use the Inventory type of items to track the cost of those items and link them to Cost of Goods Sold account. So, after you've created the Income account, the next account in the order of importance is the Cost of Goods Sold.

Activities:

- Click **Lists menu**
- Click **Item List**
- Right click in the window. Click **New**
- Type: Click **Inventory Part**
- Click **OK** (Very Important)
- Click **X** to close Item List window
- Click **Lists menu**
- Click **Chart of Accounts**
- Right click in the window. Click **New**
- Click **Other Account Types**
- Click **Cost of Goods Sold.** Click **Continue**

> You clicked Inventory Part to make sure it is on the list. Click OK to activate Cost of Goods Sold in the Chart of Accounts list. Very Important!!!

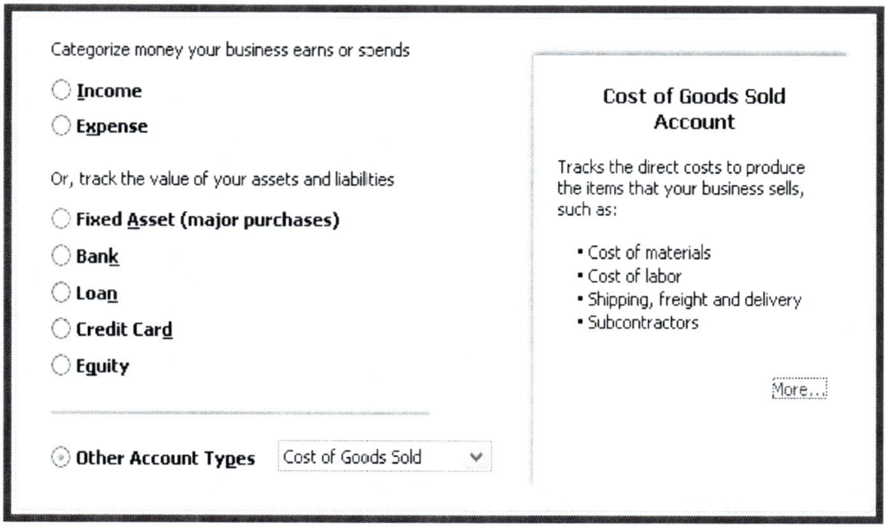

- Account Name: Type **Materials**
- Description: Type **Inventory cost of goods sold items**
- Click **Save & New**
- Account Name: Type **Supplies**
- Description: Type **Inventory cost of goods sold items**
- Click **Save & New**
- Account Name: Type **Miscellaneous**
- Description: Type **Inventory cost of goods sold items**
- Click **Save & Close**

> Actually, all 3 three accounts should be lumped into cost of goods sold but this company chose to detail them as materials, supplies and misc.

Operating Expense: Job Expense

When you have items in the warehouse you re-sell to customers you use Cost of Goods Sold account to track the costs. However, if you have items you don't re-sell to your customers; you use the Job Expenses accounts to track the cost. You should note that a service company uses Job Expense while a manufacturing company uses Job Cost. These are parts from vendors or services from subcontractor you use to provide the service or manufacture the product. After the goods are finished and are ready for re-sell you place the name of the finished products in the items list window and link them to Cost of goods sold in chart of accounts. We are practicing a service company, had it been a manufacturing company, the title of this section will be Cost of Goods Sold: Job Cost.

Activities:

- Click **Lists menu.**
- Click **Chart of Accounts**
- Right click in the window. Click **New**
- Click **Expense.** Click **Continue**
- Account Name: Type **Job Expenses**
- Click **Save & New**
- Account Name: Type **Equipment Rental**
- Click **Sub-account of:** Select **Job Expenses**
- Click **Save & New**
- Account Name: Type **Materials**
- Click **Sub-account of:** Select **Job Expenses**
- Click **Save & New**
- Account Name: Type **Supplies**
- Click **Sub-account of:** Select **Job Expenses**
- Click **Save & New**
- Account Name: Type **Delivery**
- Click **Sub-account of:** Select **Job Expenses**
- Click **Save & New**
- Account Name: Type **Subcontractors**
- Click **Sub-account of:** Select **Job Expenses**
- Click **Save & Close**
- **Look! You created expense sub-accounts**

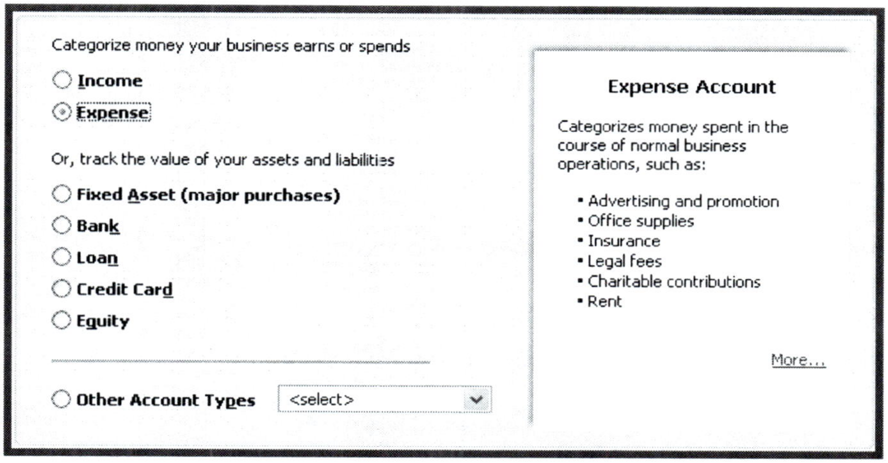

Operating Expense: Other Expense Accounts

Now we come to what we call the administrative or operational expenses. These are the expenses you paid for the entire company not to a particular product and service. It's a waste of time to track the amount of insurance premium you paid for the whole company on a particular product. In this section, you will use the account method and not the product method. You lump these expenses directly to the one account, such as the insurance expense and not spread them to different products.

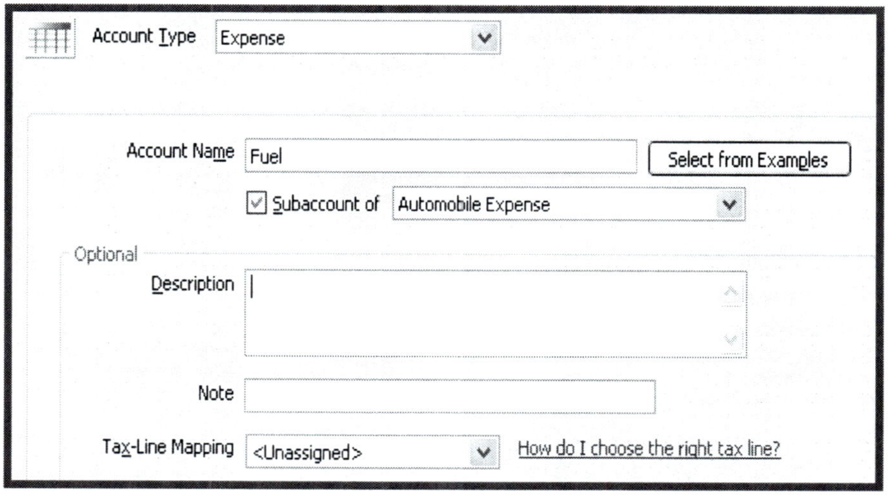

Activities:

- Right click in the Chart of Account window
- Click **New**
- Click **Expense**
- Click **Continue**
- Account Name: Type **Fuel**
- Click **Sub-account of**: Select **Automobile Expense**
- Click **Save & New**
- Account Name: Type **Insurance**
- Click **Sub-account of:** Select **Automobile Expense**
- Click **Save & New**
- Account Name: Type **License & Registration**
- Click **Sub-account of**: Select **Automobile Expense**
- Click **Save & New**
- Account Name: Type **Repairs & Maint**
- Click **Sub- account of**: Select **Automobile Expense**
- Click **Save & Close**
- **Look! You created Auto related sub-accounts**

Merging Accounts

We are going to learn how to merge two accounts into one. Before we do that, we will create a second main account with a sub-account that acts as a duplicate to the one already in the Chart of Accounts. Merge is used to clean up your Chart of Accounts or merge any unwanted account into another. We already have an account called Automobile Expense on the Chart of Account, and now you will be creating an account called Auto Expense with a sub-account, Gas.

Activities:

- In the Chart of Accounts window
- Right click in the window. Click **New**
- Click **Expense**
- Click **Continue**

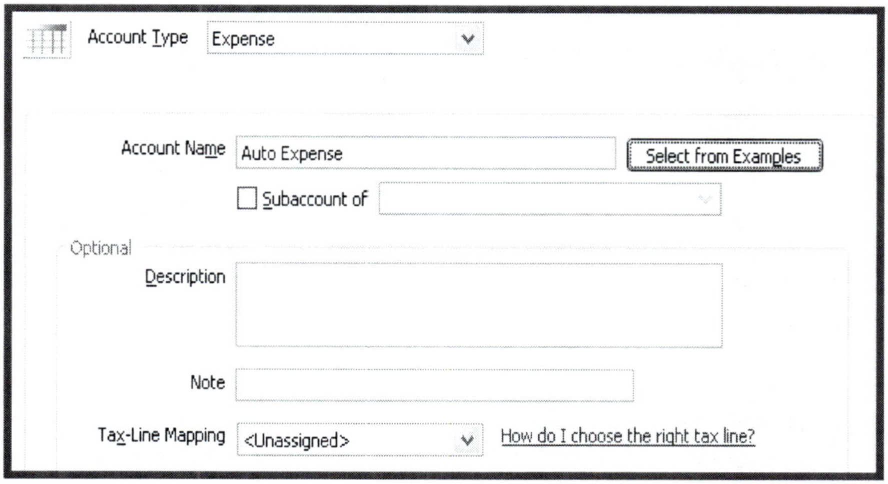

- ❖ Account Name: Type **Auto Expense** (not Automobile Expense)
- ❖ Click **Save & New**
- ❖ Account Name: Type **Gas**
- ❖ Click **Sub-account of**: Select **Auto Expense**
- ❖ Click **Save & Close**
- ❖ **Look! You have created Auto Expense with sub-account Gas**

Merging: Sub accounts

We have created the second main account, and its sub-account, Gas. The "Good" subaccount is Fuel under Automobile Expenses and the "Bad" sub-account is Gas under Auto Expenses. First, you change name Gas to Fuel and second, you merge the new Fuel to the old Fuel in Automobile Expenses. To know you're on the right track you must receive a message that says, "This name is already being used. Would you want to merge them?" Click Yes and the "Bad" account disappears.

Activities:

- ❖ In the Chart of Accounts window
- ❖ Right click **Gas** under **Auto Expense** (not **Automobile Expense)**
- ❖ Click **Edit Account**
- ❖ Account Name: Type **Fuel**
- ❖ Checkmark **Sub-account of**: Select **Automobile Expense**. (Very Important)
- ❖ Click **Save & Close**
- ❖ Click **Yes** to "This name is already…merge them?" (Very Important)
- ❖ **Look! Gas under Auto Expense is gone**
- ❖ Gas in Auto Expense is now merged with Fuel under Automobile Expense

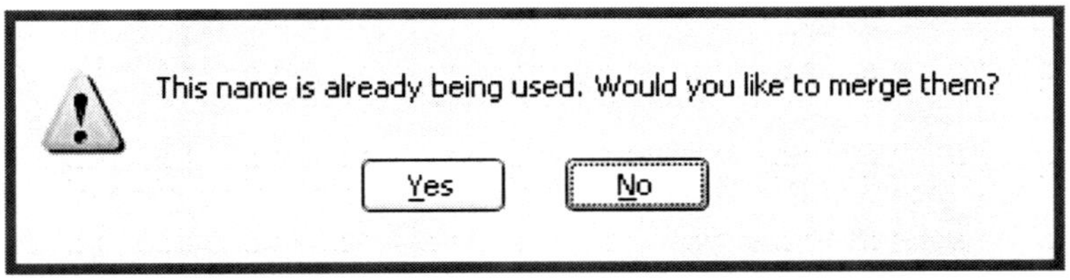

Merging: Main Accounts

We've merged the two sub-accounts; the next step is to merge two main accounts. The "Good" account is Automobile Expense and the "Bad" account is Auto Expense. After the merging process, the "Bad" account will be merged into the "Good" account. Be sure to click Yes to the message, "This name is already being used. Would you want to merge them?" You can also use the same process to merge items in the Item List, but note you cannot merge income and expense accounts.

Activities:

- In the Chart of Accounts window
- Right click on **Auto Expense**
- Click **Edit Account**
- Account Name: Type **Automobile Expense**
- Click **Save & Close**
- Click **Yes** to "The name is already…merge them?" (Very Important)
- You must see the Merge message window
- You must click Yes for merge to work
- Otherwise, the process failed
- **Look! Auto Expense has been merged with Automobile Expense**

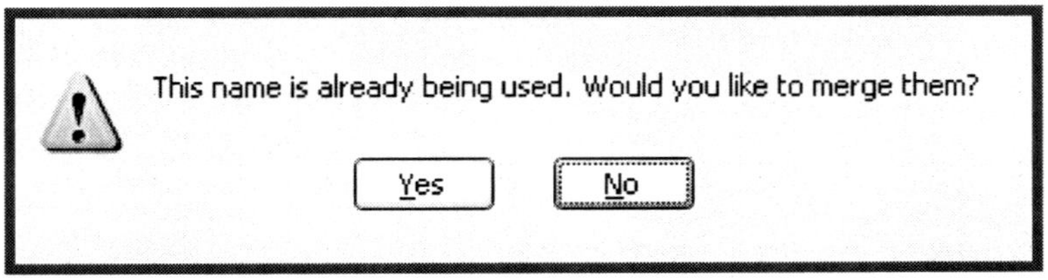

Designing Financial Statements Report

How your financial statements look depend on the way you place the accounts in the Chart of Accounts window. Materials, Labor, Supplies and Subcontractors are placed in that order and Misc is always the last. Discounts and numbers with minus signs are placed below the main account they are subtracting from. Opening balances are always on top in each section. You can move a single or a group of accounts. Your report will look very professional by designing the Chart of Account.

- In the Chart of Accounts window
- Click **Materials** under **Landscaping Services** (Very Important)
- **Place the cursor left of Materials.** You will see 4-way cross
- **Click and drag Materials** up to under Landscaping Services

> You will see long dash line as you drag up or down. You can use the same process to move the items in the item list window.

- **Move the following accounts and place them in the following order:**
- Opening Balance Income (Income section. 1st on the income accounts)
- Landscaping Services
- Materials
- Labor
- Supplies
- Subcontractors
- Equipment Rental
- Design Services
- Markup Income
- Misc Income
- Cost of Goods Sold (Cost of Goods Sold section. 1st on the cost of goods sold)
- Job Cost
- Materials
- Supplies
- Discount Received
- Miscellaneous

(Job Cost through Miscellaneous above: Link only to Manufacturing or Product Company Non Inventory items)

- Opening Balance Expense (Expense section. 1st on the expense accounts)
- Job Cost
- Materials
- Supplies
- Discount Received
- Miscellaneous

(Job Cost through Miscellaneous above: Link only to Service Company Non Inventory items)

- Automobile Expense
- Advertising and Promotion
- And a host of other operating expenses

Inventory Items

We have finished creating accounts in the Chart of Accounts window. We are now going to create items in the Items List window. The first is Inventory Items. These are items in the warehouse of which you keep as inventory. As a product or service company, you pull in two accounts when creating the inventory items. You pull in Cost of Goods Sold for the cost side and Income account for the Income side.

Activities:

> You can also design the Item List window. Make sure there is no diamond button by the word "Name" on the Item List window. If you cannot move the items, you've re-arranged the items, and must return the window to the original status.

- Click **Lists menu**.
- Click **Item List**
- Right click in the window. Click **New**
- Type: Select **Inventory Part**
- Item Name/Number: Type **Flowers**
- Description: Type **Materials**
- Cost: Type **50**. COGS Account: Select **Materials under Cost of Goods Sold**
- Sales Price: Type **75.** Tax Code: Accept **Tax**
- Income Account: Select **Materials under Landscape Services**
- Asset Account: Accept **Inventory Asset**
- Reorder Point: Type **1000**. On Hand: Type **1000**
- Total Value: Accept **50,000** as of: Type **1/1/09**. Click **Next** (right of window)

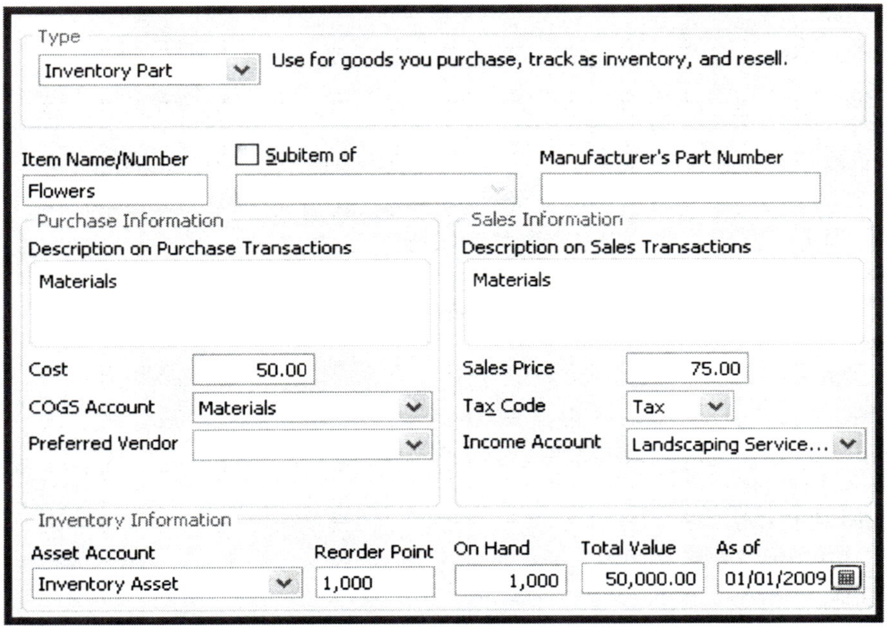

- Item Name/Number: Type **Soil**
- Description: Type **Materials**
- Cost: Type **75**. COGS Account: Accept **Cost of Goods Sold: Materials**
- Sales Price: Type **112.50.** Tax Code: Accept **Tax**
- Income Account: Accept **Landscape Services: Materials**
- Asset Account: Accept: **Inventory Asset**
- Reorder Point: Type **1000**. On Hand: Type **1000**
- Total Value: Accept **75,000** as of: Type **1/1/09**. Click **Next** (right of window)
- Item Name/Number: Type **Fertilizer**
- Description: Type **Materials**
- Cost: Type **100**. COGS Account: Accept **Cost of Goods Sold: Materials**
- Sales Price: Type **150.** Tax Code: Accept **Tax**
- Income Account: Accept **Landscape Services: Materials**
- Asset Account: Accept: **Inventory Asset**
- Reorder Point: Type **1000**. On Hand: Type **1000**
- Total Value: Accept **100,000** as of: Type **1/1/09**
- Click **OK** (right of window)

Non-inventory Items

These are materials or supplies you use in your company, but do not keep inventory of them. You just go out and buy them any time you want them for your products. You should set them up as non-inventory item, and pull in administrative expense (not cost of goods sold as we did on the inventory item) on the expense side and sales on the income side. You will click **"This item is used in assemblies…"** to pull in the two account sides, otherwise, you can only pull in the sales side.

Activities:

- Click **Lists menu**
- Click **Item List**
- Right click in the window. Click **New**
- Type: Click **Non Inventory Part**
- Item Name/Number: Type **Shrubs**
- Click **"This item is used in assemblies…"**
- Description: Type **Materials.** Cost: Type **34.** Press **Tab**
- Expense Account: Select **Materials under Job Expense**
- Sales Price: Type **51**. Tax Code: Accept **Tax**
- Income Account: Select **Materials under Landscape Services**
- Click **Next** (right of window)

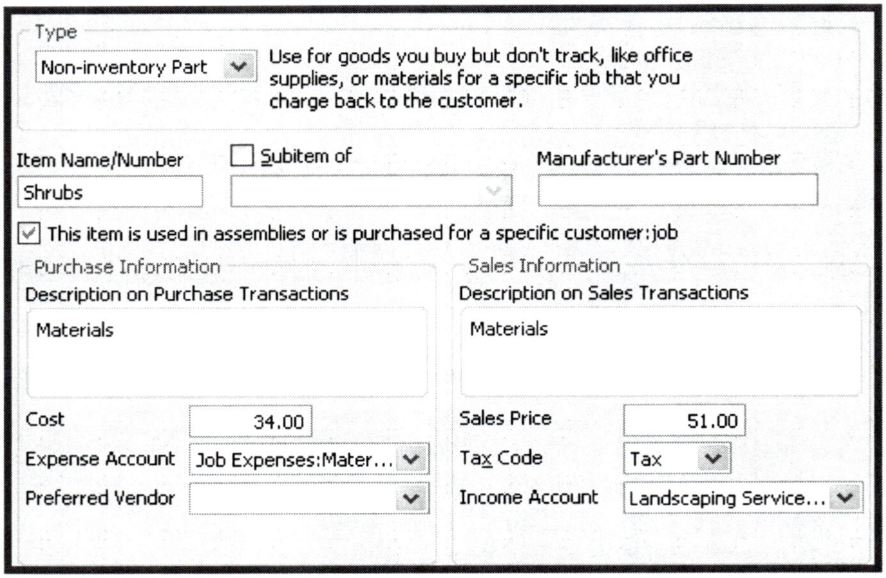

- Item Name/Number**:** Type **Wires**
- Description: Type **Materials**. Cost: Type **20**. Press **Tab**
- Expense Account**:** Accept **Job Expense: Materials**
- Sales Price: Type **30**. Tax Code: Accept **Tax**
- Income Account: Accept **Landscape Services: Materials**
- Click **Next** (right of window)
- Item Name/Number**:** Type **Holders**
- Description: Type **Supplies. Cost:** Type **15. Pres Tab**
- Expense Account**:** Select **Supplies under Job Expense**
- Sales Price: Type **20**. Tax Code: Accept **Tax**
- Income Account: Select **Supplies under Landscape Services**
- Click **Next** (right of window)
- Item Name/Number: Type **Pots**
- Description: Type **Supplies**. Cost: Type **30**. Press **Tab**
- Expense Account**:** Accept **Job Expense: Supplies**
- Price: Type **45**. Tax Code: Accept **Tax**
- Income Account: Accept **Landscape Services: Supplies**
- Click **OK** (right of window)

Service Item: Labor

There are two kinds of service labor items. One is internal or work done by the employees and the other is external or work done by subcontractors. When the work is done by employees you do not track the cost of the job unless you want to, but in general you don't. You pull in only the rate account, which is the income account for the income side of the window. It is important to complete the description box to identify that the job was done by employees and not subcontractors.

Activities:

- Click **Lists menu**.
- Click **Item List**
- Right click in the window. Click **New**
- Type: Select **Service**
- Item Name/Number: Type: **Trimming**
- Description: Type **Employee work**
- Rate: Type **100**
- Tax Code: Select **Non**
- Income Account: Select **Labor under Landscape Services**
- Click **Next** (right of window)

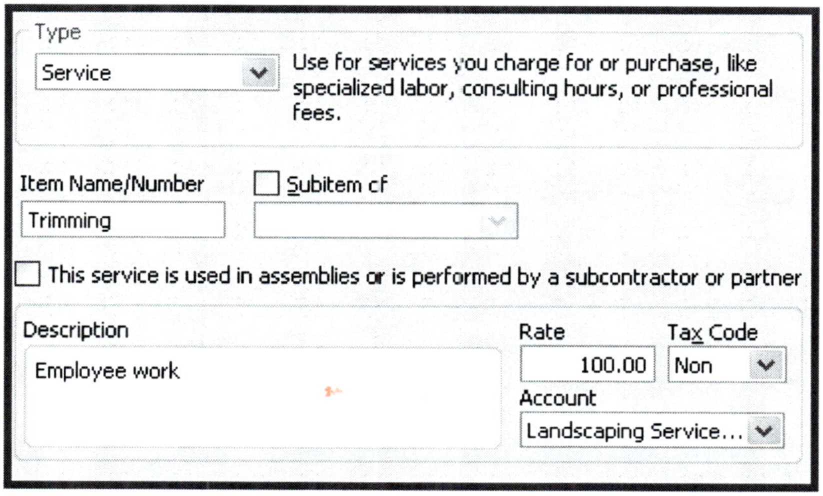

- Item Name/Number: Type: **Gardening**
- Description: Type **Employee work**
- Rate: Type **110**

- Tax Code: Accept **Non**
- Income Account: Accept **Landscape Services: Labor**
- Click **Next** (right of window)
- Item Name/Number**:** Type: **Tree Removal**
- Description: Type **Employee work**
- Rate: Type **120**
- Tax Code: Accept **Non**
- Income Account: Accept **Landscape Services: Labor**
- Click **Next** (right of window)
- Item Name/Number: Type: **Delivery**
- Description: Type **Employee work**
- Rate: Type **150**
- Tax Code: Accept **Non**
- Income Account: Accept **Landscape Services: Labor**
- Click **OK** (right of window)

Service Item: Subcontractors

If you are a company that uses subcontractors, you have to pull subcontractor accounts when creating the items. Unlike the work done by your employees, you want to keep track of the cost of subcontractors and how much you charged your customers for the work. For this purpose, you click **"This service is used in assemblies or is performed by a subcontractor or partner"** to pull in two accounts, expense/subcontractor on the expense side and income/subcontractor for the income side.

Activities:

- Click **Lists menu**.
- Click **Item List**
- Right click in the window. Click **New**
- Type: Select **Service**
- Item Name/Number**:** Type: **Installation**
- Click **This service is performed by a contractor**
- Description: Type **Subcontractor work**
- Cost:Type **200.** Expense Account**:**Select **Subcontractor under Job Expense**
- Sales Price: Type **300**
- Tax Code: Select **Non**
- Income Account: Select **Subcontractors under Landscape Services**
- Click **Next** (right of window)

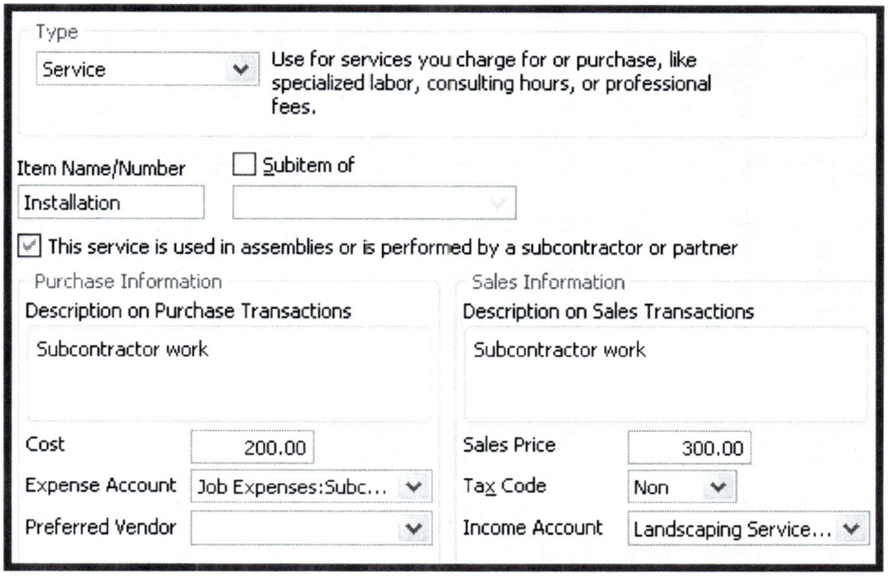

- Item Name/Number: Type: **Framing**
- Description: Type **Subcontractor work**
- Cost: Type **300.** Expense Account**:** Accept **Job Expense: Subcontractors**
- Sales Price: Type **450**
- Tax Code: Accept **Non**
- Income Account: Accept **Landscape Services: Subcontractors**
- Click **Next** (right of window)
- Item Name/Number: Type: **Decking**
- Description: Type **Subcontractor work**
- Cost: Type **400.** Expense Account**:** Accept **Job Expense: Subcontractors**
- Sales Price: Type **600**
- Tax Code: Accept **Non**
- Income Account: Accept **Landscape Services: Subcontractors**
- Click **OK** (right of window)

Fixed Asset Item List

Fixed asset items are your cars, trucks, furniture, and other properties used in running your business. You should list your fixed asset items with details. The total amount in your fixed asset listing report must match the original purchase amount on your Balance Sheet report less any depreciation. You are going to list your business tuck with its cost, description, location, and other pertinent information. Asset listing should be completed immediately following the purchase.

Activities:

- Click **Lists menu**
- Click **Fixed Asset Item List**
- Right click in the window
- Select **New**
- Asset Name/Number: Type **Business Truck**
- Asset Account: Select **Truck**
- Purchase Description. Item is: Click **New**
- Purchase Description box: Type **New** (Very Important)
- Date: Type **1/1/09**
- Cost: Type **40,000**
- Vendor/Payee: Type **American Motors**
- Asset Description: Type **Jeep Grand Cherokee**
- Click **OK** to close

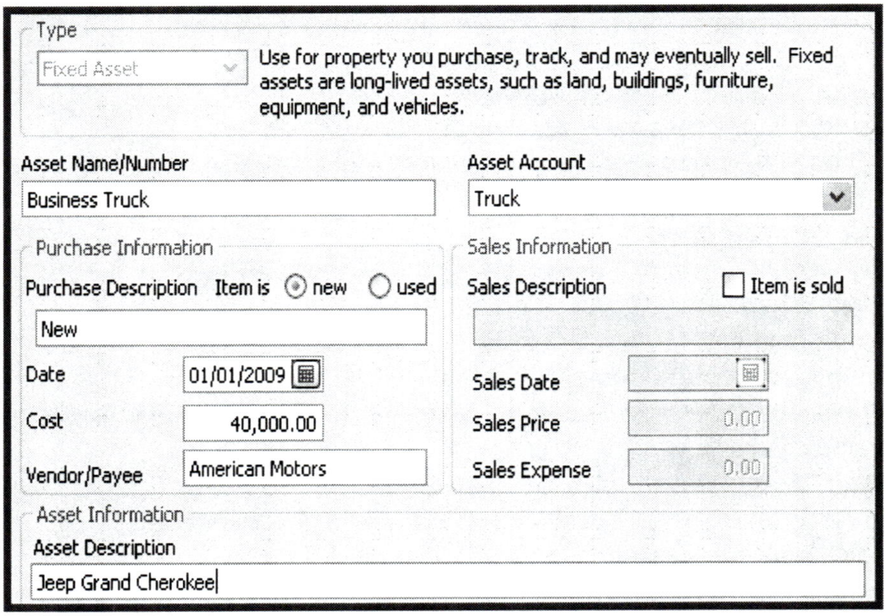

Price Level List

There are two types of price levels. One is profit and the other is nonprofit. Both price levels can be set up in the Edit menu under Sales & Customer of the Preferences submenu. For the profit level you are going to reduce the price you charge your customers by 0.0%; that is charging them full price. For non-profit customers, their prices are reduced by 50% percentage.

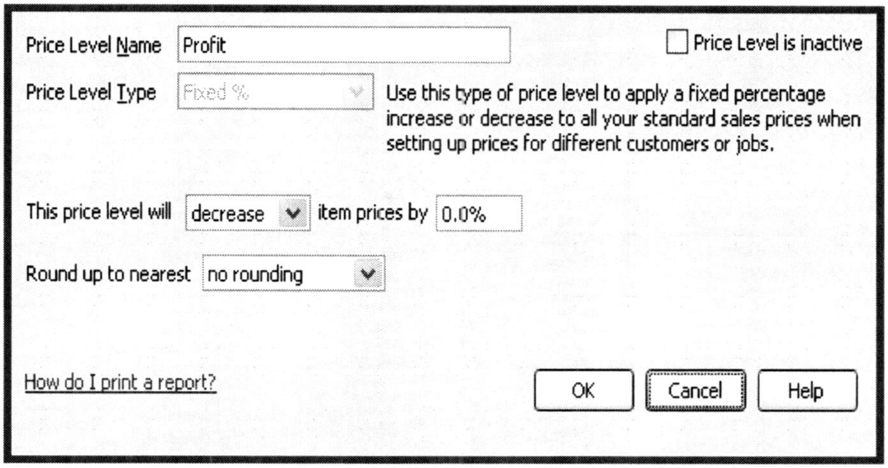

Activities:

- Click **Lists menu**
- Click **Price Level List**
- Right click in the window
- Click **New**
- Price Level Name: Type **Profit**
- Click **OK** to close window
- Right click in the window. Click **New**
- Price Level Name: Type **Non Profit Tax Exempt**
- This price level will: Accept **decrease**
- Item prices by: Type **50**. Press **Tab**
- Click **OK** to close window

Sales Tax Code List

Earlier, we talked about Sales Tax on inventory and non-inventory items because you may pay taxes to vendors to buy them in the first place. Before you enter items and tax them on your customer's invoice, you must inform QuickBooks which items are taxable and which ones are not taxable. Item like services—that come with your skills, efforts, knowledge—are not taxable. To set the default on Sales Tax, you click the Edit menu, Preferences, and open the Sales Tax Code.

Activities:

- Click **Lists menu**
- Click **Sales Tax Code List**

- Right click **Taxable Sales** in the window
- Click **Edit Sales Tax Code**
- Review Sales Tax Code window. Click **OK**
- Right click in the window
- Click **New**
- Sales Tax Code: Type **LBR**
- Description: Type **Non-Taxable Labor**
- Click **Non-Taxable**
- Click **OK**

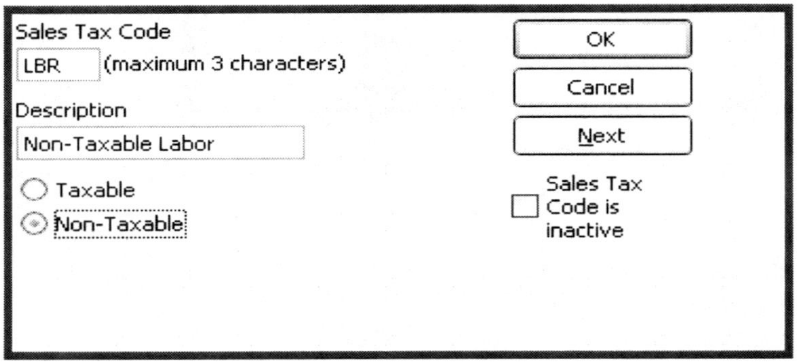

Class List

If you have different types of businesses, you should track them by classes. When you track businesses by classes you zero in on which ones that are making the most money and why; and which ones are making the least money and why. By studying your businesses by class, you are able to make adjustments in pricing, advertising, and sales. When you want to cut costs by shutting down unproductive lines of business, running your reports by class will show you which products to eliminate.

Activities:

- Click **Lists menu**
- Click **Class List**
- Right click in the window
- Click **New**
- Class Name: Type **Delivery**. Click **Next**
- Class Name: Type **Landscaping.** Click **Next**
- Class Name: Type **Maintenance**. Click **Next**

- Class Name: Type **Overhead.** Click **Next**
- Class Name: Type **Administrative**
- Click **OK**

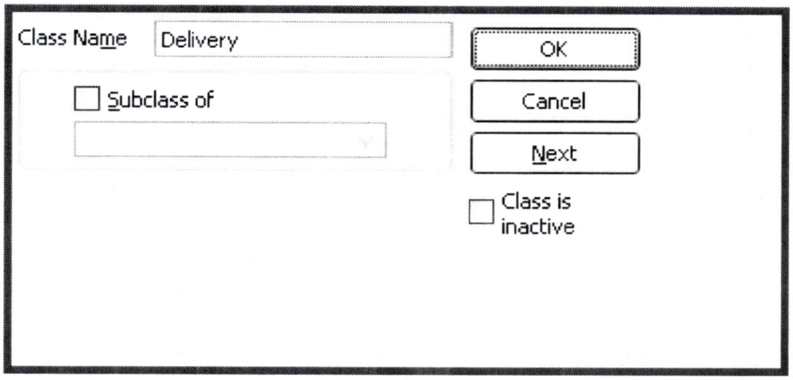

Other Names List

You use the Other Names List to add names not related to Chart of Accounts or Item List windows like Transfer to/from Checking and Transfer to/from Payroll. Remember that QuickBooks will not allow you to delete any name if it has been used in creating an invoice, bill, or linked to other accounts, especially when it involve an amount. The best way to treat such name is to make it inactive and therefore not show it in the Other Names list window.

Activities:

- Click **Lists menu**
- Click **Other Names List**
- Right click in window
- Click **New**
- Name: Type **ATM Withdrawal**. Click **Next**
- Name: Type **Deposits.** Click **Next**
- Name: Type **Transfer to Checking.** Click **Next**
- Name: Type **Transfer from Checking.** Click **Next**
- Name: Type **Transfer to Payroll.** Click **Next**
- Name: Type **Transfer from Payroll**. Click **Next**
- Name: Type **Transfer to Petty Cash.** Click **Next**
- Name: Type **Transfer from Petty Cash**
- Click **OK**

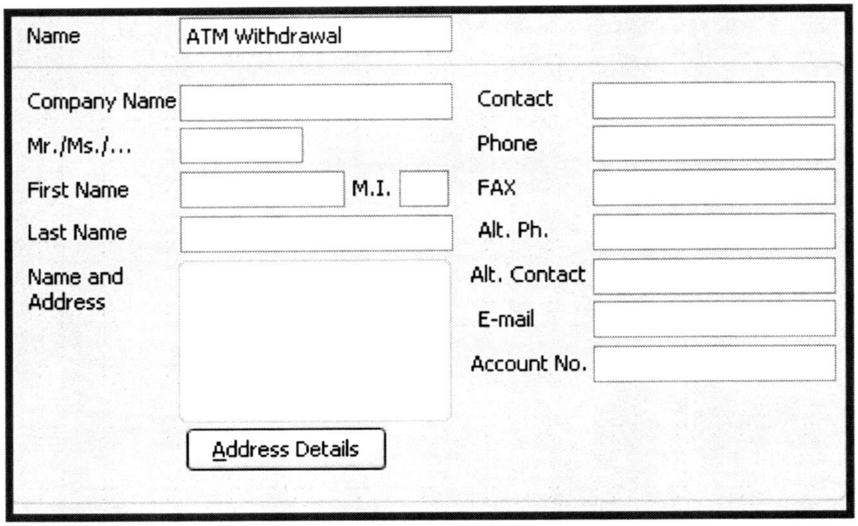

Sales Rep List

What if you divide your business into geographic territories and have to assign sales representatives to different territories? You then come to this window to make a list of these individuals. The reps will be pulled into the invoice window during the time you're completing your estimates or invoices. Most commission reports are linked to the representative in charge of the territory. You should complete this window with care to make sure the right commission is paid to right representative.

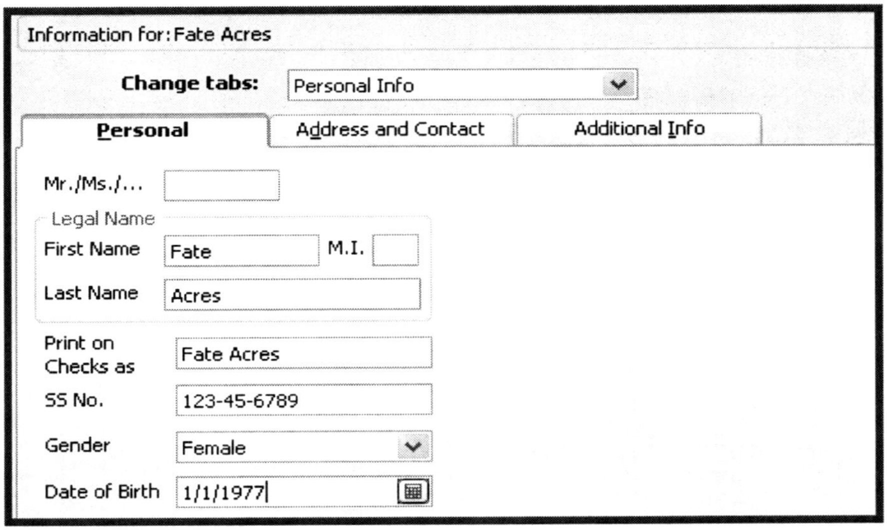

Activities:

- Click **Lists menu**
- Click **Customer & Vendor Profile Lists**
- Click **Sale Rep List**
- Right click in the window. Click **New**
- Sales Rep Name: Select **Add New**
- Click **Employee.** Click **OK**
- First Name: Type **Fate**
- Last Name: Type **Acres**. Press **Tab**
- SS No: Type **123-45-6789**
- Gender: Select **Female**
- Date of Birth: Type **1/1/1977.** Click **OK**
- Click **Leave As Is**
- Click **OK** to close New Sales Rep window

Customer Type List

Sometimes, for market planning purposes, customers are divided into types and treated differently. Some businesses may divide their customers into individual, corporate, schools and universities, and non-profit. By dividing your customers, you may be able to target a group with a special kind of pricing or advertising strategies. After the planning session is over, you should update your QuickBooks.

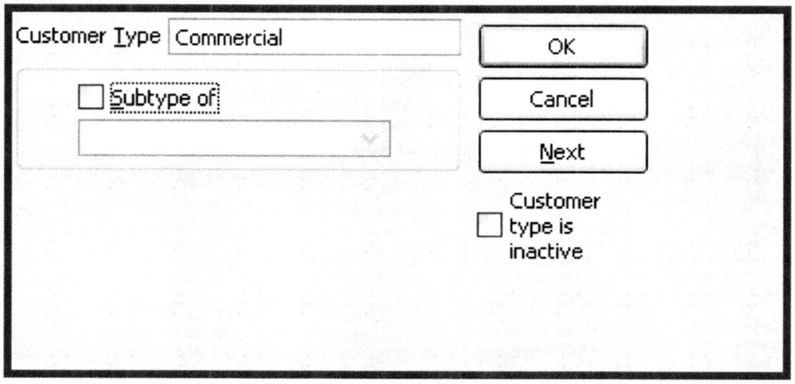

Activities:

- Click **Lists menu**
- Click **Customer & Vendor Profile Lists**
- Click **Customer Type List**
- Right click in the window. Click **New**

- Customer Type: Type **Commercial**. Click **Next**
- Customer Type: Type **Residential**. Click **Next**
- Customer Type: Type **Schools & Universities**. Click **Next**
- Customer Type: Type **Non-Profit.** Click **Next**
- Customer Type: Type **Parks & Recreation**
- Click **OK**

Vendor Type List

Before you start making payments on your bills, you should complete the Vendor Type List window. The purpose is to list your vendors so they can easily be pulled into the Bill Payment windows. Your vendors may be divided into different types like subcontractor, utilities, insurance, repairs and maintenance. You should be able to go to the Lists menu, click Customer & Vendor Profile Lists to get to Vendor Type List window.

Activities:

- Click **Lists menu**
- Click **Customer & Vendor Profile Lists**
- Click **Vendor Type List**
- Right click in the window. Click **New**
- Vendor Type: Type **Subcontractors**. Click **Next**
- Vendor Type: Type **Utilities**. Click **Next**
- Vendor Type: Type **Insurance**. Click **Next**
- Vendor Type: Type **Repairs & Maint.** Click **Next**
- Vendor Type: Type **Construction.** Click **Next**
- Vendor Type: Type **Financial Services**
- Click **OK**

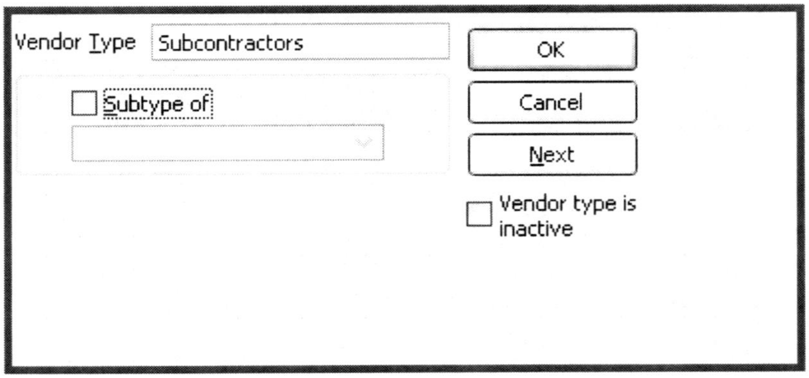

Job Type List

If you are in the services business, you might want to break down your Job into Types. One reason is because QuickBooks will want to know; another reason is that breaking your job into parts will help you to zero in on which type is getting the most or the least requests. This way you can target your cost cutting, marketing, and advertising strategies differently to get the most benefit. For example, Job Types can be broken down into Contracts, Installation, New Construction, etc.

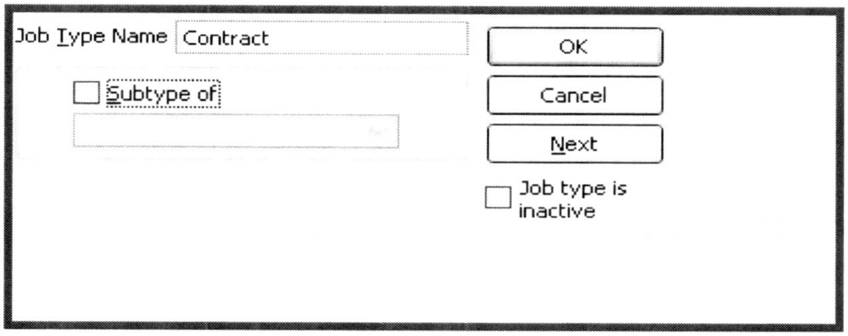

Activities:

- Click **Lists menu**
- Click **Customer & Vendor Profile Lists**
- Click **Job Type List**
- Right click in the window. Click **New**
- Job Type Name: Type **Contract**. Click **Next**
- Job Type Name: Type **Installation**. Click **Next**
- Job Type Name: Type **New Construction**
- Click **OK**

Payment Method List

If you plan on accepting payment in forms other than cash, you should complete the Payment Method List window. You have many options already pre-loaded for you in the window. For example, you have cash, check, Visa, Master card, American Express, and Discover. You may create Bank Debit Card and Electronic Fund Transfer (EFT). When you're completing the Enter Sales Receipt window, you'll be required to select the Payment Method your customer prefers.

Activities:

- Click **Lists menu**
- Click **Customer & Vendor Profile Lists**
- Click **Payment Method List**
- Right click in the window. Click **New**
- Payment Method: Type **Bank Debit Card**
- Payment Type: Select **Visa**. Click **Next**
- Payment Method: Type **EFT Electronic Funds Transfer**
- Payment Type: Select **Other**
- Click **OK**

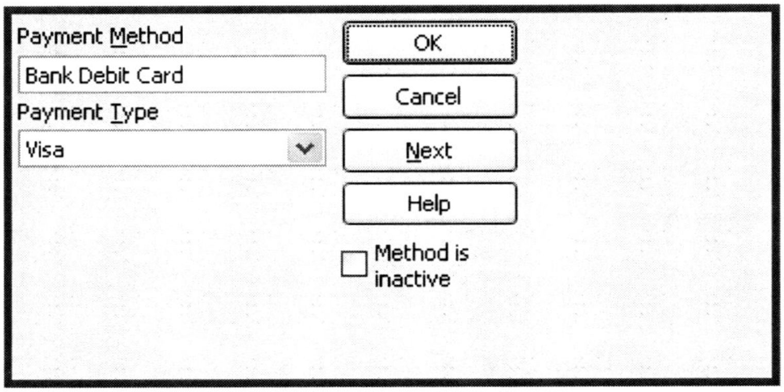

Vehicle List

Recording your assets, especially cars and trucks in the Vehicle List, is of utmost importance. The information in this report is pulled over to the Enter Vehicle Mileage and Fixed Item List windows. To get to the Vehicle List window, you should remember to click the List menu, Customer & Vendor Profile Lists and then Vehicle List. Most users cannot find this window because they think it should be listed under the List menu.

Activities:

- Click **Lists menu**
- Click **Customer & Vendor Profile Lists**
- Click **Vehicle List**
- Right click in the window. Click **New**
- Vehicle: Type **Jeep Grand Cherokee Truck**
- Description: Type **Board of Directors Truck.** Click **Next**
- Vehicle: Type **Lexus Truck**

- Description: Type **Sales Reps Truck**. Click **Next**
- Vehicle: Type **Mercedes Trailer**
- Description: Type **Distribution Trailer**
- Click **OK**

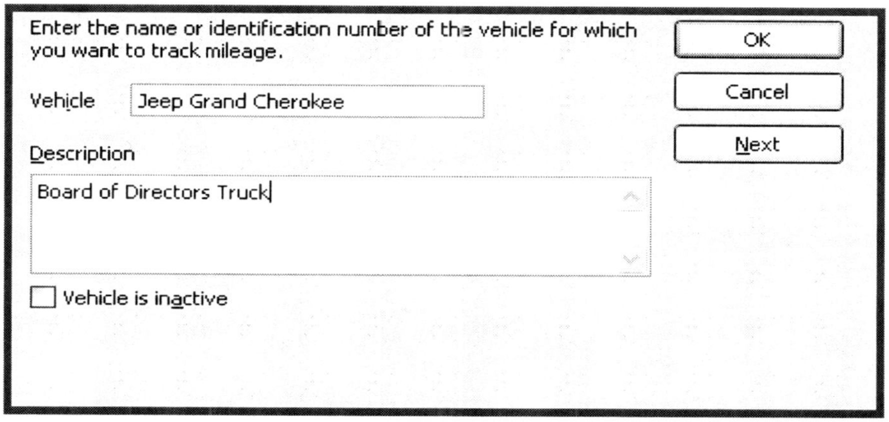

Memorized Transaction List

If you want to make sure you're on top every task and nothing falls through the cracks, memorizing your transactions should be considered seriously. After you've created identical group of transactions, you should lump them into a group. Monthly recurring bills such electric, cell phone, internet, water, gas, and other related bills are grouped together under Recurring Monthly Bills group. Normally, you select "Monthly" instead of "Never" in the "How Often" box.

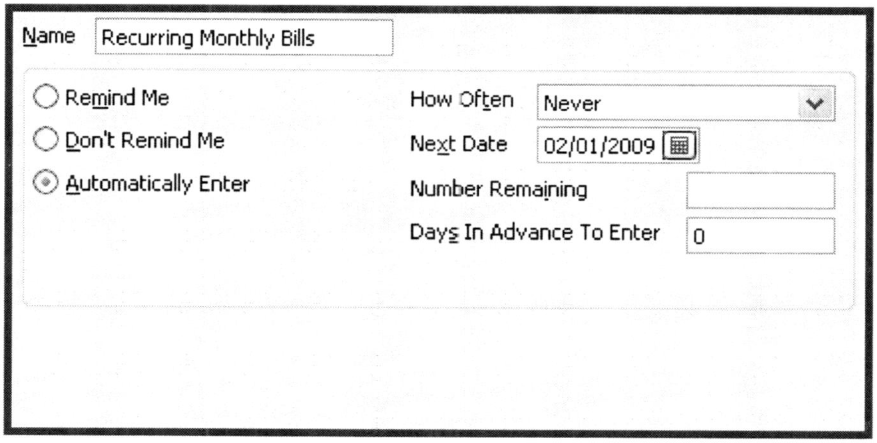

Activities:

- Click **Lists menu**
- Click **Memorized Transaction List**
- Right click in the window. Click **New Group**
- Name: Type **Recurring Monthly Bills**
- Click **Automatically Enter** option
- How Often: Accept **Never**
- When using QuickBooks for business, you should select monthly
- Next Date: Type **2/1/09.** Click **OK**
- Click **Window menu**
- Click **Close All**
- Click **Company menu**
- Click **Home Page**

Financial Results: Profit & Loss

This is one the most important chapters in terms of creating accounts and items. Accounts and lists are the backbone of accounting and finance. You created several income accounts such as the Landscaping, Markup, and the Discount accounts. You created some items in the Item List window, and imported other items from the QuickBooks sample file. Nothing you did in this chapter affected the Profit & Loss statements, until the next chapter when you will make a general journal entry.

Activities:

- Click **Reports menu**
- Click **Company & Financial**
- Click **Profit & Loss Standard**
- Date (top left): Select **This Fiscal Year**
- From: Accept **1/1/09.** To: Accept **12/31/09**
- Click **Collapse**
- **Net Income is 1,000,000**
- Click **X** to close window

Quick Company 2009

Profit & Loss

January through December 2009

	Jan - Dec 09
Ordinary Income/Expense	
Income	
Opening Balance Income	1,005,000.00
Total Income	1,005,000.00
Gross Profit	1,005,000.00
Expense	
Opening Balance Expense	5,000.00
Telephone Expense	0.00
Total Expense	5,000.00
Net Ordinary Income	1,000,000.00
Net Income	**1,000,000.00**

Financial Results: Balance Sheet

You created some accounts in this chapter, including Credit Card and Truck with its accompanying Accumulated Depreciation account. You practiced how to merge main accounts and sub-accounts. Sooner or later you will find out the Chart of Accounts, Item List, or any other list windows have accounts or items you don't want to be there. QuickBooks will then allow you to merge those accounts, but not delete them, if they are linked with other accounts. Total Assets is now $2,520,000.

Activities:

- Click **Reports menu**
- Click **Company & Financial**
- Click **Balance Sheet Standard**
- Date (top left): Select **This Fiscal Year**
- As of: Accept **12/31/09**
- Click **Collapse**
- **Total Assets is 2,520,000**
- Click **X** to close window

Quick Company 2009
Balance Sheet
As of December 31, 2009

	Dec 31, 09
ASSETS	
Current Assets	
Checking/Savings	
Money Market Account	100,000.00
USA Checking	800,000.00
USA Payroll Checking	100,000.00
USA Savings	250,000.00
Total Checking/Savings	1,250,000.00
Accounts Receivable	
Accounts Receivable	1,005,000.00
Total Accounts Receivable	1,005,000.00
Other Current Assets	
Inventory Asset	225,000.00
Total Other Current Assets	225,000.00
Total Current Assets	2,480,000.00
Fixed Assets	
Truck	40,000.00
Total Fixed Assets	40,000.00
TOTAL ASSETS	**2,520,000.00**

Review Basics of Account Numbers

You can manage your finances in QuickBooks efficiently without using account numbers. If you really want to use account numbers you must plan for it; and this section will be beneficial to you. I've seen a lot of confusion and mistakes made by clients who do not understand the intent of using account numbers. Organization is the key to using account numbers. I can look at your account and know right away if you have exceptional organization skills in accounting or not. **To turn on the account numbers, click Edit menu, Preferences,** Accounting **(left), and Company Preferences tab. Click Use account numbers, and Click OK.**

When you activate account numbers through the Edit menu, click List menu and Chart of Accounts, you will find out that QuickBooks will populate account numbers on most of your accounts. Few will not be populated, especially those accounts you created by yourself, which is a big help. All you have to do is add account numbers to the few remaining accounts. After you review the Chart of Accounts, if you decide you don't want an account number, **be sure to turn it off by** clicking **Edit menu, Preferences, Accounting (left), Company Preferences tab, Un-check Use account numbers. Click OK.**

Account Numbers

1000	Asset
2000	Liability
3000	Equity
4000	Income
5000	Expense
6000	Expense
7000	Expense
8000	Expense
9000	Other Income
9600	Other Expense

Your asset accounts will carry a number between 1000 and 1999, and your Liabilities will start from 2000 to 2999 and so on. Every time you are giving a number to any item in your books, be sure you know to which account groups it belongs. From time to time you will also be creating sub-accounts, and it is essential to know how to add serial numbers to your sub-accounts. For example, you may have the following expense and subaccounts:

Account Numbers

6000 Automobile Expenses
- 6020 Insurance
- 6021 Fuel
- 6022 Repairs & Maintenance
- 6023 Registration

Numbering Rules

- Asset and Liability accounts cannot be mixed together. For example, you cannot start assets with 1000s, liabilities with 2000s and later add an asset with 2000s or a liability with 1000s.

- All asset accounts must precede all liability accounts. For example, you cannot start assets with 1000s, liabilities with 2000s and when you think you have run out of 1000s numbers you try to squeeze an asset account with a 2000s number.

- All asset and liability accounts must precede all income and expense accounts. For example if you start assets with 1000s, liabilities with 2000s, you cannot have any income or expense with 1000s or 2000s.

- It's better to set up all your income accounts before all expense accounts, but sometimes, you can mix income with expense. For example, you may have Other Income and Other Expense in the same 9000s. In this case, start the income first and then start expense with the 9600s.

- Sub-accounts must have a higher account number. For example if the main account is 6000 all sub-accounts numbers must start with 6001. It is a good idea to allow a difference of 10 between sub-accounts, like 6010, 6020, 6030 and so on.

- If QuickBooks preloads account numbers that don't match your numbering system (for example, you have 5 digits and QuickBooks has 4 digits), you can create your own account numbers. But be sure to make QuickBooks accounts and its account numbers inactive, by right clicking on the QuickBooks account and clicking Make Account Inactive.

Chapter Summary

The Lists menu is all about creating, editing, and deleting accounts and lists. And that was the main objective of this chapter: to learn how to create new accounts and lists. In the process, we created, edited, deleted, and merged accounts and lists. A vital part of creating a new account is entering the opening balance and date. When you think about finding or creating accounts and lists, think the Lists menu.

What we accomplished:

- Reviewed the List submenus
- Reviewed chart of accounts and item lists
- Created money market account
- Created truck accounts
- Created credit card account
- Created equity account
- Created income: main accounts
- Created income: sub-accounts
- Created cost of goods sold: inventory
- Created operating expense: job expense
- Created operating expense: other expense accounts
- Merged accounts: sub accounts and main accounts

- Designed financial statements report
- Created inventory and non-inventory items
- Created labor and subcontractors items
- Practiced the fixed asset item list
- Practiced the price level list
- Practiced the sales tax code list
- Practiced the class and other names list
- Practiced the sales rep list
- Practiced the customer, vendor and job type lists
- Practiced the payment method and vehicle lists
- Created and memorized a transaction
- Processed financial statements

Financial activities

- Money Market account for $100,000
- Truck account for $40,000
- Credit Card account $500
- Inventory Asset account for a total of $225,000

Exercise 4

Complete Exercise 4 by using the following information:

1. Create bank accounts.
   Money Market Account balance 250,000 date 1/1/09

2. Create fixed asset accounts.
   Truck as main account opening balance 0.00 as of 1/1/09
   Truck at cost sub to Truck opening balance 65,450 as of 1/1/09
   Edit Accumulated Depreciation sub to Truck opening balance 0.00 as of 1/1/09

3. Create credit card accounts.
   America Express opening balance 1,500 date 1/2/09
   MasterCard opening balance 2,250 date 1/2/09
   Visa opening balance 1,725 date 1/2/09

4. Create equity accounts
   Edit Capital Stock with opening balance 1,200,000 as of 1/2/09

5. Create income accounts.
   Edit Sales to Sales & Services as main account
   Create sub account Computers
   Create sub account Office Machines
   Create sub account Household Appliances
   Create sub account Entertainment
   Create sub account Materials
   Create sub account Labor
   Create sub account Supplies
   Create sub account Subcontractors
   Create sub account Discount Given
   Edit Shipping and Delivery to Delivery as a sub to Sales & Services
   Edit Misc Income to Account Type Income as a sub to Sales & Services
   Edit Uncategorized Income to Opening Balance Income
   Edit Uncategorized Expense to Opening Balance Expense
   Create main account Interest Income

6. Create cost of goods sold accounts.
   Create main account cost of goods sold
   Activate Cost of Goods Sold as a main account as on page 93 and 94
   Create main account Job Cost
   Create Computer Parts sub account to Job Cost
   Create Office Machines Parts sub account to Job Cost
   Create Household Appliances Parts sub account to Job Cost
   Create Entertainment Parts sub account to Job Cost
   Create Materials sub account to Job Cost
   Create Supplies sub account to Job Cost
   Create Subcontractors sub account to Job Cost
   Create Miscellaneous sub account to Job Cost
   Edit Discount Received as sub to Cost of Goods Sold
   Edit Freight and Shipping to Delivery as sub account to Job Cost

6. Create expense accounts.
   Edit Payroll Expenses description: Payroll expenses with state and federal taxes
   Create Gross Wages a sub to Payroll Expenses
   Create Payroll Taxes a sub to Payroll Expenses
   Create FUTA Fed Unemp a sub to Payroll Expenses

Create SUTA State Unemp a sub to Payroll Expenses
Create Insurance Benefits a sub to Payroll Expenses
Create Retirement Benefits a sub to Payroll Expenses

7. Design your financial statements report.
   Design Equity accounts
   Design Income accounts
   Design Cost of Goods Sold account
   Design Expenses account

8. Process the following reports
   Profit & Loss Statement ending 12/31/09
   Balance Sheet Standard ending 12/31/09
   Statement of Cash Flow ending 12/31/09
   Chart of Accounts Listing as of today
   Income & Expense Graph 1/31/09
   Accounts Receivable Graph 1/31/09
   Accounts Payable Graph 1/31/09

$

Chapter 5

Company Menu

Objectives: After you've completed this chapter you will be able to:

- ✓ Explain Company submenu
- ✓ Identify the home page contents
- ✓ Identify company snapshot
- ✓ Edit company information
- ✓ Set up passwords
- ✓ Edit user's passwords
- ✓ Edit admin's password
- ✓ Set up closing date
- ✓ Remove closing date
- ✓ Process planning & budgeting
- ✓ Run Budget report
- ✓ Use the To-Do List
- ✓ Use the reminders and the alert manager
- ✓ Make general journal entries
- ✓ Enter vehicle mileage
- ✓ Process financial reports and compare results
- ✓ Explain the principles of journal entries
- ✓ Explain month-end journal entries

Review Company Menu

When you're thinking about updating Company Information such as the address, phone number, income tax form used or Federal Employment Identification Number (FEIN), remember the Company menu. In the Company Information window, selecting the right "Income Tax Form Used" will enable QuickBooks to default vital tax-related forms specifically designed for your business and industry. You can access the Chart of Accounts from the Company or Lists menus. Consistency is the key to speed. Therefore, I encourage you to access Chart of Accounts through the Lists menu.

- Click **Company menu**

The following submenus are located under the Company menu:

- **Home Page:** This is the "central nervous system" of the QuickBooks windows. The Home Page is the gateway that gives you access to most of the other windows. It has more icons than any other window. It has the following icon groups: Vendors, Customers, Employees, Company and Banking group of icons. You can always access the home page by clicking directly it on the tool bar instead of going through the Company menu.

- **Company Snapshot:** The snapshot is the summary of the financial activities of the company. It prominently displays the income and expense graph. Other financial summaries include the following: account balances, customers who owe money, vendors to pay, and reminders.

- **Advanced Reports:** You have to login to the internet to use the advanced reports.

- **Company Information:** After you've created a new company through the File menu, this is where you update the company information. Be sure any information on the company window is complete and accurate, because QuickBooks uses it to populate various forms and reports.

- **Advanced Services Administration:** These are services that QuickBooks provide to its customers online and, therefore, you should be connected to the Internet to review these services and see if they are good for you.

- **Set Up Users & Passwords:** If more than one person will be accessing your QuickBooks file, you are encouraged to set up passwords to allow limited access to only authorized persons. The Set Up Users window enables you to set up edit and delete passwords. After you've set up your own password or other employees' passwords, you should also remember to change the passwords from time to time, monthly or semiannually. Don't keep the same password for more than one year. The QuickBooks administrator has the right to change passwords and should encourage everyone to change their passwords.

- **Customer Credit Card Protection:** If you accept credit cards from your customers, you must check out this window and see how you can protect your customers' credit cards. Unless you have other protection devices, this is a service you need to look into.

- **Set Closing Date:** At the end of the accounting year, generally December or any other time approved by management, accounting books are closed, and the closing date is set. The date will prevent anyone from making entries to the previous closed year by mistake. A password should be assigned to the closing date, so that only authorized personnel can make prior year entries or adjustments.

- **Planning & Budgeting:** No business is successful without planning and budgeting. You will be able to set up a budget, project your cash flow and analyze your business using the tools under this submenu. I strongly encourage you to review your business using the Decision Tools submenu, which has the following sections: Measure Profitability, Analyze Financial Strength, Compare Debt and Ownership, Depreciate Your Assets, Manage Your Receivables, Employees, Contractors or Temp, Improve Cash Flow and Periodic Tasks.

- **To Do List:** If you don't want anything to fall through the cracks, this is the tool you will use to control your daily tasks. Periodic tasks sometimes get overlooked, but with the To Do List, all is covered. For example, you can make a note to yourself about "calling the bank to refund you the 100 they overpaid on your bank statement last month or a note to check next month's statement for 100 deposited from the bank."

- **Reminders:** Like the To Do List, Reminders will make sure the main tasks are documented to be completed at a certain time. You can use Reminders not only for yourself, but for other workers who use QuickBooks. Reminders are generated by QuickBooks based on the information on your database like invoice due date.

- **Alerts Manager:** QuickBooks has a calendar list of tax and business-related dates your company needs to meet in order to be in compliance with local and state governments' filings. You'll need to browse through this window to see these dates. QuickBooks will automatically drop an item from the list when the scheduled date has passed; you can also checkmark an item when you have completed the task before the scheduled date.

- **Chart of Accounts:** You can access Chart of Accounts from several windows, and this is one of them. It allows you to create, edit or delete accounts and account reports.

- **Make General Journal Entries:** Journal entries are the backbone of accounting and bookkeeping. However, when you are in the Company menu window, it is advisable to complete your company-related journal entries and at the end of the month when you receive your bank statements, you can then complete the bank-related journal entries.

- **Manage Currency:** This submenu allows you to turn on or turn off the currency feature. If you're dealing with international transactions, this is a submenu you should study very well.

- **Enter Vehicle Mileage:** If you have a vehicle for your business, you should practice and understand the Vehicle Mileage window. You should first create your vehicle accounts in the Chart of Accounts, so the vehicle name is pulled into the Vehicle Mileage window. You must manually record your beginning and ending mileage on paper and then transfer it to this window.

- **Prepare Letters with Envelopes:** To make your financial life easy, QuickBooks has prepared some letters for you ahead of time. All you have to do is open the windows and select and complete the required options and boxes. Take a test drive on some of these letters and see how easy it is to write a business letter, and in less time than you think. Check to see if your computer has the required Microsoft Word before you start using letters and envelopes.

Review Home Page

The Home Page is the central hub that holds major Icons and windows. It is, therefore, vital to make the Home Page your default page when QuickBooks initially opens. It has the five major menus with their Icons prominently displayed for easy access. They include the Vendor, Customer, Employees, Company, and Banking menus. With the Home Page, you don't have to access a window through the usual main menu. All you have to do is find the window you want to open on the Home Page and click on it. Let's review the contents of the Home Page.

- Click **Company menu**
- Click **Home Page**

Vendors: Vendors section has the following Icons:

- Purchase Orders
- Enter Bills
- Receive Inventory
- Enter Bills Against Inventory
- Pay Bills
- Manage Sales Tax

Customers: Customers section has the following Icons:

- Estimates
- Invoices
- Statement Charges
- Finance Charges
- Statements
- Receive Payments
- Create Sales Receipts
- Refunds & Credits

Employees: Employees section has the following Icons

- Enter Time
- Learn about Payroll Options

Company: Company section has the following Icons:

- Chart of Accounts
- Items & Services
- Adjust Quantity On Hand
- Marketing Tools

Banking: Banking section has the following Icons:

- Record Deposits
- Reconcile
- Write Checks
- Check Register
- Print Checks
- Enter Credit Card Charges

Company Snapshot

If set up preferences window correctly, QuickBooks will default you to the home page every time you logon. To get the summary of your financial activities, you click the company snapshot button on the toolbar next to the home page button. This takes you to the snapshot window, where you can view the account balances including who owes you—accounts receivable and who you owe—accounts payable. In the snapshot window you can easily see the alerts on urgent tasks.

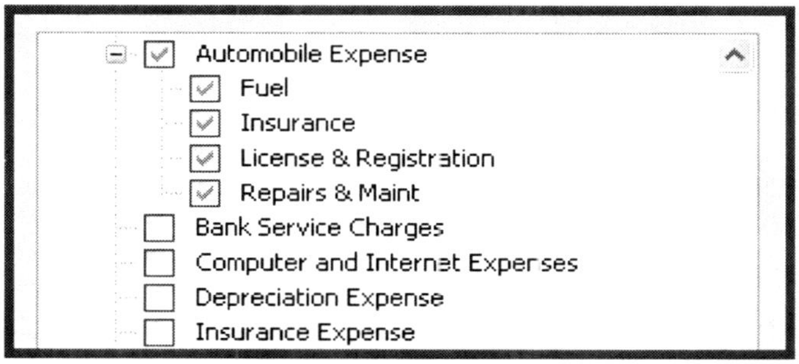

Activities:

- Click **Company menu**
- Click **Company Snapshot.** Maximize window if necessary
- Under Account Balances (bottom left). Click **Select Accounts**
- Scroll down. Checkmark **Automobile Expenses**. Click **Update**
- Under Account Balances (bottom left). Click **Go to Chart of Accounts**
- Click **X** to close the Chart of Accounts window
- Under Customers Who Owe Money. Click **Receive Payments**
- Click **X** to close Integrated Payment Processing window
- Click **X** to Customer Payment window
- Under Vendors to Pay. Click **Pay Bills**
- Click **X** to close Pay Bill window
- Under Reminders. Click **Set Preferences.** Click **X** to close Preferences

Company Information

It is highly recommended to complete as much information in your company window as possible. Information from this window is pulled to other windows and used to populate important reports. One of the most vital pieces information is the type of tax form your company uses. QuickBooks defaults the correct tax information based on the form of business you selected. Also, your Federal Employee Identification number is essential for processing tax related reports.

Activities:

- Click **Company menu**
- Click **Company Information...**
- Company Name: Accept **Quick Company 2009**
- Address: Type **123 Adam Lane**. Press **Enter**
- Type: **Dallas, TX 75000**
- Country**:** Accept **US**
- Legal Name: Type **Quick Company 2009**
- Legal Address: Type **123 Adam Lane**
- City: Type **Dallas**
- State: Press **T** twice
- Zip: Type **75000**
- Phone: Type **214-100-1000**
- Fax: Type **214-200-2000**
- E-mail: Type **accountant@quickcompany.com**
- Website: Type **www.quickcompany.com**
- Federal Employer Identification No.: Type **99-9999999** (nine 9s in total
- Contact: Type **Kelly Johnson**
- Title: Type **Director of Finance**
- Phone #: Type **214-444-3000**
- Click **OK**

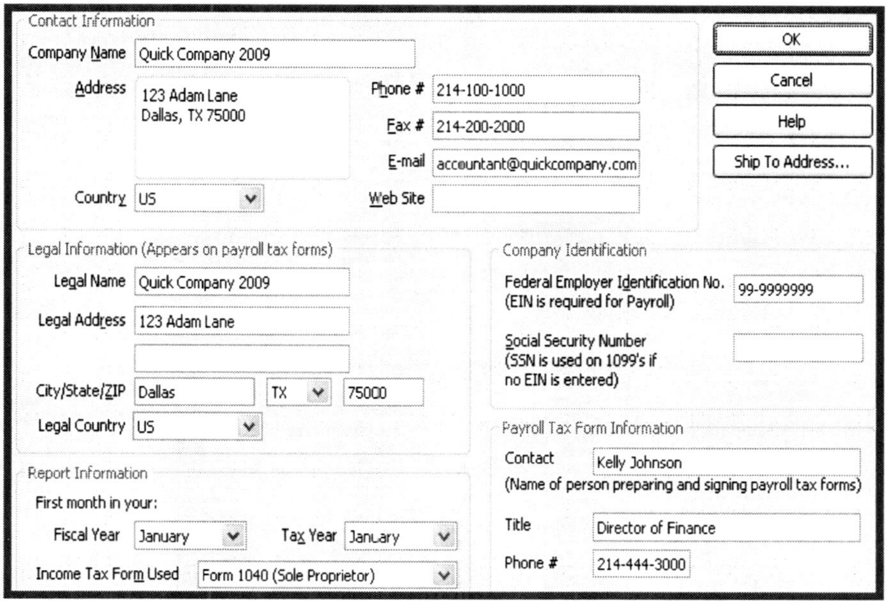

Set Up Password

Set Up Users submenu allows you to set up password for both the administrator and users. It also allows you to add, edit, delete, and view user. You will not be able to delete an administrator, but edit it only. In this exercise, you are going to create an admin and a user named Kelly. In creating Kelly's password, QuickBooks will want to know what level of rights you want to grant her. You may grant Kelly full rights to read and write every window or limited rights for a few windows.

Activities:

Click **Company menu**

- Click **Set Up Users and Passwords**
- Click **Set Up Users...**
- With Admin(logged on) highlighted
- Click **Edit User**
- User Name: Accept **Admin**
- Password: Type **admin**
- Confirm Password: Type **admin**
- Challenge Question: Select **Name of oldest nephew**
- Challenge Answer: Type **admin.** Click **Next.**
- Click **Finish**

- Click **Add User...**
- User Name: Type **Kelly**
- Password: Type **kelly**
- Confirm Password: Type **kelly.** Click **Next**
- Click **All areas of QuickBooks.** Click **Next**
- Click **Yes** to "Are you sure..."
- Review Kelly's access rights window
- Click **Finish**
- Click **Close** to User List window

If you don't want to allow the "All areas of QuickBooks" access, you can always assign selected windows.

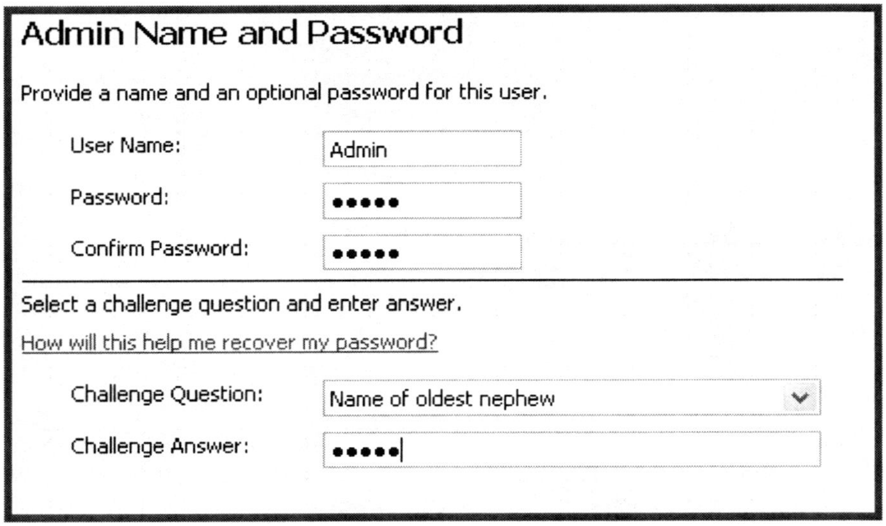

Edit User's Password

As an administrator, you have full rights—to read and write—and therefore can add, edit, and delete passwords. You can change Kelly's password, or she can do so herself if she has been assigned a password to enter the database. For Kelly to change her password, all she has to do is log on, click on Kelly and Edit User button. The administrator is the only one who can delete admin's password. To remove admin's password, you type the current password and leave the new and confirm new password boxes blank. You must select the <Select> for the challenge question.

Activities:

- Click **Company menu**
- Click **Set Up Users and Password**
- Click **Set Up Users...**

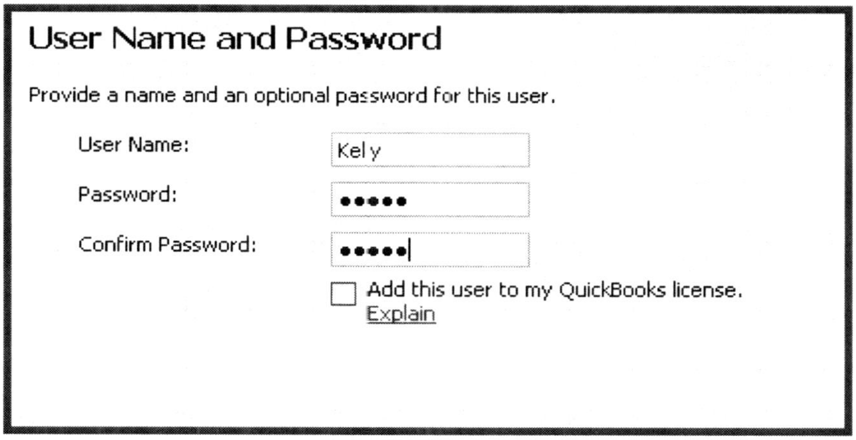

- Password: Type **admin**. Click **OK**
- Click **Kelly.**
- Click **Edit User…**
- User Name: Accept **Kelly**. Press **Tab**
- Password: Type **test**. Press **Tab**
- Confirm Password: Type **test**. Click **Next**
- Click **All areas of QuickBooks**. Click **Next**
- Click **Yes** to "Are you sure you want to give…?"
- Click **Finish**
- In the User List box. Click **Kelly.**
- Click **Delete User**
- Click **Yes** to "Are you sure you want to delete "kelly"?"
- Click **Close** to User List window

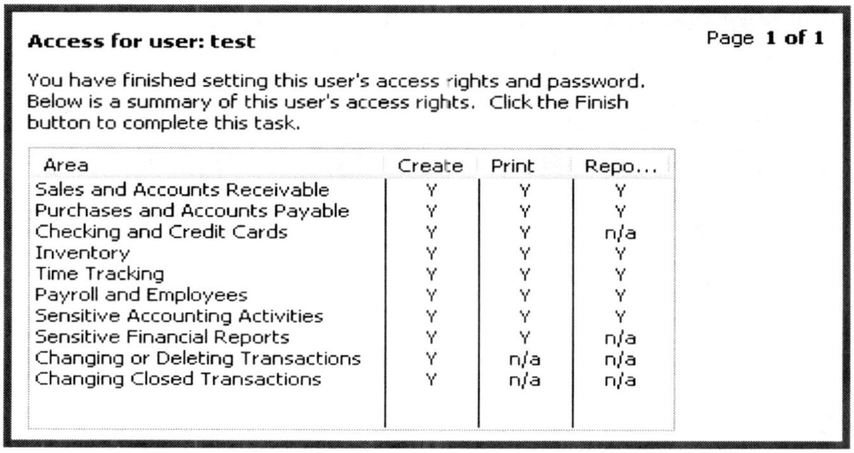

Area	Create	Print	Repo…
Sales and Accounts Receivable	Y	Y	Y
Purchases and Accounts Payable	Y	Y	Y
Checking and Credit Cards	Y	Y	n/a
Inventory	Y	Y	Y
Time Tracking	Y	Y	Y
Payroll and Employees	Y	Y	Y
Sensitive Accounting Activities	Y	Y	Y
Sensitive Financial Reports	Y	Y	n/a
Changing or Deleting Transactions	Y	n/a	n/a
Changing Closed Transactions	Y	n/a	n/a

Edit Admin's Password

The admin is the one who can add, edit or delete admin's password. To edit or remove admin's password you click the Set Up Users and Passwords and then the Change Your Password submenu, not the Set Up Users submenu. Most administrators think you can remove or delete admin password by going the Set Up Users submenu, only to find out it is not so. You must select the <Select> for the challenge question; otherwise the password is not removed.

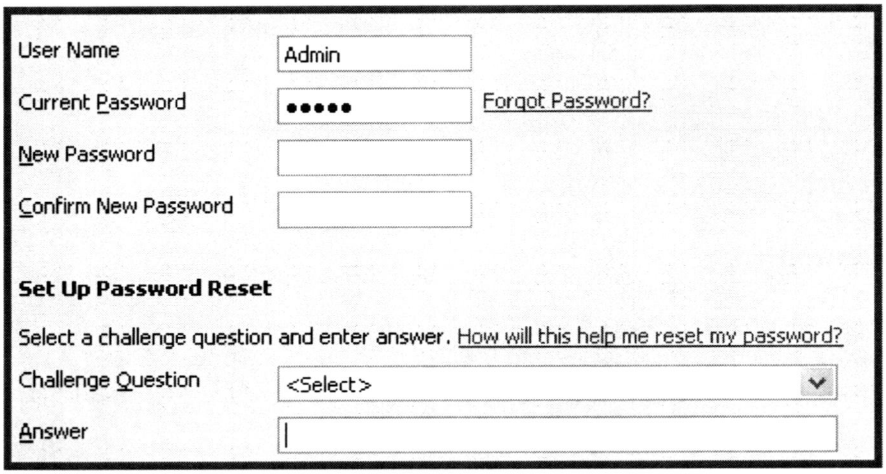

Activities:

- Click **Company menu**
- Click **Set Up Users and Passwords**
- Click **Change Your Password**
- User Name: Accept **Admin**
- Current Password: Type **admin**
- New Password: **(leave blank)**
- Confirm New Password **(leave blank)**
- Challenge Question: Select **<Select>** (Very Important)
- Challenge Answer: **(leave blank)** Click **OK**
- Click **OK** to "Your QuickBooks password…"
- That's how you remove Admin's Password

Set Closing Date

It is pertinent to know how to set up the closing date, to prevent you from erroneously keying data for the previous year. If you set up closing date correctly, any time you key transaction with previous year, QuickBooks will prompt you to enter your password. Be sure to click Cancel and change your entry to 2009 when the message window comes up. If you set the closing date/password, you must open it to enter any account's opening balances.

Activities:

- Click **Company menu**
- Click **Set Closing Date…**
- Click **Set Date/Password** (bottom of window)
- Closing Date: Type **12/31/08** (End of last year)
- Closing Date Password: Type **admin**
- Confirm Password: Type **admin**. Click **OK**
- Click **No** to "This company file does not…"
- Click **X** to close Preferences window
- Click **Lists menu.**
- Click **Chart of Accounts**
- Double click **USA Checking**
- **Highlight date for Check # 1001**:
- Type **10/10/08** (last year's date). Press **Enter**
- Click **Yes** to "You have changed…"
- **Look! QuickBooks will not allow last year's entry without password**
- Click **Cancel** to "This modification…"

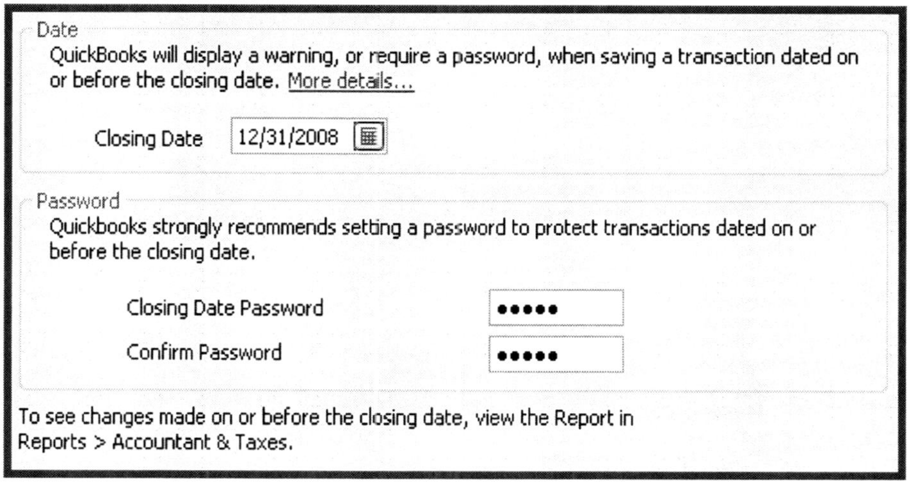

- **Highlight date again:** Type **1/1/09.** Press **Enter**
- Click **X** to close Register window.

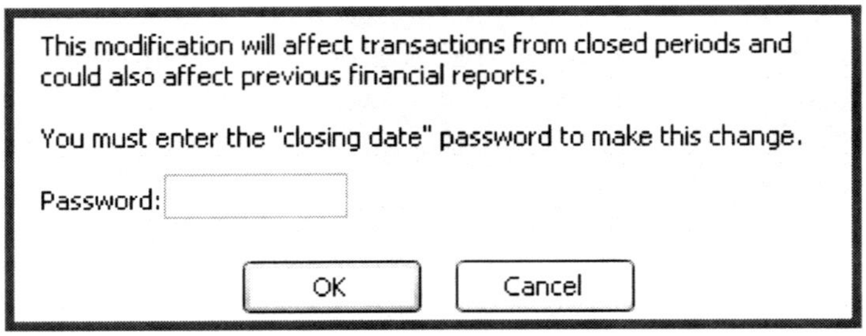

Remove Closing Date

Setting the closing date and password depends on the number of people accessing the database. If you have more than three people, it is necessary to set the closing date password. Also, it is pertinent to limit the rights of everyone but the accountant and director finance to the payroll and employees windows, which includes creating pay checks or pay stubs, printing payroll tax forms, paying or e-paying payroll taxes, accessing employees and payroll centers, and running or viewing payroll reports

Activities:

- Click **Company menu**.
- Click **Set Closing Date…**
- Click **Set Date/Password** in the main window
- Closing Date: **Highlight date**.
- Press **Delete key**

- ❖ Closing Date Password: **Highlight password**.
- ❖ Press **Delete key**
- ❖ Confirm Password: **Highlight password**.
- ❖ Press **Delete key.** Click **OK**
- ❖ Click **No** to **"This company file does not…"**
- ❖ Click **X** to close Preferences window

Planning & Budgeting

Most companies operate their businesses on budgets. Few companies can survive long without a budget. Planning and budgeting set up is the first step in the budgeting process. You go through the Company menu to set up your budget; then you choose if you want to create a budget from the previous year's data or from scratch. In this exercise, you will create a budget from scratch. The instructions below will make it easier for you to complete the budgeting process with confident.

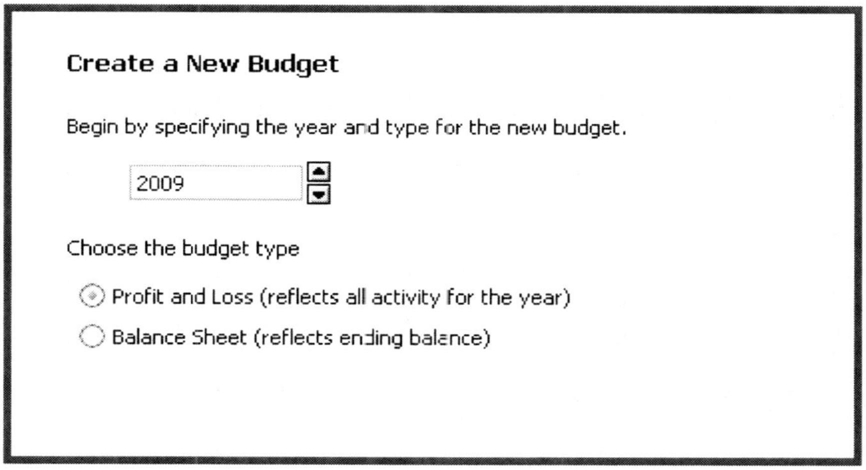

Activities:

- ❖ Click **Company menu**
- ❖ Click **Planning & Budgeting**
- ❖ Click **Set Up Budgets**
- ❖ Select **2009**
- ❖ Click **Profit and Loss...** Click **Next**
- ❖ Click **No additional criteria**. Click **Next**
- ❖ Click **Create budget from scratch**
- ❖ Click **Finish**
- ❖ Under **Jan09.** Click **Landscaping Services** line

- ❖ Type **100,000**
- ❖ Click **Copy Across** (bottom left)
- ❖ Click **Under Jan09.** Click **Cost of Goods Sold** line
- ❖ Type **40,000**
- ❖ Click **Copy Across**
- ❖ Click **Save** (bottom right of window)
- ❖ Click **OK** to close window

Account	Annual T...	Jan09	Feb09	Mar09	Apr09	May09	Jun09	Jul09	Aug09
Landscaping Services	1,200,00...	100,00...	100,00...	100,00...	100,00...	100,00...	100,00...	100,00...	100,00...
Design Services									
Equipment Rental									
Labor									
Markup Income									
Materials									
Misc Income									
Subcontractors									
Supplies									
Opening Balance In...									
Cost of Goods Sold	480,000.00	40,000...	40,000...	40,000...	40,000...	40,000...	40,000...	40,000...	40,000...
Discount Received									

Budget Report

After you have set up your budget numbers or what you expect your company to achieve in the coming year, from time to time you should run the budget report to see how you're meeting your expectations. You may want to run your report on monthly basis to hold a budget meeting or run your report on a quarterly basis. Whatever period you choose to review the report, one of the best reports to process is the Profit & Loss Budget Performance report. It shows income and expenses for the period.

Activities:

- ❖ Click **Reports menu**
- ❖ Click **Budgets**
- ❖ Click **Profit & Loss Budget Performance**
- ❖ Accept **FY 2009—Profit & Loss by Account.** Click **Next**
- ❖ Accept **Account by Month.** Click **Next**
- ❖ Click **Finish**
- ❖ Dates: Select **This Fiscal Year**
- ❖ Click **X** to close report window

	Jan - Dec 09	Budget	Jan - Dec 09	YTD Budget	Annual Budget
Quick Company 2009					
Profit & Loss Budget Performance					
January through December 2009					
Ordinary Income/Expense					
Income					
Landscaping Services	0.00	1,200,000.00	0.00	1,200,000.00	1,200,000.00
Opening Balance Income	1,005,000.00		1,005,000.00		
Total Income	1,005,000.00	1,200,000.00	1,005,000.00	1,200,000.00	1,200,000.00
Cost of Goods Sold					
Cost of Goods Sold	0.00	480,000.00	0.00	480,000.00	480,000.00
Total COGS	0.00	480,000.00	0.00	480,000.00	480,000.00
Gross Profit	1,005,000.00	720,000.00	1,005,000.00	720,000.00	720,000.00
Expense					
Opening Balance Expen...	5,000.00		5,000.00		
Telephone Expense	0.00		0.00		
Total Expense	5,000.00		5,000.00		
Net Ordinary Income	1,000,000.00	720,000.00	1,000,000.00	720,000.00	720,000.00
Net Income	**1,000,000.00**	**720,000.00**	**1,000,000.00**	**720,000.00**	**720,000.00**

To Do List

This is one function most businesses cannot do without. The To Do List has one advantage and that is your employees or associates can work from same the list and get you caught up on key financial tasks. It is easy to set it up, but the hardest part is completing the tasks you set out to do, and not procrastinate until the next day or week. Most businesses have gone out of business because they did not meet important financial deadlines. Don't let this happen to you!

Activities:

- Click **Company menu**
- Click **To Do List**
- Right click in the window. Click **New**
- Note: Type **Transfer funds to brokerage account.** Press **Tab**
- Remind me on: Type **1/10/09**. Click **Next**
- Note: Type **Call bank to refund error on bank statement.** Press **Tab**
- Remind me on: Type **1/15/09**. Click **Next**
- Note: Type **Backup QuickBooks**. Press **Tab**
- Remind me on: Type **1/31/09**. Click **OK**

- Right click on **1/10/09 for Transfer funds to...**
- Click **Edit To Do Note**
- Click **Done** (bottom right)
- Click **OK**. See Note has checkmark

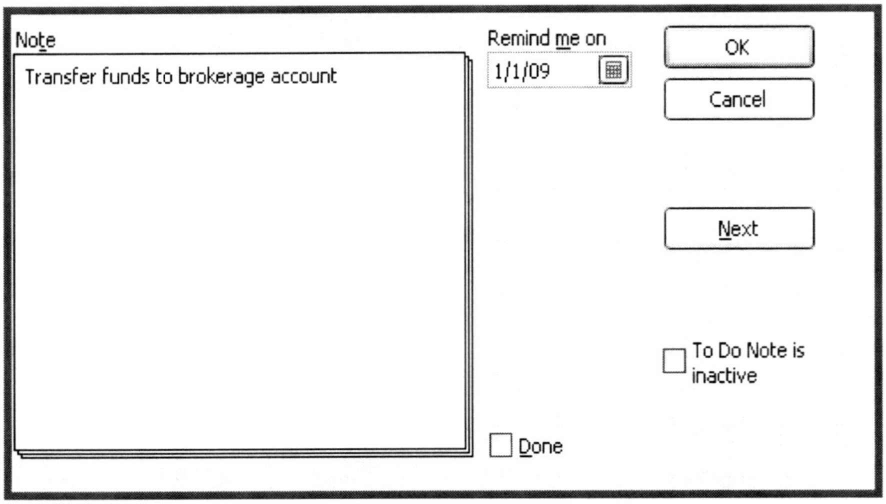

Reminders & Alert Manager

Apart from the To Do List, you have Reminders and Alert Manager. QuickBooks is doing everything possible to make sure you're on top of your financial tasks—that you get the job done—on time! One advantage of Reminders is that it will be staring you in the face every time you open your QuickBooks file, if your Preferences are set up correctly. For this reason, you must set up your Reminder in the Preferences window. Review your Reminder window daily; it's imperative!

Activities:

- Click **Company menu**
- Click **Reminders**
- Click **Collapse All** (bottom of window)
- Review window
- Click **Expand All.** Click **X** to close window
- Click **Company menu**
- Click **Alert Manager**
- Review window
- Alert Manager will remove an item when necessary
- Click **X** to close window

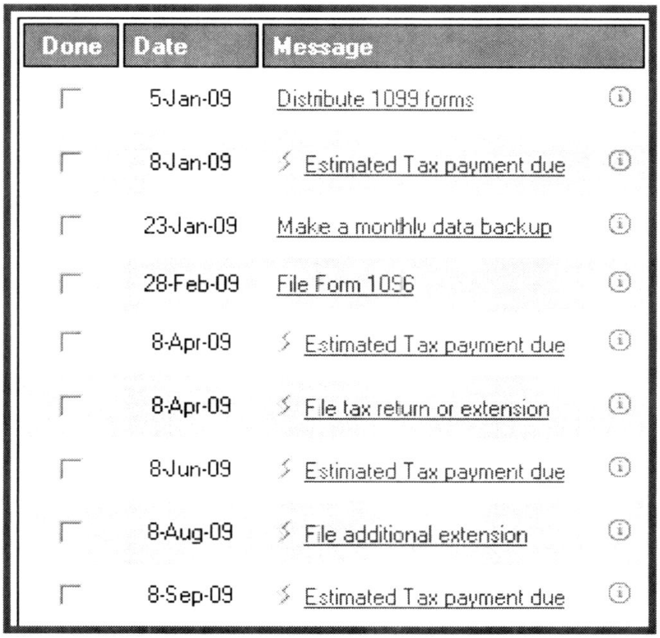

General Journal Entries

When a fixed asset loses its market value due to wear and tear, it is said to be depreciating. There are different types of depreciation methods including straight line, double declining, sum of the year's digit, and unit of production. In straight line, you divide the asset value by the number of years the asset will last and divide the result by 12 to get the monthly depreciation expense amount. Here, 40,000/5 is 8,000. You divide 8,000 by 12 to get 666.67 the monthly depreciation expense.

Activities:

- Click **Company menu**
- Click **Make General Journal Entries**
- Click **OK** to "QuickBooks now automatically assign numbers..."
- Date: Type **1/31/09** (Very Important)
- Entry No.: Accept **3**
- Click under **Account.** (left of the window
- Scroll down. Select **Depreciation Expense**
- Click under **Debit**: Type **666.67**
- Click under **Memo**: Type **Jan Depreciation on truck**
- Click under **Depreciation Expense**
- Select **Accumulated Depreciation under Truck**

- Credit: Type **666.67**
- Memo: Type **Jan Depreciation on truck**
- Click **Save & Close**. Click **OK**

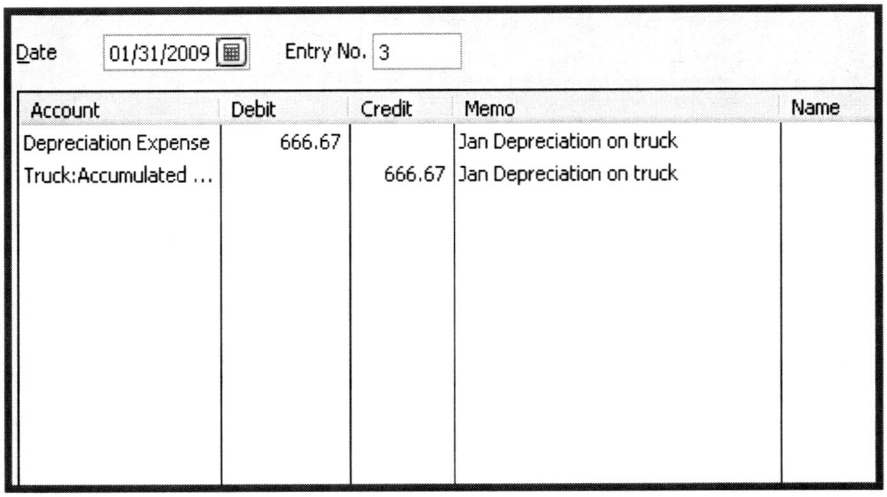

Vehicle Mileage

If you have cars and trucks, you want your staff to log in their mileage on those cars and trucks. This information is also used to send bills to customers connected to the projects. You must check and record your Trip Start and Trip End odometer readings. After you've keyed in all your data, you should be able to click the top right of the window and print a mileage report either in detail or summary format. Whatever you do, be sure you've selected the right vehicle.

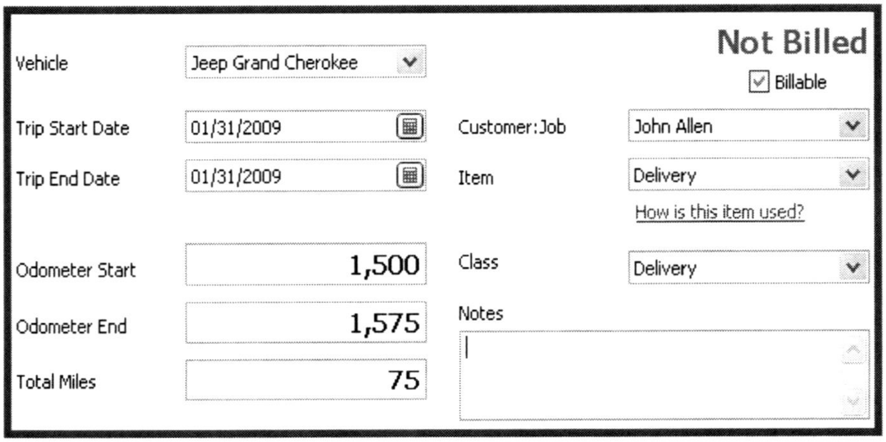

Activities:

- Click **Company menu**
- Click **Enter Vehicle Mileage**
- Vehicle: Select **Jeep Grand Cherokee Truck**
- Trip Start Date: Type **1/31/09**
- Trip End Date: Type **1/31/09**
- Odometer Start: Type **1,500**
- Odometer End: Type **1,575**. Press **Tab**
- Total Miles: Accept **75**
- Checkmark **Billable**
- Customer: Job: Select **John Allen**
- Item: Select **Delivery**
- Class: Select **Delivery**
- Click **Save & Close** (bottom right)

Financial Results: Profit & Loss

In this chapter we created a password for our financial file. I urge you to do the same on your own business file. It's always good to make it difficult for intruders to invade your privacy. We introduced the Depreciation Expense, by making a General Journal entry for $666.67, to reduce the value of the Truck asset. Every month, the truck value is decreased and the Depreciation Expense account is increased by the same amount. If you did not select This Fiscal Year from the Date down arrow you might not get the same result.

Activities:

- Click **Reports menu**
- Click **Company & Financial**
- Click **Profit & Loss Standard**
- Date (top left): Select **This Fiscal Year**
- From: Accept **1/1/09.** To: Accept **12/31/09**
- **Net Income is 999,333.33**
- Click **X** to close window

Quick Company 2009
Profit & Loss
January through December 2009

	Jan - Dec 09
Ordinary Income/Expense	
Income	
Opening Balance Income	1,005,000.00
Total Income	1,005,000.00
Gross Profit	1,005,000.00
Expense	
Opening Balance Expense	5,000.00
Depreciation Expense	666.67
Telephone Expense	0.00
Total Expense	5,666.67
Net Ordinary Income	999,333.33
Net Income	**999,333.33**

Financial Results: Balance Sheet

Anytime you depreciate an asset account, you reduce the account balance. As you continue to depreciate the asset account, the Accumulated Depreciation balance will continue to increase while the asset balance will continue to decrease by the same amount. So every month, you must check the both the Profit & Loss and the Balance Sheet statements to make sure these amounts are pulling into these reports. Total Truck account has decreased by $666.67 and Total Asset is $2,519,333.33

Activities:

- Click **Reports menu**
- Click **Company & Financial**
- Click **Balance Sheet Standard**
- Date (top left): Click down arrow
- Select **This Fiscal Year**
- As of: Accept **12/31/09**
- Click **Collapse**
- **Total Assets is 2,519,333.33**
- Click **X** to close window

Quick Company 2009
Balance Sheet
As of December 31, 2009

	Dec 31, 09
ASSETS	
Current Assets	
Checking/Savings	
Money Market Account	100,000.00
USA Checking	800,000.00
USA Payroll Checking	100,000.00
USA Savings	250,000.00
Total Checking/Savings	1,250,000.00
Accounts Receivable	
Accounts Receivable	1,005,000.00
Total Accounts Receivable	1,005,000.00
Other Current Assets	
Inventory Asset	225,000.00
Total Other Current Assets	225,000.00
Total Current Assets	2,480,000.00
Fixed Assets	
Truck	39,333.33
Total Fixed Assets	39,333.33
TOTAL ASSETS	**2,519,333.33**

Review Principles of Journal Entries

There are five major accounts in accounting. However, sometimes accountants create minor accounts to explain the nature of these five accounts. For instance, asset is one of the five major accounts, but sometimes accountants create current assets, fixed assets, and other assets to explain how liquid these assets are.

Five major accounts:

- Assets
- Liabilities
- Equity
- Income
- Expenses

Debits and Credits:

Newcomers to the accounting profession would find this section a little hard to understand initially more than any other part of accounting. In fact, this is one of the most significant sections of the entire book, because debit and credit are what happen to most numbers that enter the QuickBooks software. I'm going to give you the summary of debits and credits, and once you understand this simple principle, every facet of accounting job will so easy to you.

Debits and Credits Picture:

Increase(Debit)	**Increase(Credit)**
Assets	**Liabilities**
	Equity
Expenses	**Income**
Decrease (Credit)	**Decrease (Debit)**

Every accountant has this same picture you're looking at, burnt into his or her mind, and once you understand and can remember this picture, the rest of accounting is history! I'll explain the picture in a minute, but let me repeat what I said before: All accounts in the accounting profession are created from these five accounts. All you have to do is remember these five accounts, and any time you see an account, you just find out which account it was created from. Once you understand how to debit and credit these five accounts, you will understand how to debit and credit thousands of accounts you or anyone else can create from these five accounts. It's that easy!

Explanation to Debit and Credits Picture:

Increase (Debit)	Increase (Credit)
Assets	Liabilities
	Equities
Expenses	Income
Decrease (Credit)	Decrease (Debit)

- First, remember there are only five major accounts
- Assets and Expenses on the left
- Liabilities, Equities, and Income on the right
- On the Left side Increase is Debit
- On the right side Increase is Credit
- Increase on Assets and Expenses is Debit and the opposite is true
- Decrease on Assets and Expenses is Credit
- Increase on Liabilities, Equities and Income is Credit and the opposite is true
- Decrease on Liabilities, Equities and Income is Debit
- If you think Assets and Expenses increases you think Debit
- If you think Liabilities, Equities and Income increases you think Credit
- Can you close your eyes and see this picture? That's all you need
- Increase Debit. Increase Credit. That's it! And the opposite is true.

Using Debits and Credits Picture in Journal Entry:

Increase (Debit)	Increase (Credit)
Assets	Liabilities
	Equity
Expenses	Income
Decrease (Credit)	Decrease (Debit)

Assets and Equity:
You can get clues about a journal entry by talking to yourself about what happened. For example, you might say, "I put money in the checking account—Asset, which is on the left side," or "I took out a loan--Liability, which is on the right side."

What if you, as the owner, bring money into the business and put it in the bank account called USA Checking in the amount of 50,000?

You will increase USA Checking (an Asset) by 50,000 and will increase the Owner's accounts Equity). When you increase asset, you Debit it. And when you increase equity, you Credit it.

USA Checking	50,000	
Owner's Investments		50,000

Assets and Expenses:

Now you have funds in the bank account USA Checking. What if it's the end of the month and you wrote a check from USA Checking to pay a telephone bill for 450? You will decrease USA Checking (an Asset) by 450 and will increase the telephone bill accounts (an Expense). When you decrease asset, you Credit it; and when you increase expense, you Debit it.

USA Checking		450
Telephone Expense	450	

Assets and Liabilities:

What if go out and buy Inventory for 65,786 for your business, they give you a bill and you promised to pay the account within 30 days.

You will increase Inventory (an Asset) by 65,786 and also increase Accounts Payable (a Liability). When you increase asset you, Debit it; and when you increase liability, you Credit it.

Inventory Asset	65,786	
Accounts Payable		67,786

Assets and Income:

What if one of your customers sends you a check for consulting services for 23,450 and you put it in USA Checking account?

You will increase USA Checking (an Asset) by 23,450 and will increase Consulting Income (an Income). When you increase asset, you Debit it; and when you increase income, you Credit it.

USA Checking	23,450	
Consulting Income		23,450

Assets and Assets:

Up until now I've been talking about Assets and other accounts, now let's see what happened when you used asset to buy asset. For example, you went to a store and bought a computer for 3,500 with a check.

When you pay by check, you decreased USA Checking (an Asset) by 3,500 and increase Computer account (an Asset). When you decrease asset you, Credit it; and when you increase asset, you Debit it.

USA Checking		3,500
Computer	3,500	

Examples of Accounts:

Click Lists menu. Click Chart of Accounts. Review some accounts examples.

a. Examples of Assets: Cash, Checking account, Savings account, Accounts Receivables, Other Current Assets, Fixed (Long Term) Assets
b. Examples of Liabilities: Accounts Payable, Credit Card, Other Current Liabilities, Long Term Liabilities
c. Examples of Equity: Beginning Equity, Owner's Contribution, Owners Distribution, Retained Earnings, Other Equity accounts
d. Examples of Income: Landscaping, Materials, Supplies, Subcontractors, Sales, Services, Uncategorized
e. Examples of Expenses: Cost of Goods Sold, Materials, Supplies, Automobile, Insurance, Telephone, Taxes, Utilities, Uncategorized

To perform the journal entries, you click Company menu, then, click Make General Journal entries. You are now in the journal entry window.

Practice makes perfect!

The difference between you and I is time. I've been using the same principle I'm teaching you here for many years now—it's no magic at all. Believe me, as soon as you understand this simple principle, and use it over and over again, it will be as easy as ABC. I've just given you few examples, every other journal entries will follow similar pattern. You can use the same thought pattern I've used here to make practically any journal entries. Remember QuickBooks is designed to make these entries for you, all the hard work has been done, I'm just showing what is going on behind the scenes, should you want to make one these entries yourself. This stuff is very easy with practice!

Review Month-End Journal Entries

From time to time you may make journal entries such as when you bought asset or pay for expenses with your personal money. You have to make a journal entry to bring in that money into the business as Debit to Checking and Credit to Owners Contribution. However, in this section we are looking at monthly entries you have to make because business activities. You don't have to worry too much about accounting and journal entries; QuickBooks has done all the work for you. However, there are few entries you would have to do yourself and my job is to make sure you understand, step by step, how to make these few entries. Relax and have fun—this is so easy! I'll start here with the company related entries, when you get to the Banking menu, I'll explain those entries also. You may test these journal entries only in the Testing Company file not in the Quick Payroll file. There are four basic entries in this section:

Company basic entries:

- Depreciation
- Inventory Supplies
- Prepaid Expenses
- Payroll (aka Wages)

Depreciation:

As you manage your business with your fixed assets—truck, building or furniture—these assets are losing value. Accountants would say these assets are depreciating in value (the opposite of appreciating in value). Accounting rules allow you to reduce your income every month by the amount your asset is depreciating in value. Initially, you created a Truck account in the Chart of Account window for 40,000. Let's find out how QuickBooks made the journal entry. Click Repots menu. Click Company & Financial. Click Balance Sheet Standard. Double click 40,000 for Original Truck Price. Double click 40,000 again. Double click GENJRNL (left of 1st row). Look! QuickBooks made the following entries for you:

Truck: Original Truck Price	40,000	
Opening Bal Equity		40,000

As we calculated somewhere in the previous pages, if your monthly depreciation amount is 666.67. Then your job is to make the following entries:

Deprecation Expense	666.67	
Accumulated Depreciation-Truck		666.67

Inventory Asset:

When you set up your Inventory Parts in the Item List window under the List menu, QuickBooks made the following entries for Inventory Asset of 50,000.

Inventory Asset	50,000	
Opening Bal Equity- Adjustment		50,000

As you continue to use the supplies, the number and the value will continue to go down. If you set the quantity box, QuickBooks should be able to track of your inventory balance on your Balance Sheet report. If you did not set the quantity box, QuickBooks will not track of your inventory, you have to go to the warehouse and count the remainder of your inventory. When you subtract what is left from what you started with, the difference is what you used. If you used 4,500 of Material Inventory, your job would be to make the following entries, but QuickBooks made the entries for you because you told QuickBooks to track your inventory.

Inventory: Materials		4,500
Cost of Good Sold: Materials	4,500	

Click Reports menu. Click Company & Financial. Click Balance Sheet Standard, you will see Inventory Asset has gone down by 4,500. Click Reports menu. Click Company & Financial. Click Profit & Loss Standard, Date: Select This Fiscal Year, you will see Cost of Good Sold has 4,500.

Prepaid Expenses:
If you own assets such as a Truck or Building, you should have insurance on those assets. Sometimes, the insurance company will prorate the insurance bill into monthly payments, which they can withdraw from your checking account by EFT (electronic fund transfer). In this case, you have no journal entry problem. However, if you wrote a one-time check for 10,500 to the insurance company for one year you must write the check in the Check Register, but you should first create an account called prepaid insurance in the Chart of Account window with 0.00 opening balance, and then pull that account into the check register. QuickBooks will then make the following entries for you:

USA Checking		10,500
Prepaid Insurance	10,500	

As each month passes by, you divide the annual lump sum of 10,500 into 12 and book the result of 875 every month. You will make the following monthly entries:

Insurance Expense	875.00	
Prepaid Insurance		875.00

Click Reports menu. Click Company & Financial. Click Balance Sheet Standard, you will see Prepaid Insurance has gone down by 875. Click Reports menu. Click Company & Financial. Click Profit & Loss Standard, Date: Select This Fiscal Year. You will see Insurance Expense has 875.00

Wages:
If you have December 31 as the end of your fiscal year—as most companies do—sometimes, that date will fall in the middle of the week, say, on a Tuesday. What if you have an employee who earns $20 an hour and worked from Monday, December 29, 2008 through Friday, January 2, 2009 the next year? You will accrue the Monday, Tuesday, and Wednesday in the 2008 financial statement, because the services have been performed but not paid for yet till Friday of 2009.

Your entry for the three days (Monday and Wednesday) that fell in 2008 financial statement, but were not paid for, will be 24 hours at 20 an hour.

Payroll Expense	480.00	
Payroll Liabilities		480.00

Summary:
These are the four basic end-of-the-period journal entries you will have to make in the Company menu. Any other journal entries that come along will follow one these four basic entries. All you have to do is follow the same thinking pattern and you will be OK. It is not hard once you take one of these examples and repeat it over and over again—be it Depreciation, Inventory Supplies, Prepaid Expenses, or Payroll Payable.

Chapter Summary

Most Company menu activities are office administration in nature, how to update the Company Information, how to setup and update password windows for users and administrator. We looked at the Make General Journal Entries window which is important because you will be using it frequently. If you pay a bill with your personal check, you will first use the Enter Bills window under Vendor menu; then you make a Journal Entry with a Debit to Checking Account and a Credit to Owners Equity. Finally, you pay the bill with the amount you just posted to the Checking Account.

What we accomplished:

- Reviewed Company submenus
- Reviewed the home page
- Browsed company snapshot
- Updated company information
- Set up passwords
- Edited user's password
- Edited admin's password
- Set the closing date
- Remove the closing date
- Prepared planning and budgeting
- Ran Budget report
- Practiced the To-Do list
- Used reminders and the alert manager
- Made general journal entries
- Completed the vehicle mileage window
- Processed financial statements
- Reviewed the principles of journal entries
- Reviewed month-end journal entries

Additional Financial activities:

- Depreciation Entry for $666.67

Exercise 5

Complete Exercise 5 by using the following information:

1. Create service items link to chart of accounts labor under sales & services
   Item: Site Training. Description: Labor group. Rate 100
   Item: Installation. Description: Labor group. Rate 150
   Item: Repairs. Description: Labor group. Rate 200
   Item: Computer Setup. Description: Labor group. Rate 250

2. Create inventory items link to cost of goods sold and sales & services.
   Item: Desktop. Description: Computer group
   Cost 500 price 950. Reorder 100 on hand 1100 date 1/2/09
   Item: Laptop. Description: Computer group
   Cost 400 price 820. Reorder 100 on hand 1100 date 1/2/09
   Item: Printers. Description: Office machines group

Cost 230 price 460. Reorder 100 on hand 1100 date 1/2/09
Item: Fax Machines. Description: Office machines group
Cost 150 price 300. Reorder 100 on hand 1100 date 1/2/09

Item: Big Screen Wall. Description: Entertainment group
Cost 600 price 950. Reorder 200 on hand 1500 date 1/5/09
Item: Big Screen Stand. Description: Entertainment group
Cost 1000 price 1550. Reorder 200 on hand 1500 date 1/5/09

Item: Refrigerator. Description: Household appliances group
Cost 750 price 1500. Reorder 500 on hand 2000 date 1/5/09
Item: Oven. Description: Household appliances group
Cost 650 price 1350. Reorder 500 on hand 2000 date 1/5/09
Item: Microwave. Description: Household appliances group
Cost 200 price 400. Reorder 500 on hand 2000 date 1/5/09

3. Create non inventory items link to chart of account job cost
   Item: Computer Parts. Description: Computer group. Price 300.
   Item: Office Machines Parts. Description: Office Machines group. Price 100
   Item: Household Appliances Parts. Descr: Household Appliances group. Price 250
   Item: Entertainment Parts. Description: Entertainment group. Price 200

   Item: Wires. Description: Material group. Price 45
   Item: Cable. Description: Material group. Price 25
   Item: Boxes. Description: Supplies group. Price 45

4. Create other charge items link to chart of account income.
   Item: 10% Discount Given. Description: Sales & services group
   Amount or %: -10% (Type with %)

5. Set up the following list by referring to the page or using the data given below.
   Price Level List as on page 106
   Sales Tax Code List as on page 107

   For Class List use the following class list:
   Computers
   Office Machines
   Entertainment
   Household Appliances

Other Name List as on page 109

Customer Type List use following customer type list:
Corporate
Schools & University
Churches

For Vendor Type List use the following vendor type list:
Transportation
Utilities
Insurance
Repairs & Maintenance
Financial Services

For Job Type List use the following job type list:
Computer Parts
Office Machines Parts
Household Appliances Parts
Entertainment Parts

For Payment Method List as on page 113

6. Prepare general journal entry under the company menu
   January entry 5 yrs Straight line on Truck $65,450 date 1/31/09 as on page 142

6. Process the following reports
   Profit & Loss Statement ending 12/31/09
   Balance Sheet Standard ending 12/31/09
   Statement of Cash Flow ending 12/31/09
   Inventory Valuation Summary 1/31/09
   Inventory Stock Status by Item 1/31/09
   Physical Inventory Worksheet 1/31/09
   Account Listing as of Today
   Item Price List as of Today
   Item Listing as of Today

$

Chapter 6

Customers Menu

Objectives: After you've completed this chapter, you will be able to:

- ✓ Describe Customers submenus
- ✓ Identify customer center contents
- ✓ Create new customers
- ✓ Create customer jobs
- ✓ Prepare estimates
- ✓ Process invoices
- ✓ Complete sales receipts
- ✓ Complete credit memos/refunds
- ✓ Create statement charges
- ✓ Access finance charges
- ✓ Create customer statements
- ✓ Receive payments
- ✓ Make Deposits
- ✓ Complete the weekly timesheet and time single activity
- ✓ Process the change items prices
- ✓ Void and delete invoice with and without payment
- ✓ Create A/R & sales graphs
- ✓ Save customer balance details on pdf
- ✓ Process financial reports and compare results

Review Customers Submenus

Most businesses sell goods and services to Customers and collect payments from them. The purpose of the Customers menu is to help you complete all customer related windows with the right information. When you think about creating, editing or deleting a customer, you think the Customers menu. When you get used to the Customers menu and its functions, navigating the customer windows will be easy. I cannot emphasize consistency enough in accessing Customer windows through the menu; this way you don't waste your time running back and forth from one window to another.

- Click **Customer menu**

The following submenus are located under the Customers menu:

- **Customer Center:** This is the door office to other customer windows. It holds all the information about each customer. The windows in the Customer Center will allow you to create, edit or delete customers. You can delete a new customer, but if sales and payments are connected to that customer, QuickBooks will not allow you to delete it. It is recommended that you make the customer inactive.

- **Create Estimates:** Your customer may request an estimate for a particular job or project; this way the customer can evaluate whether to choose you over other Vendors. Estimate is a precursor to an invoice, since the customer is going to review your invoice based on the estimated price of the items you previously quoted. So be sure your prices are correct; most customers don't like surprises.

- **Create Invoices:** Before you can sell anything to your customer, an invoice window should be completed. The customer invoice window is user-friendly and easy to navigate as long as you have completed the appropriate List menu windows; you can pull the right information into the customer's invoice.

- **Enter Sales Receipts:** When a customer pays immediately and the transaction is completed in one shot, it is best to use the sales receipts. With sales receipt, your customer is not going to owe you in the future; rather payment is made in full at the moment. You don't need an invoice an item again after you've completed the Sales Receipt.

- **Enter Statement Charges:** The job of this window is to accumulate charges until the end of the month. If you are performing consulting services for a customer, every time you incur a charge, you may enter the charge daily or wait till the end of the month. You enter the charges directly in the register and receive payment in the receive payment window as usual. At the end of the month you will print a statement that shows all the charges.

- **Create Statements:** After you've entered all your charges, at the end of the month you are ready to send a statement to the customer. It is recommended that you make sure all charges from all departments are entered on the statements—if you have more than one department. Your customer would not like to see last month's activities on this month's statement.

- **Assess Finance Charges:** After you've sent invoices to your customers, not all the customers will pay off their invoices at the end of the month. After 30, 60 or 90 days, you will start charging late fees on those outstanding invoices at the percentage you pre-set in QuickBooks. You then run the Assess Finance Charges process to update customer balances with the late fees and a new invoice will be sent out next month with late fees included.

- **Receive Payments:** This is not receiving payment in the mail, but completing the Receive Payment window. It allows you to enter the payment for the right customer. I cannot overemphasize the importance of pulling the right customer for the right payment. You could assess late fees to the wrong customer because you have applied another's payment to the wrong customer. It is recommended to double check your work after this window is completed.

- **Create Credit Memos/Refunds:** If you sell merchandise to a customer, you may specify FOB shipping point. This means the customer is responsible for the goods as soon as it leaves your dock. Another option is to specify FOB Destination, which means you are responsible for the goods till they arrive at the customer's dock. If this is the case, then you will be issuing credit memos or refunds for all damaged goods in transit; because you are responsible for the goods until they arrive at the customer's dock. If you can, it is a good practice to avoid all FOB Destination arrangements.

- **Add Credit Card Processing:** A small business will be quick in receiving payment much faster if you can sign up for credit card processing. The only drawback is the fees from the credit card issuer, which may be exorbitant.

- **Enter Time:** If you have hourly employee, at the end of every week, you will fill out a Time Card for him or her in QuickBooks. There are two ways of recording time. The first one is the use of the Weekly Timesheet. It has a one-week period, Monday through Sunday, where you can enter the 8 hours worked for one day. The second tool is the Time/Enter Single Activity. It allows you to complete a day's job by time clock.

- **Item List:** We've discussed Item List under the Item menu. Item List window allows you to create items that pull to other windows and reports.

- **Change Item Prices:** Item prices are not carved in stone; it changes from month to month or from year to year. QuickBooks has made it possible for you to change a list of product prices with a click of a button. It is recommended to use the percentage method of increasing prices across the board, so you don't have to manually increase prices on thousands of individual items.

Review Customer Center

Anytime you have a problem with a customer, the first place you should think about is the Customers menu, and the next place is the Customer Center. They have all the activities that pertain to a customer. If you're at the Home Page, you can access the Customer Center by clicking the Customers button. However, if you're at any other window the best move is to click the Customers menu and then Customer Center. Let's review the contents of the Customer Center windows.

- Click Customers menu
- Click Customer Center

Activities buttons and windows: You will find the following activities when you open the Customer Center window:

- New Customer & Job
- New Transaction
- Print
- Excel
- Word
- Customer & Job
- View
- Transaction
- Edit Customer

- Edit Notes
- Show
- Filter By
- Date

Report for this Customer: Customer reports are located at the right side of the window and they include the following:

- QuickReport
- Open Balance
- Show Estimates

Right Click: When you right click the left side of the Customer Center window, you will find the following options:

- Find
- Use
- Refresh
- Edit Customer: Job
- Add Job
- Make Customer: Job Inactive
- Re-sort List
- Hierarchical View
- Flat View
- Customize Columns
- Show Full Customer List only
- Create Invoice
- Create Estimates
- Show Estimates
- Receive Payments
- Make Deposits
- Enter Sales Receipts
- Enter Statement Changes
- Create Credit Memos/Refunds
- Create Statements
- Access Finance Charges
- Use Register

Customer Information: Adams Address

As soon as you've signed a contract with a customer, the next step is to load the customer data in the system. You should not wait to take care of this task because you will be overwhelmed when you decide to send out invoices and you discover the customer is not available in QuickBooks. When creating a new customer, you should supply as much information as possible. The particular information you skip may be the one you'll need most on an invoice or report.

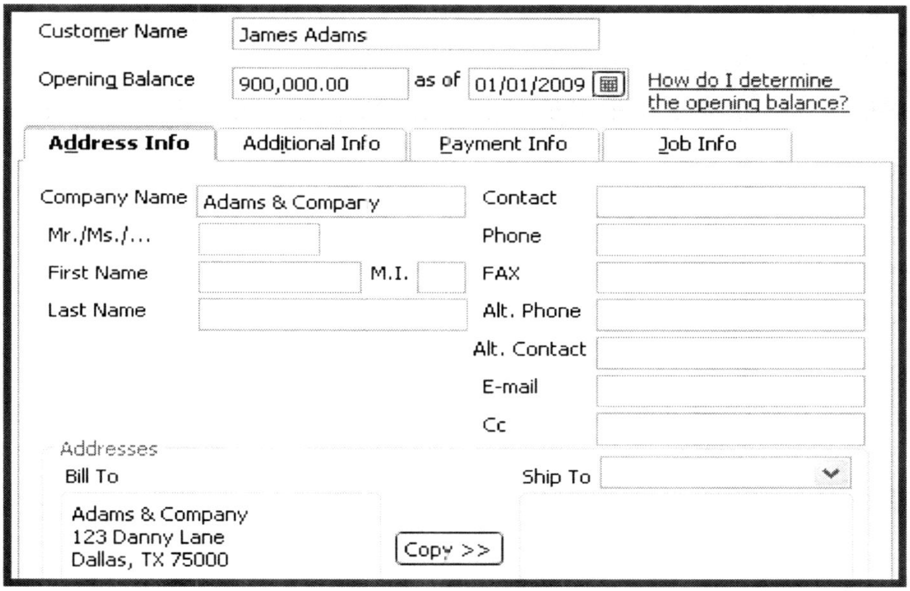

Activities:

- Click **Customers menu**
- Click **Customer Center**
- Right click in the window
- Click **New Customer**
- Customer Name: Type **James Adams**
- Opening Balance: Type **900,000** as of: Type **1/1/09**
- Company Name: Type **Adams & Company**
- Click in Bill To box. Accept **Adams & Company**. Press **Enter**
- Type **123 Danny Lane, Dallas, TX 75000**
- Click **OK**

Customer Information: Adams Additional Info

In the Lists menu, we touched briefly on a customer's address information. In this section, we are going provide detail information about a customer. Remember the more data you can provide about a customer, the more knowledgeable you are about that customer and the more reports you will be able to pull about that customer in the future. Additional Info tab and the Job Info tab are excellent places to furnish some vitally important data about your customers—use them wisely!

Activities:

- Double click **James Adams**
- Contact: Type **Kenny Moore**
- Phone: Type **214-300-1111**
- Fax: Type **214-300-2222**
- E-mail: **kmoore@adamscompany.com**

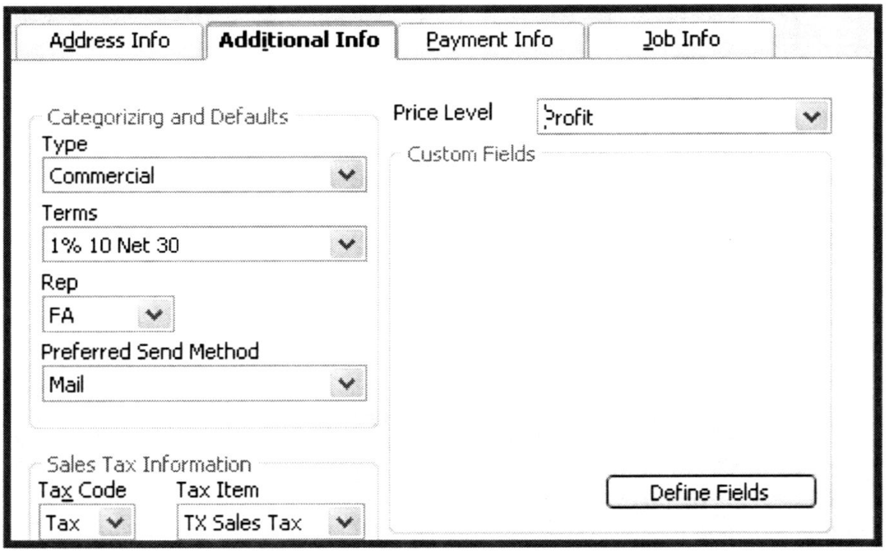

- Click **Additional Info** tab
- Type Select **Commercial**
- Terms: Select **1% 10 Net 30**
- Rep: Select **FA**
- Preferred Send Method: Select **Mail**
- Tax Code: Select **Tax**
- Tax Item: Select **TX Sales Tax**

❖ Price Level (top right): Select **Profit**
❖ Click **Payment Info** tab

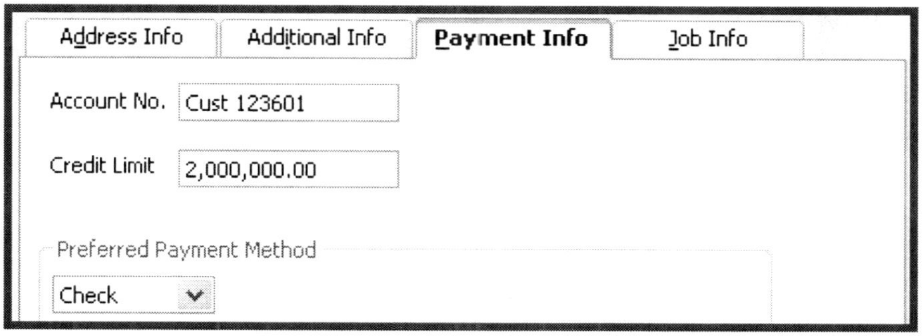

❖ Account No: Type **Cust 123601**
❖ Credit Limit: Type **2,000,000**
❖ Preferred Payment Method: Type **Check**
❖ Click **Job Info** tab
❖ Job Status: Select **In Progress**
❖ Start Date: Type **1/1/09**
❖ Projected Date: Type **12/31/09**
❖ End Date: (Leave blank)
❖ Description: Type **Flower Beds**
❖ Job Type: Select **New Construction**
❖ Click **OK**

Customer Information: Allen

Customer details are easy to collect by having the customer fill out a questionnaire or a Customer Profile Sheet. In this exercise, we have full profile on John Allen, including his address, phone number, and e-mail address. On the Additional Info tab, we entered him as a commercial customer, and his payment term is 1% 10 net 30. It means that John Allen can take a 1% discount if he pays within 10 days of the invoice date; otherwise, the entire amount is due in 30 days.

Activities:

❖ Double click **John Allen**
❖ Company Name: Type **Allen Enterprises**
❖ Click in "Bill To" box
❖ Accept **Allen Enterprises**. Press **Enter**
❖ Type **5000 Allen Road**. Press **Enter**

- ❖ **Dallas, TX 75000**
- ❖ Contact: Type **Tammy Mitchell**
- ❖ Phone **214-611-1100**
- ❖ Fax**: 214-611-2200**
- ❖ E-mail: Type **tmitchell@allen.com**
- ❖ Click **Additional Info** tab (top)
- ❖ Type: Select **Commercial**
- ❖ Term: Select **1% 10 Net 30**
- ❖ Rep: Select **FA**
- ❖ Preferred Send Method: Select **Mail**
- ❖ Tax Code: Select **Tax**
- ❖ Tax Item: Select **TX Sales Tax**
- ❖ Price Level: Select **Profit**

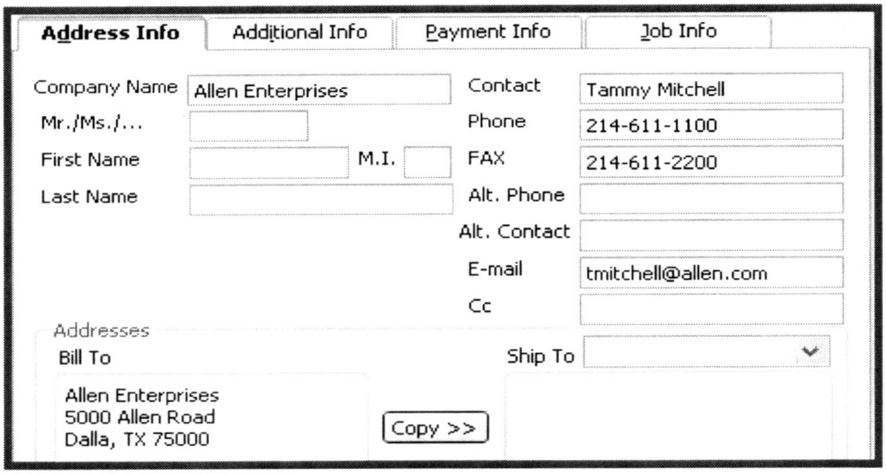

- ❖ Click **Payment Info** tab
- ❖ Account No: Type. **Cust 123789**
- ❖ Credit Limit: Type **350,000**
- ❖ Preferred Payment Method: Select **Check**
- ❖ Click **Job Info** tab
- ❖ Job Status: Select **In Progress**
- ❖ Start Date: Type **1/1/09**
- ❖ Projected Date: Type **12/31/09**
- ❖ End Date: **(Leave blank)**
- ❖ Job Description: Type **Installation**
- ❖ Job Type: Select **Installation**
- ❖ Click **OK**

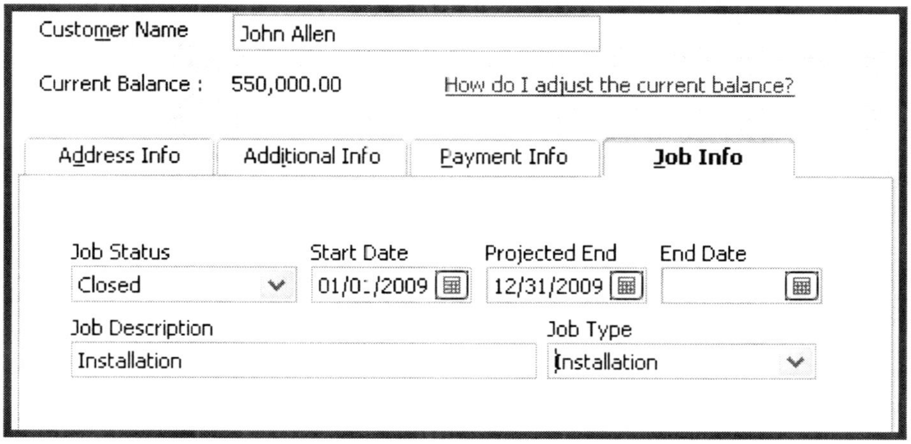

Customer Information: Brown

Customer details involve completing most of the boxes on a customer window. Essential customer information includes the contact name, phone number and e-mail address. The purpose is to know who to contact when there is a question about an invoice or a payment. Contacting a company by e-mail is regarded as a legitimate business tool, admissible in court in times of financial disputes. Customer number and credit limit should be readily available for future reference as needed.

Activities:

- Double click **Tommy Brown**
- Company Name: Type **Tommy & Sons**
- Click in "Bill To" box
- Accept **Tommy & Sons.** Press **Enter**
- Type **1000 Camp Road.** Press **Enter**
- **Dallas, TX 75000**
- Contact: Type **Jake Sanders**
- Phone: **214-114-1000**
- Fax**: 214-114-2000**
- E-mail: Type **jsanders@tommy.com**
- Click **Additional Info** tab
- Type: Select **Commercial**
- Term: Select **1% 10 Net 30**
- Rep: Select **FA**
- Preferred Send Method: **E-mail**
- Tax Code: Select **Tax**.
- Tax Item: Select **TX Sales Tax**

- Price level: **Profit**
- Click **Payment Info** tab
- Account No: Type. **Cust 123741**
- Credit Limit: Type **550,000**
- Preferred Payment Method: Select **Check**
- Click **Job Info** tab
- Job Status: Select **In Progress**
- Start Date: Type **1/1/09**
- Projected Date: Type **12/31/09**
- End Date: (Leave blank)
- Job Description: Type **Installation**
- Job Type: Select **Installation**
- Click **OK**

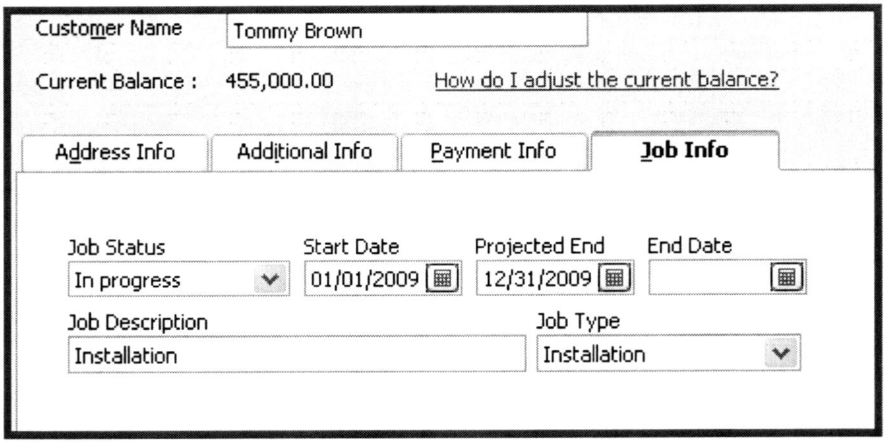

Customer Information: US Machines

Information in the Customer List window is pulled into other windows, such as the Customer Contact Listing and the Customer Phone List windows, where you can find the customer name, bill to, contact phone number, and fax number. This information is pulled from the Customer List window, if it is provided at the time the window is being completed. When you type the customer's name in the Company Name box and press tab key, the "Bill To" box is populated.

Activities:

- ❖ Right click in the Customer Center window
- ❖ Click **New Customer**
- ❖ Customer Name: Type **US Machines**

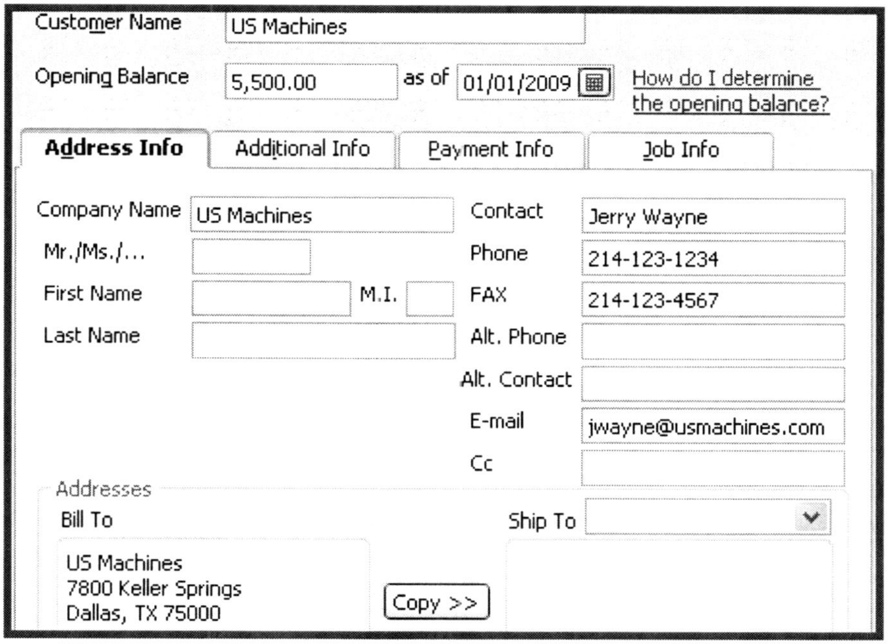

- ❖ Opening Balance: Type **5,500** as of: Type **1/1/09**
- ❖ Company Name: Type **US Machines**
- ❖ Click in "Bill To" box: Accept **US Machines**
- ❖ Type **7800 Keller Springs, Dallas, TX 75000**
- ❖ Contact: Type **Jenny Wayne**
- ❖ Phone: Type **214-123-1234**
- ❖ Fax: Type **214-123-4567**
- ❖ E-mail: Type **jwayne@usmachines.com**
- ❖ Click **Additional Info** tab
- ❖ Type: Select **Commercial**
- ❖ Term: Select **1% 10 net 30**
- ❖ Rep: Select **FA**
- ❖ Preferred Send Method: Select **Mail**
- ❖ Tax Code: Select **Tax**
- ❖ Tax Item: Select **TX Sales Tax**
- ❖ Price Level: Select **Profit**

- Click **Payment Info** tab
- Account No: Type **Cust 123456**
- Credit Limit: Type **500,000**
- Preferred Payment Method: Select **Bank Debit Card**
- Click **Job Info** tab
- Job Status: Select **In progress**
- Start Date: Type **1/1/09.** Projected End: Type **12/31/2010** (next year)
- Job Description: **Water Pipes**
- Job Type: Select **New Construction**. Click **OK**

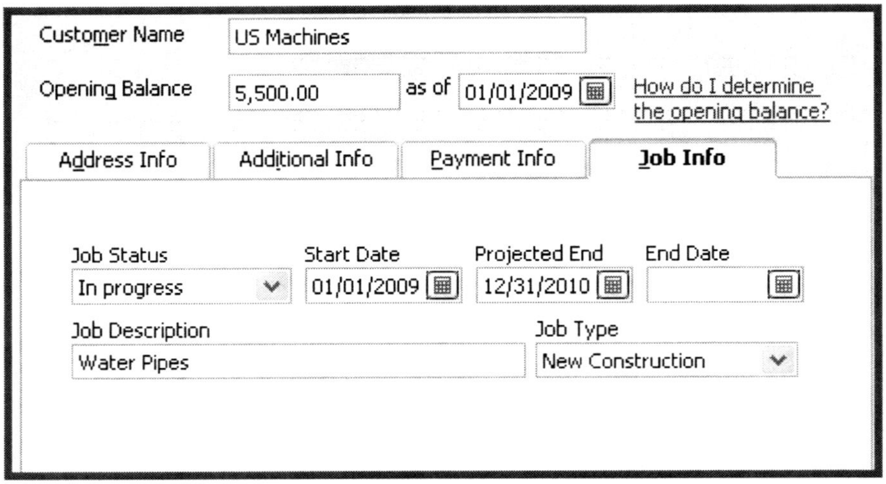

Customer Information: Johnson

Creating a Customer Job is helpful when the customer has more than one location. We are going to create two job sites for this customer. Most of the time you would complete the Bill To and Ship To boxes. The Bill To is the headquarters and the Ship To is the branch location. When you create Customer Jobs, the total in the headquarters, in this case Jerry Johnson is the addition of the amounts from the branches. The job name is the branch location and the customer is the headquarters.

Activities:

- Right click in the Customer Center window
- Click **New Customer**
- Customer Name: Type **Jerry Johnson**
- Opening Balance: Type **0.00** as of: Type **1/1/09**
- Company Name: Type **Johnson & Company**

- Click in Bill To box: Accept **Johnson & Company**. Press **Enter**
- Type **145 Johnson Lane.** Press **Enter**
- Type **Dallas, TX 75000**
- Contact: Type **Jerry Johnson**
- Phone: Type **214-111-5000**
- Fax: Type **214-111-6000**
- E-mail: Type **jjohnson@jj.com**
- Click **Additional Info** tab
- Type: Select **Commercial**
- Terms: Type **1% 10 Net 30**
- Rep: Select **FA**
- Preferred Send Method: Select **Mail**
- Tax Code: Select **Tax**
- Tax Item: Select **TX Sales Tax**
- Price Level: Select **Profit**
- Click **OK** to close window

Johnson's Information: Job Auto Sales

You've created the customer by providing the customer name, opening balance, address information, bill to, and additional information. Payment Info and Job Info tabs should be left alone at this time. The purpose of the Ship To, Payment Info, and Job Info tabs is to specify the particular location with a different account number. Account numbers for individual locations are recommended to track activities of those locations. Be sure to match the Ship To box with the name of the job.

Activities:

- Right click **Jerry Johnson**
- Click **Add Job**
- Job Name: Type **123 Main St**
- Opening Balance: Type **1,500** as of: Type **1/1/09**
- Ship To (middle right): Select **Add New**
- Address Name: Type **Jerry Auto Sales**
- Address: Type **123 Main St**
- City: **Dallas**
- State: **TX**
- Zip: **75000.** Click **OK**

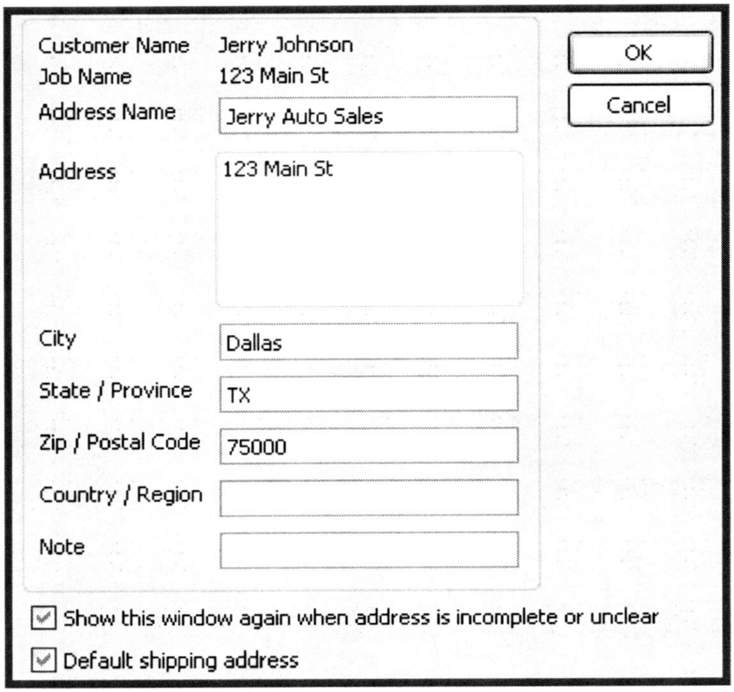

- Click **Payment Info** tab
- Account No: Type **Cust 123800**
- Credit Limit: Type **100,000**
- Preferred Payment Method: Select **Check**
- Click **Job Info** tab
- Job Status: Select **In Progress**
- Start Date: Type **1/1/09**
- Projected End: Type **12/31/09**
- Job Description: Type **Installation**
- Job Type: Type **Installation**
- Click **OK** to close window

Johnson's Information: Job Auto Parts

After you've added the customer's headquarter, all you do is use most of the same information to complete the branch offices. The key customer windows are the Ship To, Job Name, Address Name, Customer Number, and the Job Information. If you are dealing with a customer's residential address, you should click the Additional Info tab and select Residential or Other names for the Customer Type box. Additional Info tab data for the headquarter and branches are different.

Activities:

- Right click **Jerry Johnson**
- Click **Add Job**
- Job Name: Type **456 Koven Road**
- Opening Balance: Type **2,500** as of: Type **1/1/09**
- Ship To (middle right): Click Select **Add New**
- Address Name: Type **Jerry Auto Parts**
- Address: Type **456 Koven Road**
- City: **Dallas**
- State: **TX**
- Zip: **75000.** Click **OK**
- Click **Payment Info** tab
- Account No: Type **Cust 123801**
- Credit Limit: Type **100,000**
- Preferred Payment Method: Select **Check**
- Click **Job Info** tab
- Job Status: Type **In Progress**
- Start Date: Type **1/1/09**
- Projected End: Type **12/31/09**
- Job Description: Type **Installation**
- Job Type: Type **Installation**
- Click **OK** to close window

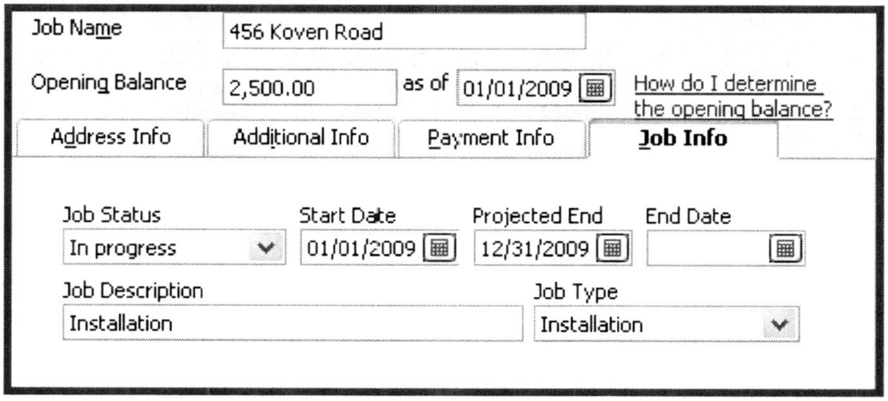

Estimates

Most companies will require you to send estimates or bids before a contract is awarded. If allowed, send your estimate by e-mail for quick consideration. A late estimate is a bad business practice and should be avoided at all costs. Your estimate should contain essential information, such as the item name, description, cost, amount, etc. If you don't want markup to show on your estimate, go to Edit, Preferences, Time & Expenses, Company Preferences tab, type 0.00 for the Default Markup %. You will need to type the correct price by hand in the Item list window.

Activities:

- Click **Customers menu**.
- Click **Create Estimates**
- Customer: Job: Select **James Adams**
- Class: Select **Landscaping**
- Date: Type **1/2/09.** Estimate #: Accept **1**
- Name/Address: Accept default

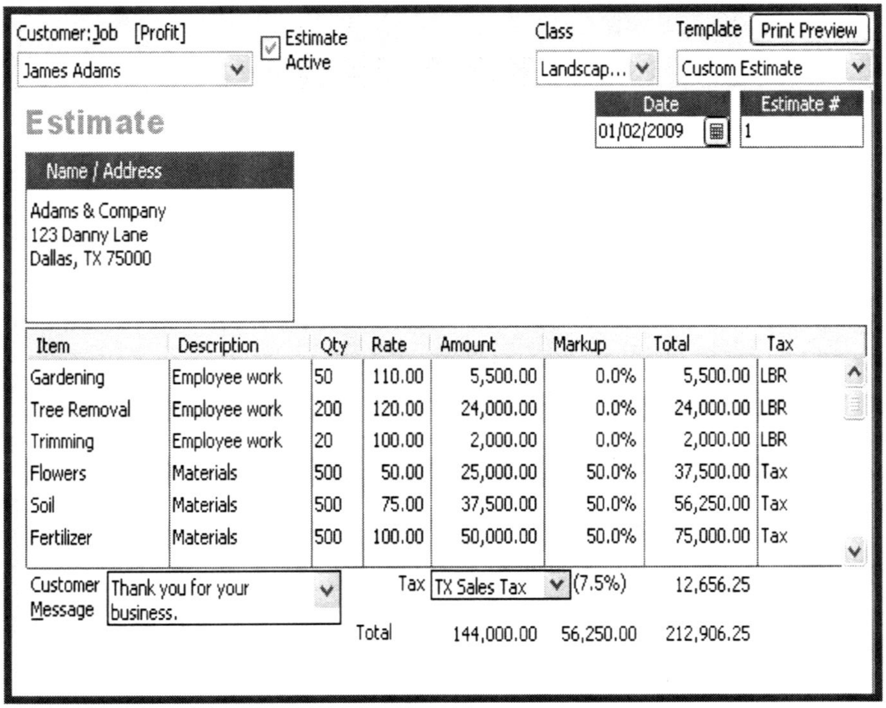

Customer:Job [Profit] James Adams | Estimate Active | Class Landscap... | Template Custom Estimate | Print Preview

Estimate | Date 01/02/2009 | Estimate # 1

Name / Address
Adams & Company
123 Danny Lane
Dallas, TX 75000

Item	Description	Qty	Rate	Amount	Markup	Total	Tax
Gardening	Employee work	50	110.00	5,500.00	0.0%	5,500.00	LBR
Tree Removal	Employee work	200	120.00	24,000.00	0.0%	24,000.00	LBR
Trimming	Employee work	20	100.00	2,000.00	0.0%	2,000.00	LBR
Flowers	Materials	500	50.00	25,000.00	50.0%	37,500.00	Tax
Soil	Materials	500	75.00	37,500.00	50.0%	56,250.00	Tax
Fertilizer	Materials	500	100.00	50,000.00	50.0%	75,000.00	Tax

Customer Message: Thank you for your business. | Tax TX Sales Tax (7.5%) 12,656.25

Total 144,000.00 56,250.00 212,906.25

- Click under **Item**: Select **Gardening**
- Qty: Type **50**
- Tax (end of row): Select **LBR**
- Select **Tree Removal**
- Qty: Type **200.** Tax: Select **LBR**
- Select **Trimming**

- ❖ Qty: Type **20.** Tax: Select **LBR**
- ❖ Select **Flowers**
- ❖ Qty: Type **500.** Tax: Select **Tax**
- ❖ Select **Soil**
- ❖ Qty: Type **500.** Tax: Select **Tax**
- ❖ Select **Fertilizer**
- ❖ Qty: Type **500.** Tax: Select **Tax**
- ❖ Customer Message: Select **Thank you for your business**
- ❖ Checkmark **To be e-mailed box** (bottom left)
- ❖ Customer Tax Code: Accept **Tax**
- ❖ Tax: Accept **TX Sales Tax**(7.5%)
- ❖ **Look! Total Tax is 12,656.25. Total Estimate is 212,906.25**
- ❖ Click **Print Preview** (top right of window)
- ❖ Click **Zoom In.** Click **Close**
- ❖ Click **Save & Close**

Invoices

An invoice must have the customer's name and address, with shipping and billing addresses if they are different. The terms of payment should be provided, along with a purchase order number. Product data are required to be accurate including the item name, item number, quantities, prices, and sales tax amount. You must have inventory on hand from vendors before you can invoice an inventory item. Otherwise, the only items you could invoice are labor or non-inventory items.

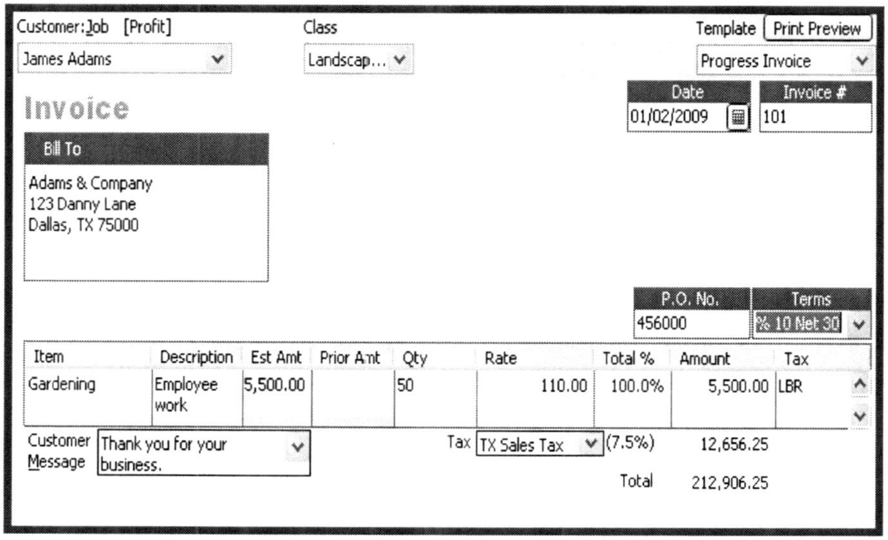

Activities:

- Click **Customers menu**
- Click **Create Invoices**
- Customer: Job: Select **James Adams**
- In Available Estimates window
- Customer Job: Accept **James Adams.** Click **OK**
- Click **"Create Invoice for the entire…"** Click **OK**
- Class: Select **Landscaping**
- Date: Accept **1/2/09**
- Invoice: Type **101**
- P. O. No: Type **456000**
- Terms: Accept **1% 10 Net 30**
- Customer Message: Accept **Thank you for your business**
- Checkmark **To be Printed** (bottom left)
- Checkmark **To be e-mailed**
- Customer Tax Code: Accept **Tax**
- **Look! Total Tax is 12,656.25. Total Invoice is 212,906.25**
- Click **Save & Close**

Sales Receipt: Allen

As was mentioned earlier, taxes are collected on some items but not on others. Sales of your skills, effort, profession, and other intangibles are non-taxable, and sales of tangible items are taxable, especially if you pay sales tax to buy the item from a vendor. You have to charge the same sales tax to customers, unless county rates are different. Invoices are sent to customers and payments are received later, but with sales receipts, payments are received now—that is the major difference.

Activities:

- Click **Customers menu**
- Click **Enter Sales Receipt**
- Click **X** on QuickBooks Web Browser
- Customer: Job: Select **John Allen**
- Click **OK** to "The customer or the job you've selected…"
- Click **Mileage** tab
- Checkmark **1/31/09 Delivery** (left of window). Click **OK**
- Class: Select **Landscaping**
- Date: Type **1/2/09**
- Sales No: Type **1001**
- Check No: Type **987**

- Payment Method: Accept **Check**
- Under Item (left) Select **Delivery**
- Description: Type **Delivery of materials**
- Tax: Select **LBR**. Qty: Accept **75**
- Select **Flowers**
- Tax: Select **Tax**. Qty: Type **450**
- Select **Soil**
- Tax: Select **Tax.** Qty: Type **450**
- Select **Fertilizer**
- Tax: Select **Tax**. Qty: Type **450**
- Customer Message: Select **Thank you for your business**
- Checkmark **To be printed**
- Checkmark **To be e-mailed**
- Customer Tax Code: Accept **Tax**
- **Look! Total Tax is 11,390.63. Total Receipt is 174,515.63**
- Click **Save & Close**

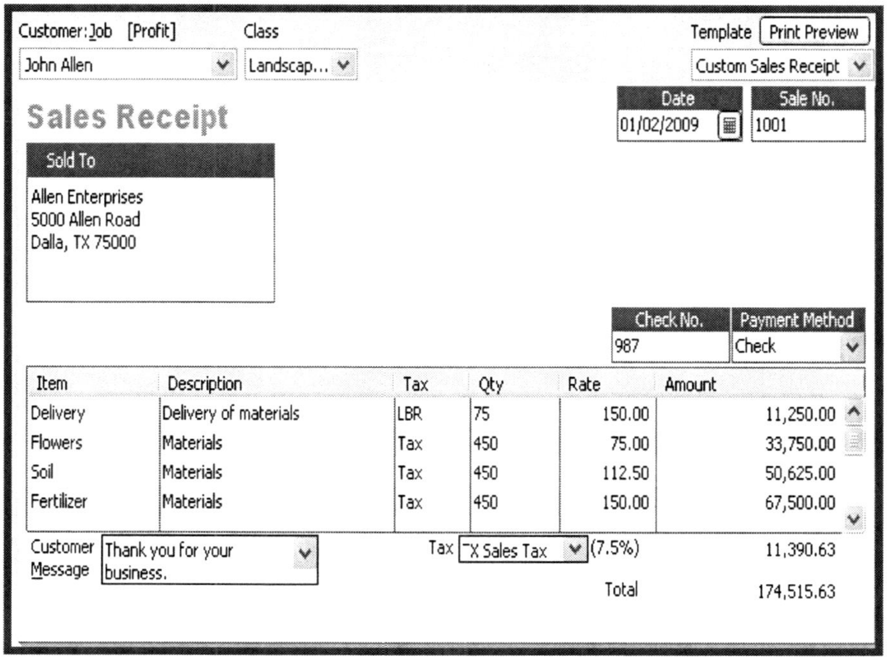

Sales Receipt: Brown

When you made a cash sale for either cash or check, you use the Enter Sales Receipt window. You use the same Sales Receipt form for taxable and non-taxable items. Be sure the name of the item, the number of the item, the quantity, the price and the total amount paid on the receipt are all communicated on the receipt. The Payment method is documented for auditing and banking purposes. Sales receipts by checks should be separated from those of credit cards and other payment types.

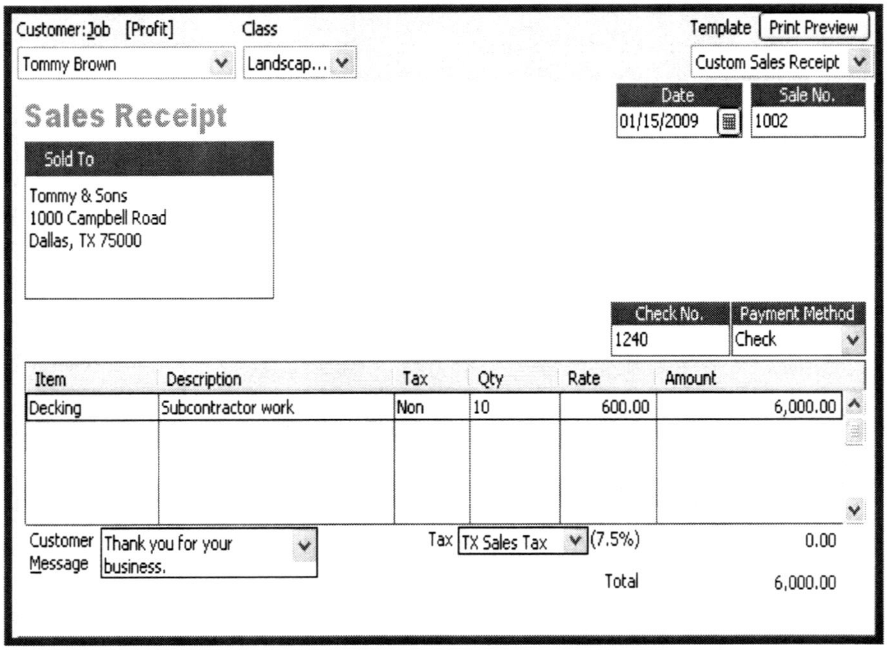

Activities:

- Click **Customers menu**
- Click **Enter Sales Receipt**
- Click **X** on QuickBooks Web Browser
- Customer: Job: Select **Tommy Brown**
- Class: Select **Landscaping**
- Date: Type **1/15/09**
- Sales No: Accept **1002**
- Check No: Type **1240**
- Payment Method: Accept **Check**
- Click under **Item** (left of window): Select **Decking**
- Tax: Accept **Non**

- Qty: Type **10**
- Customer Message: Select **Thank you for your business**
- Checkmark **To be printed**
- Uncheck **To be e-mailed** (Very Important)
- Customer Tax Code: Accept **Tax**
- **Look! Total Tax is 0.00. Total Receipt is 6,000**
- Click **Save & Close**

Credit Memos/Refunds

When customers return merchandise to you, credit memos are sent to them. If they have future purchases, you can reduce the invoice amount by these credit memos, and payments are made on the remaining balances. Make sure a customer did not apply a memo twice. Applying duplicate Credit Memo is possible. In the example below, you are applying a Credit Memo by clicking on the "Apply to an invoice" window that comes up after you clicked the Save & Close button.

Activities:

- Click **Customers menu**
- Click **Create Credit Memos/Refunds**
- Customer: Job: Select **James Adams**
- Class: Select **Landscaping**
- Date: Type **1/2/09**

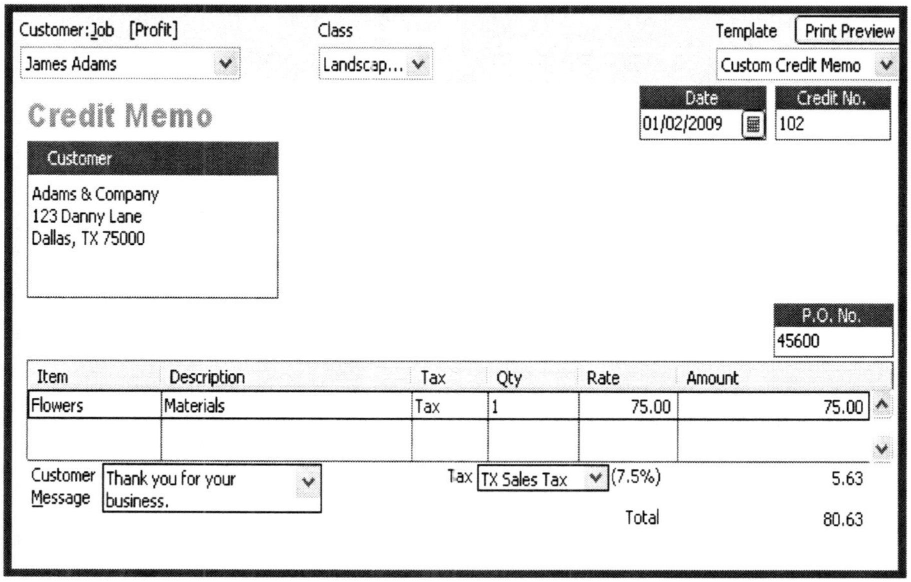

- ❖ Credit No: Accept **102**
- ❖ P. O. No: Type **456000**
- ❖ Click under Item: (left of window) Select **Flowers**
- ❖ Tax: Accept **Tax**
- ❖ Qty: Type **1**
- ❖ Customer Message: Select **Thank you for your business**
- ❖ Checkmark **To be printed**
- ❖ Checkmark **To be e-mailed**
- ❖ Customer Tax Code: Accept **Tax**
- ❖ **Look! Total Tax is 5.63. Total Credit is 80.63**
- ❖ Click **Save & Close**
- ❖ Click **Apply to an Invoice.** Click **OK**
- ❖ Checkmark **1/1/09 Amt Applied 80.63**
- ❖ Click **Done**

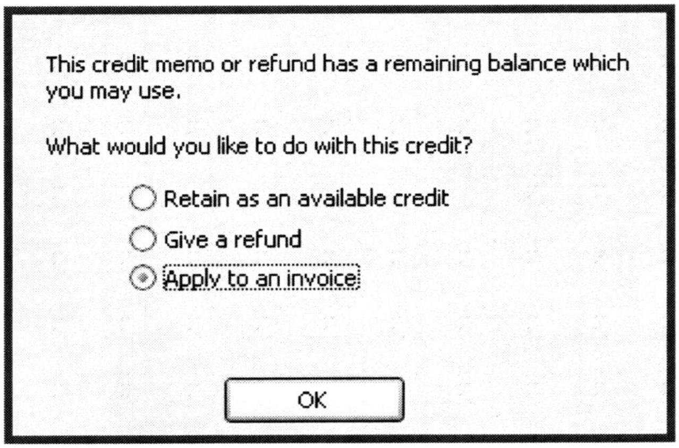

Statement Charges

There are three ways of billing your customers: Invoices, Sales Receipts, and Statements. In a Statement, you enter activities in the register as they come in from different departments until the end of the month. At the end of the month, you send one statement to the customer that lists all the entries for the month. Be sure all activities are collected from all departments before the final statement goes to the customer. No one likes previous months' entries on current month's statement.

Activities:

- ❖ Click **Customers menu**
- ❖ Click **Enter Statement Charges**

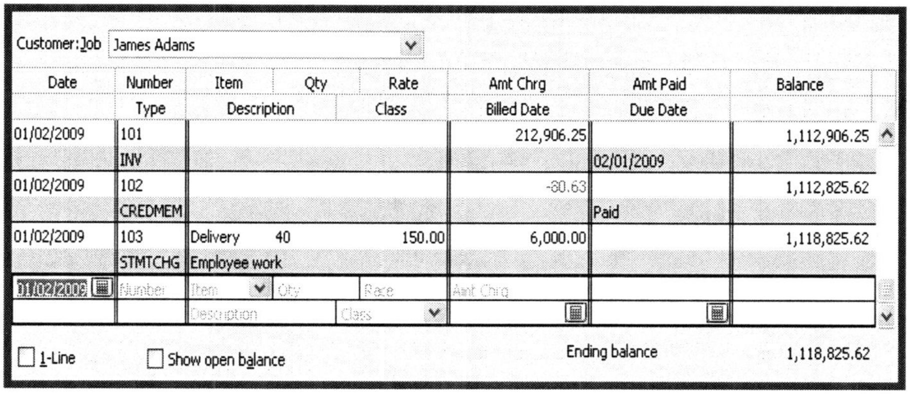

- ❖ Customer: Job: Select **James Adams**
- ❖ In the Register. On the last blank line
- ❖ Date: Accept **1/2/09**
- ❖ Click **under the Number column**
- ❖ Number: Type **103**
- ❖ Item: Select **Delivery**
- ❖ Qty: Type **40**. Press **Tab**. **Look! Amount is 6,000**
- ❖ Click **Record** (bottom right of window)
- ❖ **Look! Accounts Receivable balance is 1,118,825.62**
- ❖ Click **X** to close window

Finance Charges

If you have to assess finance charges to your customers, you must have a collection policy that stipulates the percentage of interest charged on past due invoices and the grace period before finance charges are added to customer's Invoices. No business will be happy to see finance charges without knowledge of your collection policy. To set your finance charge, go to Edit menu and then Preferences and provide the Annual Interest Rate, the Minimum Finance Charge, and the Grace Period.

Activities:

- ❖ Click **Customers menu**
- ❖ Click **Assess Finance Charges**
- ❖ Assessment Date: Type **2/1/09**. Press **Tab**
- ❖ Template: Accept **Finance Charge**
- ❖ Click **Mark All** (bottom left of window)
- ❖ Click **Assess Charges** (bottom right of window)

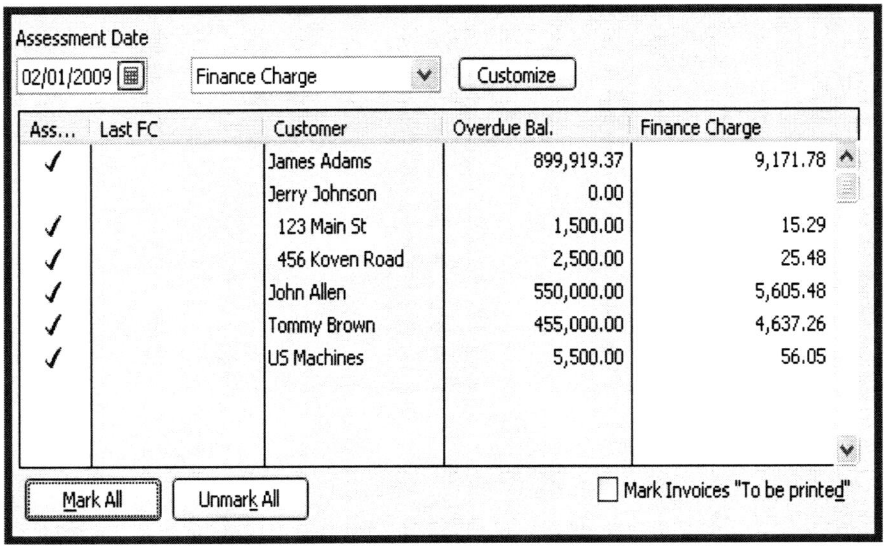

Assessment Date 02/01/2009 | Finance Charge | Customize

Ass...	Last FC	Customer	Overdue Bal.	Finance Charge
✓		James Adams	899,919.37	9,171.78
		Jerry Johnson	0.00	
✓		123 Main St	1,500.00	15.29
✓		456 Koven Road	2,500.00	25.48
✓		John Allen	550,000.00	5,605.48
✓		Tommy Brown	455,000.00	4,637.26
✓		US Machines	5,500.00	56.05

Mark All | Unmark All | Mark Invoices "To be printed"

- Click **Reports menu**
- Click **Company & Financial**
- Click **Profit & Loss Standard**
- Date: Select **This Fiscal Year**
- Double click **Misc Income for 19,511.34**
- **Look! These are the Finance Charges**
- Click **X** to close Transaction Detail by Account window

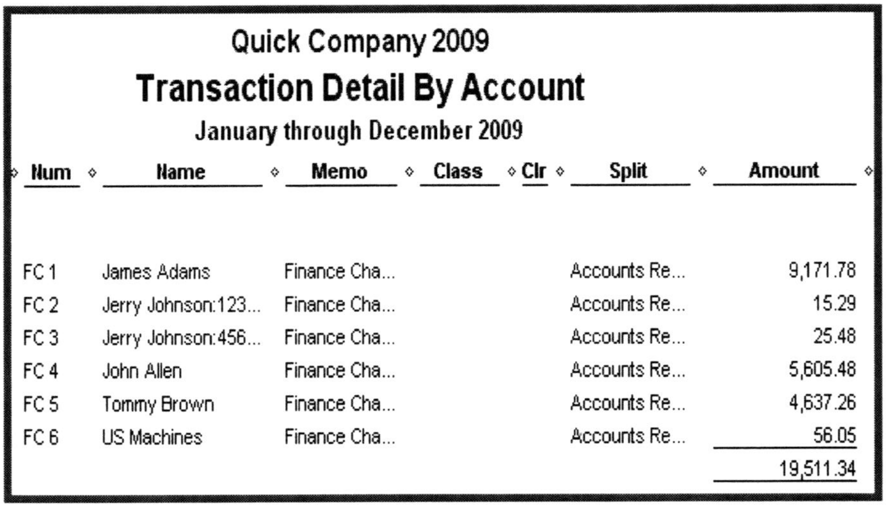

Quick Company 2009

Transaction Detail By Account

January through December 2009

Num	Name	Memo	Class	Clr	Split	Amount
FC 1	James Adams	Finance Cha...			Accounts Re...	9,171.78
FC 2	Jerry Johnson:123...	Finance Cha...			Accounts Re...	15.29
FC 3	Jerry Johnson:456...	Finance Cha...			Accounts Re...	25.48
FC 4	John Allen	Finance Cha...			Accounts Re...	5,605.48
FC 5	Tommy Brown	Finance Cha...			Accounts Re...	4,637.26
FC 6	US Machines	Finance Cha...			Accounts Re...	56.05
						19,511.34

Customer Statements

After you've entered all the transactions for the month in the register. At the end of the month, you are ready to review and print the final statement that goes to the customer. The statement's total must match the total of the individual charges. It is easy to send a statement to a customer without adding an entry charge. It is not a good business practice to have differences from the two totals, which is why you must have a reviewer to audit statements before they are dispatched to customers.

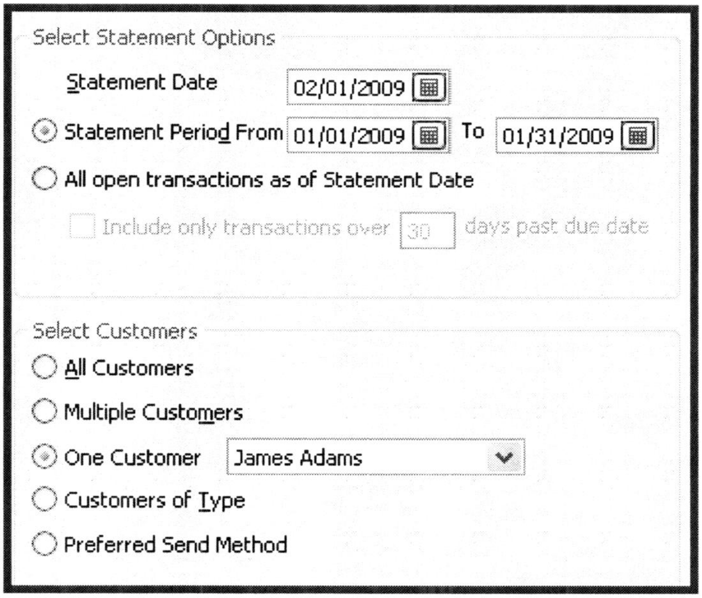

Activities:

- Click **Customers menu**
- Click **Create Statements…**
- Statement Date: Type **2/1/2009**
- Statement Period From: Type **1/1/09**. To: Type **1/31/09**
- Click **One Customer**. Click **Down arrow**
- Select **James Adams**
- Click **Preview**. (bottom left)
- Click **Zoom In** (top of the window)
- Click **Close or Print** if printer is ready
- Click **Close** on Create Statement window

Receive Payments

When you receive a payment from your customer, you must pull the customer's invoices and apply the check to the outstanding balances. Sometimes, one check will cover a number of invoices and at other times one check will cover just one invoice. Completing the Receive Payment window is easy, because as soon as you pull up the invoice, QuickBooks does the rest with the click of a button. It is recommended to select the Method of Payment, and if a check was received, type the check number.

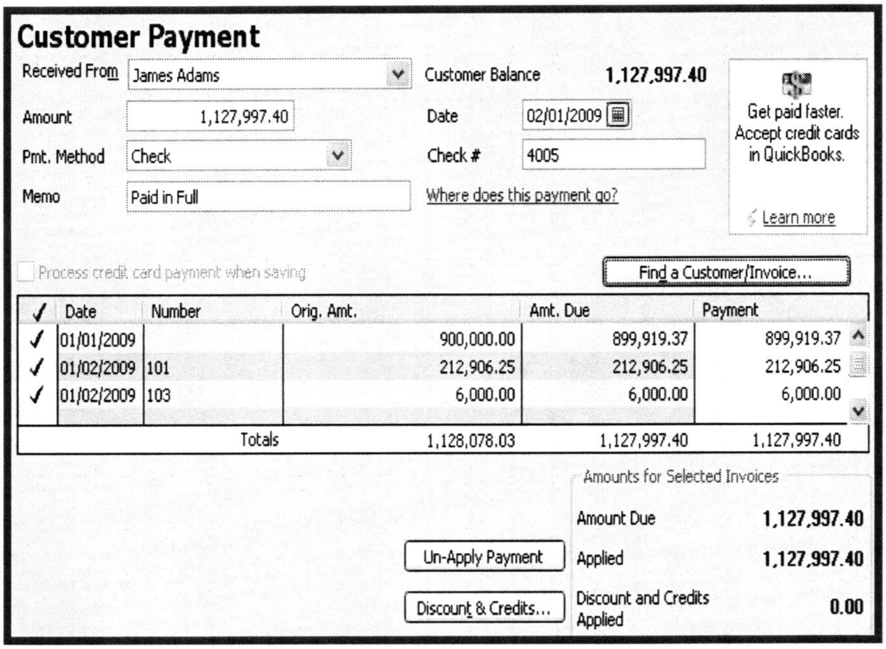

Activities:

- Click **Customers menu**
- Click **Receive Payments**
- Click **X** on QuickBooks Web Browser
- Receive From: Select **James Adams**
- Customer Balance: Accept **1,127,997.40**
- Amount: Type **1,127,997.40**
- Date: Accept **2/1/09**
- Pmt Method: Select **Check**
- Check #: Type **4005**
- Memo: Type **Paid in Full**

- ❖ Checkmark **all entries**
- ❖ Amount Due (bottom right): **1,127,997.40**
- ❖ Click **Save & Close**

Make Deposits

After you have received payment from a customer in the Receive Payment window, the amount is sent to the Undeposited Funds account in the Chart of Accounts. You should open the Chart of Accounts and confirm that the amount is in the Undeposited Funds account. Now go to the Banking menu and open the Make Deposit window. One of the most important steps is to make sure you select the right checking account where the payment is to be deposited. QuickBooks will move the amount from the Undeposited Funds account to the checking account of your choice.

Activities:

- ❖ Click **Lists menu**
- ❖ Click **Chart of Accounts**
- ❖ **Undeposited Funds** (top) balance is **1,308,513.03**
- ❖ Click **Banking menu**
- ❖ Click **Make Deposits**
- ❖ View Payment method type: Accept **All Types**
- ❖ Checkmark 1st payment **#1001 for 174,515.63.** Click **OK**

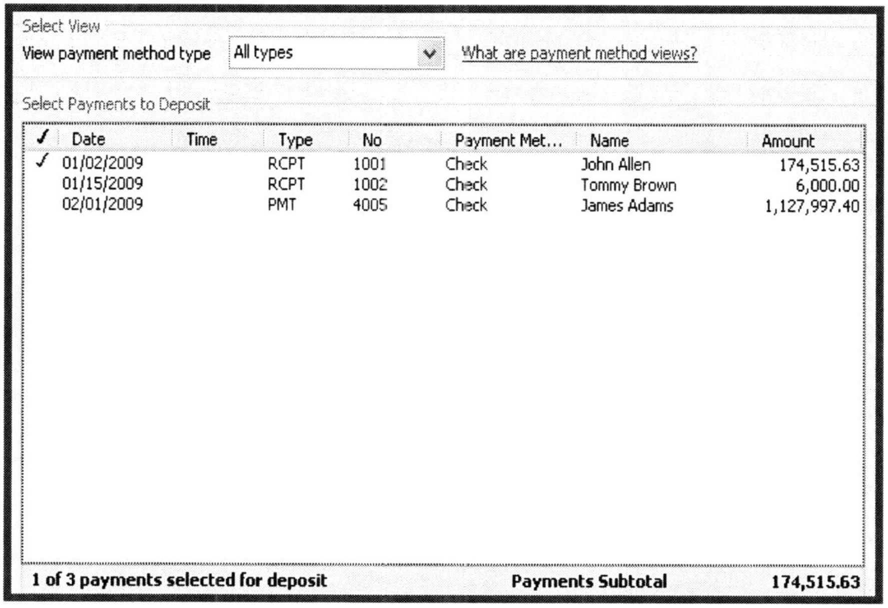

Deposit To: Select **USA Checking**

- Date: Type **1/15/09**
- Memo: Accept **Deposit**
- Click **Print down arrow (**top of window)
- Select **Deposit Slip…**
- Click **Preview** (right)
- Click **Zoom In**
- Click **Close or Print** if printer is ready
- Click **X** on Print Deposit window
- Click **Save & Close** (bottom right of window)
- Click **Lists menu**
- Click **Chart of Accounts**
- **Undeposited Funds the balance is now 1,133,997.40**
- Undeposited Funds balance is decreased by 174,515.63
- Funds are now deposited to USA Checking account

Deposit Summary 12/31/2008

Summary of Deposits to USA Checking on 01/15/2009

Chk No.	PmtMethod	Rcd From	Memo	Amount
987	Check	John Allen		174,515.63
			Deposit Subtotal:	174,515.63
			Less Cash Back:	
			Deposit Total:	174,515.63

Weekly Timesheet

There are two ways of tracking time, the Weekly and the Single Time Activity. In the Weekly Timesheet, you have one week in a row, starting form Monday through Sunday. The total is at the far right end of the row, which populates as you press the Tab key on your keyboard. The Weekly Timesheet is employee specific, that is, you have to document one employee at a time. You can use the Copy Last Week button to copy last week's timesheet into this week's timesheet, if both are the same.

Activities:

- ❖ Click **Customers menu**
- ❖ Click **Enter Time**
- ❖ Click **Use Weekly Timesheet**

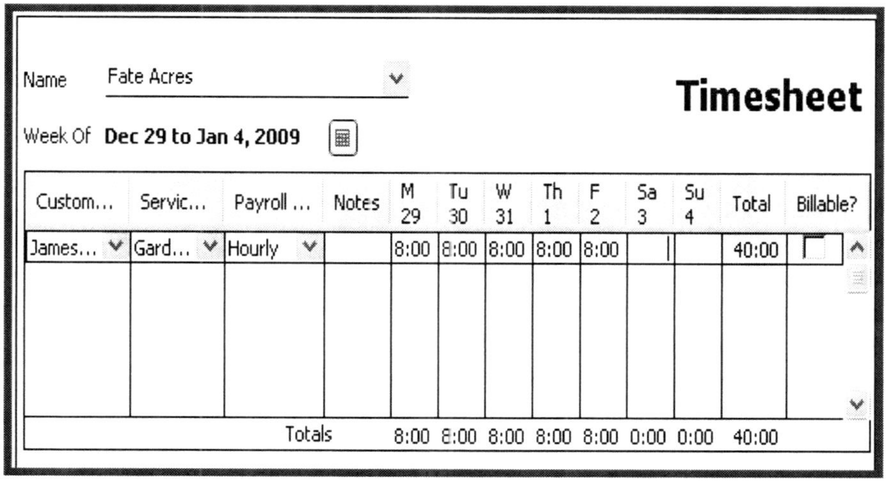

- ❖ Name: Select **Fate Acres**
- ❖ Click **Yes** to "Would you like…" (Very Important)
- ❖ Week of: Click **Date button.** Click arrow **to December 2008**
- ❖ Click **29** (Last Monday For Dec 29 to Jan 4,2009)
- ❖ Click under **Customer: Job** (left of window)
- ❖ Select **James Adams**. Service Item: Select **Gardening**
- ❖ Payroll Item: Select **Add New**
- ❖ Click **Hourly Wages**. Click **Next**
- ❖ Click **Regular Pay**. Click **Next**
- ❖ Enter name: Type **Hourly**. Click **Next**
- ❖ Enter the Account: Accept **Payroll Expenses**
- ❖ Click **Finish**. Click **OK**
- ❖ From **Monday 29** to **Friday 4.** Type **8.00**. Press **Tab each time**
- ❖ Total: Accept **40**. Uncheck **Billable**. Click **Save & Close**

Time/Enter Single Activity

The second way of tracking time is the Single Time Activity timesheet. As the name implies, you have to use this process for a single activity. This window is handy and useful if you want to time yourself on any activity on which you're working, in or out of QuickBooks. You must accept today's date for the time clock to work, and the time starts ticking as soon as you press the Start button located at the bottom left of the window. You press the Stop button as soon as the task is completed.

Activities:

- Click **Customers menu**
- Click **Enter Time**
- Click **Time/Enter Single Activity**…
- Date: Type **1/2/09**
- Name: Select **Fate Acres**
- Customer: Job: Select **John Allen**
- Service Item: Select **Installation**
- Duration box: Type **0:33** (with colon)
- Uncheck **Billable**(top right)
- Payroll Item: Select **Hourly.** Click **OK**
- Normally, you click Start button (bottom left of window)
- And then click Stop when you've finished your work
- Click **Save & Close** to close window

You normally accept today's date, which is the day you're performing the task for your company.

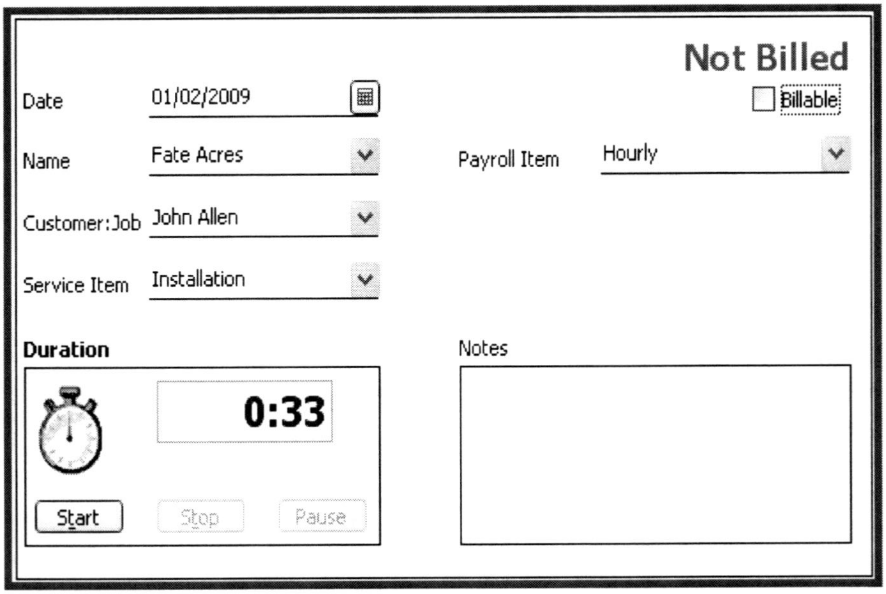

Change Item Prices

You see it happen all the time; a company decides it wants to increase prices by 5%. If you have hundreds of items to sell, it will take a long time to manually change the individual item prices. QuickBooks has done it again! With the click of a button, your entire line of product prices is changed instantaneously. You have to go to the Change Item Prices window, complete the percentage increase box, and select how you want the increase—based on current price or unit cost.

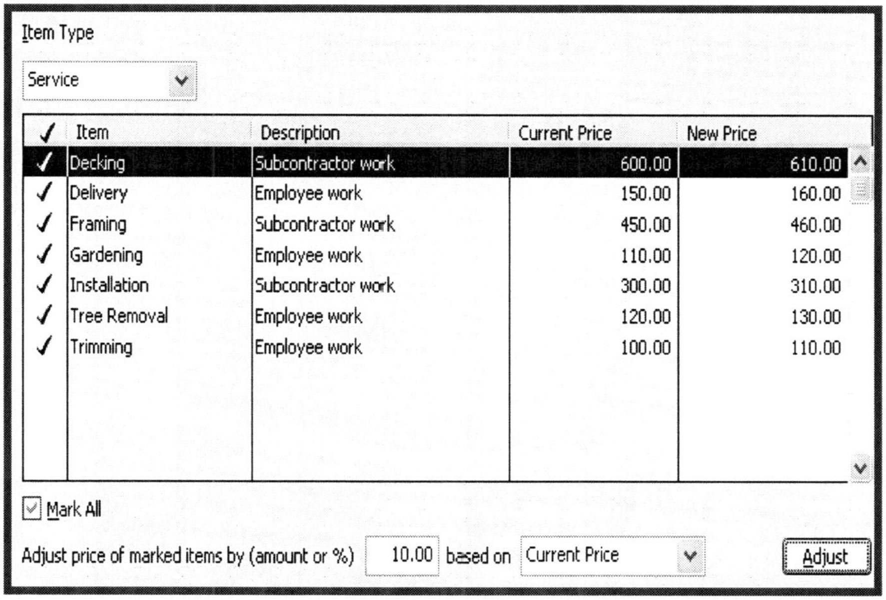

Activities:

- Click **Customers menu**
- Click **Change Item Prices**
- Item Type: Accept **Service.** Press **Tab**
- **Look! Decking Current Price is 600.00**
- **Look! New Price column to the right is empty**
- Checkmark **Mark All** (bottom left of window)
- **Adjust price of marked items...)**: Type **10.** Press **Tab**
- Based on: Accept **Current Price**
- Click **Adjust** (bottom right of window)
- **Look! New prices are displayed with 10 increase**
- Click **OK** (bottom) to save changes

Delete Invoice without Payment

When create an invoice and payment has not been received from the customer, you may discover it was a wrong customer you wrote the check to. QuickBooks will give you the option to edit, void or delete the invoice. **In this section, will pull up James Adams to see that he has no unpaid invoice before and after this exercise**. We will void the invoice and not delete it yet so we can have an invoice to work with in the next page, at which time we will void and delete it.

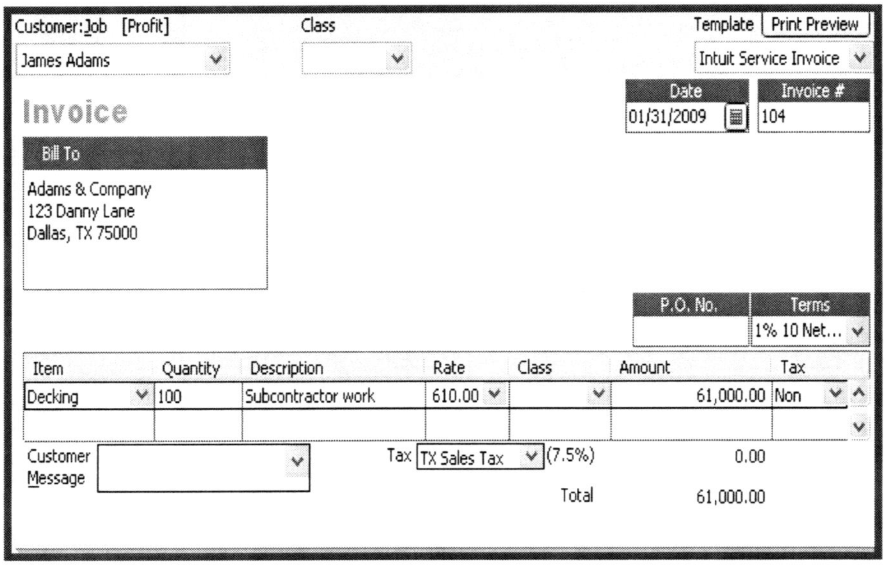

Activities:

- Click **Customers menu**
- Click **Create Invoices**
- Customer: Job: Select **James Adams**
- Date: Type **1/31/09**
- Invoice #: Accept **104**
- In the lower window. Click under **Item** (left of window): Select **Decking**
- Quantity: Type **100**. Balance Due (bottom right): **61,000.00**
- Click **Save & Close**
- Click **Customers menu**
- Click **Create Invoices**
- Click **Previous** button to Invoice #104 for 61,000
- Click **Edit menu**

- Click **Void Invoice**
- **Look! Balance Due is 0.00** (Bottom right of window)
- Click **Save & Close**
- Click **Yes** to "You have changes transaction…"
- Click **Customers menu**
- Click **Receive Payments**
- Click **X** on QuickBooks Web Browser
- Receive From: Select **James Adams**
- **Look! James Adams has no unpaid invoices to pay, invoice is deleted**
- Click **X** to close Customer Payment window
- Click **No** to "You have not recorded…"

Invoice with Payment

Sometimes, you may create an invoice and received a payment from the customer, but later discovered the amount on the invoice was wrong. Now, you have to decide whether to re-issue another invoice with the right amount and delete the old invoice or issue a credit memo. Remember the best place to delete an invoice and the check you received on that invoice is in the accounts receivable register. Click on the invoice or check and then click on the Edit menu and Delete invoice or check.

Activities:

- Click **Customers menu**
- Click **Create Invoices**
- Click **Previous** button to Invoice #104 for 0.00
- Quantity (bottom window): Type **100**. Press **Tab**.
- Balance Due: Accept **61,000**
- See how easy you can re-create a voided invoice
- Click **Save & Close**
- Click **Yes** to "You have changed…"
- Click **Customers menu.**
- Click **Receive Payments**
- Click **X** on QuickBooks Web Browser
- Receive From: Select **James Adams**
- Amount: Type **61,000.** Press **Tab.**
- In the lower window. Accept **Checkmark** left of date on #104
- Click **Save & Close**

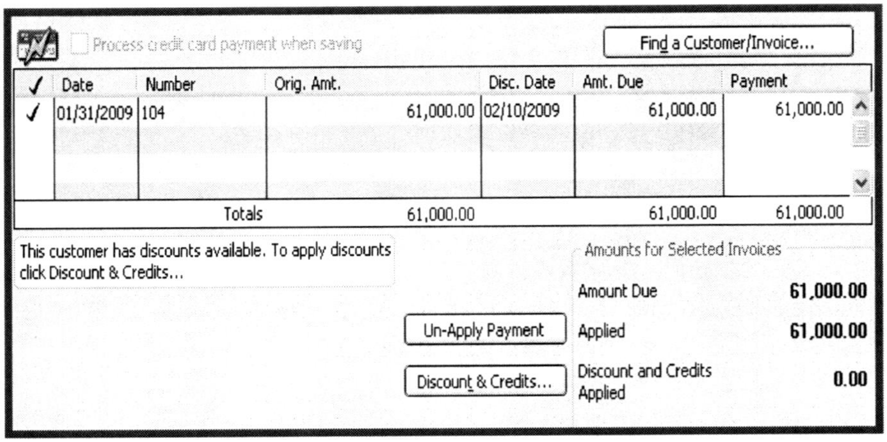

Delete Invoice with Payment

After you've created an invoice and received the payment, QuickBooks still gives you the option to void or delete the invoice. The only difference between voiding and deleting an invoice that has or has not been paid is that you have to delete the payment after deleting the invoice. In this section, we will first pull up the voided invoice and re-create it to a new invoice, receive the payment from the customer, void and delete the invoice, and then delete the payment. **We will pull up James Adams to see he has no unpaid invoices before and after this exercise.**

Activities:

- Click **Customers menu**
- Click **Create Invoices**
- Click **Previous** button to Invoice #104 for 61,000
- Click **Edit menu.** Click **Void Invoice**
- **Look! Balance Due is 0.00** (Bottom right of window)
- Click **Edit menu.** Click **Delete Invoice**
- Click **OK to** "There are payments…"
- Click **X** to close window
- Click **Lists menu**
- Click **Chart of Accounts**
- Double click **Accounts Receivable**
- Click **1/31/2009 James Adam PMT for 61,000**
- Click **Edit menu.** Click **Delete Payment**
- Click **OK** to "Are you sure…"
- Click **Customers menu**
- Click **Receive Payments**

- Click **X** on QuickBooks Web Browser
- Receive From: Select **James Adams**
- **Look! James Adams has no unpaid invoices to pay**
- Click **X** to close Customer Payment window
- Click **No** to "You have not recorded…"

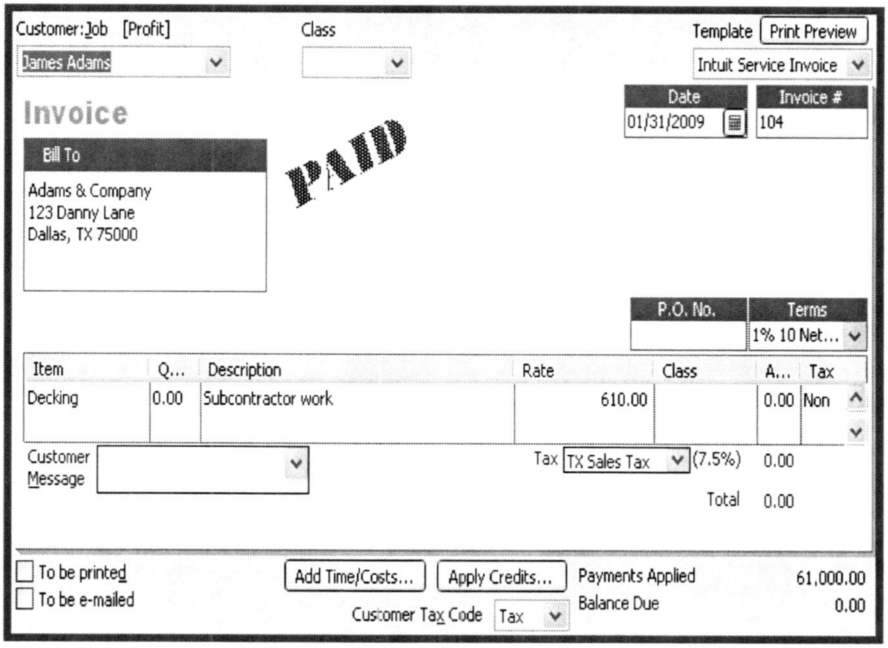

Accounts Receivable Graph

Customer invoice sales are tracked by QuickBooks and used to update the Accounts Receivable balance. Furthermore, Accounts Receivable can be presented in an aging format. The purpose of the Accounts Receivable Graph is to present the balances by aging format in bar chart and by customer by pie chart. If you want to get the details of the individual bar chart, you double click on it. If you want to get the details of the individual the pie chart, you double click on it also.

Activities:

- Click **Reports menu**
- Click **Customers & Receivables**
- Click **Accounts Receivable Graph**
- Click **Date**..(top left of window): Type **12/31/09.** Click **OK**

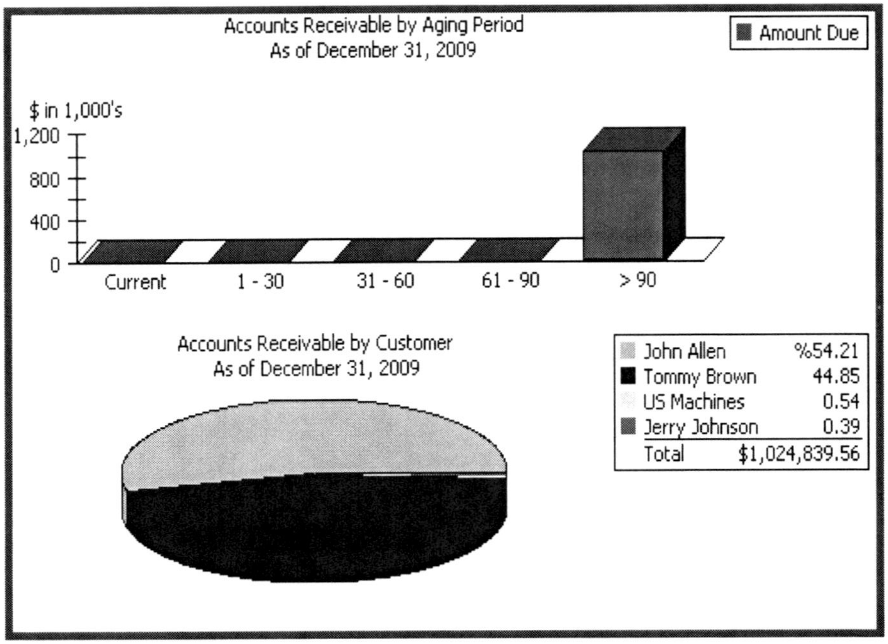

- ❖ Click **Print**
- ❖ Click **Landscape**
- ❖ Click **Cancel** or Print if Printer is ready
- ❖ Click **X** to close Graph window

Sales Graph

Company sales include the invoice and cash sales. So, QuickBooks uses the account sales to track all sales activities. The purpose of the sales graph is to pictorially present these summaries in bar chart and pie chart. When the charts are first displayed, they are by items. You need to click the By Customer button located at the top left of the window to see the graphs by customer. If you want to view the graphs by reps, you click the By Rep button also located at the top left of the window.

Activities:

- ❖ Click **Reports menu**
- ❖ Click **Sales**
- ❖ Click **Sales Graph**
- ❖ Click **Date**..(top left of window)
- ❖ Graph Dates: Select **This Year.** Click **OK**

- ❖ Click **By Item** (top left of window)
- ❖ Click **By Customer**
- ❖ Click **By Rep**
- ❖ Click **Print**. Click **Landscape**
- ❖ Click **Cancel** or **Print** if Printer is ready
- ❖ Click **X** to close Graph window

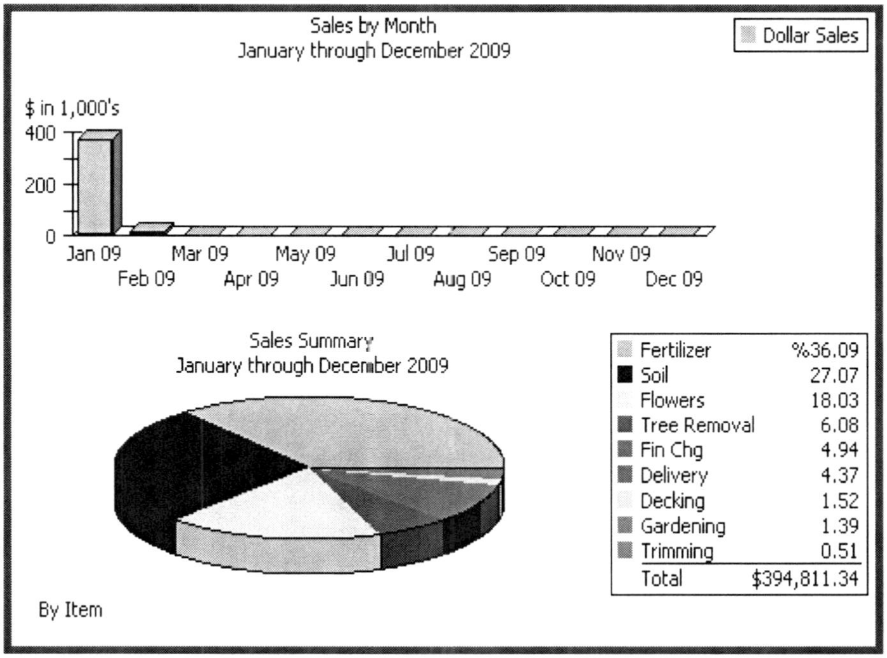

Customer Balance on PDF

If you want to increase your cash flow you must be on top of your account receivables. Some customers will pay you on time without being asked to do so. For other customers, you have to remind them of their outstanding balance before they will send you a check. You should run your aging summary report to see who is 30 days past due. As soon as a customer is 30 days past due, you should run the customer balance report as shown below and email it immediately. You can also open an invoice, save it as a PDF and email to a customer.

Activities:

- ❖ Click **Customers menu**
- ❖ Click **Customer Center**

- Click **James Adams** in the left window
- In the bottom right window
- Show: Select **Balance Details**
- Right click in the bottom right window
- Click **View as a Report**
- Dates: Select **This Fiscal Year**
- Click **File menu**
- Click **Save as PDF…**
- Save in: Select **Desktop**
- File name: Type **James Adams Balance Details**
- Click **Save**
- Click **X** to close Balance Details window
- Minimize all windows to see James Adams' pdf
- Double click **James Adams** pdf to open
- Click red **X** to close pdf
- Maximize QuickBooks

Quick Company 2009
Balance Details for James Adams
January through December 2009

Type	Num	Date	Due Date	Aging	Amount
Jan - Dec 09					
Invoice	FC 1	2/1/2009	2/1/2009		9,171.78
Payment	4005	2/1/2009			-1,127,997.40
Invoice	101	1/2/2009	2/1/2009		212,906.25
Credit Memo	102	1/2/2009	1/2/2009		-80.63
Stmt Charge	103	1/2/2009			6,000.00
Invoice		1/1/2009	1/1/2009		900,000.00
Jan - Dec 09					**0.00**

Financial Results: Profit & Loss

Customers menu has more activities than any other menus in terms of dealing with a customer. We created new customers, estimates, invoices, and received payments. Estimates do not affect financial statements until they are turned into invoices. Payments for invoices were received from customers. We invoiced Design Services, Decks & Patios, Installations, Maintenance & Repairs, and other services. These activities affected the Profit & Loss statement and Net Income is $2,089,944.67

Activities:

- ❖ Click **Reports menu**
- ❖ Click **Company & Financial**

Quick Company 2009
Profit & Loss
January through December 2009

	Jan - Dec 09
Ordinary Income/Expense	
Income	
Opening Balance Income	1,914,500.00
Landscaping Services	394,811.34
Total Income	2,309,311.34
Cost of Goods Sold	
Materials	213,700.00
Total COGS	213,700.00
Gross Profit	2,095,611.34
Expense	
Opening Balance Expense	5,000.00
Depreciation Expense	666.67
Telephone Expense	0.00
Total Expense	5,666.67
Net Ordinary Income	2,089,944.67
Net Income	**2,089,944.67**

- ❖ Click **Profit & Loss Standard**
- ❖ Date: Select **This Fiscal Year**
- ❖ From: Accept **1/1/09**. To: Accept **12/31/09**
- ❖ Click **Collapse**
- ❖ **Net Income is 2,089,944.67**
- ❖ Click **X** to close window

Financial Results: Balance Sheet

When you sell goods and services to customers, you send invoices for those goods and services. If payments are not received at the same time the invoices are created, Accounts Receivable, a Balance Sheet account is affected. As customers make payments, you receive them in the Receive Payments window. If the Preferences windows are set up correctly, payments are sent automatically to Undeposited Funds. You can see Undeposited Fund now has a balance and Total Assets is $3,633,985.92

Activities:

- Click **Reports menu**
- Click **Company & Financial**
- Click **Balance Sheet Standard**
- Date: Select **This Fiscal Year**
- As of: Accept **12/31/09**
- Click **Collapse**
- **Total Assets is 3,633,985.92**
- Click **X** to close window

Quick Company 2009

Balance Sheet

As of December 31, 2009

	Dec 31, 09
ASSETS	
Current Assets	
Checking/Savings	
Money Market Account	100,000.00
USA Checking	974,515.63
USA Payroll Checking	100,000.00
USA Savings	250,000.00
Total Checking/Savings	1,424,515.63
Accounts Receivable	
Accounts Receivable	1,024,839.56
Total Accounts Receivable	1,024,839.56
Other Current Assets	
Inventory Asset	11,300.00
Undeposited Funds	1,133,997.40
Total Other Current Assets	1,145,297.40
Total Current Assets	3,594,652.59
Fixed Assets	
Truck	39,333.33
Total Fixed Assets	39,333.33
TOTAL ASSETS	**3,633,985.92**

Chapter Summary

Customer menu is all about sales activities and receipt of payments from the customers. Your ending balance from your previous books is your opening balance in QuickBooks. If you have a few invoices it is better to enter them individually through the Create Invoices window. If you have too many invoices, it is easier to enter the total amount per customer in the Opening Balance box.

What we accomplished:

- Reviewed Customers submenus
- Reviewed customer center
- Created customers
- Created customer jobs
- Created estimates
- Created invoices
- Processed sales receipts
- Generated credit memo
- Entered statement charges
- Assessed finance charges
- Created customer statement
- Received payments
- Deposited checks to the bank
- Completed weekly timesheets
- Completed time single activity
- Processed price adjustments
- Deleted invoices with and without payments
- Generated A/R and sales graphs
- Saved customer balance details on pdf
- Processed financial statements

Additional Financial activities:

- Opening sales for James Adams 900,000
- Opening sales for US Machines 5,500
- Opening sales for Jerry Johnson's two locations 4,000
- Invoice #101 for James Adams 200,250
- Sales Receipt #1001 for John Allen 163,125
- Sales Receipt #1002 for Tommy Brown 6,000
- Credit Memo #102 for James Adams 75
- Statement Charges #103 for James Adams 6,000
- Finance Charges FCs on Overdue Invoices 19,511.24
- Cost of Goods Sold to James Adams was 112,450
- Cost of Good Sold to John Allen was 101,250
- Received Payment from James Adams 1,127,997
- Deposited Check to the bank from John Allen 174,515.63

Exercise 6

Complete Exercise 6 by using the following information:

1. Edit all customer with 7.5% Texas State tax in the Additional Info tab

2. Create invoice for the following customers
   Jenny Lane LLC. Class: Computer. Date 1/1/09 invoice #101
   Item: Computer Desktop. Qty 1000
   Item: Computer Laptop. Qty 1000
   Item: Computer Setup. Qty 1

   Luke Walsh Company. Class: Household App. Date 1/1/09 invoice #102
   Item: Refrigerator. Qty 1000
   Item: Microwave. Qty 1000
   Item: Oven. Qty 1000
   Apply 10% Discount

3. Receive payment from the following customers
   Jenny Lane LLC all outstanding date 1/5/09
   John Arlington all outstanding date 1/5/09
   Luke Walsh Company for only 250,000 date 1/5/09

4. Process the following reports
   Profit & Loss Statement ending 12/31/09
   Balance Sheet Standard ending 12/31/09
   Statement of Cash Flow ending 12/31/09
   Customer Balance Details 1/31/09
   Collections Report 1/31/09
   Transaction List by Customer 1/31/09
   Sales by Customer Detail 1/31/09
   Sales by Item Summary 1/31/09
   Sales Graph 1/31/09
   Job Profitability Detail Jenny Lane LLC 1/31/09
   Item Profitability 1/31/09

$

Chapter 7

Vendors Menu

Objectives: After you've completed this chapter, you will be able to:

- ✓ Explain Vendors submenus
- ✓ Identify vendor center contents
- ✓ Complete vendor information
- ✓ Prepare purchase orders
- ✓ Receive inventory with bill
- ✓ Receive inventory without bill
- ✓ Enter bills for received inventory
- ✓ Pay inventory bills
- ✓ Enter operating expense bills
- ✓ Pay operating expense bills and sales tax
- ✓ Generate sales tax liability report
- ✓ Generate sales tax revenue summary report
- ✓ Complete the physical inventory worksheet
- ✓ Create the inventory adjustment accounts
- ✓ Perform inventory quality/value adjustment process
- ✓ Process tax forms
- ✓ Delete bills with and without payment
- ✓ Generated Accounts Payable graph
- ✓ Save vendor balance details on pdf
- ✓ Process financial reports and compare results

Review Vendor Submenus

Vendor management is crucial to the success of your business. Vendors want your money more than you can imagine, and controlling them and their bills is essential to your bottom line and your cash flow. The Vendors menu is the gateway to vendor-related activities and reports. You want to ask for estimates and bids to select the most cost effective vendors to work with. You should take discounts from your vendors when offered. If I were to show you the math on the savings when you take discounts from your vendors, it would be outstanding and no bank can come close in lending you money at that rate.

- Click **Vendors menu**

The following submenus are found under the Vendors menu:

- **Vendor Center:** The Center allows you to see the summary of vendor activities in one window, including address, credit limit, account number, contact information, e-mail address, phone number, fax number, and terms of payment.

- **Enter Bills:** Before you pay your bill you are encouraged to first enter the bill in the Enter Bills window. You will be able to enter the vendor name, date, amount, terms, expense account or items as the case may be. Make it a practice to first enter bills before writing checks, that way at any point in time; you can see outstanding or unpaid bills.

- **Pay Bills:** Before you pay a bill remember to subtract any discounts from the vendor for early payments which is a reduction on cost of goods sold or cost of purchases. After you've entered the bills in the Enter Bills window, you come to the Pay Bills window, pull up the same bill you've just entered and pay it. When you open the Pay Bills window, all unpaid bills are displayed in front of you. Select the bill or bills you want to pay and click Pay Now.

- **Sales Tax:** When you sell products to your customers, if you collect sales tax, at the end of the tax period you must remit the collection to the appropriate government agency. You come to the Sales Tax submenu to pay the bills and perform other sales tax activities, including adjust sales tax due, and review sales tax liabilities.

- **Create Purchase Orders:** If you set up your reorder point correctly in the Edit menu, Preferences, QuickBooks will prompt you when you reach the reorder point. At that time, you will come to the Create Purchase Orders window to fill out the inventories you want from your vendors. Be sure to click the To Be e-mail box so you can be able to e-mail your Purchase Orders to the vendors instead of using the postal service, which is not cost effective.

- **Receive Item and Enter Bill:** After the Purchase Order is e-mailed to the vendor; items you requested are shipped to you immediately. Because the vendors ship the items and enclosed a bill, you are going to receive the items and at the same time Enter the Bills. You must make absolutely certain that you key in the invoice number when you enter bill; you don't pay duplicate bills.

- **Receive Items:** If the vendor forgot to enclose the bills when shipping the items, you have to go to the Receive Items window, pull up the vendor and receive the items. In this case the Ref No. must be left blank because you do not have the bill number from the vendor. This is imperative to remember.

- **Enter Bill for Received Items:** After you've received the Items, and later you received the bill from the vendor, it is time now to enter the bill number on the Ref No. line. This is important because you do not want to issue two or more checks on the same bill.

- **Inventory Activities:** This is where you manage you inventory quantities. You will be able to enter new items, adjust quantity/value on hand, and take a physical inventory count of your products.

- **Print 1099s/1096:** Some of your vendors will qualify for Form 1099 or Form 1096, especially, your subcontractors. You must click the "Vendor Eligible of 1099" in the Additional Info tab when creating or editing the vendor information. To activate the Form 1099/1096, you must set up the Edit menu, Preferences, and Tax: 1099 window.

- **Item List:** You can access the Item List through the Vendor menu. This window allows you to create new items, and edit or delete old items. At the bottom of the window are the following activities: Items, Activities, Reports, and Excel. Don't forget to always right click in any list window to see what activities are available for you. When you right click in the Item List window, you will get almost the same submenus as if you had clicked the Vendors menu.

Review Vendor Center

It is easier to access the Vendor Center if you're already in the Home Page by clicking the Vendors button. Depending on the nature of your business, you may have fewer vendors than customers. Though the Customer and Vendor Centers windows are similar, generally, there are more activities in the Customer Center window than the Vendor Center window. Let's review the contents of the Vendor Center window.

- Click **Vendors menu**
- Click **Vendor Center**

Activities buttons and windows: You will find the following activities when you open the Vendor Center window

- New Vendor
- New Transaction
- Print
- Excel
- Word
- Vendor tab
- View down arrow
- Transaction tab
- Edit Vendor
- Edit Notes
- Show down arrow
- Filter By down arrow
- Date down arrow

Report for this Vendor: Vendor reports are located at the right side of the window and they include the following:

- QuickReport
- Open Balance

Right Click: When you right click the left side of the Vendor Center window, you will find the following options:

- Find
- Use
- Refresh
- Edit Vendor
- New Vendor
- Make Vendor Inactive
- Customize Columns
- Show Full Customer List Only
- Write Checks
- Enter Bills
- Pay Bills
- Enter Credit Card Charges
- Create Purchase Orders
- Receive Items & Enter Bills
- Receive Items
- Enter Bill for Received Items

Vendor Information: Telephone America

Like the Customer Detail window, it is essential to provide vendor data and information as detailed as possible, because vendor profile in this window is globally pulled to other windows and reports. The vendor's physical address should be double checked after entry, since other departments, especially the shipping department depend on its accuracy. Telephone and fax numbers should not be overlooked either, and must be updated frequently as information changes and becomes available. Note also that QuickBooks will allow you to enter just the vendor's name without other information. When you have a customer who is also a vendor you have to modify the names such as John Doe Customer for a customer and John Doe Vendor for a vendor.

Activities:

- Click **Vendors menu**
- Click **Vendor Center**
- Double click **Telephone America**
- Company Name: Type **Telephone America**
- Click **in Name and Address box**:
- Accept **Telephone America**. Press **Enter**
- Type **4700 Welling Circle.** Press **Enter**
- Type **Dallas, TX.75000**
- Contact: Type **Susan Sanchez**

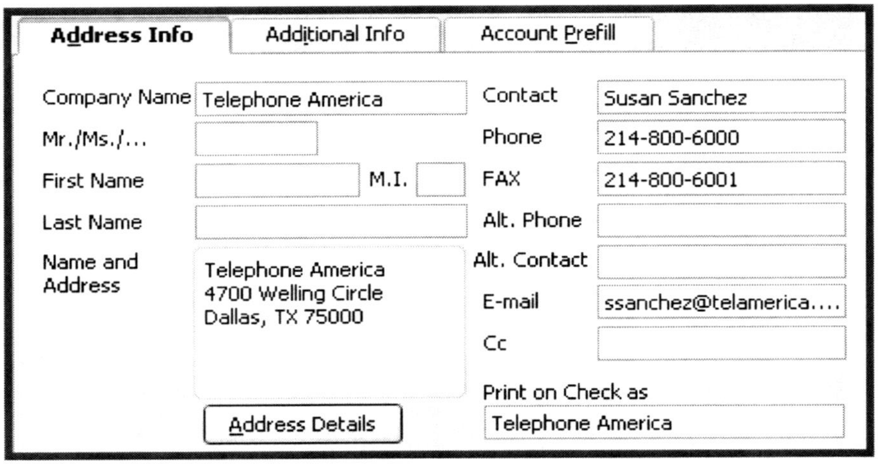

- ❖ Phone: Type **214-800-6000**
- ❖ Fax: Type **214-800-6001**
- ❖ E-mail: Type **ssanchez@ telamerica.com**
- ❖ Click **Additional Info** tab
- ❖ Account No: Type **Vend 123745**
- ❖ Type: Select **Utilities**
- ❖ Term: Select **Due on receipt**
- ❖ Credit Limit: Type **100,000**
- ❖ Tax ID: Type **73-9876543**
- ❖ Click **OK**

Vendor Information: US Supplies

Most of the time, the Vendor Name and Company Name boxes are the same, if there is any reason both boxes are not be the same, then make sure you provide the correct company name. QuickBooks uses the company name to populate the name & address and the "Print on Check as" boxes. In essence, the company name box is more legitimate than the vendor name, since you will see that name on a check being sent to a vendor. Provide any opening balance amount and remember QuickBooks calls this Uncategorized Expense unless you change the account name.

Activities:

- ❖ Right click in the Vendor Center window
- ❖ Select **New Vendor**
- ❖ Vendor Name: Type **US Supplies**
- ❖ Opening Balance: Type **1,500** as of: Type **1/1/09**

- Company Name: Type **US Supplies**. Press **Tab**
- Click in Name and Address: Accept **US Supplies**. Press **Enter**
- Type **1234 Downing Rd**, Press **Enter**
- Type **Dallas, TX 75000**
- Contact: Type **Andrea Felton**
- Phone: Type **214-100-1234**
- Fax: Type **214-100-4567**
- E-mail: Type **afelton@ussupplies.com**
- Click **Additional Info** tab
- Account No: Type **Vend 123456**
- Type: Select **Supplier**
- Terms: Select **2% 10 Net 30**
- Credit Limit: Type **500,000**
- Tax ID: Type **73-1234566**
- Checkmark **Vendor eligible for 1099**
- Click **OK**

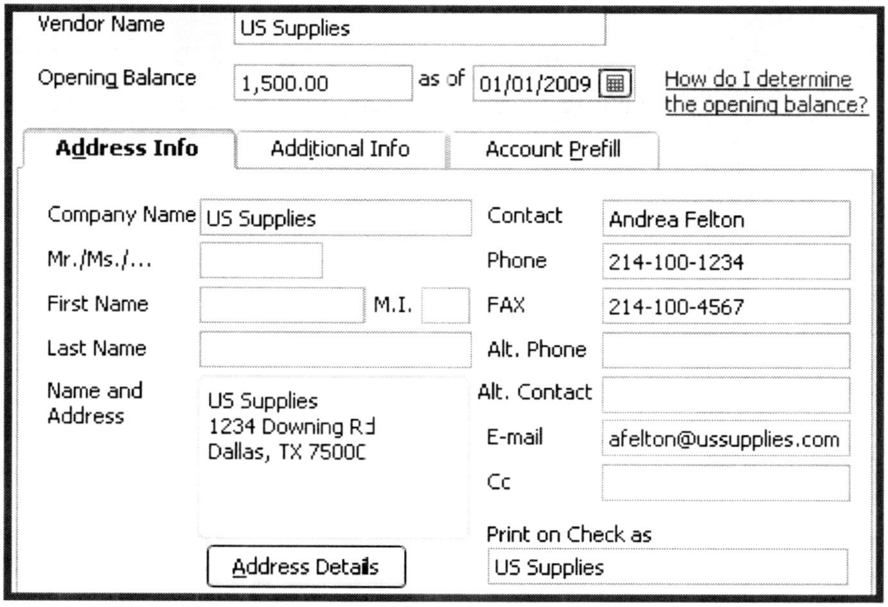

Vendor Information: Payroll Services

Some payroll related vendors are government agencies and others are private companies. Government agencies include the Internal Revenue Service and state and local government agencies in charge of collecting sales tax. In the private sector, these are the banks and other financial institutions. Most of the time a company can contract with these financial institutions to manage employee and employer funds and, therefore, have fiduciary responsibilities to the funds entrusted in their care.

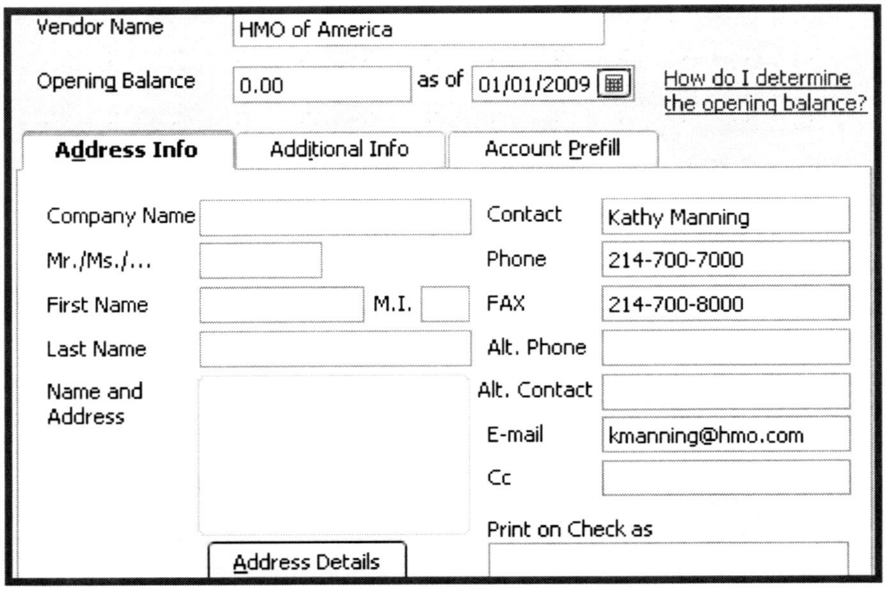

Activities:

- Right click in the Vendor Center window
- Click **New Vendor**
- Vendor Name: Type **HMO of America**
- Opening Balance: Type **0.00** as of: Type **1/1/09**
- Contact: Type **Kathy Manning**
- Phone: Type **214-700-7000**
- Fax: Type **214-700-8000**
- E-mail: Type **kmanning@hmo.com**
- Click **Next**
- Vendor Name: Type **Money Mgt of America**
- Opening Balance: Type **0.00** as of: Type **1/1/09**
- Contact: Type **Tony Casey**
- Phone: Type **214-600-6000**
- Fax: **Type 214-600-7000**
- E-mail: Type **tcasey@mma.com**
- Click **Next**
- Vendor Name: Type **US Treasury**

- ❖ Opening Balance: Type **0.00** as of: Type **1/1/09**
- ❖ Contact: Type **Joe Lekey**
- ❖ Phone: Type **214-600-1040**
- ❖ Fax: Type **214-700-1040**
- ❖ E-mail: Type **jlekey@ustreasury.gov**. Click **Next**
- ❖ Vendor Name: Type **TX – Unemployment Company**
- ❖ Opening Balance: Type **0.00** as of: Type **1/1/09.** Click **OK**

Purchase Orders

When you send purchase orders to your vendor for products and services, they are expected to fill your order right away. Make sure you want these items, because your vendors are going to operate on that assumption. If you set up your re-order point for each product, the task of completing and sending an e-mail with your purchase order is a breeze. Always match your purchase order with the invoice to compare prices and quantity on what you requested and what was finally sent and charged to you.

Activities:

- ❖ Click **Vendors menu**
- ❖ Click **Create Purchase Orders**
- ❖ Vendor: Select **US Supplies**
- ❖ Class: Select **Landscaping**

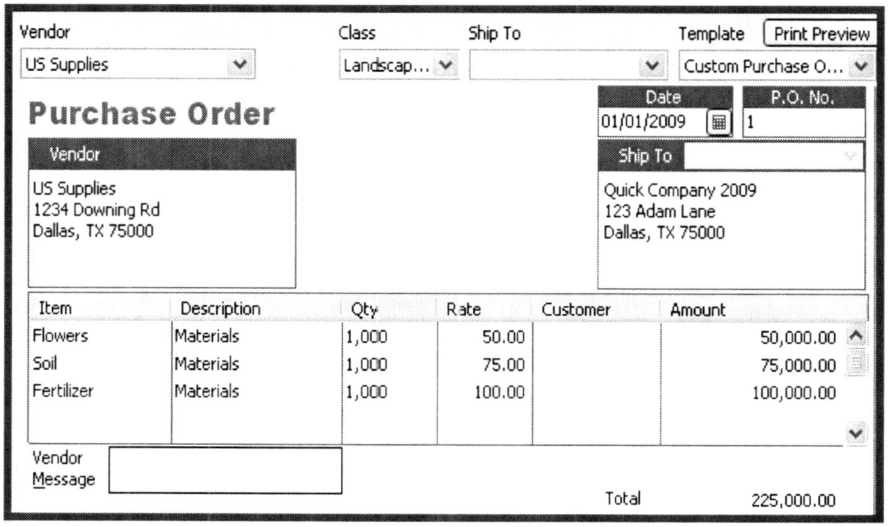

- Date: Type **1/1/09**
- P. O. No.: Accept **1**
- Vendor Address: Accept **US Supplies**
- Ship To Address: Accept **Quick Company 2009** (your company's name)
- Click under **Item**: Select **Flowers**
- Qty: Type **1000**. Press **Tab**
- Select **Soil**
- Qty: Type **1000**. Press **Tab**
- Select **Fertilizer**
- Qty: Type **1000**. Press **Tab**
- Checkmark **To be printed**
- Checkmark **To be e-mailed**
- **Look! Total amount is 225,000.00**
- Click **Save & Close**

Inventory with Bill

It is possible to receive inventory from your vendor without any bills, and other times, the vendor will remember to ship inventory with the bill. When you receive inventory with a bill, you match the bill with the purchase order. If the bill was completed correctly, you will see your purchase order number typed on the bill itself. When the purchase order number is not typed, you must type it yourself on the bill for references purposes. Click Save & Close and your work are done.

Activities:

- Click **Vendors menu**
- Click **Receive Items and Enter Bill**
- Click **Bill** (top left)
- Vendor: Select **US Supplies** (If you see US Supplies. Press Tab)
- Click **Yes** to "Open Purchase order exist…".
- Checkmark **1/1/09 for PO No. 1.** Click **OK**
- Date: Accept **1/1/09**
- Ref No.: Type **Ussup 1201** (this is the bill number)
- Bill Due: Accept **1/31/09**
- Term: Accept **2% 10 Net 30**
- Discount Date: Accept **1/11/09**
- Flower Qty: Type **800 (not 1000).** Press **Tab**
- Amount: Accept **40,000**
- Soil Qty: Type **800 (not 1000).** Press **Tab**
- Amount: Accept **60,000**

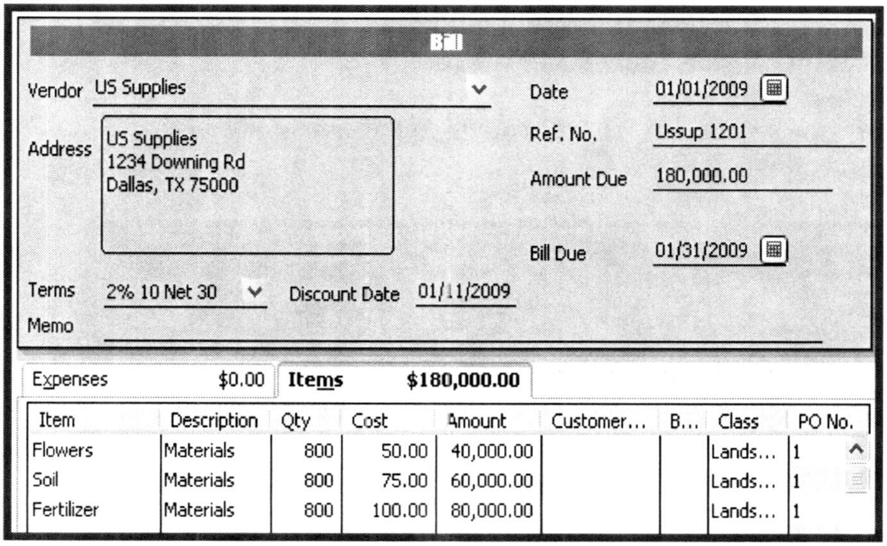

Bill

Vendor US Supplies — Date 01/01/2009

Address: US Supplies, 1234 Downing Rd, Dallas, TX 75000 — Ref. No. Ussup 1201

Amount Due 180,000.00

Bill Due 01/31/2009

Terms 2% 10 Net 30 — Discount Date 01/11/2009

Memo

Expenses $0.00 — Items $180,000.00

Item	Description	Qty	Cost	Amount	Customer...	B...	Class	PO No.
Flowers	Materials	800	50.00	40,000.00			Lands...	1
Soil	Materials	800	75.00	60,000.00			Lands...	1
Fertilizer	Materials	800	100.00	80,000.00			Lands...	1

- Fertilizer Qty: Type **800 (not 1000).** Press **Tab**
- Amount: Accept **80,000**
- Amount Due (top right): Accept **180,000**
- Click **Save & Close**

Inventory without Bill

When you receive inventory without a bill, you create a bill yourself, but this time it is called Item Receipt. What you're doing in essence is documenting what you received from the vendor. For practical purposes, the driver of vehicle should be present to witness the inventory count and sign off on what he or she delivered to you. Because you did not receive the bill from the vendor, you will leave the Ref. No. (Reference Number) box blank until you receive a bill from the vendor.

Activities:

- Click **Vendors menu**
- Select **Receive Items**
- Vendor: Select **US Supplies** (if you see US Supplies. Press Tab)
- Click **Yes** to "Open Purchase order exists…"
- Checkmark **1/1/09 for PO No. 1.** Click **OK**
- Date: Accept **1/1/09**
- Ref No.: **Leave blank**
- You did not receive bill yet only the inventory
- Amount Due: Accept **45,000**

Because you did not receive the bill you leave the box empty until the bill comes in.

- Memo: Accept **Received items** (bill to follow)
- Item: Accept **Flower, Soil and Fertilizer**
- Qty: Accept **200** for each
- Amount: Accept **10,000, 15,000 and 20,000** respectively
- Click **Save & Close**

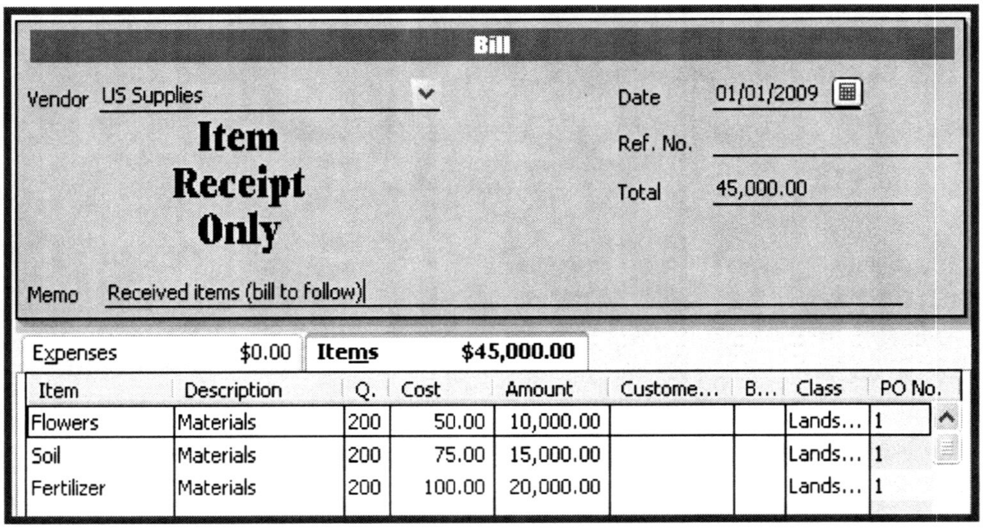

Enter Bill for Received Inventory

Sometimes, the vendor will send you inventory ahead of the bill. And when you finally receive the bill, you will match the content of the bill with Item Receipt you previously created. One of the most significant activities in this section is to type the bill number on the Ref. No. line. Typing the bill number and using the Item Receipt you previously created, will prevent you from paying on a duplicate bill; and believe me, it happens all the time. Watch out for mistakes like this one!

Activities:

- Click **Vendors menu**
- Click **Enter Bill for Received Items**
- Vendor: Select **US Supplies**
- Click **1/1/09 with "Receive item…"** Click **OK**
- Vendor: Accept **US Supplies**
- Date: Accept **1/1/09**
- Ref No.: Type **Ussup 1201**.
- Amount Due: Accept **45,000**

If you set up your preferences correctly, QuickBooks will not allow duplicate invoice numbers.

- ❖ Click **Save & Close**
- ❖ Click **Yes** to "You have changed the transactions…?"
- ❖ Click **Cancel** to "Another Bill already has number USA 1201"
- ❖ If you did not get the message above, you typed the wrong Ref No.
- ❖ Ref No: Type **Ussup 1375**.(we tested with a duplicate Ref No above)
- ❖ Click **Save & Close**.
- ❖ Click **Yes**

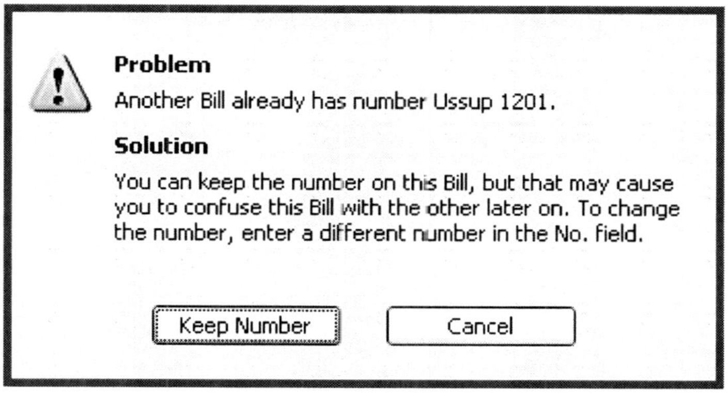

Pay Inventory Bill

When inventory has been previously recorded with a receipt number, by the due date you're ready to pay the bill. But before you pay the bill, find out if there's a cash discount for early payment. You should seriously consider paying on time to take advantage of any discounts; otherwise, you pay the bill by the due date. Make it a habit of making payments from previously recorded bills. This policy will prevent you from paying an invoice twice, since the Payment window will blank and empty.

Activities:

- ❖ Click **Vendors menu**
- ❖ Click **Pay Bills**
- ❖ Show bills(top left): Click **Show all bills**
- ❖ Checkmark **the three US Supplies bills** boxes
- ❖ Amount Due: Accept **231,500**
- ❖ Disc Used: Accept **4,530**
- ❖ Amount to Pay: Accept **221,970**
- ❖ Payment Date: Type **1/2/09**
- ❖ Payment Method: Accept **Check** (bottom left)
- ❖ Click **To be printed**

- ❖ Payment Account: Accept **USA Checking** (bottom left)
- ❖ Ending Balance: Accept **752,545.63**
- ❖ Click **Pay Selected Bills.** Click **Done**

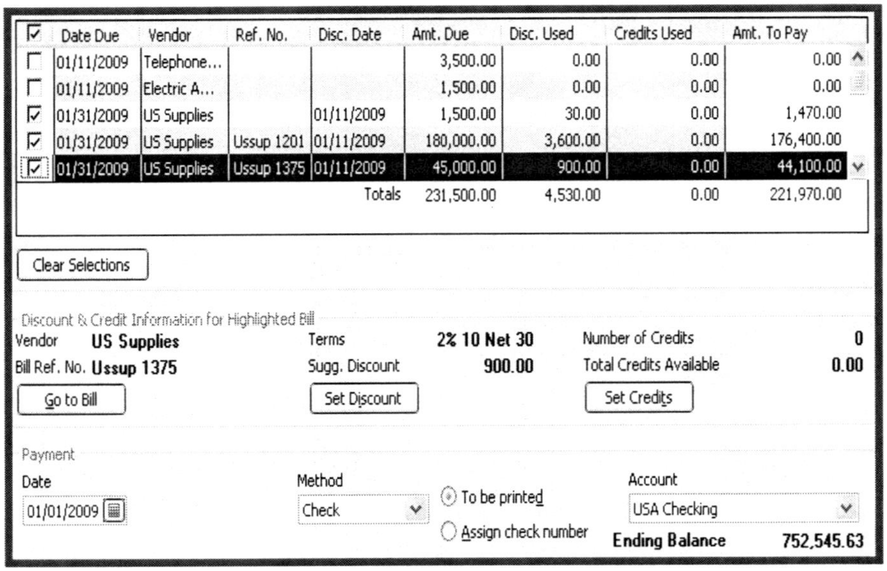

Enter Operating Expense Bill

You have two types of bills, inventory and office related bills. Take a look at the Enter Bill window, there are two tabs, one is Expenses and the other is Items. You use one of these tabs depending on the item you are going to bill for. For example, if you are going to record an administrative expense, you use the Expenses tab, but if you're going to record an inventory bill you use the Items tab. You cannot pull in items with income account only, but expense and income or expense only accounts.

Activities:

- ❖ Click **Vendors menu**
- ❖ Click **Enter Bills**
- ❖ Click **Bill** (top left of window)
- ❖ Vendor: Select **Telephone America**
- ❖ Date: Type **1/2/09**
- ❖ Ref. No.: Type **Cell 12978**
- ❖ Amount Due: Type **459.00**

- ❖ Bill Due: Accept **1/2/09**
- ❖ Term: Accept **Due on receipt**
- ❖ Click under Account: Select **Telephone Expense**
- ❖ Amount: Accept **459.00**
- ❖ Memo: **January cell phone**
- ❖ Note! You are in **Expenses tab** not **Item tab** which is for product expenses
- ❖ Click **Save & Close** (bottom right of window)

Operating expenses will take you to the expense tab and inventories will take you to the items tab.

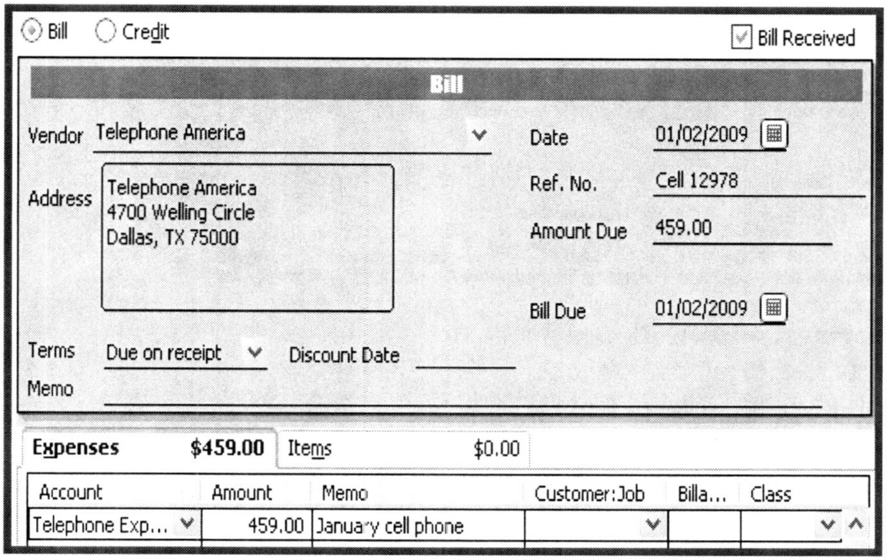

Pay Operating Expense Bill

After you've entered an office related bill into QuickBooks, the totals of individual bills are matched with totals on the vendor reports. Payments to vendors are processed in the Pay Bills window, and bills are pulled up according to the cutoff date, mainly at the end of the month. You view all bills by clicking the Show All Bills, but be sure to select those bills that came before the due date, unless you are paying the bills in advance to take advantage of discounts from the vendor.

Activities:

- ❖ Click **Vendors menu**
- ❖ Click **Pay Bills**
- ❖ Click **Show all bills** boxes (top left of window):
- ❖ Sort Bills By: Accept **Due Date**
- ❖ Checkmark **the two Telephone America bills**
- ❖ Amt. Due (column): Accept **5,459**

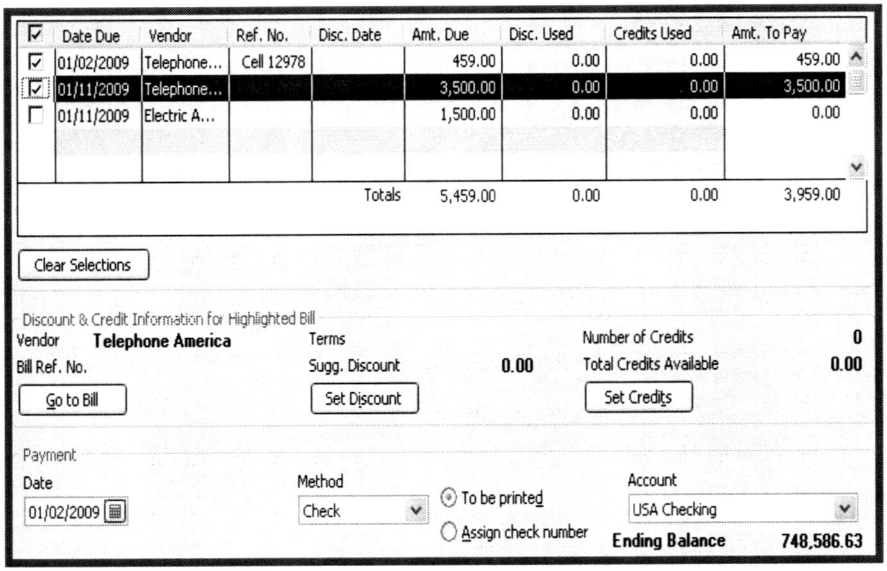

- ❖ Amt To Pay (column): Accept **3,959**
- ❖ Payment Date: Type **1/2/09**
- ❖ Payment Method: Accept **Check**
- ❖ Click **To be printed**
- ❖ Payment Account: Accept **USA Checking** (bottom left)
- ❖ Ending Balance: Accept **748,586.63**
- ❖ Click **Pay Selected Bills.** Click **Done**

Pay Sales Tax

Sales Tax Liability must be handled with care. The name of the government agency where the check is sent must be documented in the Vendor Detail window; otherwise the vendor's name will not be available in the Pay Bills window. Before a check is processed to a government agency the Sales Tax Liability report must be reviewed to make sure it matches with the vendor account balance. If any differences exist, adjusting entries must be made first before the check is issued.

Activities:

- ❖ Click **Vendors menu**
- ❖ Click **Sales Tax**
- ❖ Click **Pay Sales Tax…**
- ❖ Pay From Account: Accept **USA Checking.** Press **Tab**
- ❖ Check Date: Type **1/10/09**. Press **Tab**

- ❖ Show sales tax due through: Type **3/31/09**. Press **Tab**
- ❖ Checkmark **TX Sales Tax for 24,041.25**
- ❖ Amt. Due: Accept **24,041.25**
- ❖ Amt Paid: Accept **24,041.25**
- ❖ Ending Bank Balance: Accept **724,545.38**
- ❖ Checkmark **To be printed** (bottom left of window)
- ❖ Click **OK** to close window

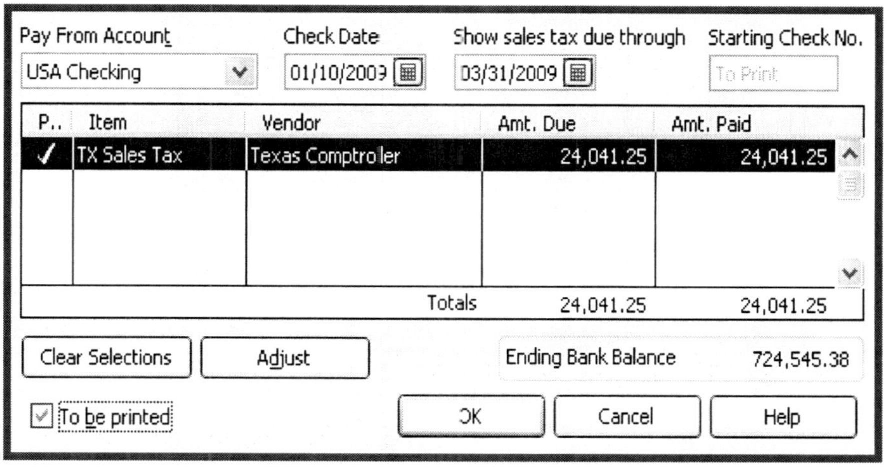

Sales Tax Liability Report

In the Sales Tax Liability report you are mainly after the amount of tax that is owed to the government agency, while in the Sales Tax Revenue Summary, you are after the total sales that is generated for the period. For audit purposes, you want to make sure that total customer sales for the period—month, quarter, or year—matches the total Sales Tax Revenue Summary for the same period. If there are differences between the revenue summary and the customer total, an adjusting entry is needed.

Activities:

- ❖ Click **Vendors menu**
- ❖ Click **Sales Tax**
- ❖ Click **Sales Tax Liability**
- ❖ Date (top left of window): Select **This Calendar Year**
- ❖ **Look! Tax Collected is 24,041.25**
- ❖ Click **Memorize** (top left of window)

- Name: Accept **Sales Tax Liability**
- Checkmark **Save in Memorized Report Group**
- Accept **Accountant**. Click **OK**
- Click **X** to close report window

Quick Company 2009

Sales Tax Liability

January through December 2009

	Total Sa...	Non-Ta...	Taxable...	Tax Rate	Tax Co...	Sales T... As of D...
Texas Comptroller						
TX Sales Tax	375,300.00	54,750.00	320,550.00	7.5%	24,041.25	0.00
Total Texas Comptroller	375,300.00	54,750.00	320,550.00		24,041.25	0.00
TOTAL	**375,300.00**	**54,750.00**	**320,550.00**		**24,041.25**	**0.00**

Sales Tax Revenue Summary Report

The Sales Tax Revenue Summary report is important in terms of auditing your sales tax activities. Because you want to be sure of the amount of tax you're sending to the government, the Sales Tax Revenue Summary report must match the Sales by Customer Summary report located under the Reports menu, Sales. This is one way to audit your sales tax payment. The Sales Tax Revenue Summary report has two columns, one is taxable sales and the other is non-taxable sales.

Activities:

- Click **Vendors menu**
- Click **Sales Tax**
- Click **Sales Tax Revenue Summary**
- Date (top left of window): Select **This Calendar Year**
- **Look! Taxable Sales is 320,550.00**
- Click **Memorize** (top left of window)
- Name: Accept **Sales Tax Revenue Summary**
- Checkmark **Save in Memorized Report Group**
- Accept **Accountant**. Click **OK**
- Click **X** to close report window

Quick Company 2009

Sales Tax Revenue Summary

January through December 2009

	Taxable Sales	Non-Taxable...	Non-Taxable...	TOTAL
Texas Comptroller				
TX Sales Tax	320,550.00	42,750.00	12,000.00	375,300.00
Total Texas Comptroller	320,550.00	42,750.00	12,000.00	375,300.00
TOTAL	**320,550.00**	**42,750.00**	**12,000.00**	**375,300.00**

Physical Inventory Worksheet

When you first receive inventory from your vendors, they are stored in the warehouse. At the end of the month you take inventory count to find out how many items are left. In theory, the number of inventory items you started with minus the ones you sold should equal the number of items left in the warehouse. In practice, it doesn't always turn out that way. For example, you might have damaged items that will not count as good items. You print this worksheet for the inventory count.

Activities:

- Click **Vendors menu**
- Click **Inventory Activities**

Quick Company 2009

Physical Inventory Worksheet

All Transactions

	Item Description	Pref Vendor	On Hand	Physical Count
Inventory				
Fertilizer	Materials		1,050	____________
Flowers	Materials		1,051	____________
Soil	Materials		1,050	____________

- Click **Physical Inventory Worksheet**
- Click **Print** (top of window)
- Click **Preview** (right of window)
- Click **Zoom In**
- Click **Close or Print** if printer is ready
- Click **X** to close Print Reports window
- Click **X** to close Physical Inventory Worksheet
- Normally you go to the warehouse and count inventory
- We assume the count for Fertilizer is 1000 not 1050 and Soil is 1100 not 1050
- Normally you write these number on the worksheet
- Adjustment is next page

Normally, you take the inventory worksheet to the warehouse where you count and note the inventory #s on the worksheet.

Inventory Adjustment Accounts

What if you started with 100 items and you sold 10; you should have 90 left in the warehouse. And what if at the end of the month, with Physical Inventory Worksheet you printed from the previous exercise, you go to the warehouse and counted 85 instead of 90. It means 5 items are missing or damaged. You must now create Adjustment Accounts that reduce the number of items to 85. You'll first create two accounts; one is Adjustment to Incr (Increase) Inventory and the other Adjustment to Decr (Decrease) Inventory.

Activities:

- Click **Lists menu**
- Click **Chart of Accounts. Maximize window**
- Right click in the window. Click **New**
- Click **Income.** Click **Continue**
- Account Name: Type **Adjustment to Incr Inventory**
- Description: Type **When the Total Value of Adjustment is positive**
- Click **Save & New**
- Account Type: Select **Expense** (Very Important)
- Account Name: Type **Adjustment to Decr Inventory**
- Description: Type **When the Total Value of Adjustment is negative**
- Click **Save & Close**
- Click **X** to close Chart of Accounts

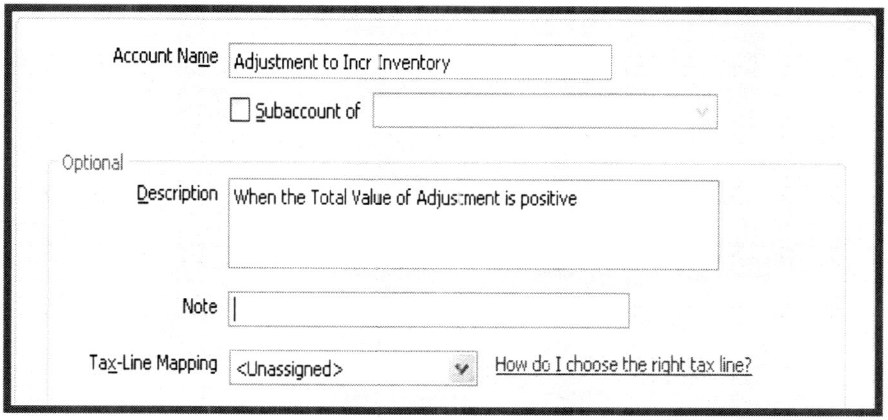

Inventory Adjustment

After you've created the two adjustment accounts, you're now ready to adjust the inventory to match warehouse count. The Adjustment window will greet you with the Current Qty—which is the third column. The fourth column is the New Qty column; this is where you type in the number from the Physical Inventory Worksheet. The final column is the Qty Difference which calculates the difference between the Current and New quantities; a total amount is displayed at the bottom of the window.

Activities:

When the Total Value of Adjustment (bottom right of the window) is negative you decrease the inventory and when the Total Value is positive you increase the inventory.

- Click **Vendors menu**
- Click **Inventory Activities**
- Click **Adjust Quantity/Value on hand**
- Adjustment Date: Type **1/31/09**
- Ref. No.: Accept **1**
- Click under **New Qty** for Fertilizer: Type **1000**. Press **Tab**
- Click under **New Qty** for Soil: Type **1100**. Press **Tab**
- Total Value of Adjustment (bottom right): Accept **-1,250**
- Because Total Value of Adjustment (bottom right) is negative
- Adjustment Account (top left): Select **Adjustment to Decr Inventory**
- Click **Save & Close**

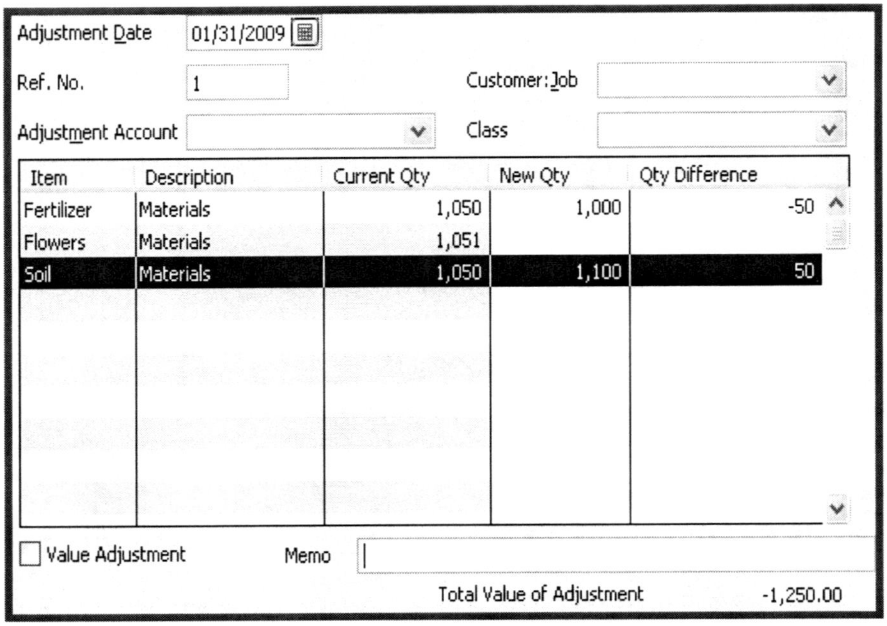

Tax Forms

When you're setting up your new vendors, some will qualify to receive Form 1099, especially, your subcontractors. Their windows should have a checkmark to receive Form 1099. Remember, if you did not check this box for the respective vendor, QuickBooks will not issue Form 1099 to that vendor. At the end of the year, you must run the Form 1099 report; and you may select the "Only 1099 Vendors" window. **Be sure to select Last Calendar Year in the Dates window**.

Activities:

- Click **Vendors menu**
- Click **Print 1099/1096**
- Click **Run Report under #1**
- Review Report
- Click **X** to close window
- Click **Map Accounts under #2**
- Review window
- Click **X** to close window
- Click **Run Report under #3**
- Dates (top left): Select **This Calendar Year**
- 1099 Option: Accept **Only 1099 vendors**

- **Look! US Supplies has 217,440.00**
- Click **X** to close
- Click **Print 1099 under #4**
- Please specify date range: Select **This Calendar Year**
- Click **OK**
- Click **OK** again
- There's no 1099s last year to pay this year
- Click **Close** (bottom right)

Quick Company 2009

Vendor 1099 Review

January 2, 2009

Vendor	Tax ID	Eligible for 1099	Address
Electric America		No	
HMO of America		No	
Money Mgt of America		No	
Telephone America	73-9876543	No	Telephone America 4700 Welling Circle Dallas, TX 75000
Texas Comptroller		No	
TX-Uemployment Company		No	
US Supplies	73-1234566	Yes	US Supplies 1234 Downing Rd Dallas, TX 75000
US Treasury		No	

Delete Bill without Payment

Sometimes, you may finish creating a bill only to find out there is something wrong with it—maybe you paid the wrong amount or some other reasons. QuickBooks has options for you to edit, void or delete the bill. In this exercise, you will only void the bill so you can have something to delete in the next practice page. You will also pull up America Auto Services to see there are no bills before and after this exercise. Because we have not sent out the check, there is no problem with voiding the check.

Activities:

- Click **Vendors menu**
- Click **Enter Bills**
- Vendor: Select **Add New**
- Vendor Name: Type **America Auto Service.** Click **OK**
- Date: Type **1/31/09**
- Ref. No.: Type **Testing void**

- Amount: Type **5,000**
- Click **under Account**: Select **Repairs & Maint under Automobile**
- Click **Save & Close**
- Click **Vendors menu**
- Click **Enter Bills**
- Click **Previous to America Auto Service for 5,000**
- Click **Edit menu**
- Click **Void Bill**
- **Look! Amount Due is 0.00**
- Click **Save & Close**
- Click **Yes** to "You have changed…"
- Click **Vendors menu**
- Click **Pay Bills**
- **Look! There is no bills for America Auto Service**
- Click **X** to close window

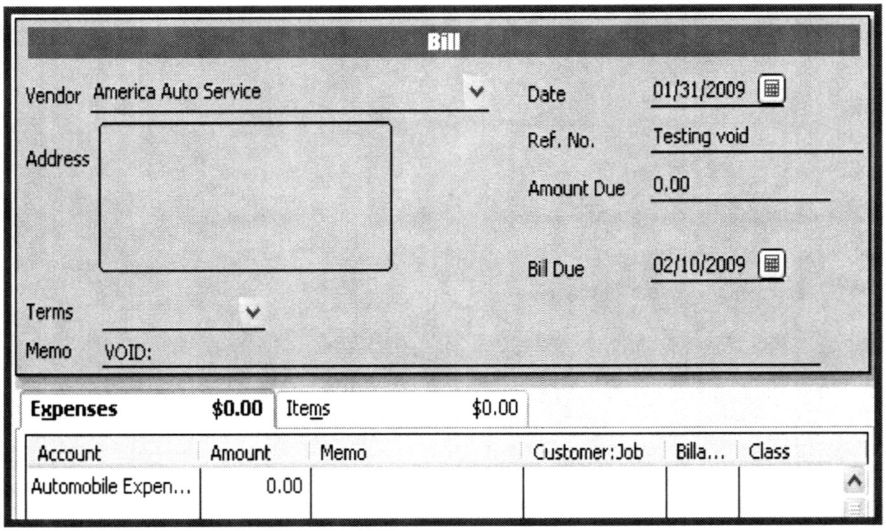

Bill with Payment

In this practice and the next, you will see how easy it is to create a bill, issue a check to a vendor, and later delete the bill and the check. Practically, almost any bill can be deleted from the system even if you have issued a check on that bill. Always remember the best place to delete a bill and the check you paid on that bill is in the accounts payable register window. After you've selected the bill or the check, you click the Edit menu and Delete bill or check.

Activities:

- Click **Vendors menu**
- Click **Enter Bills**
- Click **Previous button to America Auto Service Testing Void for 0.00**
- Amount: Type **5,000.** Press **Tab**
- See how easy you can re-create a voided bill
- Click **Save & Close**
- Click **Yes** to "You have changed…"
- Click **Vendors menu**
- Click **Pay Bills**
- Checkmark **America Auto Service for 5,000**
- Click **Pay Selected Bills** (bottom right of window)
- Click **Done**

In QuickBooks, it's very easy to void a bill and re-create it into another bill by just typing a new amount.

Delete Bill with Payment

You may create a bill and make payment, but before you send out the check you discover the check was for the wrong amount. Though the bill has been marked paid, QuickBooks will allow you to edit, void or delete the bill. In this exercise you will pull up the previous bill you voided, re-create it to a new bill, make payment on the bill, void and delete it. The main difference when the bill has been paid is to delete the payment in the Accounts Payable window. You will pull up American Auto Service to see that there are no bills before and after this exercise.

Activities:

- Click **Vendors menu**
- Click **Enter Bills**
- Click **Previous to America Auto Service for 5,000.00**
- Click **Edit menu.** Click **Void Bill**
- **Look! Amount Due is 0.00**
- Click **Edit menu.** Click **Delete Bill**
- Click **OK** to "This bill has been paid…"
- Click **X** to close Check window
- Click **Lists menu**
- Click **Chart of Accounts**
- Double click **Accounts Payable** to open register
- Click **1/31/09 America Auto Service for 5,000**
- Click **Edit menu.** Click **Delete Bill Pmt-Check**
- Click **OK** to "Are you sure…?"

- ❖ Click **Vendors menu**
- ❖ Click **Pay Bills**
- ❖ **Look! There is no bill for America Auto Service**
- ❖ Click **X** to close Pay Bills window

Date	Number / Type	Vendor / Account Memo	Due Date	Billed	✓	Paid	Balance
01/01/2009	Ussup 137	US Supplies	Paid	45,000.00			5,000.00
	BILL	-split-					
01/02/2009		Telephone America				3,959.00	1,041.00
	BILLPMT	USA Chec					
01/02/2009	Cell 12978	Telephone America	Paid	459.00			1,500.00
	BILL	Telephone					
01/31/2009		America Auto Service				5,000.00	-3,500.00
	BILLPMT	USA Chec					
Splits						Ending balance	-3,500.00

Accounts Payable Graph

As you pay your bills, QuickBooks tracks your payments and updates the Account Payable balance. If you want to see how long you have owed certain bill, the best place to come is the Accounts Payable graph. The graph presents Accounts Payable balances by aging in bar chart and by customer in pie chart. You double click the bar chart to see the details of the bar chart and double click the pie chart to see the details of the pie chart.

Activities:

- ❖ Click **Reports menu**
- ❖ Click **Vendors & Payables**
- ❖ Click **Accounts Payable Graph**
- ❖ Click **Date**..(top left of window): Show Aging as of: Type **12/31/09.**
- ❖ Click **OK**
- ❖ Click **Print**.
- ❖ Click **Landscape**
- ❖ Click **Cancel** or Print if Printer is ready
- ❖ Click **X** to close Graph window

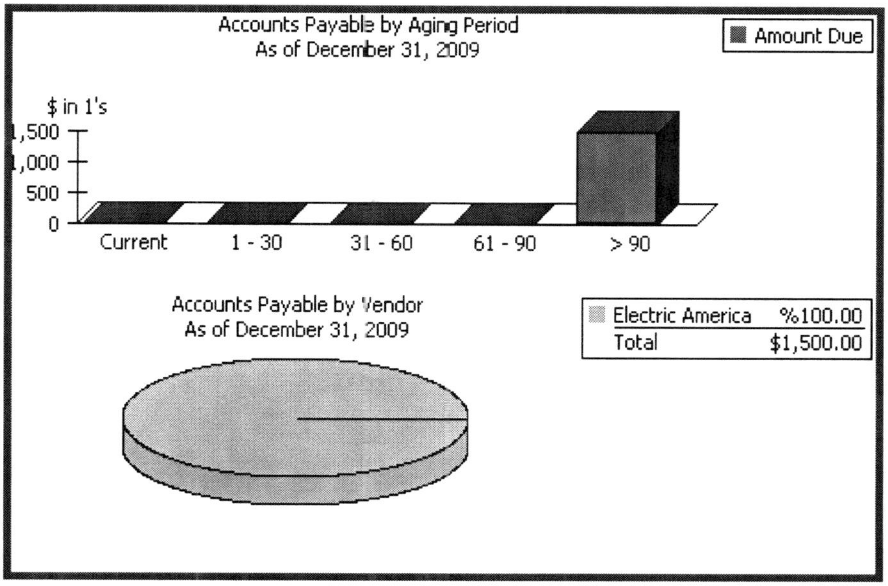

Vendor Balance on PDF

Sometimes, a vendor may call you for payment on a particular invoice. You have to research the invoice to see if it has been paid or not. If the invoice has been paid you have to run, print, and enclose the vendor balance details to the vendor. The report will show the check number and the date of payment. You may also run this report any time you are paying a vendor on an outstanding balance. That way the vendor can see what invoice is outstanding and what matching check amount is enclosed. You can also open a bill, save it as a PDF and email to a customer.

Activities:

- Click **Vendors menu**
- Click **Vendor Center**
- Click **Electric America** in the left window
- In the bottom right window
- Show: Select **Balance Details**
- Right click in the bottom right window
- Click **View as a Report**
- Dates: Select **This Fiscal Year**
- Click **File menu**
- Click **Save as PDF…**
- Save in: Select **Desktop**

- ❖ File name: Type **Electric America Balance Details**
- ❖ Click **Save**
- ❖ Click **X** to close Balance Details window
- ❖ Minimize all windows to see Electric America's pdf
- ❖ Double click **Electric America** pdf to open
- ❖ Click red **X** to close pdf
- ❖ Maximize QuickBooks

Quick Company 2009

Balance Details for Electric America

January through December 2009

Type	Date	Due Date	Aging	Amount	Open Balance
Jan - Dec 09					
Bill	01/01/2009	01/11/2009	354	1,500.00	1,500.00
Jan - Dec 09				**1,500.00**	**1,500.00**

Financial Results: Profit & Loss

In the Vendors menu, we created a purchase order; and like the estimates in the Customers menu, it does not affect the financial statements until the purchase order is turned into a bill. Only then will a customer send payments. We made an adjusting entry on inventory, which affected the Profit & Loss statement. We had several other activities that affected Profit & Loss statement. Gross Profit is now $2,100,141.34, and Net Income is now $2,091,265.67.

Activities:

- ❖ Click **Reports menu**
- ❖ Click **Company & Financial**
- ❖ Click **Profit & Loss Standard**
- ❖ Date: Select **This Fiscal Year**
- ❖ From: Accept **1/1/09.** To: Accept **12/31/09**
- ❖ Click **Collapse**
- ❖ **Net Income is 2,091,265.67**
- ❖ Click **X** to close window

Quick Company 2009
Profit & Loss
January through December 2009

	Jan - Dec 09
Ordinary Income/Expense	
Income	
Opening Balance Income	1,914,500.00
Landscaping Services	394,811.34
Total Income	2,309,311.34
Cost of Goods Sold	
Materials	213,700.00
Discount Received	-4,530.00
Total COGS	209,170.00
Gross Profit	2,100,141.34
Expense	
Adjustment to Decr Inventory	1,250.00
Opening Balance Expense	6,500.00
Depreciation Expense	666.67
Telephone Expense	459.00
Total Expense	8,875.67
Net Ordinary Income	2,091,265.67
Net Income	**2,091,265.67**

Financial Results: Balance Sheet

When you buy goods and services from vendors, they send you bills for those goods and services. If payments are not made at the same time then the bills become accounts payable, a Balance Sheet account is affected. In this chapter, cash decreased when we paid US Supplies, Telephone America, and Texas Comptroller in the amount of $221,970, $3,959, and $24,041.25 respectively. Inventory asset now stands at $235,050 and Asset balance is now $3,607,765.67.

Activities:

- Click **Reports menu**
- Click **Company & Financial**
- Click **Balance Sheet Standard**
- Date: Select **This Fiscal Year**
- As of: Accept **12/31/09**

- Click **Collapse**
- **Total Assets is 3,607,765.67**
- Click **X** to close window

Quick Company 2009
Balance Sheet
As of December 31, 2009

	Dec 31, 09
ASSETS	
Current Assets	
Checking/Savings	
Money Market Account	100,000.00
USA Checking	724,545.38
USA Payroll Checking	100,000.00
USA Savings	250,000.00
Total Checking/Savings	1,174,545.38
Accounts Receivable	
Accounts Receivable	1,024,839.56
Total Accounts Receivable	1,024,839.56
Other Current Assets	
Inventory Asset	235,050.00
Undeposited Funds	1,133,997.40
Total Other Current Assets	1,369,047.40
Total Current Assets	3,568,432.34
Fixed Assets	
Truck	39,333.33
Total Fixed Assets	39,333.33
TOTAL ASSETS	**3,607,765.67**

Chapter Summary

Anytime you have a problem with a vendor, the first place you should think about is the Vendors menu, and the next place is the Vendor Center window. It has all the activities that pertain to your vendors. The Vendor Center window allows you to create edit and delete vendors, but you must know how to go about doing these, and the processes will be easy since you've practiced with some examples.

What we accomplished:

- Reviewed Vendors submenus
- Reviewed Vendor Center contents
- Created Vendors Information
- Completed Purchase Order
- Received Inventory with bills
- Received Inventory without bills
- Entered Bills for received Inventory
- Paid Inventory Bill
- Recorded Operating Office Bills
- Paid Operating Office Bills
- Recorded Payment for Sales Tax
- Generated Sales Tax Liability Reports
- Ran Sales Tax Revenue Summary Reports
- Completed a Physical Inventory Worksheet
- Created Inventor Adjustment accounts
- Entered the Inventory Quantity Adjustment
- Generated Tax Forms 1099 & 1096
- Deleted Bills with and without payment
- Generated Account Payable graph
- Saved vendor balance details on pdf
- Processed financial statements

Additional Financial activities:

- Opening Bill for US Supplies 1,500
- Inventory from US Supplies 225,000
- Discount from US Supplies 4,530
- Payment to US Supplies 221,970
- Bill from Telephone America 459
- Payment to Telephone America 3,959
- Payment to Comptroller 24,041.25
- Decrease in Inventory 1,250

Exercise 7

Complete Exercise 7 by using the following information:

1. Create new supply vendors
   General Supply Company Inc. opening balance 0.00 date 1/1/09
   First National Supplies. opening balance 0.00 date 1/1/09

2. Create new payroll vendors
   US Treasury. opening balance 0.00 date 1/1/09
   TX-Unemployment. opening balance 0.00 date 1/1/09
   HMO of America. opening balance 0.00 date 1/1/09
   Money Mgt of America. opening balance 0.00 date 1/1/09

3. Create the following bills using the receive items and enter bill window
   First National Supplies. Date 1/2/09 Ref #01022009
   Item: Computer Parts. Qty 1000
   Item: Office Machines Parts. Qty 1000
   Item: Wires. Qty 100
   Item: Cable. Qty 100
   Item: Boxes. Qty 100

   General Supply Company Inc. Date 1/5/09 Ref #01052009
   Item: Household Appliances Parts. Qty 1000
   Item: Entertainment Parts. Qty 1000
   Item: Wires. Qty 100
   Item: Cable. Qty 100
   Item: Boxes. Qty 100

4. Process the following reports
   Profit & Loss Statement ending 12/31/09
   Balance Sheet Standard ending 12/31/09
   Statement of Cash Flow ending 12/31/09
   AP Summary 1/31/09
   Vendor Balance Summary 1/31/09
   Sales Tax Liability 12/31/09
   Sales Tax Revenue Summary 12/31/09
   Purchase by Vendor Detail 1/31/09
   Purchase by Item Summary 1/31/09
   Inventory Valuation Summary 1/31/09
   Inventory Stock Status by Item 1/31/09

$

Chapter 8

Employees Menu

Objectives: After you've completed this chapter, you will be able to:

- ✓ Describe Employees submenus
- ✓ Identify employees center contents
- ✓ Set up free trial payroll subscription
- ✓ Set up payroll & employee preferences
- ✓ Enter employee time tracking
- ✓ Create employees payroll checks
- ✓ Print employees pay stubs
- ✓ Manage payroll items
- ✓ Pay payroll liabilities
- ✓ Process financial reports and compare results

Review Employees Submenus

You should register with QuickPayroll before you can use some of the Payroll & Employees windows. However, if you have not registered, you should be able to perform the employees' related activities in this chapter. It's one thing to run your business and deal with other businesses; it is another when you have to deal with a government agency. It is a serious offence to collect payroll taxes from employees and not remit them to the government. Therefore, Employees menu is sometimes considered a legal window; if you treat it that way—you have nothing to worry about! Sometimes, you may not want to worry about doing your payroll yourself, but find a payroll service company to handle it for you. It is a matter of cost benefit analysis; it's what is good for your company that counts.

- Click **Employees menu**

The following submenus are found under the Employees menu:

- **Employee Center:** The center lets you to create new employees, edit, find, and delete employees. It has other activities that help you manage your employees, like completing the Timesheet and printing reports.

- **Enter Time:** For hourly employees, you must fill out or enter their time before they are paid. You open the Use Weekly Timesheet to enter a one week's hours on each line. The timesheet is then processed for payment.

- **Pay Employees:** After you have completed employee timesheet for an hourly employee and have updated payroll information for a salaried employee, you come to this window to pay employees. You must enter the pay period, the payroll checking account or other accounts, and the check date. The window will default all the employees you are suppose to pay.

- **Edit/Void Paychecks:** The window allows you to edit or void any checks you created. After you the "Show Paycheck from and through" boxes, QuickBooks will display all the checks within that period. You then click on the check and click the edit or void buttons.

- **Payroll Taxes and Liabilities:** As soon as you pay employees, QuickBooks will automatically generate employees' taxes, if your preferences are set correctly. Not only taxes, QuickBooks will also generate employees' deductions, such as 401(k), health and dental premiums and other deductions that were made from employees' paycheck. These deductions are then transmitted to the respective management companies. The window allows you to pay payroll liabilities, adjust payroll liabilities, and deposit refund of liabilities.

- **Payroll Forms:** You can be able to view your federal payroll forms from this window. Remember, you can only view this form on 2005 data if you did not subscribe to QuickBooks Payroll. The forms you can view include Annual Form 940/940-EZ, Quarterly Form 941/Schedule B, Interview for your Form 941/Schedule B, and Annual Form W-2/W-3 Wage and Tax Statement/ Transmittal.

- **Payroll Services Options:** This window provides the services options from QuickBooks including: Learn about payroll options, order payroll service, enter payroll service key, and run payroll checkup.

- **Payroll Setup:** This is one of the major windows under the Employees menu. It allows you to set up the payroll and employees preferences. It helps you to set up the payroll items which QuickBooks uses to during paycheck processing.

- **Manage Payroll Items:** Managing your payroll items is all about creating new items, editing or deleting old items. The major submenus are new payroll item and view/edit payroll item list.

Review Employee Center

As noted earlier, most of the buttons in the Employees menu will not be activated if you are not registered for the QuickBooks Payroll services. If you are at the Home Page window, you can access to the Employee Center by clicking on the Employees button located at the left of the window. Let's review the contents of the Employee Center window.

- Click Employees menu
- Click Employee Center

Activities buttons and windows: You will find the following activities when you open the Employee Center window

- New Employee
- Manage Employees Information
- Print

- Enter Time
- Excel
- Word
- Employees tab
- Transaction tab
- View down arrow
- Edit Employee
- Edit Notes
- Show down arrow
- Date down arrow

Report for this Employee: Employee reports are located at the right side of the window and they include the following:

- QuickReport
- Payroll Summary
- Paid Time Off Report
- Payroll Transaction Detail
- Learn About Payroll

Right Click: When you right click the left side of the Employee Center window, you will find the following options:

- Find
- Use
- Refresh
- Edit Employee
- New Employee
- Employee Default
- Delete Employee
- Make Employee Inactive
- Customize Columns
- Show Full Customer List Only

Free Trial Payroll Subscription

If you want to use QuickBooks Payroll to calculate your payroll figures and prepare your tax forms that go to the government agencies, it is advisable to subscribe to the QuickBooks Payroll. However, if you just want to calculate the payroll figures and complete the government tax forms yourself by hand, QuickBooks Payroll will allow to do just that very easily. Before the payroll setup, click the Employees menu to see you have three submenus, but after the setup, you will have more submenus.

Activities:

- Click **Employees menu**
- **Look! You have three submenus**
- Click **Help menu**
- Click **QuickBooks Help**
- Click **Search** tab (top left of window)
- In the white box: Type **manual calculation**
- Click **Forward** arrow
- Click "**Calculate payroll taxes manually…**" (left window)
- In the bottom window. Scroll down
- Click "**manual payroll calculation**"
- In the bottom window. Scroll down
- Click "**Set my company file to use manual calculation**"
- Click **OK** to "You must now calculate…"
- You're now setup for payroll processing
- Click **X** to close QuickBooks Help window

Hourly

Setting up the Payroll default items is our first task in creating the payroll database. After we've created the New Employee's window and have completed the necessary employee's information, our first set up is the Hourly Wage, which is for the hourly employees. For that reason, the first window will default Hourly Wages. In the next window, for the question, "Is this item for regular, overtime, sick or vacation pay?" we will click Regular Pay and continue to complete the rest of the windows. The name of the item is Hourly.

Activities:

- Click **Employees menu**
- **Look! You now have more submenus**
- Click **Edit menu**

- ❖ Click **Preferences**
- ❖ Click **Payroll & Employees** (left of the window)
- ❖ Click **Company Preferences** tab
- ❖ Click **Employee Defaults** (bottom right)
- ❖ In Earnings box
- ❖ Click under Item Name: Select **Hourly**

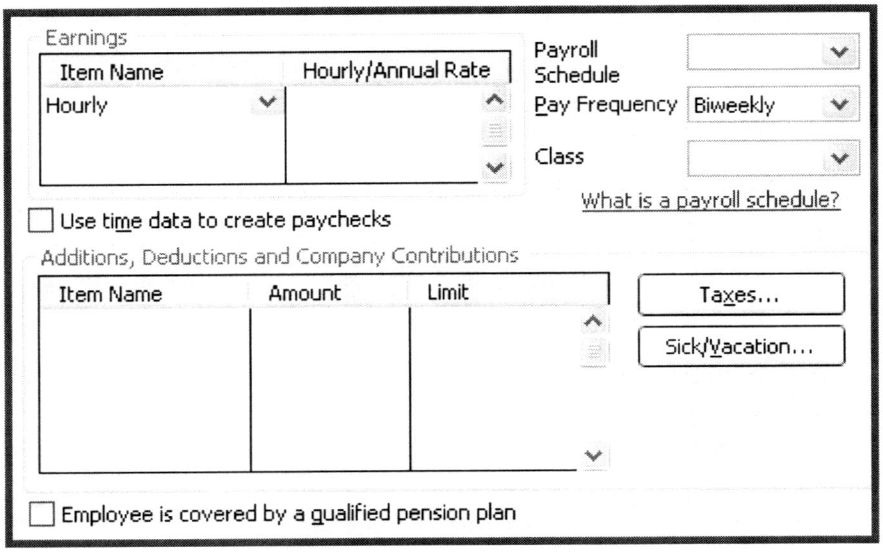

Overtime & Sick Hourly

Our next preference is Overtime and since this is for an hourly employee, we accept Hourly Wages. And in the next window for the question, "Is this item for regular, overtime, sick or vacation pay?" We will click Overtime Pay and after the Overtime, item we set up Sick Pay. Since the item is for an hourly employee, we accept Hourly Wages and in the next window for the question, "Is this item for regular, overtime, sick or vacation pay?" We click Sick Pay

Activities:

- ❖ In Earnings box
- ❖ Click under **Hourly**
- ❖ Click **Add New**
- ❖ Click **Hourly Wages**. Click **Next**
- ❖ Click **Overtime Pay**. Click **Next**
- ❖ Enter Name: Type **Overtime Hourly**. Click. **Next**

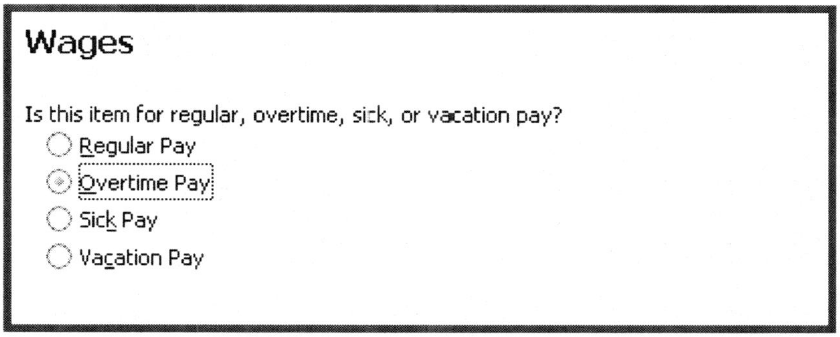

- Click **Time-and-a-half**. Click **Next**
- Enter account: Accept **Payroll Expense**
- Click **Finish**
- Click under **Overtime Hourly**
- Click **Add New**
- Accept **Hourly Wages.** Click **Next**
- Click **Sick Pay.** Click **Next**
- Enter Name: Type **Sick Hourly**. Click **Next**
- Enter account: Accept **Payroll Expense**
- Click **Finish**

Vacation Hourly

Our next preference is setting up the Vacation Pay, and since this is for an hourly employee, we accept Hourly Wages. In the next window for the question, "Is this item for regular, overtime, sick or vacation pay?" We click Vacation Pay. After Vacation Pay, we set up the Annual Salary. Since the item is for a salaried employee, we will accept Annual Salary, and in the next window for the question, "Is this item for regular, overtime, sick or vacation pay?" We click Regular Pay.

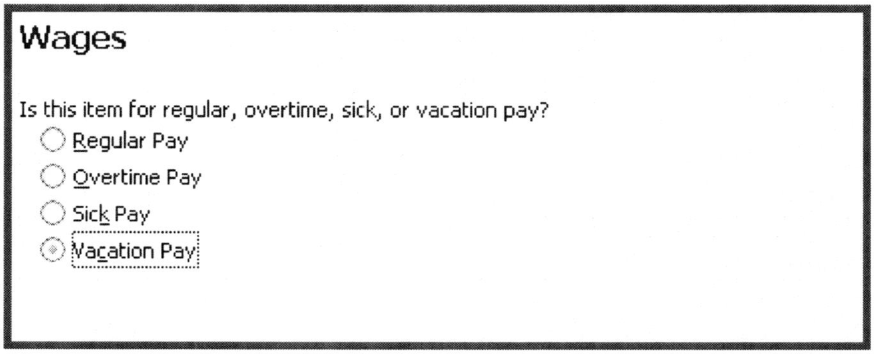

Activities:

- Click under **Sick Hourly**
- Click **Add New**
- Click **Hourly Wages**. Click **Next**
- Click **Vacation Pay**. Click **Next**
- Enter Name: Type **Vacation Hourly**. Click. **Next**
- Enter account: Accept **Payroll Expense**
- Click **Finish**

Salary

After the Vacation Hourly, we will set up Salary and since this is for a salaried employee, we select Regular Pay and then type Salary. After the Salary, we set up the Sick Salary. We start first by clicking Annual Salary; followed by Sick Pay, then thee actual name is Sick Salary. After Sick Salary, we set up Vacation Salary, but starts with Annual Salary followed by Sick Pay and the actual name Vacation Salary. You always Payroll as the expense account.

Activities:

- Click under **Vacation Hourly**
- Click **Add New**
- Click **Annual Salary.** Click **Next**
- Click **Regular Pay**. Click **Next**
- Enter Name: Type **Salary**. Click **Next**
- Enter account: Accept **Payroll Expense**
- Click **Finish**
- Click under **Salary**
- Click **Add New**
- Accept **Annual Salary**. Click **Next**
- Click **Sick Pay**. Click **Next**
- Enter Name: Type **Sick Salary.** Click. **Next**
- Enter account: Accept **Payroll Expense**
- Click **Finish**
- Click under **Sick Salary**
- Click **Add New**
- Accept **Annual Salary**. Click **Next**
- Click **Vacation Pay**. Click **Next**
- Enter Name: Type **Vacation Salary**. Click **Next**
- Enter account: Accept **Payroll Expense**
- Click **Finish**

Commission & Bonus

After the Vacation Salary, we will set up Commission for both an hourly wage earner and a salary employee. For this reason, in the first window we will click Commission. In the next window there is no question for, "Is this item for regular, overtime, sick or vacation pay?" Rather, we are taken to the name window, which is also Commission. In the account window we accept the defaulted account name, which is Payroll Expense. The percentage of the commission we will use is 5%

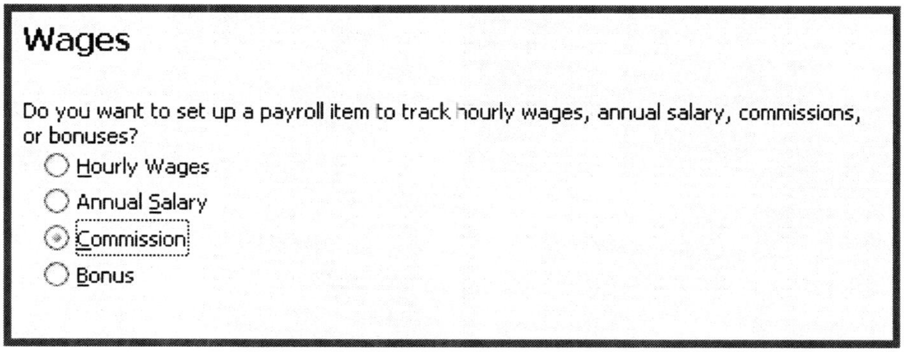

Activities:

- Click under **Vacation Salary**
- Click **Add New**
- Click **Commission.** Click **Next**
- Enter Name: Type **Commission.** Click **Next**
- Enter account: Accept **Payroll Expense.** Click **Next**
- Default %: Type **10% (must type %)**. Press **Tab**
- Click **Finish**
- Click under **Commission**
- Click **Add New**
- Click **Bonus.** Click **Next**
- Enter Name: Type **Bonus**
- Click **Next**
- Enter account: Accept **Payroll Expense**
- Click **Finish**
- Pay Frequency (right of Earnings box):
- Accept **Biweekly**

Job & Mileage Reimbursement

Up until now we have been clicking under the Earnings box, from now on, we are going to be clicking under the Addition…box. Job Reimbursement is the next item we have to set up in the payroll database, and the item is an addition to both an hourly wage earner and a salary employee. For this reason, in the first window we click Additions. In the next window, we are taken to the Enter Name window, where we will create Job Reimburse and Mileage Reimbursement.

Activities:

- ❖ You're still in the Employee Default window
- ❖ In Additions, Deductions and Company Contribution box
- ❖ Click under **Item Name**
- ❖ Click **Add New**
- ❖ Click **Addition**. Click **Next**
- ❖ Enter Name: Type **Job Related Reimburse**. Click **Next**
- ❖ Enter account: Accept **Payroll Expense**. Click **Next**
- ❖ Tax Tracking: Accept **Compensation**. Click **Next**
- ❖ Taxes. Accept **Checkmarks on all**. Click **Next**

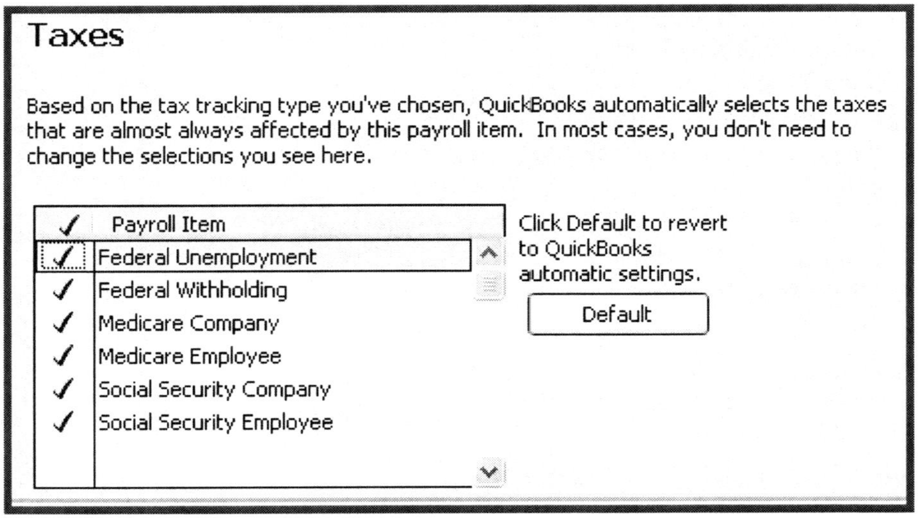

- ❖ Calculate based on qty. Click **Neither**. Click **Next**
- ❖ Default rate: **0.00**
- ❖ Default Limit: **Leave Blank**
- ❖ Click **Finish**
- ❖ Click under **Job Related Reimburse**

- Click **Add New**
- Click **Addition**. Click **Next**
- Enter Name: Type **Mileage Reimbursement.** Click **Next**
- Expense account: Select **Payroll Expense.** Click **Next**
- Tax Tracking: Select **None**. Click **Next**
- Taxes. **Leave Blank.** Click **Next**

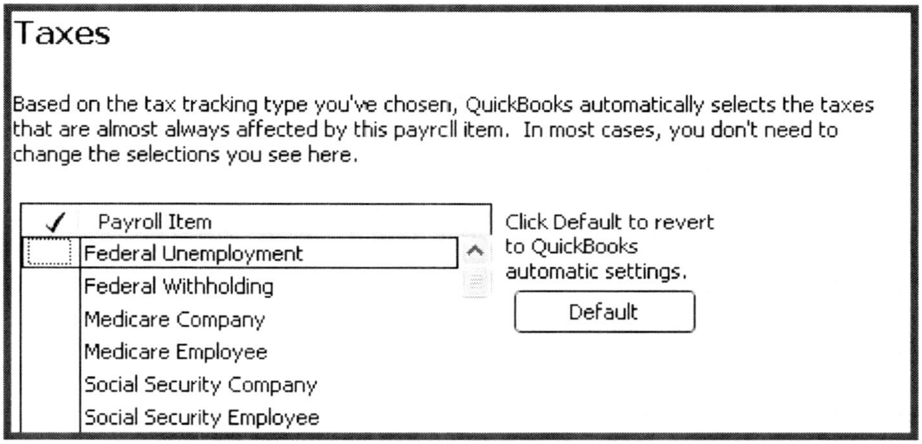

- Calculate based on qty: Click **Neither**. Click **Next**
- Gross vs. net: Click **net pay.** Click **Next**
- Default rate: **0.00**.
- Default Limit: **Leave Blank**
- Click **Finish**

Insurance

After the Mileage Reimbursement, our next payroll item is Health Insurance. This item is a deduction from both an Hourly Wage Earner and a Salary Employee. For this reason we click Deduction in the first window. Then, we are taken to the "Enter name for deduction" window, and the name of the deduction is Health Insurance. The next window will ask us to enter the name of the agency, and this time we will select HMO of America because it has been set up already as a vendor.

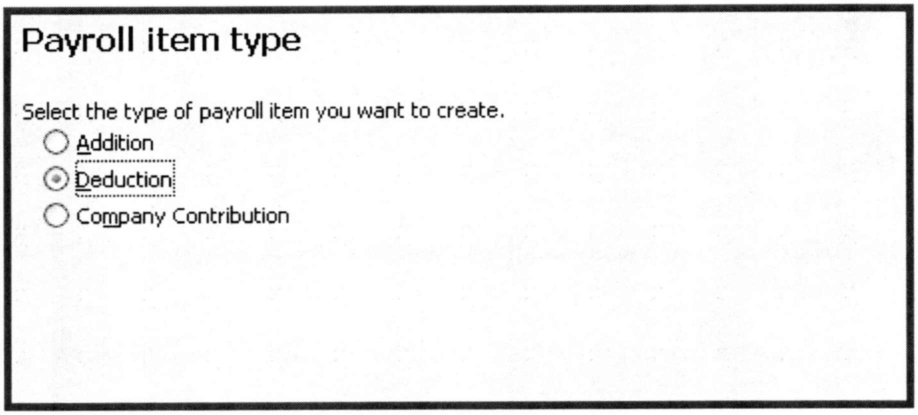

Activities:

- Click under **Mileage Reimbursement**
- Click **Add New**
- Click **Deduction**. Click **Next**
- Enter Name: Type **Health Insurance.** Click **Next**
- Enter Name of Agency: Select **HMO of America**
- Liability account: Accept **Payroll Liabilities**. Click **Next**
- Tax Tracking: Select **Premium only/125** (bottom of window). Click **Next**
- Taxes. Accept **Checkmarks on all**. Click **Next**
- Calculate based on qty. Click **Neither**. Click **Next**
- Default rate: **0.00**
- Default Limit: **Leave Blank**
- Click **Finish**
- Click **OK**
- Click under **Health Insurance**
- Click **Add New**
- Accept **Deduction**. Click **Next**
- Enter Name: Type **Dental Insurance.** Click **Next**
- Enter Name of Agency: Select **HMO of America**
- Liability account: Accept **Payroll Liabilities**. Click **Next**
- Tax Tracking: Select **Premium only/125** (bottom of window). Click **Next**
- Taxes. Accept **Checkmarks on all**. Click **Next**
- Calculate based on qty. Click **Neither**. Click **Next**
- Default rate: **0.00**
- Default Limit: **Leave Blank**
- Click **Finish**
- Click **OK**

Taxes

The next step is setting Taxes for both Federal and State. The Tax button is located at the bottom right of the window. When you click on it, you will be taken to the Federal tax tab. First you have to identify the filing status—single, married, married using single, or don't withhold. Finally, you accept all the defaults in the window except the Advanced Earned Income Credit. From the Federal window, you will be taken to the State tab, where you provide information about state work status.

Activities:

- Click **Taxes**…(right of the window)
- Click **Federal** tab
- Checkmark **Medicare**
- Checkmark **Social Security**
- Checkmark **Federal Unemployment Tax (company paid)**

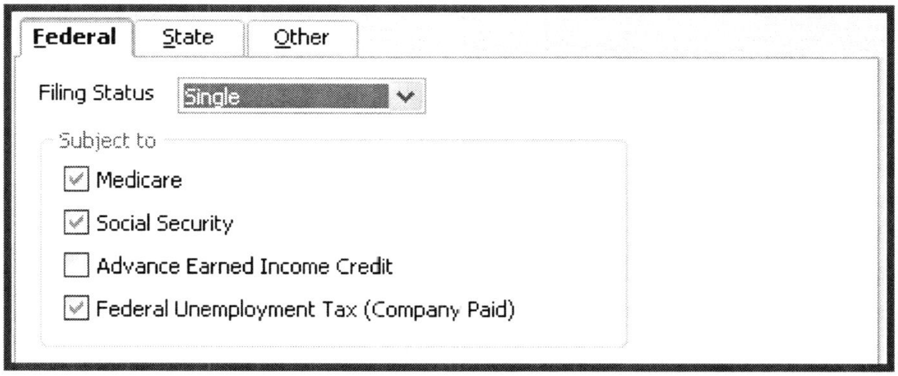

- Click **State** tab
- State worked**:** Press **T twice for TX**
- Checkmark **SUI (Company Paid)**
- State Subject to Withholding**:** Select **TX.** Press **Tab** (Very Important)
- Click **OK**
- Click **Set Up** to "TX-Unemployment…"

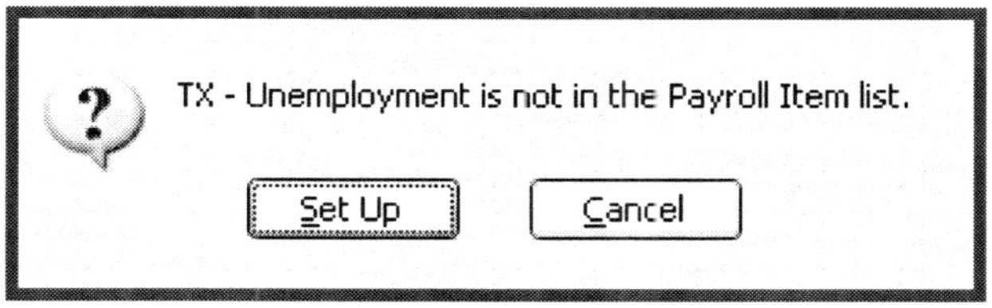

- ❖ Name: Accept **TX-Unemployment Company**. Click **Next**
- ❖ Enter Name of Agency: Select **TX-Unemployment Company**
- ❖ Liability Account: Accept **Payroll Liabilities**
- ❖ Expense Account: Accept **Payroll Expense.** Click **Next**
- ❖ Company Tax rate: Accept **2.7% for all quarters**. Click **Next**

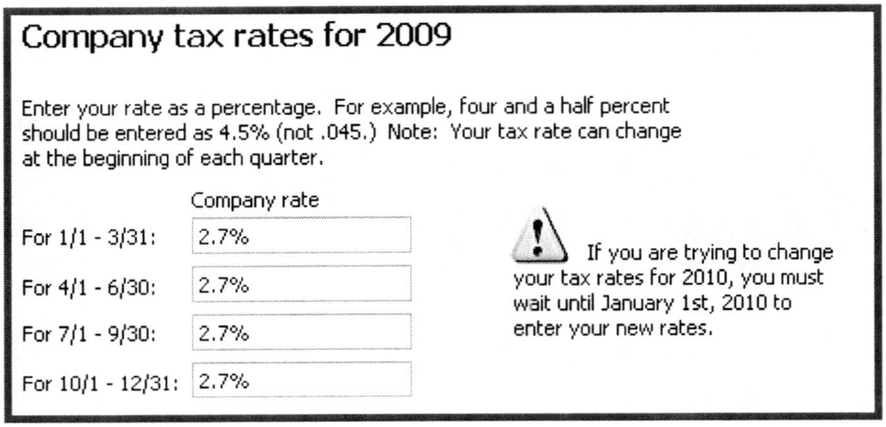

- ❖ Taxable Compensation: Accept **Checkmark on all items**. Click **Next**
- ❖ Checkmark **Dental Insurance**
- ❖ Checkmark **Health Insurance**
- ❖ Click **Finish**
- ❖ Click **OK** to "You can set up…"
- ❖ You're now in Employee Defaults window

Sick Leave

Next to Taxes is the Sick & Vacation default button. Your employees will not be 100% healthy throughout the year, so you should make room for sick time. Also, you don't expect them to work from January to December without any vacation. For this reason you should make room for vacation period. First, you have to decide when the accrual period will start. This is at the beginning of the fiscal year for most company, and for others, it starts from February or July.

Activities:

- ❖ Click **Sick/Vacation…** (right of the window)
- ❖ Sick Accrued Period: Select **Every paycheck**
- ❖ Hours accrued per paycheck: Type **4**
- ❖ Maximum number of hours: Type **104**

- ❖ Checkmark **Reset hours each New Year?**
- ❖ Vacation Accrual Period: Select **Every paycheck**
- ❖ Hours accrued per paycheck: Type **4**
- ❖ Maximum number of hours: Type **104**
- ❖ Checkmark **Reset hours each New Year**
- ❖ Click **OK** to close Sick & Vacation
- ❖ Click **OK** to close Employee Defaults window
- ❖ Click **OK** to close Preferences window

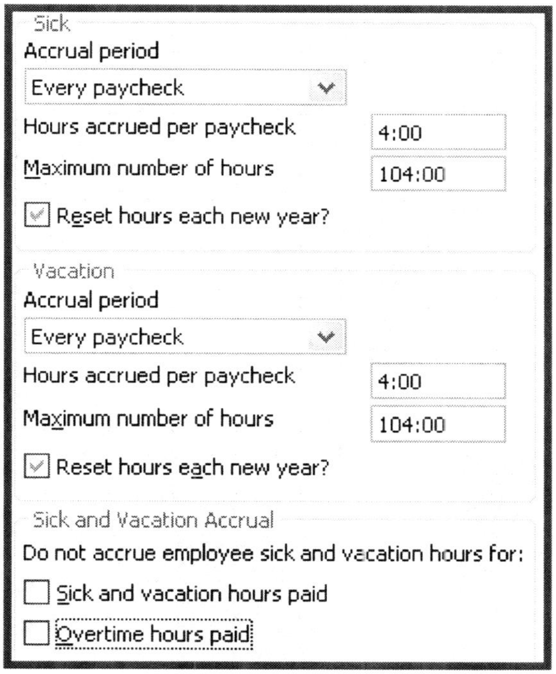

Fate's Information

Before you can pay your employees, their personal information must be loaded in the database. This basic information is used to populate most of the windows about the employees. Some of these windows are the Paycheck, Employee Contact, and Employee Taxes. You started with Fate Acres' personal information in the previous chapters, now you are going to add more information that is necessary to process Fate's Payroll checks. You document as much information as possible.

Activities:

- Click **Employees menu**
- Click **Employee Center**
- Double click **Fate Acres** in the window
- Change tabs: Select **Personal Info**
- Click **Address and Contact** tab
- Address: Type **123 Danny Lane**
- City: Type **Dallas**
- State: Type **TX**
- Zip: Type **75000**
- Phone: Type **214-123-1000**
- E-mail: Type **facres@quickcompany.com**
- Change tabs: Select **Payroll and Compensation Info**
- In Earnings box: **Delete any defaulted items**
- Select **Hourly**. Type **50** for Rate
- Select **Overtime Hourly.** Accept **75** for Rate
- Select **Commission.** Press **Tab.** Click Rate. Accept **10%**
- Select **Bonus.** Type **0.00**
- Checkmark **Use time data to create paychecks.** (Very Important)
- In Addition…box. **Delete any defaulted items**
- Select **Health Insurance.** Type **-20** for Amount. Type **-520** for Limit
- Select **Dental Insurance.** Type **-10** for Amount. **Type -260** for Limit
- Pay Frequency (right of Earnings box): Accept **Biweekly**

The 520 is 20 multiply by 26 paydays and 260 is 10 multiply by 26 paydays.

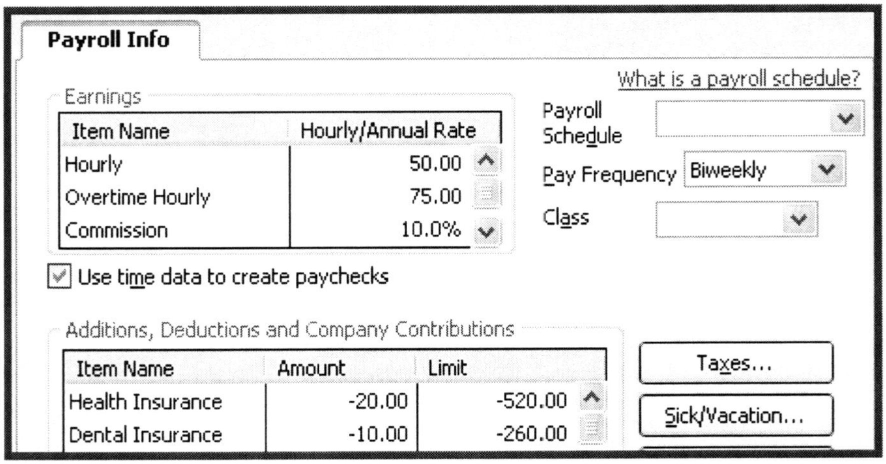

Fate's Taxes, Sick & Vacation

After an employee's personal information are loaded, your next step is to load the tax and tax-related data. In this window, you will be providing the Federal Tax information such as the Marital Status, Family Allowance—that is the number of persons in your household; you want to declare for tax purposes. You also have the option of selecting Medicare, Social Security, Advance Earned Income Credit, and the Federal Unemployment Tax and finally the state tax information.

Activities:

- Click **Taxes**… (right of Additions box)
- Click **Federal** tab
- Filing Status: Select **Married**
- Allowances: Type **2**

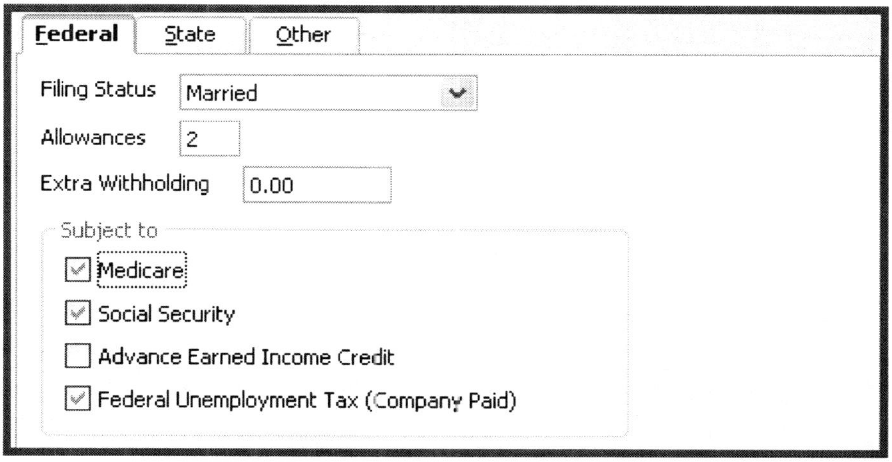

- Extra Withholding: Accept **0.00**
- Checkmark **Medicare**
- Checkmark **Social Security**
- Checkmark **Federal Unemployment tax**.
- Click **State** tab
- State Worked: Select **TX**
- Checkmark **SUI (Company Paid)**
- State Subject to Withholding: Select **TX**. Press **Tab**. Click **OK**
- Click **Sick/Vacation**…(right of window)
- In Sick box. Accrual period: Select **Every paycheck**
- Hours accrued per paycheck: Type **4**

- Maximum number of hours: Type **104**
- Checkmark **Reset hours each new year?**
- Begin accruing sick time on : Type **1/1/09**
- In Vacation box. Accrued period: Accept **Every paycheck**
- Hours accrued per paycheck: Type **4**
- Maximum number of hours: Type **104**
- Checkmark **Reset hours each new year?**
- Begin accruing vacation time on: Type **1/1/09**
- Click **OK**
- Click **OK** again to close Edit Employee window

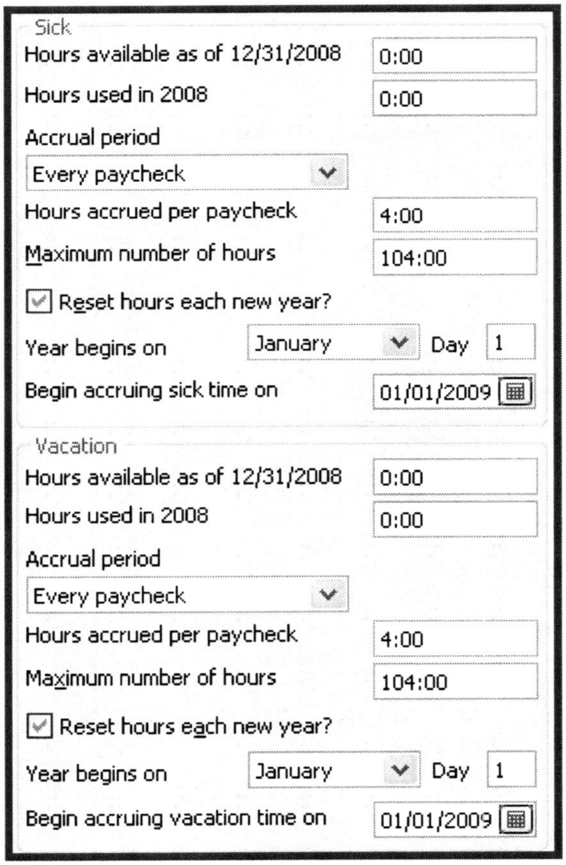

Jerry's Information

Up to this point we have been talking about an Hourly Employee—Fate Acres. We are now going to see a salary employee and learn what information QuickBooks needs to process an accurate payroll forms. Like an hourly employee, you will furnish the employee's address, phone, and e-mail address. In the Additional Info tab, you will provide the employee's number, if any. Documenting an employee without these personal data is a prerequisite to disaster when a paycheck is processed.

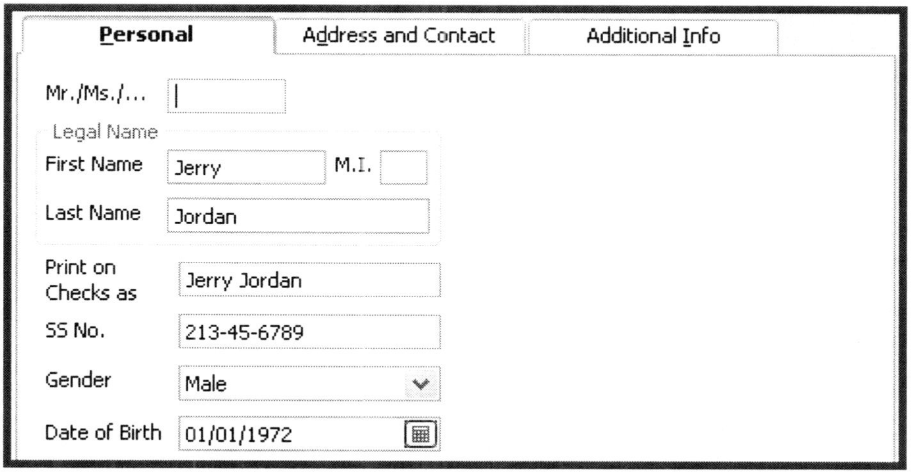

Activities:

- Right click in the Employee Center window
- Click **New Employee**
- Change tabs**:** Accept **Personal Info**
- First Name: Type **Jerry**
- Last Name: Type **Jordan**
- SS No. Type **213-45-6789**
- Gender: Select **Male**
- Date of Birth: Type **1/1/1972**
- Click **Address and Contact** tab
- Address: Type **456 Kenton St.**
- City: Type **Dallas**
- State: Type **TX**.
- Zip: Type **75000**
- Phone: Type **214-111-1000**
- E-mail: Type **jjordan@quickcompany.com**

- Change tabs: Select **Payroll and Compensation Info**
- In the Earning box: **Delete any defaulted items**
- Select **Salary.** Type **100,000** for Rate
- Select **Commission**. Press **Tab**. Accept **10%** for Rate
- Select **Bonus.** Type **0.00** for Rate
- Checkmark **Use time data to create paychecks.** (Very Important)
- In the Additions, Deductions…: **Delete any defaulted items**
- Select **Health Insurance**. Type **-20**. for Amount. Type **-520** for Limit
- Select **Dental Insurance.** Type **-10**. for Amount. Type **-260** for Limit
- Pay Frequency (right of Earnings box): Accept **Biweekly**

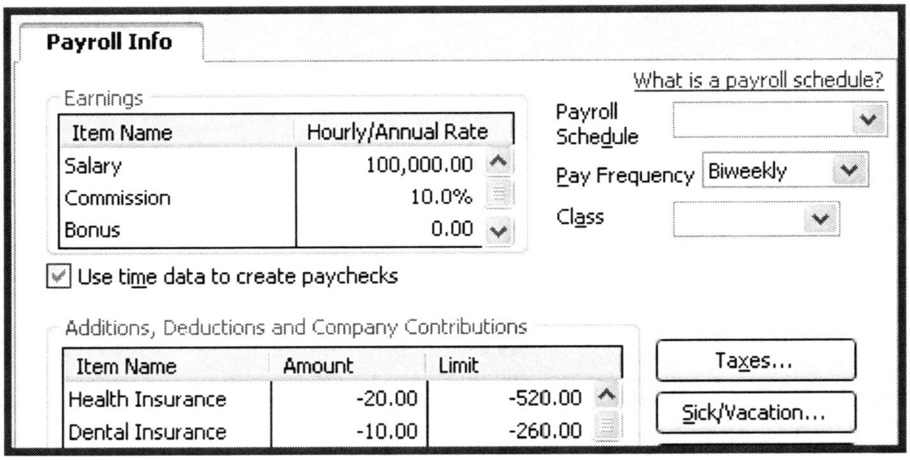

Jerry's Taxes, Sick & Vacation

Our salary employee is Jerry Jordan, and for federal tax purposes, his Filing Status will be disclosed. In this case he is married with a child, therefore, his allowance is three—that is the number of persons in his household he wants to claim for income tax purposes. You will select Medicare, Social Security, and Federal Unemployment options for him. When you click the State tab, you will supply his State tax basic information. Tax data must be double checked for accuracy.

Activities:

- Click **Taxes**… (right of Additions)
- Click **Federal** tab
- Filing Status: Select **Married**
- Allowances: Type **3**

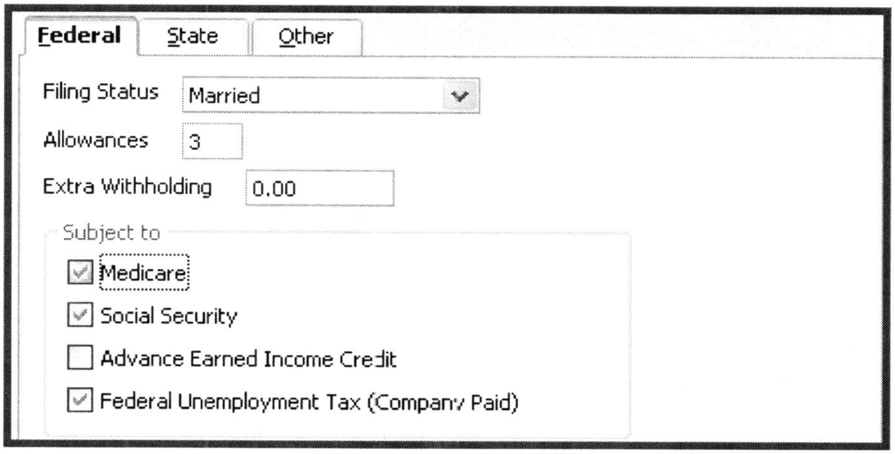

- Extra Withholding: Accept **0.00**
- Checkmark **Medicare**
- Checkmark **Social Security**
- Checkmark **Federal Unemployment tax**
- Click **State** tab. State Worked: Accept **TX**
- Checkmark **Click SUI (Company Paid)**
- State Subject to Withholding: Accept **TX**. Click **OK**
- Click **Sick/Vacation**…(right of window)
- In Sick box. Accrual period: Accept **Every paycheck**
- Hours accrued per paycheck: Accept **4**
- Maximum number of hours: Type **104**
- Checkmark **Reset hours each new year?**
- Begin accruing sick time on : Type **1/1/09** (Very Important)
- In Vacation box. Accrued period: Select **Every paycheck**
- Hours accrued per paycheck: Type **4**
- Maximum number of hours: Type **104**
- Checkmark **Reset hours each new year?**
- Begin accruing vacation time on: Type **1/1/09**. (Very important) Click **OK**
- Click **OK** to close New Employee window
- Click **Leave As Is**

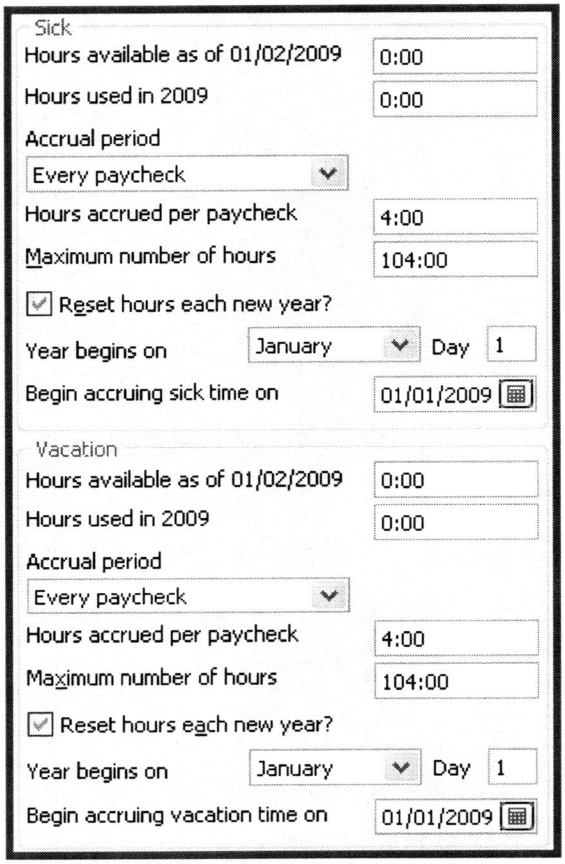

Time Tracking

It is not possible to pay an hourly employee without a Timecard or a Timesheet. A Timesheet is not applicable to a salary officer, unless it's used for other purposes. You will need to click the Set Date button to identify the date range of your timesheet—from Monday to Sunday. You then need to type the number of hours for one day at a time. If you have previously completed a Timesheet, you can click the Copy Last Sheet button that allows you copy the previous Timesheet to a new sheet.

Activities:

- Click **Employee menu**
- Click **Enter Time**
- Click **Use Weekly Timesheet**

- ❖ Name: Select **Fate Acres**
- ❖ Week of: Click **Date button.** Click **Arrow to January 2009**
- ❖ Click **January 5, 2009** (1st Monday For Jan 5 to Jan 11,2009
- ❖ Click **Copy Last Sheet** (bottom left of window)
- ❖ Delete **0:33 on Friday 9**
- ❖ Total hours: Accept **40:00**
- ❖ Click **Save & Close**
- ❖ Click **Yes** to "Row without a duration will not be saved…?"
- ❖ Click **Edit menu**
- ❖ Click **Use Calculator**
- ❖ Minimize Calculator to the Taskbar

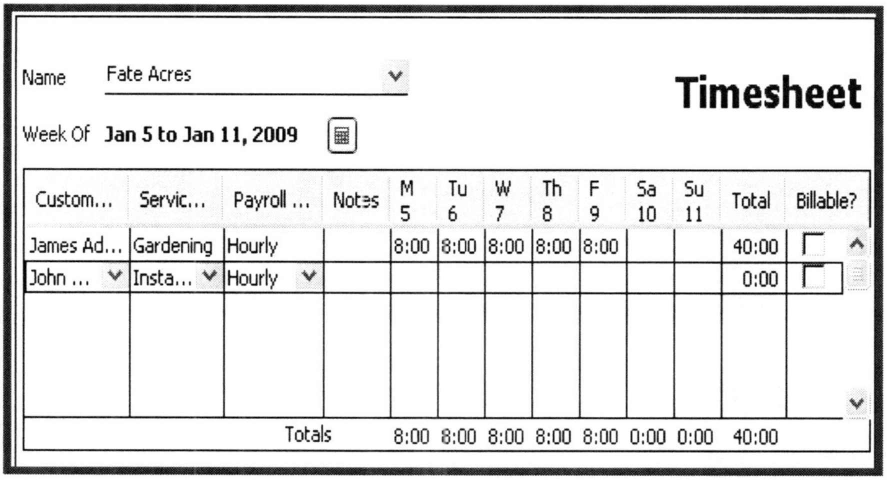

Pay Fate Acres

After you've completed the Timesheet to determine how many hours an employee has worked, the next step is to pay the employee. Click the Employees menu and Pay Employee to see the Pay window. Provide the check date, pay period and then click the Create button; you will be taken to the Preview Paycheck window. You may decide to hire a Payroll Services company. By the Pay Day, the company will send you a Summary Payroll report on each employee.

Activities:

- ❖ Click **Employees menu**
- ❖ Click **Pay Employees**
- ❖ Click **No** to "You aren't signed up…"
- ❖ Pay Period Ends: Highlight box. Type **1/11/2009**. Press **Tab**.

- Click **Yes** to “If you’re using time tracking …”
- Check Date: Highlight box. Type **1/11/2009.** Bank balance: **100,000**
- Checkmark **Fate Acres** (left of window). Accept **Hourly 80:33**
- Click **underlined Fate Acres in blue**
- In the Earnings box.
- Accept **Hourly**: Accept **50** for Rate. Accept **80** for Hours
- Select **Overtime Hourly**: Accept **75** for Rate. Type **1:04** for Hours
- Select **Commission**: Accept **10%** for Rate. Type **50,000** for Quantity

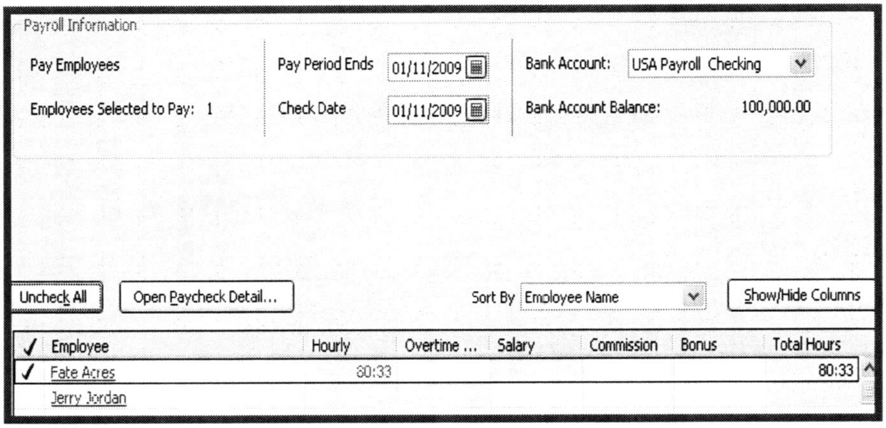

- Select **Bonus**: Type **10,000** for Rate
- In the Other Payroll Items box
- Accept **Health Insurance**: Type **-20**
- Accept **Dental Insurance**: Type **-10**
- In the Company Summary box
- Social Security: Type **1,181.10**
- Medicare: Type **276.23**
- Federal Unemployment: Type **56.00**
- TX – Unemployment: Type **243.00**
- In the Employee Summary box. Add the following:
- Federal Withholding: Type **5,380.00**
- Social Security: Type **1,181.10**
- Medicare: Type **276.23**
- **Look! Check Amount (right of window) is $12,212.67**
- **Company Summary total is 1,756.33. Maximize Calculator and confirm!**
- Click **Save & Close** on Preview Paycheck window
- Click **Continue** (bottom right). Click **Create Paychecks**
- Click **Close** to Confirmation window

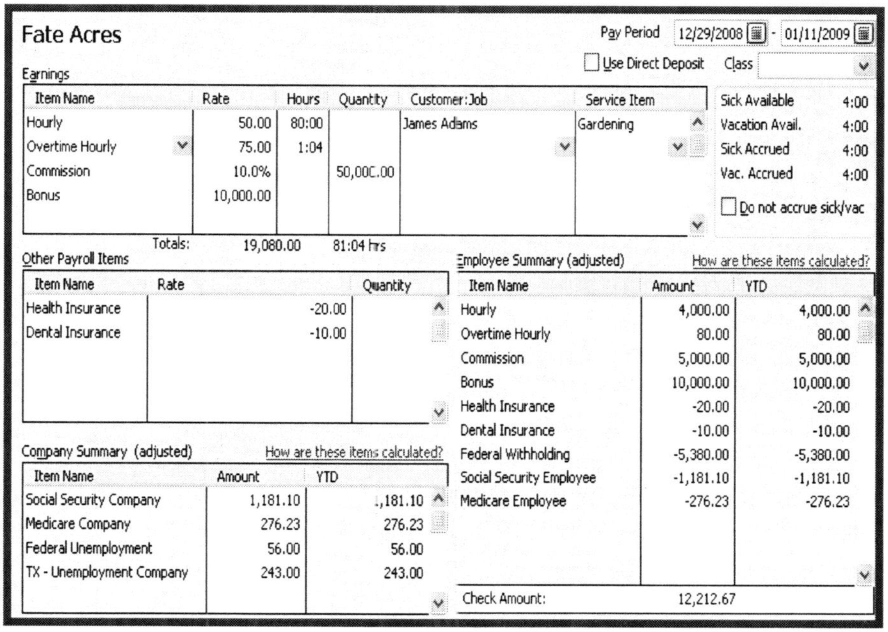

Pay Jerry Jordan

To pay an hourly employee, you must prepare a Timesheet. However, with a salaried employee, it very easy and you don't need a Timesheet. All you do is click the Pay Employees submenu under the Employees menu and the salaried employee's name is populated in the window. You will need to click Jerry Jordan in the window and proceed to complete the rest of the window as instructed below. Be sure to select the Payroll account from which Jerry's check is paid from.

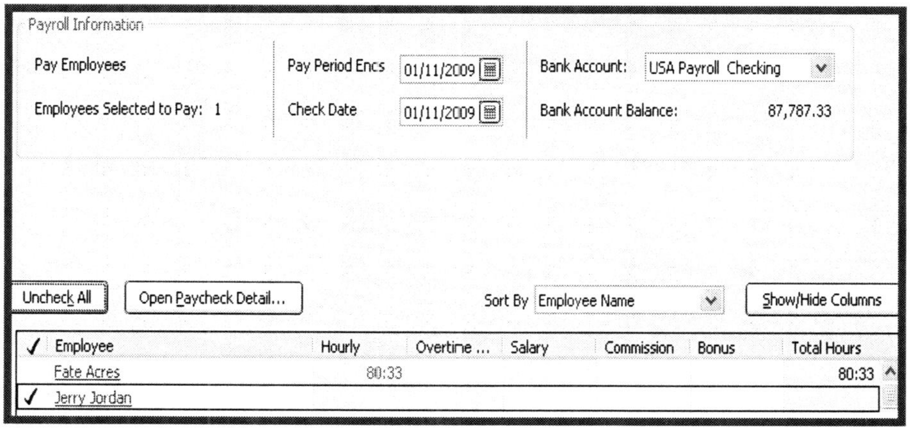

Activities:

- Click **Employees menu**
- Click **Pay Employees**
- Pay Period Ends: Highlight box. Type **1/11/2009**. Press **Tab**
- Click **Yes** to "If you're using time tracking..." Bank Balance **87,787.33**
- Check Date: Highlight box. Type **1/11/2009**.
- Checkmark **Jerry Jordan** (left of window)
- Click **underlined Jerry Jordan**
- In the Earnings box.
- Select **Salary:** Accept **3,846.15** for Rate. Type **80** for Hours
- Select **Commission:** Accept **10%** for Rate. **100,000** for Quantity
- Select **Bonus**: Type **20,000** for Rate
- In the Other Payroll Items box
- Select **Health Insurance:** Accept **-20**
- Select **Dental Insurance**: Accept **-10**
- In the Company Summary (adjusted) box
- Social Security: Type **2,096.60**
- Medicare: Type **490.33**
- Federal Unemployment: Type **56.00**
- TX Unemployment: Type **243.00**
- In the Employee Summary (adjusted). Add the following:
- Federal Withholding: Type **10,501.00**
- Social Security: Type **2,096.60**
- Medicare: Type **490.33**
- **Look! Check Amount (right of window) is $20,728.22**
- **Company Summary total is 2,885.93. Maximize Calculator and confirm!**
- Click **Save & Close** on Preview Paycheck window
- Click **Continue** (bottom right). Click **Create Paychecks**
- Click **Close** to Confirmation window

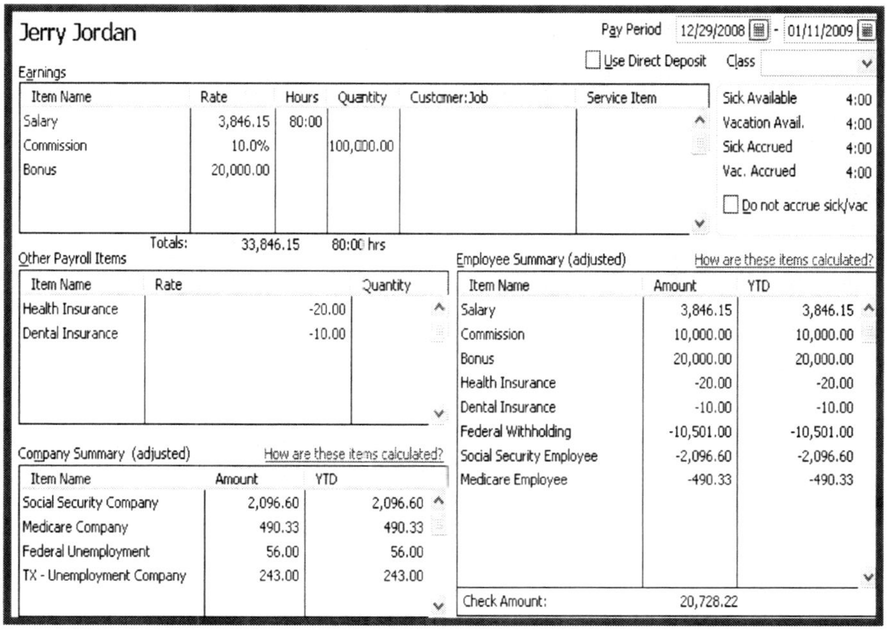

Print Pay Stubs

Previously, you paid an hourly employee, the next step is to print the pay stub and forward a copy of the pay stub and the check to the employee by mail or by hand. QuickBooks gives you the option to print one check or a batch of checks at one time. Make sure you double check that the check amount matches the pay stub amount. You might you the total method, that is adding all the amounts on a pay stub batch and the amounts on a pay check batch and two must match.

Activities:

- Click **Employees menu**
- Click **Employee Center**
- Click **Fate Acres** (left of window)
- Click **Print down arrow** (top of window)
- Click **Print/Email Paystubs**
- Bank Account: Select **USA Payroll Checking**
- Date: Type **12/29/08** Thru **1/11/09**
- Show (bottom left): Click **Both**
- Click **Select All** (right of window)
- Click **Preview**
- Click **Zoom In on Fate's Pay Stub**

- ❖ Click **Next page to Jerry's Pay Stub**
- ❖ Click **Close** or **Print** if Printer is ready.
- ❖ Click **X** to close Select Pay Stubs window

Fate's Pay Stubs

Quick Company 2009
123 Adam Lane
Dallas, TX 75000

Fate Acres
123 Danny Lane
Dallas, TX 75000

Employee Pay Stub   Check number: Pay Period: 12/29/2008 - 01/11/2009   Pay Date: 01/11/2009

Employee	SSN	Status (Fed/State)	Allowances/Extra
Fate Acres, 123 Danny Lane, Dallas, TX 75000	***-**-6789	Married/(none)	Fed-2/0/TX-0/0

Earnings and Hours	Qty	Rate	Current	YTD Amount
Hourly	80:00	50.00	4,000.00	4,000.00
Overtime Hourly	1:04	75.00	80.00	80.00
Commission	50,000.00	10.00%	5,000.00	5,000.00
Bonus		10,000.00	10,000.00	10,000.00
			19,080.00	19,080.00

Paid Time Off	YTD Used	Available
Sick	0:00	4:00
Vacation	0:00	4:00

Deductions From Gross	Current	YTD Amount
Health Insurance	-20.00	-20.00
Dental Insurance	-10.00	-10.00
	-30.00	-30.00

Taxes	Current	YTD Amount
Federal Withholding	-5,380.00	-5,380.00
Social Security Employee	-1,181.10	-1,181.10
Medicare Employee	-276.23	-276.23
	-6,837.33	-6,837.33

Net Pay	12,212.67	12,212.67

Jerry's Pay Stubs

Quick Company 2009
123 Adam Lane
Dallas, TX 75000

Jerry Jordan
456 Kenton St
Dallas, TX 75000

Employee Pay Stub   Check number: Pay Period: 12/29/2008 - 01/11/2009   Pay Date: 01/11/2009

Employee	SSN	Status (Fed/State)	Allowances/Extra
Jerry Jordan, 456 Kenton St, Dallas, TX 75000	***-**-6789	Married/(none)	Fed-3/0/TX-0/0

Earnings and Hours	Qty	Rate	Current	YTD Amount
Salary	80:00		3,846.15	3,846.15
Commission	100,000...	10.00%	10,000.00	10,000.00
Bonus		20,000.00	20,000.00	20,000.00
			33,846.15	33,846.15

Deductions From Gross	Current	YTD Amount
Health Insurance	-20.00	-20.00
Dental Insurance	-10.00	-10.00
	-30.00	-30.00

Taxes	Current	YTD Amount
Federal Withholding	-10,501.00	-10,501.00
Social Security Employee	-2,098.60	-2,098.60
Medicare Employee	-490.33	-490.33
	-13,087.93	-13,087.93

	Current	YTD Amount
Net Pay	20,728.22	20,728.22

Paid Time Off	YTD Used	Available
Sick	0:00	4:00
Vacation	0:00	4:00

Manage Payroll Items

Managing Payroll Items is all about viewing, adding, removing, and editing the payroll items. There are several ways of opening the window. One way is to click the Employees menu, Manage Payroll Items, and View/Edit Payroll Items List. Another option is to click the Lists menu, and then the Payroll Item List. You edit the payroll items to add vendor name to all deductions—federal and state items. The "Payable To" column for these items must show the vendor name.

Activities:

- Click **Employees menu**
- Click **Manage Payroll Items**
- Click **View/Edit Payroll Item List**
- Double click **Federal Unemployment**
- Enter name…: Accept **Federal Unemployment.** Click **Next**
- Enter name of agency: Select **US Treasury**
- **Continue to click Next to Pre-tax deduction** window
- Click **Finish**
- Double click **Federal Withholding**
- Enter name…: Accept **Federal Withholding.** Click **Next**
- Enter name of agency: Select **US Treasury**
- **Continue to click Next till you see Pre-tax deduction** window
- Click **Finish**
- The rest of **Payable To** are completed with US Treasury
- Click **X** to close Payroll Item List window

Advance Earned …	Federal Tax			Advance EIC Pa…	US Treasury	99-9999999
Federal Unemplo…	Federal Tax	0.8%	7,000.00	FUTA	US Treasury	99-9999999
Federal Withholding	Federal Tax			Federal	US Treasury	99-9999999
Medicare Company	Federal Tax	1.45%		Comp. Medicare	US Treasury	99-9999999
Medicare Employee	Federal Tax	1.45%		Medicare	US Treasury	99-9999999
Social Security C…	Federal Tax	6.2%	102,000.00	Comp. SS Tax	US Treasury	99-9999999
Social Security E…	Federal Tax	6.2%	-102,000.00	SS Tax	US Treasury	99-9999999
TX - Unemployme…	State Une…	2.7%	9,000.00	Comp. SUI	TX-Unemployme…	

Pay Payroll Liabilities

Every time you pay employees, automatically payroll liabilities are generated. You are going through these processes to understand the steps involve in payroll liabilities processing, and also to realize how easy the actual work is after you have completed the payroll set up. Again, you open the Payroll Liabilities window, and select the liabilities you want to pay; making sure the figure in "Amount to Pay" column has everyone you want to pay.

Activities:

- Click **Employees menu**
- Click **Payroll Taxes and Liabilities**
- Click **Pay Payroll Liabilities**
- Dates: From: Type **12/29/08.** Through: Type **1/11/09.** Click **OK**
- Checkmark **To be printed**

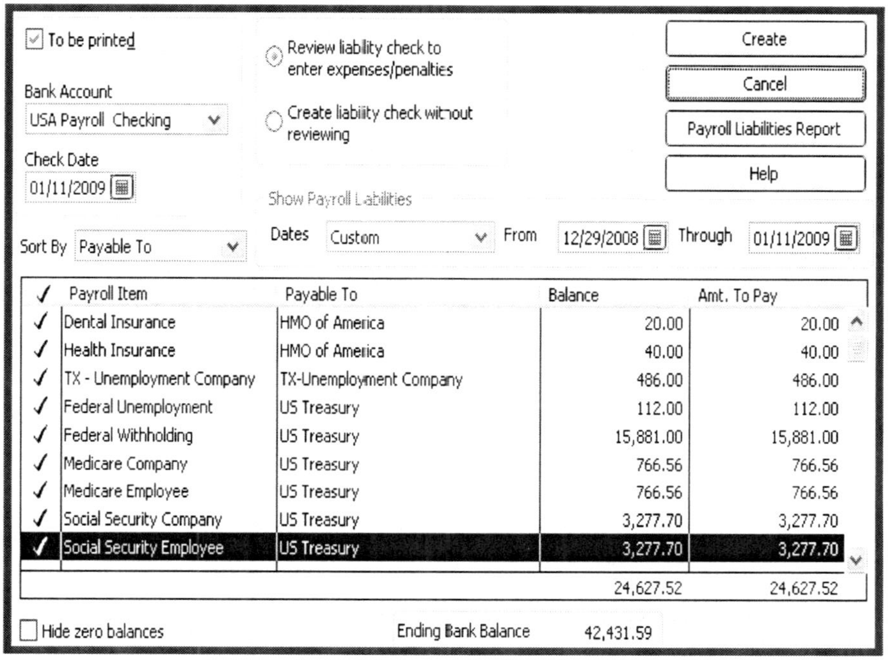

- Click **Review liability check to enter…**
- Bank Account: Accept **USA Payroll Checking**
- Check Date: Type **1/11/09** .
- Show Liabilities. Dates: From: Accept **12/29/08**. Thru: Type **1/11/09**.
- **Checkmark all liabilities with numbers**
- Total Balance: Accept **24,627.52**
- Total Amt. To Pay: Accept **24,627.52**
- Ending Bank Balance: Accept **42,431.59**
- Click **Create** (top right of window)
- Click **Save & Close** on the check window

Financial Results: Profit & Loss

If you have employees, whether you choose to run your payroll in-house or contract with an outside vendor, you would see the effects of payroll activities on your Profit & Loss statements. In this chapter, we prepared Timesheet and paid employees. We also processed checks for vendors. These payments reduced the payroll account and brought the Gross Profit to $2,100,141.34 and Net Income is $2,033,697.26.

Quick Company 2009
Profit & Loss
January through December 2009

	Jan - Dec 09
Ordinary Income/Expense	
Income	
Opening Balance Income	1,914,500.00
Landscaping Services	394,811.34
Total Income	2,309,311.34
Cost of Goods Sold	
Materials	213,700.00
Discount Received	-4,530.00
Total COGS	209,170.00
Gross Profit	2,100,141.34
Expense	
Adjustment to Decr Inventory	1,250.00
Opening Balance Expense	6,500.00
Depreciation Expense	666.67
Payroll Expenses	57,568.41
Telephone Expense	459.00
Total Expense	66,444.08
Net Ordinary Income	2,033,697.26
Net Income	**2,033,697.26**

Activities:

- Click **Reports menu**
- Click **Company & Financial**
- Click **Profit & Loss Standard**
- Date: Select **This Fiscal Year**
- From: Accept **1/1/09.** To: Accept **12/31/09**
- Click **Collapse**
- **Net Income is 2,033,697.26**
- Click **X** to close window

Financial Results: Balance Sheet

As you issue the payroll checks from the Payroll Checking account, the Balance Sheet statement is affected. If you paid employees and the Payroll Checking is still the same, that's a red flag you have issued payroll checks from the wrong account. If the checks are available, zero them out and re-issue checks from the right account, otherwise, you will need a journal entry to move money to the payroll account. Payroll Checking balance is $42,431.59 and Total Assets is now $3,550,197.26.

Activities:

- Click **Reports menu**
- Click **Company & Financial**
- Click **Balance Sheet Standard**
- Date: Select **This Fiscal Year**
- As of: Accept **12/31/09**
- Click **Collapse**
- **Total Assets is 3,550,197.26**
- Click **X** to close window

Quick Company 2009

Balance Sheet

As of December 31, 2009

	Dec 31, 09
ASSETS	
Current Assets	
Checking/Savings	
Money Market Account	100,000.00
USA Checking	724,545.38
USA Payroll Checking	42,431.59
USA Savings	250,000.00
Total Checking/Savings	1,116,976.97
Accounts Receivable	
Accounts Receivable	1,024,839.56
Total Accounts Receivable	1,024,839.56
Other Current Assets	
Inventory Asset	235,050.00
Undeposited Funds	1,133,997.40
Total Other Current Assets	1,369,047.40
Total Current Assets	3,510,863.93
Fixed Assets	
Truck	39,333.33
Total Fixed Assets	39,333.33
TOTAL ASSETS	**3,550,197.26**

Chapter Summary

We presented the basic Payroll processing windows. You will see more windows if you sign up with QuickPayroll software. The chapter takes you through the setup windows you will encounter, and the only step left to process the paychecks. Once you understand the basic foundation, completing the remaining steps is a breeze. Also, if you decide to sign up for a Payroll Service company, you learned how to take the service company's report and load them into QuickBooks.

What we accomplished:

- Reviewed Employees submenus
- Reviewed employee center contents
- Activated free trial payroll subscription
- Completed the payroll & employees Preferences setup
- Created an employee timesheet
- Created employees payroll checks
- Processed employees pay stubs
- Managed payroll items
- Pay payroll liabilities
- Processed financial statements

Financial activities:

- Payroll Payment to Fate 12,212.67
- Payroll Payment to Jerry 20,728.22
- Payroll Payment to HMO 60.00
- Payroll Payment to TX-Unemployment 486.00
- Payroll Payment to US Treasury 24,081.52

Exercise 8

This exercise will show you how to record payroll transactions if you are using a payroll processing company. At the end of every pay period, the company will send you the files to pay employees and vendors and record the payroll transactions in your books. Complete Exercise 8 by using the following information:

1. In the vendor center window create new employees
   Kate Anderson, opening balance 0.00 date 1/2/09
   John Safeway, opening balance 0.00 date 1/2/09

2. In the <u>vendor enter bill</u> window create checks for these employees and vendors
   Kate Anderson. Date 1/2/09. Amount 12,212.67. Expense a/c Gross Wages
   John Safeway. Date 1/2/09. Amount 20,728.22. Expense a/c Gross Wages

   US Treasury. Date 1/2/09. Amount 23,969.52. Expense a/c Payroll Taxes
   US Treasury. Date 1/2/09. Amount 112.00. Expense a/c FUTA Fed Unemp
   TX-Unemployment. Date 1/2/09. Amount 486. Expense a/c SUTA State Unemp
   HMO of America. Date 1/2/09. Amount 60.00. Expense a/c Health Premium

3. In the <u>vendor pay bills</u> window pay these bills from <u>payroll checking a/c</u>
   Kate Anderson 12,212.67 date 1/5/09
   John Safeway 20,728.22 date 1/5/09
   US Treasury 23,969.52 date 1/5/09
   US Treasury 112.00 date 1/5/09
   TX-Unemployment date 1/5/09
   HMO of America date 1/5/09

4. Process the following reports
   Profit & Loss Statement ending 12/31/09
   Balance Sheet Standard ending 12/31/09
   Statement of Cash Flow ending 12/31/09
   Transaction List by Vendor 1/31/09
   Account Listing 1/31/09
   Trial Balance 1/31/09

$

Chapter 9

Banking Menu

Objectives: After you've completed this chapter, you will be able to:

- ✓ Explain Banking submenus
- ✓ Write checks
- ✓ Record credit card charges
- ✓ Process single checks
- ✓ Process batch checks
- ✓ Use the Go To function
- ✓ Generate the register reports
- ✓ Edit the check register
- ✓ Process the register QuickReport
- ✓ Use the sort function
- ✓ Use the split entry function
- ✓ Make deposits
- ✓ Transfer funds
- ✓ Complete the loan manager process
- ✓ Analyze bank statement
- ✓ Make General Journal entries
- ✓ Reconcile the bank statements
- ✓ Process financial reports and compare results
- ✓ Explain bank reconciliation steps
- ✓ Identify bank reconciliation entries

Review Banking Submenus

As you work through this book, you will discover there are windows you have not used that are significant to you. On one occasion, I saw a client writing deposit slips by hand, when all he could have done is go to the Deposit window and click the Print down arrow located at the top of the window and click Print Deposit Slip.

- Click **Banking menu**

The following activities are found under the Banking menu:

- **Write Checks:** Before you use this window, be sure you have completed the vendor list—that is, you have listed all your vendors, because the Write Checks window will need the vendor's name on the checks. You may also add the vendor as you write the checks. It's important to identify the expense account or the item name you are writing the check for. The Write Checks window will also show you the checking account you are writing check from and the current balance. Make sure you select the right checking account and that you have enough balance to cover the amount of the check you're writing.

- **Order Checks & Envelopes:** If you plan to write a large number of checks and you plan to automate the check writing process in your QuickBooks software, it would be wise to order checks and envelopes from QuickBooks. This submenu will allow you to setup a check reorder reminder. QuickBooks will prompt you to reorder checks as soon as you reach that check number.

- **Enter Credit Card Changes:** If you are going to have volumes of credit card charges or activities, by far this is one of most significant windows you need to understand. It will be cost effective to download your credit card charges rather than manually entering the credit card charges into the account. The Credit Card Charges window will give you the name of the credit card and the current balance. Be sure to select the right credit card name.

- **Use Register:** You can write a check directly from the check register window or straight from the Write Check window as we discussed above. Using the check register is faster, because you don't have to deal with all the details as in the Write Checks window. You will need to select or type the right check number.

- **Make Deposits:** The Making Deposit window is easy is to use; the checks you collected from the customers are now listed in the Make Deposit window. In making a deposit, you are transferring the money to the Undeposited Funds account in the Chart of Account. After the deposit process is completed, the Undeposited Fund account will be zero, and the checking account where you deposited the checks will be higher.

- **Transfer Funds:** Transferring funds does not mean the funds have been moved physically to the receiving account. You must write a check, call the bank, or go online, to actually complete the process of moving the money to the right account. You can check the balances of the sending and receiving accounts before and after the process in the Chart of Accounts to make sure the results are what you intended. The sending account is decreased and the receiving account is increased.

- **Reconcile:** Every month you will use the reconcile window to balance or match the amount in your QuickBooks file with the amount in the bank. If there is any difference, you will have to make a journal entry to make QuickBooks agree with the bank account. If the bank over-paid a check this month, you will credit the checking account and debit Other Expense and call the bank refund your account with the overpayment. Next month when the bank refunds your money, you debit the checking account and credit Other Income.

- **Online Banking:** More companies are conducting businesses online, and should do the same. Check with your bank to see what is required to allow to you to pay and receive money online.

- **Loan Manager:** After you have created your loan account in the Chart of Accounts, you can come to the Loan Manger window to give complete details of the loan. The Loan Manager will allow you to add more loans, review loan summary and payment schedules. One of the best features is the "What if Scenarios," which allows you to play what will happen if your loan amount, loan percentage (term), payment amount or payment period changes.

- **Other Names List**: This window allows you create names that are not related to other windows. Names such as Transfer From Checking, Transfer To Checking, Transfer From Savings, Transfer To Savings, and ATM Withdrawal are created in this window. You can think of other names; any odd names you're not used to or you don't know will go with the Chart of Accounts or Item Lists windows.

Write Check

There are several ways of reaching the Write Check window. You can either go through the Edit menu and click the Use Register or open the Chart of Account from the Lists menu and click to open the check register. The final way is to go through the Banking menu and click the Write Check submenu. The route you choose depends on where you are and what you are doing at the time. If you are working on bank-related tasks, you may open the Write Check window from the Banking menu.

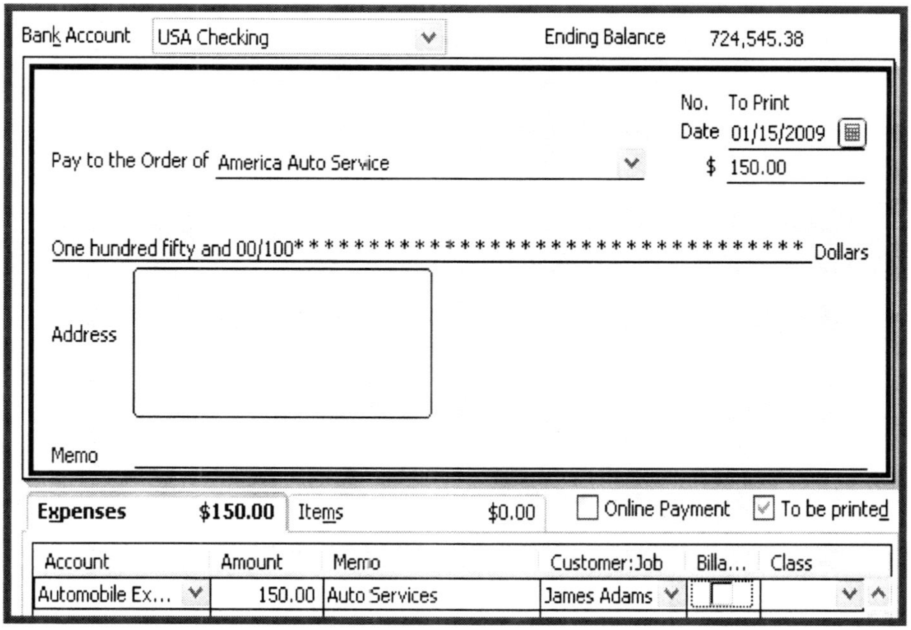

Activities:

- Click **Banking menu**
- Click **Write Checks**
- Bank Account: Accept **USA Checking**
- Ending Balance: Accept **724,545.38**
- Date: Type **1/15/09**
- Pay to the Order of: Select **American Auto Services**
- Amount: Type **150.** Press **Tab**
- Click **under Account** (left of window):
- Select **Repairs/Maint under Automobile Expense**. Press **Tab**
- Amount: Accept **150**
- Memo: Type **Auto Services**
- Customer: Job: Select **James Adams.** Uncheck **Billable**

- ❖ Checkmark **To be Printed**
- ❖ Click **Save & Close**

Enter Credit Card Charges

As we move toward a cashless society, most future purchases will be in the form of Credit Card charges. Most companies have thousands of dollars in Credit Card charges. There are two ways of entering Credit Card charges: The first is to manually enter one single charge into the Credit Card window. The second and fastest way of entering Credit Card charges—is to download the transactions online. The benefit more than offsets the cost of setting it up with the online company.

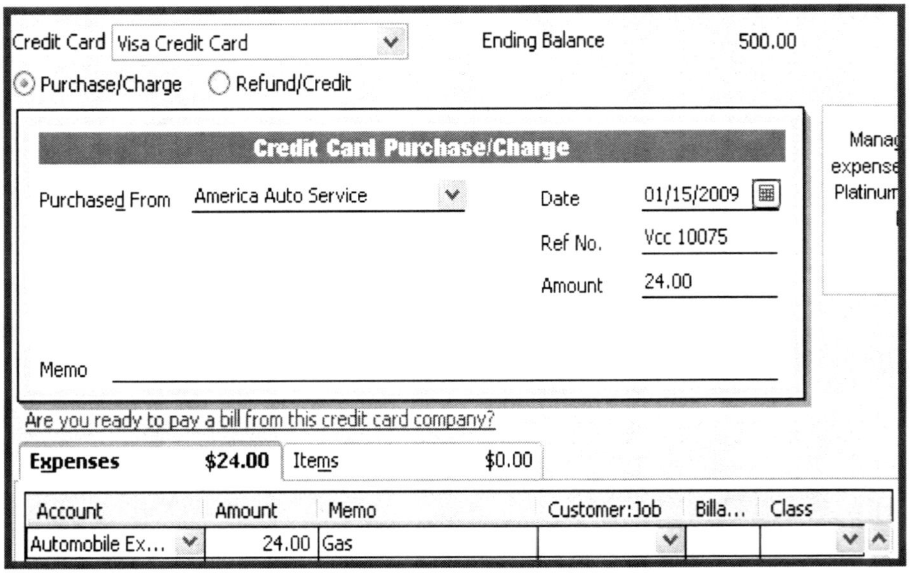

Activities:

- ❖ Click **Banking menu**
- ❖ Click **Enter Credit Card Charges**
- ❖ Credit Card: Accept **Visa Credit Card**
- ❖ Click **Purchase/Charge**
- ❖ Purchase From: Select **American Auto Services**
- ❖ Date: Accept **1/15/09**
- ❖ Ref No.: Type **Vcc 10075.** Amount: Type **24**
- ❖ Click **under Account** (left of window)
- ❖ Select **Fuel under Automobile Expenses**. Press **Tab**
- ❖ Amount: Accept **24**

- ❖ Memo: Type **Gas**
- ❖ Customer: Job: Select **James Adams**
- ❖ Click **Save & Close**

Print Single Checks

From time to time you may want to write a single check to a vendor. In that case, you have to process the single check by itself. QuickBooks has another option that allows you to write and print one single check. As always, you must make sure you are printing from the right bank account using the next check serial number. All you have to do is pull up the single check with the right date. Then you click Print from the Print drop-down window located at the top of the window.

Activities:

- ❖ Click **Banking menu**
- ❖ Click **Use Register**
- ❖ Select Account: Select **USA Checking**. Click **OK**
- ❖ Date: Type **1/15/09**
- ❖ Number: Accept **1003**
- ❖ Payee: Type **American Auto Services**
- ❖ Amount: Type **250**
- ❖ Account: Click **Repairs/Maint under Automobile Exp**
- ❖ Double click **CHK** in the Number/Type
- ❖ Bank Account: Select **USA Checking**
- ❖ Checkmark **To be printed** (right)
- ❖ Click **Print down arrow** (top left of window)
- ❖ Select **Print**…(top)
- ❖ Printed Check Number: Type **1003.** Click **OK**
- ❖ Check Style: Click **Voucher** (left of window)

Date	Number / Type	Payee / Account	Memo	Payment	✓	Deposit	Balance
01/15/2009	DEP	Undeposited Fund: Deposit				174,515.63	724,545.38
01/15/2009	To Print / CHK	America Auto Service / Automobile Expen:		150.00			724,395.38
01/15/2009	To Print / CHK	America Auto Service / Automobile Expen:		250.00			724,145.38
01/15/2009	Number	Payee / Account	Memo	Payment		Deposit	
Splits						Ending balance	724,145.38

- ❖ Click **Cancel**
- ❖ Click **Save & Close**
- ❖ Click **Yes** to "You have changed…"

Print Batch Checks

Most companies have a particular day of the month when they process all checks, except the Payroll checks that are processed twice a month. During that day of the month, all checks to vendors are written from a designated checking account. Normally, for a single check, you open the check register, preview and print one check. However, printing a batch of checks will save time when you have more than one check. Most large companies use batch system of printing checks.

Activities:

- ❖ You're still in USA Checking register window
- ❖ Double click **BILLPMT for US Supplies for $221,970.00**
- ❖ Bank Account: Select **USA Checking**
- ❖ Ending Balance: Accept **724,145.38**
- ❖ Checkmark **To be Printed** (right of window)
- ❖ Click **Print down arrow** (top left of window)
- ❖ Select **Print Batch**

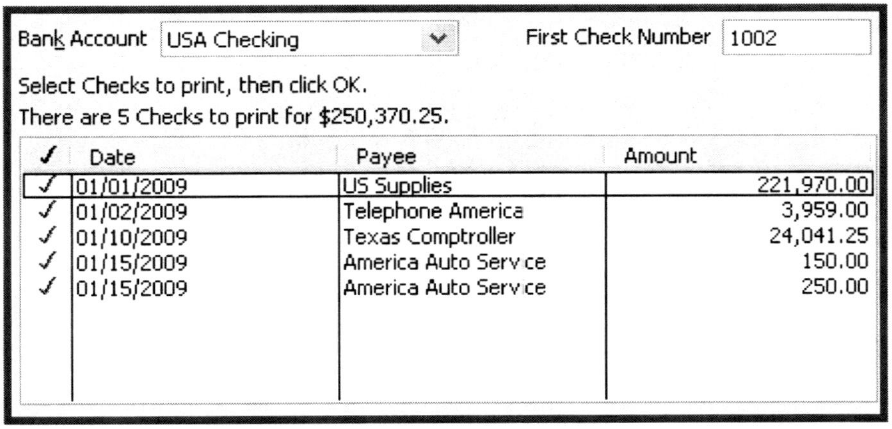

- ❖ Bank Account: Accept **USA Checking**
- ❖ First Check Number: Type **1002**
- ❖ Click **Select All** (right of window). Click **OK**
- ❖ Check Style: Click **Voucher**
- ❖ Click **Cancel**

- Click **X** to "Select Checks to Print" windows.
- Click **Save & Close** Bill Payment window

Go To Register

It is easy to scroll up and down the check register or any other register when you have few entries. However, when you have hundreds or thousands of entries, it is difficult to find a vendor by scrolling the register. The best way to search for a payee is to use the Go To function. Just click the Go To button located at the top left of the Register. In the "Which Field" box, select the option you want to search such as the payee, number/reference, memo, and amount.

Activities:

- You're still in USA Checking register window
- Click on **Opening Balance Equity** for 800,000 (the first register entry)
- Click **Go To** (top left of window)
- Click, Hold and Drag the **Go To blue bar** to the right of window
- Which Field: Accept **Payee/Name**
- Search For: Select **Telephone America**. Click **Next**
- **Look! Search line goes to the 1st Telephone America**
- Click **Next** again
- **Look! Search line goes to the 2nd Telephone America**
- Click **X** to close Go To window

Register Report

This is the most used report in the register. It is handy when you want to review a Register report for a certain period of time, like from the beginning to the ending of the month. The best aspect of the report is that it will give you the register balance for that time period. To get a correct running balance, you must sort with the date ascending that way the dates are displayed with the beginning dates at the top and the ending dates at the bottom of the check register.

Activities:

- ❖ You're still in USA Checking register window
- ❖ Click **Print…** (top left of window)
- ❖ From: Type **1/1/09**
- ❖ Through: Type **12/31/09**
- ❖ Click **OK**
- ❖ Click **Preview** (right of window)
- ❖ Click **Zoom In**. Look! Balance is **724,145.38**
- ❖ Click **Close or Print** if printer is ready
- ❖ Click **X** to close Print List window

Quick Company 2009

Register: USA Checking

From 01/01/2009 through 12/31/2009

Sorted by: Date, Type, Number/Ref

Date	Number	Payee	Account	Memo	Payment	C	Deposit	Balance
01/01/2009			Opening Balance Equity	Account Openi...		X	800,000.00	800,000.00
01/01/2009	1001	Telephone America	Telephone Expense	VOID:		X		800,000.00
01/01/2009	To Print	US Supplies	-split-	Vend 123456	221,970.00			578,030.00
01/02/2009	To Print	Telephone America	Accounts Payable	Vend 123745	3,959.00			574,071.00
01/10/2009	To Print	Texas Comptroller	Sales Tax Payable		24,041.25			550,029.75
01/15/2009			Undeposited Funds	Deposit			174,515.63	724,545.38
01/15/2009	To Print	America Auto Service	Automobile Expense:R...		150.00			724,395.38
01/15/2009	To Print	America Auto Service	Automobile Expense:R...		250.00			724,145.38

Edit Check Register

Manually changing the check number is possible when it comes to the transactions on your check register. Sometimes, you will discover incorrect or insufficient information on a check. At that point it is not necessary to void the check, but to edit the check by correcting the information on the check. If, for example, the check has not been printed or reconciled with the bank statement and the amount is wrong, you can correct it right on the check.

Activities:

- ❖ You're still in USA Checking register window
- ❖ Highlight **To Print** to US Supplies for **221,970.00**
- ❖ Type **1002.** Click **Record**
- ❖ Click **Yes** to "You have changed…"

- Highlight **To Print** to Telephone America for **3,959.00**
- Type **1003.** Click **Record**
- Click **Yes** to "You have changed…"
- Highlight **To Print** to Texas Comptroller for **24,041.25**
- Type **1004.** Click **Record**
- Click **Yes** to "You have changed…"
- Highlight **To Print** to American Auto Service for **150.00**
- Type **1005.** Click **Record**
- Click **Yes** to "You have changed…"
- Highlight **To Print** to American Auto Service for **250.00**
- Type **1006.** Click **Record**
- Click **Yes** to "You have changed…"

Register QuickReport

The second most used report in the check register is the QuickReport. If you want to see all the checks you've written to a vendor or to see what bills from a vendor are still unpaid, the QuickReport is your best ally. Click on the vendor and then QuickReport at the top of the register window, and voila! All the entries on that vendor are displayed on the screen in matter of seconds. The best part is you will also have the total amount of the checks you've written to this one vendor.

Activities:

- You're still in USA Checking register window
- Click **Telephone America check # 1001 for 0.00**
- Click **QuickReport**. (top of window)
- Date (top left of window): Select **This Fiscal Year**

Quick Company 2009

Register QuickReport

January through December 2009

Type	Date	Num	Memo	Account	Clr	Split	Amount
Telephone America							
Check	01/01/2009	1001	VOID:	USA Checking	✓	Telephone Ex...	0.00
Bill Pmt -Check	01/02/2009	1003	Vend 123745	USA Checking		Accounts Pa...	-3,959.00
Total Telephone America							-3,959.00
TOTAL							**-3,959.00**

- ❖ Click **Print**...(top left of window)
- ❖ Click **Preview** (right of window)
- ❖ Click **Zoom In**
- ❖ Click **Close or Print** if printer is ready
- ❖ Click **X** to close Print Reports window
- ❖ Click **X** to close Quick Report window

Sort Register

For bookkeepers, it is always a good idea to sort the entries on your check register Order Entered, that way you don't lose the last entry you made just because the date came much earlier than other checks. The last entry will always be at the bottom of the register, for easy access if you want to make corrections. When you sort by Amount (largest first), the payment column is in ascending order and when you sort by Amount (smallest first) the deposit is in ascending order.

Activities:

- ❖ You're still in USA Checking register window
- ❖ Sort by (bottom left): Accept **Date, Type, Number**
- ❖ Look! Register is listed by Date ascending order
- ❖ Sort by: Select **Amount (largest first)**
- ❖ Look! Payment column is ascending order. Deposit is descending order

Date	Number / Type	Payee / Account	Memo	Payment
01/01/2009		Payee		Payment
	DEP	Opening Balance Equity	Account Opening Balance	
01/15/2009				
	DEP	Undeposited Funds	Deposit	
01/01/2009	1001	Telephone America		0.00
	CHK	Telephone Expense	VOID:	
01/15/2009	1005	America Auto Service		150.00
	CHK	Automobile Expense:Repairs & Maint		
01/15/2009	1006	America Auto Service		250.00
	CHK	Automobile Expense:Repairs & Maint		
01/02/2009	1003	Telephone America		3,959.00
	BILLPMT	Accounts Payable	Vend 123745	
01/10/2009	1004	Texas Comptroller		24,041.25
	TAXPMT	Sales Tax Payable		
01/01/2009	1002	US Supplies		221,970.00
	BILLPMT	-split-	Vend 123456	

- ❖ Sort by: Select **Amount (Smallest first)**
- ❖ Look! Payment column is descending order. Deposit is ascending order

- Sort by: Select **Number/Ref**. Register is listed by check number
- Sort by: **Date, Type, Number**
- Register lists is returned to original sort condition

Split Entry

You use the Split entry function to separate a bill, when one bill from the same vendor can be posted to different accounts. In this age of superstores and Supercenters, it is easy to make purchases that fall into different categories. For example, if you buy an item for your business automobile, like a floor mat, and some printer paper for office use. You will have two categories and the Split function will help you to categorize the expense into automobile and office expenses.

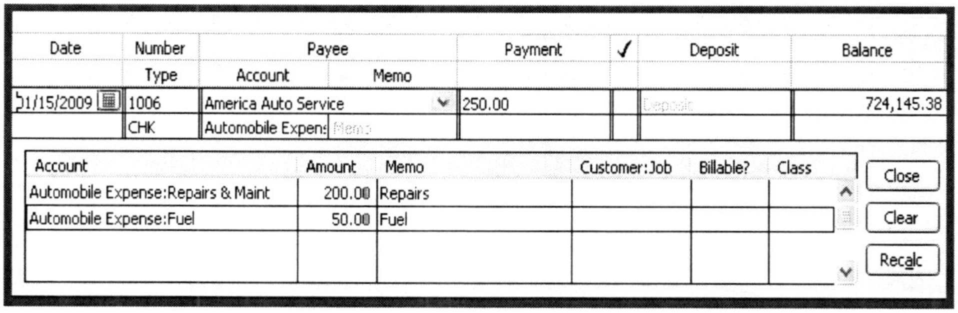

Activities:

- You're still in USA Checking register window
- Click **Check # 1006 for American Auto Services for 250**
- Click **Splits** (bottom left of window)
- In Split window. Click **under Account** (left of window)
- Accept **Automobile Expense/Repairs & Maint**. Press **Tab**
- Amount: Type **200**. Press **Tab.** Memo: Type **Repairs**
- Click **under Automobile Expense/Repair**
- Account. Select **Fuel**. Press **Tab**
- Amount: Accept **50**. Press **Tab.** Memo: Type **Fuel**
- Click **Close** to Split window (right)
- Click **Record** (bottom right)
- Click **Yes** to "You have changed…"

Make Deposits

If you must go the bank regularly, this section is for you. As you receive checks from customers and enter them through the Receive Payments window, the Chart of Accounts window will show the deposits are accumulating in the Undeposited Funds account. When you are ready to go the bank, you go to the Make Deposit window and print the two deposit slips—one for you and the other for the bank staff. After deposits, funds are moved from Undeposited Funds to Checking.

Activities:

- ❖ Click **Lists menu**
- ❖ Click **Chart of Accounts**
- ❖ **Look! Undeposited Funds balance is 1,133,997.40**
- ❖ Click **X** to close Chart of Account window
- ❖ Click **Banking menu**
- ❖ Click **Make Deposits**
- ❖ View Payment method type: Accept **All Types**
- ❖ Click **Select All** (bottom left)
- ❖ **Look! Payment Subtotal is 1,133,997.40.** Click **OK**

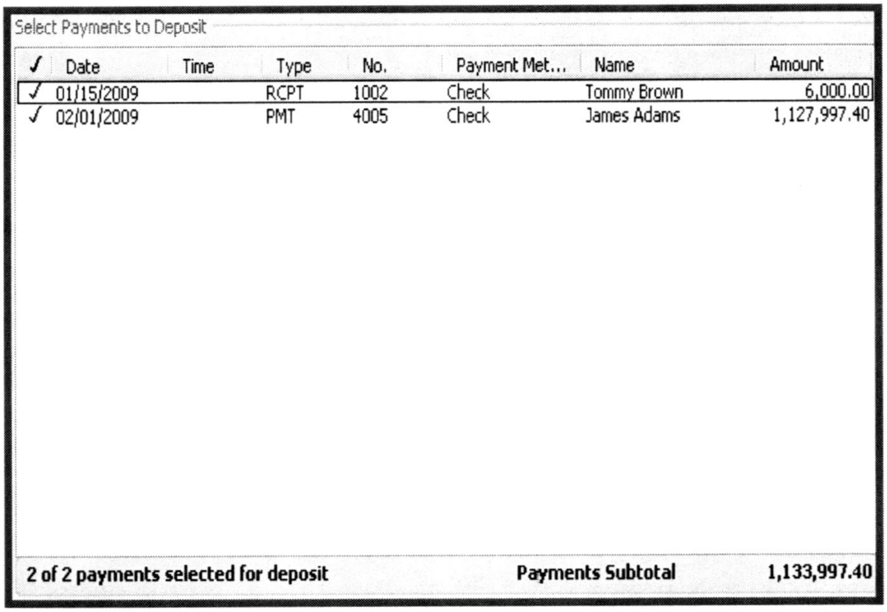

- ❖ Click **Print Down arrow** (top left of window)
- ❖ Select **Deposit Slip**

- Click **Preview** (right)
- Click **Zoom In**

Deposit Summary 1/2/2009

Summary of Deposits to USA Checking on 01/15/2009

Chk No.	PmtMethod	Rcd From	Memo	Amount
1240	Check	Tommy Brown		6,000.00
4005	Check	James Adams	Paid in Full	1,127,997.40
			Deposit Subtotal:	1,133,997.40
			Less Cash Back:	
			Deposit Total:	1,133,997.40

- Click **Close or Print** if printer is ready
- Click **X** to close Print Deposit Slip window
- Click **Save & Close** (bottom right of window)
- Click **Lists menu**
- Click **Chart of Accounts**
- **Look! Undeposited Funds balance is now 0.00**
- Funds are deposited to the checking account

Transfer Funds

As you open multiple bank accounts, the best way to move money between those accounts is by Fund Transfer process. For example, you can move money from business checking account where you deposit checks from customers to other accounts such as payroll account. Because the payroll account does not receive deposits from customers, a good way to fund it, is through the Transfer Funds window. Remember, you also do the actual transfers between accounts at the bank.

Activities:

- Click **Lists menu**
- Click **Chart of Accounts**
- Right click in the window. Click **New**
- Click **Bank**
- Click **Continue**
- Account Name: Type **Petty Cash**
- Click **Enter Opening Balance**

- Statement Ending Balance: Type **0.00**
- Statement Ending Date: Type **1/1/09.** Click **OK**
- Click **Save & Close.** Click **No** to "Set up online services…"
- Click **Banking menu**. Click **Transfer Funds**
- Date: Type **1/15/09**
- Transfer Funds From: Select **USA Checking**
- Transfer Funds To: Select **Petty Cash**
- Transfer Amount $: Type **100.00.** Press **Tab**
- Account Balance: Accept **1,858,142.78**
- Click **Save & Close**

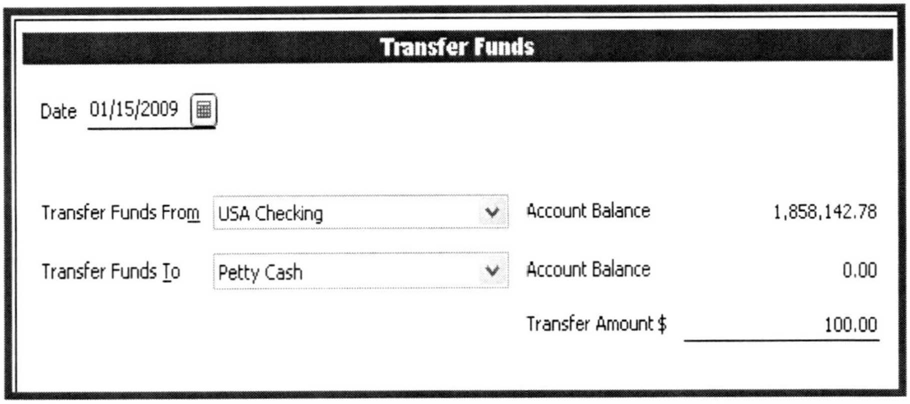

Loan Manager: Account

The Loan Manager is one of the most powerful tools in your QuickBooks software. The manager will help you to track the activities of different loans, all in one place, at the same time. Tracking interest, principal amount and due dates are easier with the Loan Manager. You can set up new loans, add, edit, and remove loans. The first step in setting up the Loan Manager is creating the loan account in the Chart of Accounts window under the Lists menu.

Activities:

- Click **Lists menu**
- Click **Chart of Accounts**
- Right Click in the window
- Click **New**
- Click **Other Account Types**
- Select **Long Term Liability**
- Click **Continue**

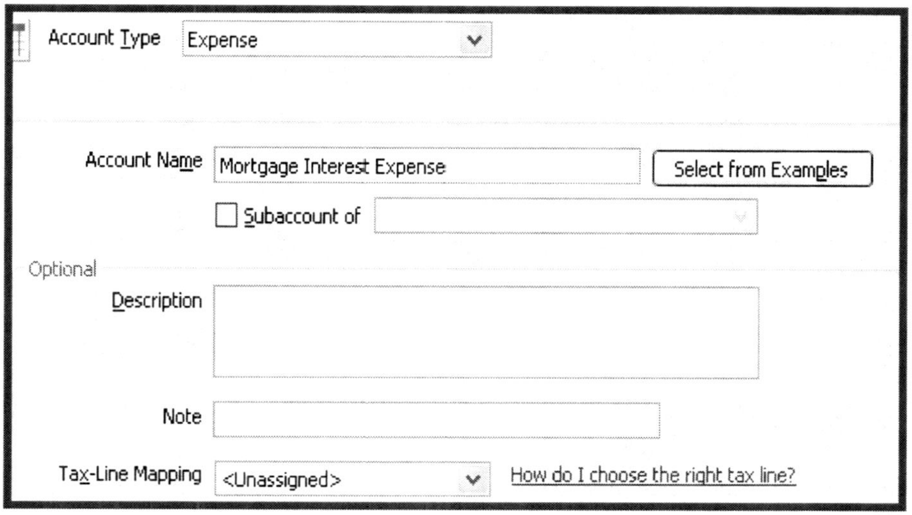

- Account Name: Type **Mortgage Loan**
- Click **Enter Opening Balance…**
- Opening Balance: Type **500,000** as of: Type **1/1/09.** Click **OK**
- Click **Save and New** (right of window)
- Account Type: Select **Expense** (Very Important)
- Account Name: Type **Mortgage Interest Expense**
- Click **Save & Close**
- Click **X** to close Chart of Account window

Loan Manager: Lender

The next phase is furnishing the lender's basic information. As always it is imperative to provide lender's information as completely as possible for payment processing. When the Address Info tab is opened, you will be able to enter the lender's information, which includes the name of the lender, opening balance, date, address, phone number, and the contact person or the loan officer. You will need to click the Additional Info tab to enter the account number of the loan.

Activities:

- Click **Vendors menu**
- Click **Vendor Center**
- Right Click in the Vendor's window. Click **New Vendor**
- Vendor Name: Type **Mortgage Bank of Dallas**
- Opening Balance: Type **0.00** as of: Type **1/1/09**
- Click **OK**

Loan Calculator

Loan calculation is a very powerful process you need to understand how it works in QuickBooks. Just about any loans you may have can be calculated using the loan manager. Open the loan manager and click the "What if Scenarios" button and you will be taken to the window where you will input just a few information and QuickBooks will do the rest. You don't have to look for a complex financial calculator anymore, but open your QuickBooks loan manager.

Activities:

- Click **Banking menu**
- Click **Loan Manager**
- Click **What if Scenarios** (bottom of window)
- Amount Borrowed: Type **500,000**
- Origination date: Type **1/1/09**
- Term: Type **360**
- Payment Amount: Accept **0.00**
- Payment period: Accept **Monthly**

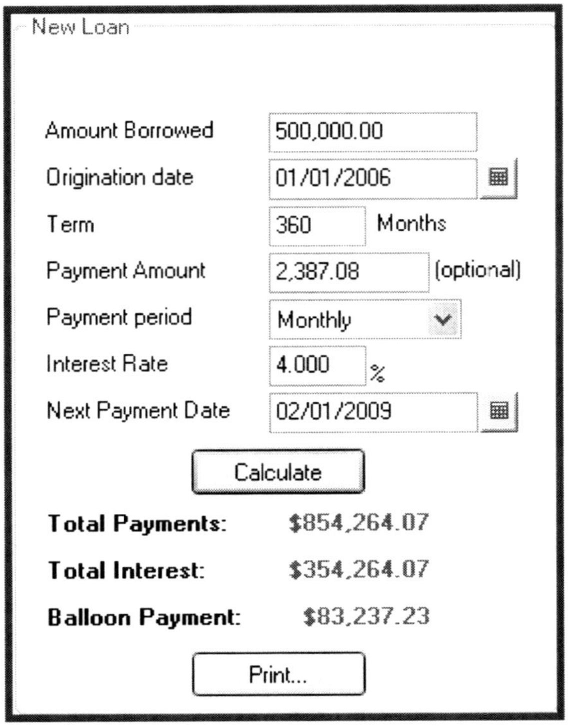

- Interest rate: Type **4**
- Next Payment Date: Type **2/1/09**
- Click **Calculate**
- Payment Amount: **2387.09**. (middle of window)
- Click **OK** to close window

Loan Manager: Loan

After you've added the loan in the Chart of Accounts and the name of the lender in the Vendor's List, it is time to add a loan to the Loan Manager. When you open the manager window, you would click the "Add a Loan" button located at the top right of the window. Note: The best place to delete any account is in the register. In this case, you open the Mortgage Loan account in the Chart of Account and delete the opening balance from the Edit menu with the Delete General Journal submenu.

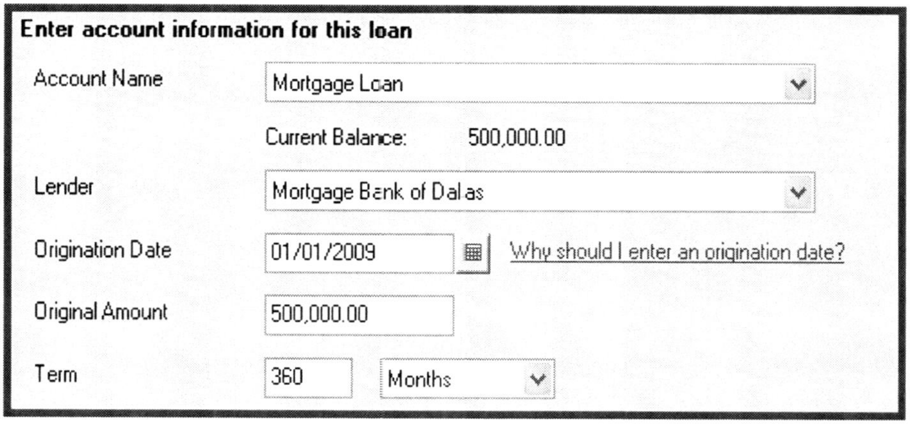

Activities:

- You're still in the Loan Manager
- Click **Add a Loan**...(right of window)
- Account Name: Select **Mortgage Loan**
- Current Balance: Accept **500,000**
- Lender: Select **Mortgage Bank of Dallas**
- Origination Date: Type **1/1/09**
- Original Amount: **500,000**
- Terms: Type **360**. Select **Months**. Click **Next**

- Due Date: Type **2/1/09**
- Payment Amount: Type **2,387.08** (calculated from previous page)
- Payment Period: Select **Monthly**. Click **Next**
- Interest Rate: Type **4**
- Compound Period: Accept **Monthly**
- Payment Account: Select **USA Checking**
- Interest Expense Account: **Mortgage Interest Expense**
- Fees/Charges Exp Account: Select **Bank Service Charges**
- Click **Finish**

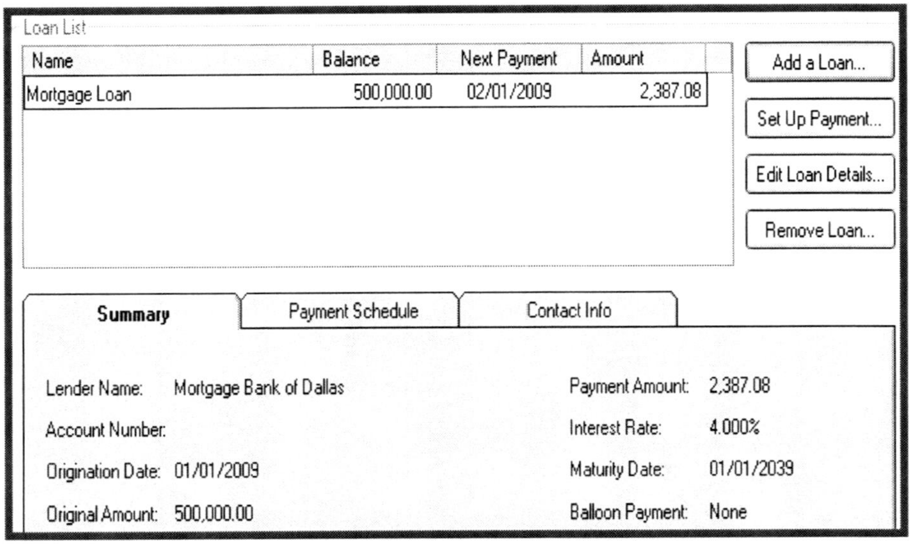

- Click **Summary** tab. Review window
- Click **Payment Schedule** tab
- Scroll to the bottom.
- **You must see Payment # 360 with Balance 0.00**
- Click **Close** to Loan Manager

Bank Statement

The first thing you do when you open a bank statement is to look at the customer name and the ending date. You don't want to be reconciling another company's bank statements or an old statement sent to you in error.

Bank of United States of America
1234 North Banking Lane
Dallas, TX 75000
1-800-123-9999

Director of Finance
Quick Company
123 Adam Lane
Dallas, TX 75000

Customer Activities for the Month Ending 1/31/2009

Beginning Balance			800,000.00
Deposits:			
1/01/2009	1,133,997.40		
1/15/09	174,515.63		
Total Deposits			1,308,513.03
Withdrawals:			
1/2/2009	CK#1002	221,970.00	
1/2/2009	CK#1003	3,959.00	
1/10/2009	CK#1004	24,041.25	
1/15/2009	CH#1005	100.00	
1/15/2009	CK#1006	260.00	
1/15/2009	TFR to X2855	100.00	
Total Withdrawals			250,419.25
Ending Balance 1/31/2009			1,858,082.78

General Journal Entry

General Journal Entries are made under the Company menu. Every month, you will make two types of journal entries. The first are asset related, when you adjust the actual balance with book balance. The second are bank related, when you adjust the bank statement with book balance. After you reviewed the bank statements, you found out the balance did not match the check register. Immediately, you start the reconciliation to find what entries in the bank statements are not in the books or what entries are wrong in either the bank statements or your book. In this case you found out the bank paid two checks incorrectly. Your job at this point is to make entries to agree with the bank statement, later you email the bank to make corrections and afterwards you match their corrections in next month statements.

Activities:

> The key is to do the opposite!
>
> Bank Overpayment you reduce your cash
> Bank Underpayment you increase your cash.

- Click **Company menu**
- Click **Make General Journal Entries**. Click **OK**
- Date: Type **1/31/09**. Entry: Accept **5**
- Click under **Account** (left of window)
- Select **USA Checking.** Debit: Type **50**
- Memo: Type **Underpayment**
- Under USA Checking. Select **Repair/Maint under Automobile Exp**
- Credit: Accept **50**. Memo: Type **Underpayment**
- Under Automobile Expense… Select **Fuel under Automobile Expense**
- Debit: Type **10**. Memo: Type **Overpayment**
- Under Automobile Expense... Select **USA Checking**.
- Credit: Accept **10.** Memo: Type **Overpayment**
- Click **Save & Close**

Date 01/31/2009 Entry No. 5

Account	Debit	Credit	Memo
USA Checking	50.00		Underpayment
Automobile Expense:Repairs & ...		50.00	Underpayment
Automobile Expense:Fuel	10.00		Overpayment
USA Checking		10.00	Overpayment

Bank Reconciliation

As explained earlier, as soon as you receive your statement from the bank, you should look for entries on the statement that are not on the company's check register and entries that are on the check register that are not on the bank statement. Examples are interest income, interest expense, bank fees, deposits and checks that have not been entered either by you or the bank. In the Reconciliation window, you will type the balance on the bank statement, in this case **$1,858,082.78** which matches your check register balance after you've made the journal entries; then click the Mark All button, the Difference (bottom right of the window) must be 0.00.

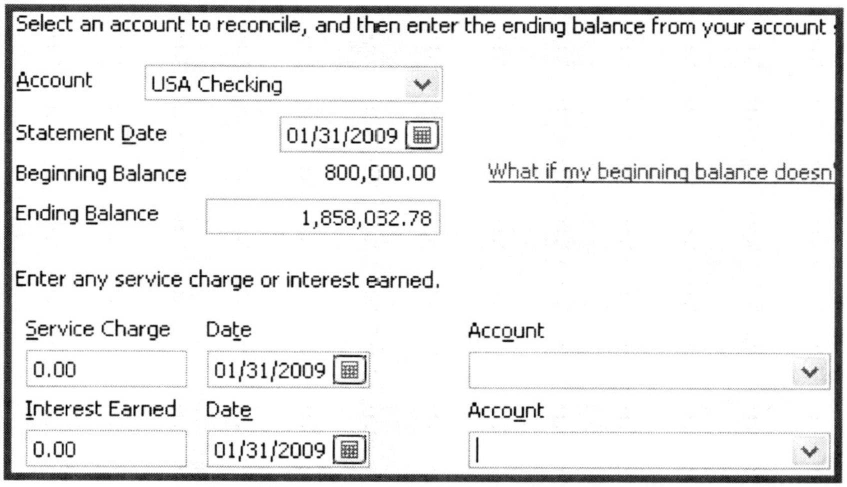

Activities:

- Click **Banking menu**
- Click **Reconcile**
- Account: Select **USA Checking**
- Statement Date: Type **1/31/09**
- Ending Balance: Type **1,858,082.78** (from bank statement). Press **Tab**
- Click **Continue** (bottom of window)
- Click **Mark All** (middle of window)
- **Difference (bottom right of window): Must be 0.00**
- Click **Reconcile Now** (bottom right of window) (Very Important)

For period: 01/31/2009 ☐ Hide transactions after the statement's end date

Checks and Payments

✓	Date ▲	C...	Payee	Amount
✓	01/01/2009	1002	US Supplies	221,970.00
✓	01/02/2009	1003	Telephone Ame...	3,959.00
✓	01/10/2009	1004	Texas Comptroller	24,041.25
✓	01/15/2009			100.00
✓	01/15/2009	1005	America Auto S...	150.00
✓	01/15/2009	1006	America Auto S...	250.00
✓	01/31/2009	5		10.00

Deposits and Other Credits

✓	Date ▲	C...	Memo	Type	Amount
✓	01/01/2...	1001	VOID:	CHK	0.00
✓	01/15/2...		Deposit	DEP	174,515.63
✓	01/15/2...		Deposit	DEP	1,133,997.40
✓	01/31/2...	5	Underpay...	GENJRNL	50.00

Mark All | Unmark All | Go To | Columns to Display...

Beginning Balance	800,000.00
Items you have marked cleared	
4 Deposits and Other Credits	1,308,563.03
7 Checks and Payments	250,480.25

Modify

Service Charge	0.00
Interest Earned	0.00
Ending Balance	1,858,082.78
Cleared Balance	1,858,082.78
Difference	0.00

- Click **Both**
- Click **Display**
- Click **OK** to "This report display current..."
- Click **X** to close Reconciliation Summary
- **You must have Checkmark on all entries**
- Congratulations!
- Click **X** to close Reconciliation Detail window

Checks and Payments - 7 items						
Bill Pmt -Check	01/01/2009	1002	US Supplies	✓	-221,970.00	-221,970.00
Bill Pmt -Check	01/02/2009	1003	Telephone America	✓	-3,959.00	-225,929.00
Sales Tax Paym...	01/10/2009	1004	Texas Comptroller	✓	-24,041.25	-249,970.25
Check	01/15/2009	1006	America Auto Serv...	✓	-250.00	-250,220.25
Check	01/15/2009	1005	America Auto Serv...	✓	-150.00	-250,370.25
Transfer	01/15/2009			✓	-100.00	-250,470.25
General Journal	01/31/2009	5		✓	-10.00	-250,480.25
Total Checks and Payments					-250,480.25	-250,480.25
Deposits and Credits - 4 items						
Check	01/01/2009	1001	Telephone America	✓	0.00	0.00
Deposit	01/15/2009			✓	174,515.63	174,515.63
Deposit	01/15/2009			✓	1,133,997.40	1,308,513.03
General Journal	01/31/2009	5		✓	50.00	1,308,563.03
Total Deposits and Credits					1,308,563.03	1,308,563.03

Financial: Profit & Loss

In the Banking menu, most of the activities are bank account related. We learned how to write and print both single and batch checks. If you have multiple checks, processing checks in a batch is easier and more efficient. We had three expenses, two were checks and one was a credit card charge for a total of $424. We also had an overpayment and underpayment by the bank for a total of $40. Those activities net to a total of $384 and our Net Income is now $2,033,313.26

Quick Company 2009
Profit & Loss
January through December 2009

	Jan - Dec 09
Ordinary Income/Expense	
Income	
Opening Balance Income	1,914,500.00
Landscaping Services	394,811.34
Total Income	2,309,311.34
Cost of Goods Sold	
Materials	213,700.00
Discount Received	-4,530.00
Total COGS	209,170.00
Gross Profit	2,100,141.34
Expense	
Adjustment to Decr Inventory	1,250.00
Opening Balance Expense	6,500.00
Automobile Expense	384.00
Depreciation Expense	666.67
Payroll Expenses	57,568.41
Telephone Expense	459.00
Total Expense	66,828.08
Net Ordinary Income	2,033,313.26
Net Income	**2,033,313.26**

Activities:

- Click **Reports menu**
- Click **Company & Financial**
- Click **Profit & Loss Standard**
- Date: Select **This Fiscal Year**
- From: Accept **1/1/09.** To: Accept **12/31/09**
- Click **Collapse**
- **Net Income is 2,033,313.26**
- Click **X** to close window

Financial: Balance Sheet

We created and funded a Petty Cash account. We printed the deposit slips and sent the checks to the bank. The Undeposited Fund disappeared from the Balance Sheet report and the balance went into checking account. After deposit make sure Undeposited Fund balance is zero in the Chart of Accounts. The $500,000 Building loan went into a liability account. Our checking account balance went down by $360. Current Assets are $3,488,108.18 and Total Assets is $3,549,837.26.

Activities:

- Click **Reports menu**
- Click **Company & Financial**
- Click **Balance Sheet Standard**
- Date: Select **This Fiscal Year**
- As of: Accept **12/31/09**
- Click **Collapse**
- **Total Assets is 3,549,837.26**
- Click **X** to close window

Quick Company 2009
Balance Sheet
As of December 31, 2009

	Dec 31, 09
ASSETS	
Current Assets	
Checking/Savings	
Petty Cash	100.00
Money Market Account	100,000.00
USA Checking	1,858,082.78
USA Payroll Checking	42,431.59
USA Savings	250,000.00
Total Checking/Savings	2,250,614.37
Accounts Receivable	
Accounts Receivable	1,024,839.56
Total Accounts Receivable	1,024,839.56
Other Current Assets	
Inventory Asset	235,050.00
Total Other Current Assets	235,050.00
Total Current Assets	3,510,503.93
Fixed Assets	
Truck	39,333.33
Total Fixed Assets	39,333.33
TOTAL ASSETS	**3,549,837.26**

Review Bank Reconciliation Steps

Reconciling your bank statement in QuickBooks is different from reconciling your bank statement in Quicken. With QuickBooks, most of your checks will be written from your bills; that is, if you set up to pay from bills. You should make it a policy of entering your bills first and then writing checks from bills. In Quicken, if you don't automate your checks, you will first write check on your check books and then manually key in your checks to the check register, this is where most mistakes are made—just remember this, and you'll be OK!

Reconciliation Process:

When you open your bank statement, use the following steps to get started and complete the Reconcile window. In the beginning, you will be running the first trial to see if your bank reconciliation difference is 0.00. If it's not zero, then you will start the correction and reconciliation process to get you to 0.00, by clicking a checkmark on each entry in the window.

- Click Banking menu
- Click Reconcile
- Account: Select the right account
- Statement Date: Type statement date from bank statement
- End Balance: Type the amount from bank statement
- Service Charge: Type amount and date from statement, select Interest exp
- Interest Earned: Type amount and date from statement, select Interest Inc
- Click Continue (bottom of window) to the Reconcile window
- Click Mark All button (bottom of window)
- Difference (bottom right of window): Must be 0.00
- If it's not 0.00. Click Unmark All (bottom right of window)
- Click Modify (bottom right of window) to go back to reconcile window

Major reconciling areas:

Since you are using QuickBooks and entering your bills first before writing checks, you would have few reconciliation problems, and if you do, they would come from these areas:

- Entering wrong amounts from the bank statement to the Reconcile window
- Deposits by bank to your account, you don't know about e.g. Interest earned
- Withdraw by bank from your account, you don't know about e.g. Service fees
- You wrote a check to a vendor in a hurry, not recorded in the check register

- Someone wrote a check to him/herself, not recorded in the check register
- Bank overpaid or underpaid on a check by mistake

Minor reconciling areas:

Sometimes the bank will make a mistake in paying a check and what they will list on your statement is what they paid is different from what is actually on the check. And sometimes, when you're entering amounts from the statement to the reconciling window or making a journal entry, what you entered might be different from what is actually on the statement. You will be able to find these errors if you use the following steps or look in the following areas:

- Error of Commission: In 23.45 you typed 230.45 or 203.45
- Error of Omission: In 23.45, you type 20.00 and left out 3.45 or .45 or 5
- Error of Transposition: In 23.45, you typed 32.45 or type 23.54
- Error of Multiple Mistakes: Difference is 99.99 you left out 1 cent and 100
- Wrong Journal entry: You enter amount as debit when it should be credit.
- Duplicate checks: You mistakenly wrote two checks to the same vendor.

Entering amount from bank statement:

When you click Modify, and you're taken back to the Reconcile window, you are now ready to verify and confirm that the amounts you've just entered from the bank statement and the amounts on Reconcile window are the same. Check the following:

- Account: Verify you are in the right account
- Beginning Balance: Check last month's statement ending balance and beginning balance you just entered are the same
- Ending Balance: Verify you typed the correct Ending Balance
- Service Charge: Verify you typed the correct total of all Service Charge
- Interest Earned: Verify you typed the correct total of all Interest Earned
- Click Continue to go back to the Reconcile window

Deposits by Bank into your account:

Run your finger through the bank statement and click checkmarks on deposit entries on the Reconcile window. You are looking to see if there are outstanding deposit entries without checkmarks.

- Click Report menu, Banking, Deposit Details, and Date down arrow. Select Custom. Type beginning and ending date on the bank statement

- Make sure the entry you are looking for is not in the Deposit Details
- Make a journal entry for that entry. I'll discuss how later on in another section

Withdrawal by Bank from your account:
Run your finger through the bank statement and click checkmarks on checks and withdrawals on the Reconcile window. You are looking to see if there are outstanding checks and withdrawals without checkmarks.

- Click Report menu, Banking, Check Details, and Date down arrow. Select Custom. Type beginning and ending date on the bank statement
- Make sure the entry you are looking for is not in the Check Details...
- Make a journal entry for that entry. I'll discuss how later on in another section

You wrote checks to vendors not recorded:
After you have clicked checkmarks on the deposits and withdrawals on the Reconcile window from the bank statement, you will find a check on the statement that is not a Reconcile window.

- You may have written a COD (Cash on Delivery) check and forget to record it
- Click Report menu, Banking, Check Details, and Date down arrow. Select Custom. Type beginning and ending date on the bank statement
- Make sure the entry you are looking for is not in the Check Details report
- Make a journal entry for that entry. I'll discuss how later on in another section

Someone wrote a check to him/herself:
After you have clicked checkmarks on the deposits and withdrawals on the Reconcile window from the bank statement, you will find a check on the statement that is not a Reconcile window.

- This may be a missing check. Someone found the company checkbook and wrote a check to him/herself and forged the company's signature.
- Find the actual check from the bank statement envelope or request a copy of the check from your bank. Contact your banker immediately for fraud.
- Click Report menu, Banking, Missing Checks, and Date down arrow. Select Custom. Type beginning and ending date on the bank statement

- Make sure the entry you are looking for is not in the Check Details
- Make a journal entry for that entry. I'll discuss how to later on in another section

Bank overpaid or underpaid a check:
After you have clicked checkmarks on all the deposits and withdrawals on the Reconcile window from the bank statement, you will NOT find a check on the statement that is not a reconcile window. That is, you have clicked all the entries and you still have a difference at the bottom right of the Reconcile window.

- Your problem may be an overpayment or underpayment
- You will be using the error finding process such as Error of Commission, Error of Omission, Error of Transposition, and Error of Multiple Mistakes, which I'll discuss later on in another section

Error of Commission:
If you've clicked all the entries from the bank statement to the Reconcile window and you still have a difference at the bottom right of the window.

- Divide your difference by 2. If you can divide the difference without a remainder, you may have a commission problem at the end of the number. If you can divide the difference by 3 or 9 without a remainder, you may also have a commission problem
- You are looking for the amount on the statement that is longer than the one on the Reconcile window. Instead of 20 bank may have paid 200 (the mistake is at end of the number) or instead of 45 bank paid 405 (the mistake is at the middle of the number)
- When you find it, you will make a journal entry

Error of Omission:
If you've clicked all the from the bank statement to the Reconcile window and you still have a difference at the bottom right of the window.

- Divide your difference by 2. If you can divide the difference without a remainder, you may have an omission problem at end of the number. If you can divide the difference by 3 or 9 without a remainder, you may also have an omission problem
- You are looking for the amount on the statement that is shorter than the one on the Reconcile window. Instead of 200 bank may have paid 20 (the mistake is at the end of the number) or instead of 203 bank paid 23 (the mistake is at

the middle of the number)
- When you find it, make a journal entry

Error of Transposition:
If you've clicked all the from the bank statement to the Reconcile window and you still have a difference at the bottom right of the window.

- Divide your difference by 3 or 9. If you can divide the difference without a remainder, you may a transposition problem.
- You are looking for the amount on the statement that has the amount switched around. Instead of 245 bank paid 254
- After you find it, make a journal entry

Error of Multiple Mistakes:
If you've clicked all the entries from the bank statement to the Reconcile window and you still have a difference at the bottom right of the window.

- If your difference has few pennies to round to a whole number, for example 99.99 or any amount closer, you may have a problem of multiple mistakes.
- You first have to look for the amount which makes the difference a whole number, in this case 1 cent. Run your finger through the last digits amount on the bank statement. When you find the 1 cent, then you start looking for the 100.00, which is easy to find, by using the error of commission and omission as explained above.
- When you find it, you will make a journal entry

Wrong Journal Entry:
After you have clicked checkmarks on the deposits and withdrawals on the Reconcile window from the bank statement, you will find a check or a deposit on the statement that is not a Reconcile window. In other words, if there is an unchecked deposit on the bank statement, look for the same amount in the Reconcile window check column. And if there is an unchecked withdrawal on the bank statement, look for the same amount in the Reconcile window deposit column. You credited deposit instead of debiting it, and you debited withdrawal instead of crediting it.

- Divide your difference by 2. If you can divide the difference without a remainder, you may have a problem of wrong journal entry. You have entered a deposit as a withdrawal or a withdrawal as a deposit.
- Look on the bank statement to see if you can find one half of the amount of

the difference. For example, if the difference at the bottom right of the Reconcile window is 200, look for 100 on the bank statement and in the middle of the Reconcile window.

- When you find it, you will make two journal entries: one to reverse the mistake you made and another to make the right journal entry.

Duplicate Checks:
For some reason you may have written two checks to the same vendor. Maybe the first as a COD and later, you wrote another check thinking that the vendor had not been paid.

Click Report menu, Banking, Missing Checks, and Date down arrow. Select Custom. Type beginning and ending date on the bank statement

- You are looking at the check number column to see if you will see duplicated check numbers
- If you discovered you wrote two checks and voided one of them, but before you put a stop payment with your bank, the check had already been cashed, now you have a duplicate check problem
- You will need to reverse the voided check to be able to match the bank statement, therefore, you need a journal entry

Review Bank Reconciliation Entries

We have discussed the potential problems you will encounter while reconciling your bank statement. Now is the time to talk about how to correct them. The goal is to make journal entries for those amounts you found on the bank statement. In other words, you are adding to the Reconcile window any amount the bank added to your bank statement without your knowledge and you subtract from the Reconcile window any amount the bank subtracted from your bank statement. When you're finished, the Reconcile window should have every amount on your bank statement; clicked with checkmarks and the bottom difference must be 0.00.

Earlier, I said there are at least two times you are going to make journal entries. The first one is at the end of the month, when you are making the company related journal entries. The second is when you receive your bank statements and you are making bank related journal entries. We talked about company related journal entries; let's look at the following bank related journal entries.

Entering amount from bank statement:
You will not need a journal entry. All you have to do is click the Modify button. You will be taken to Begin Reconciliation window, where you can make the corrections needed, if any. Just enter the correct TOTAL of all Services Charge or the TOTAL of all Interest Earned amounts. QuickBooks will make the journal entry for you, in case you need to know what QuickBooks did, if you have to do it yourself next time.

For total Service Charges of 125, QuickBooks would make the following entries:

USA Checking		125.00
Service Charges Expense	125.00	

For total interest income of 535, QuickBooks would make the following entries:

USA Checking	535.00	
Interest Income		535.00

Deposits by Bank into your account:
If the bank deposited electronic fund transfer (EFT) into your checking from a customer for consulting services you provided in the amount of 150,000, you will increase or debit the checking account (the bank deposited the cash) and decrease or credit the services (the customer is paying for them). Make the following entries:

USA Checking	150,000	
Consulting Income		150,000

Withdrawal by Bank from your account:
What if one of your customers sent you a check for 2,450.50, you deposited the check in USA Checking account, and later the check was returned to the bank because of NSF (Non Sufficient Funds)? The bank will now withdraw that same amount from your account. You will decrease or credit the account the bank withdrew the cash from; increase or debit the Consulting Income. Make the following entries:

USA Checking		2,450.50
Consulting Income	2,450.50	

Or you can move the entries around, like I did below; it's still the same thing. I used the above method to make it easy for you to follow and understand by starting with USA Checking first:

Consulting Income	2,450.50	
USA Checking		2,450.50

You wrote checks to vendors not recorded:
You wrote a COD (cash on delivery) check for 3,782.12 in a hurry for office supplies you ordered and later found out you had not recorded it. You will decrease or credit the checking account from which you wrote the COD check; increase or debit the Office Supplies you are paying for. Make the following entries:

USA Checking		3,782.12
Office Supplies	3,782.12	

Someone wrote a check to himself/herself:
After you find out someone wrote a 50,000 check to himself/herself, you must make an entry to record the check and balance with the bank statement while you go after the person who forged the check. You decrease or credit the checking account from which the thief wrote the check; and increase or debit Other expenses. You used Other expenses because the account has nothing to do with other accounts in the Chart of Accounts. Make the following entries:

USA Checking		50,000.00
Other Expenses	50,000.00	

Bank overpaid or underpaid a check:
When you find out the bank overpaid on a check, if the amount is too small (depending on your company policy), such as less than a dollar, you write if off. However, if the amount is more than a dollar, you make the entry and call the bank for a refund. Whether it is a small or large amount, you must make a journal entry to balance with the bank statement. If the bank overpaid by 50 cents, you decrease or credit the checking account from which the bank overpaid; and increase or debit Other expenses. Make the following entries:

USA Checking		0.50
Other Expenses	0.50	

If bank underpaid by 50 cents, you will increase or debit the checking account from which the bank overpaid; and decrease or credit Other expenses. Make the following entries:

USA Checking	0.50	
Other Expenses		0.50

Error of Commission:
This is like the overpayment above. For instance the bank paid 200 instead of paying 20. The difference is 180; that is why you can divide the difference by 2, 3 or 9. You will decrease or credit the checking, from which the bank overpaid; and increase or debit Other Expenses. Make the following entries:

USA Checking		180.00
Other Expenses	180.00	

Error of Omission:
This mistake is like the underpayment above. For instance: Instead of 900, the bank paid 90. The difference is 810, which is why you should divide the difference by 2, 3 or 9. You will increase or debit the checking account from which the bank overpaid; and decrease or credit Other Expenses. Make the following entries:

USA Checking	810.00	
Other Expenses		810.00

Error of Transposition:
This is a common mistake made by anyone who is new to the accounting or bookkeeping industry. For instance: Instead of 245, the bank paid 254. The difference is 9, that is why you can divide the difference by 3 or 9. This is an overpayment of 9. You will decrease or credit the checking account from which the bank overpaid; and increase or debit Other Expenses. Make the following entries:

USA Checking		9.00
Other Expenses	9.00	

Error of Multiple Mistakes:
In this case the bank made two mistakes in the same month on the same account. It can be tricky to find this mistake, but with practice it is easy to find. If you have one round amount you did not click, such as 200, but if the difference is 199.99, then you know you are looking at multiple mistakes. Find the 1 cent and then click the 200 in the Reconcile window—you don't need journal entry. Another example: Instead of 500.20, the bank paid 500.21 (a difference and overpayment of 1 cent), and instead of 5,200 the bank paid 5,000 (a difference and underpayment of 200). If you net the overpayment of 1 cent and the underpayment of 200, you get an underpayment of 199.99. To book the overpayment of 1 cent, you will decrease or credit the checking from which the bank overpaid and increase or debit other expenses. The entries are:

USA Checking		0.01
Other Expenses	0.01	

To book the underpayment of 200, you will increase or debit the checking, from which the bank overpaid; and decrease or credit Other Expenses. Make the following entries:

USA Checking	200.00	
Other Expenses		200.00

Wrong Journal Entry:
What if, after you have completed any of the above journal entries, you go to the Reconcile window and still you're not in balance? You may have made a mistake by reversing the debit and credit entries:

USA Checking		100.00
Other Expenses	100.00	

Instead of booking 100 to debit USA Checking, you booked a credit. You are now faced with double mistake or multiple mistakes. Any time you make a wrong journal entry it will take you two entries to make your entries right. The first one is to correct the mistake you made, and the second one is to make the entry you were going to make in the first place. Your difference will be 200, which is why you should divide the difference by 2 to find the number that is causing the problem. To correct the 100 mistake, you will increase or debit USA Checking; and decrease or credit Other Expenses. Make the following entries:

USA Checking	100.00	
Other Expenses		100.00

To book the entry of 100 you were going to make in the first place, you will increase or debit USA Checking and decrease or credit other expenses. Make the following entries:

USA Checking	100.00	
Other Expenses		100.00

Duplicate Checks:
What if you find out you wrote another check after you wrote a COD check to the same vendor for 3,782.12 and you immediately void the second check from

QuickBooks? And before you can get to the bank, the two checks have been cashed? You have to reverse the check you've just voided. When you write the second check, this is the entry QuickBooks makes for you:

USA Checking		3,782.12
Office Supplies	3,782.12	

When you void the second check, this is the entry QuickBooks makes for you:

USA Checking	3,782.12	
Office Supplies		3,782.12

When you find out from the bank statement that the vendor cashed the two checks, you have to reverse the check you voided and call the vendor to send you a refund for cashing two checks. You will decrease or credit the checking account from which you wrote the second check; and increase or debit the Office Supplies you are paying for. Make the following entries to reverse the check you voided:

USA Checking		3,782.12
Office Supplies	3,782.12	

Chapter Summary

If your Bank Statement balance is not the same with your checking accounts balance for example, find out the reason. If it's a customer deposit that is on statement but not the books; create an invoice, receive the payment and deposit the check to make the books balance. If it's a vendor check that is not on the books, create a bill and make the payment so the amount is withdrawn from your checking account to make the books balance. All others you have to make journal entries to make the books balance with the bank statements.

What we accomplished:

- Reviewed Banking submenus
- Wrote checks
- Entered credit card charges
- Processed single and batch check
- Practiced the Go To function
- Ran the register report
- Edited the check register
- Processed the QuickReport window
- Practiced the sort function
- Practiced the split functions
- Made deposit and Transferred funds
- Completed the Loan Manager windows
- Processed General Journal entries
- Reconciled bank statement
- Processed financial statements
- Reviewed bank reconciliation steps
- Reviewed bank reconciliation journal entries

Additional Financial activities:

- America Auto Service by Check 150
- America Auto Service by Credit Card 24
- America Auto Service by Check 250
- Undeposited Funds to Checking 1,133,997.40
- Transfer Funds Petty Cash 100
- Created a Mortgage Loan for 500,000
- Made Journal Entry for Underpayment 50
- Made Journal Entry for Overpayment 10

Exercise 9

Complete Exercise 9 by using the following information:

1. You received a Checking bank statement and the balance is 3,809,804.75
   You're going to balance the Checking register of 929,451.00 with the bank

2. You saw an amount for 2,878,018.75 in the bank statement
   Make a deposit for the total balance in Undeposited Funds of 2,878,018.75
   Date 1/2/09

3. You saw an overpayment by the bank on check #1005 for 100
   Make a journal entry of 100 for cash and telephone expense

4. You saw an underpayment by the bank on check #1006 for 90
   Make a journal entry of 90 for cash and insurance expense

5. You saw interest income for 2,345 on the statement but not on the register
   Make a journal entry of 2,345 for cash and interest income

6. Perform the reconciliation process statement ending date 1/31/09
   To match your check register balance with bank balance of 3,809,804.75

7. Process the following reports
   Profit & Loss Statement ending 12/31/09
   Balance Sheet Standard ending 12/31/09
   Statement of Cash Flow ending 12/31/09
   Deposit Detail Checking 1/31/09
   Previous Reconciliation Summary Checking ending 1/31/09
   Previous Reconciliation Detail Checking ending 1/31/09
   Register Report Checking ending 1/31/09
   Register Report Payroll ending 1/31/09
   Register QuickReport for US Treasury ending 1/31/09

$

Chapter 10

Reports Menu

Objectives: After you've completed this chapter, you will be able to:

- ✓ Explain Report submenus
- ✓ Identify report center contents
- ✓ Process multiple reports
- ✓ Generate reports under the following submenus:
- ✓ Company & Financial
- ✓ Customer & Receivables
- ✓ Sales
- ✓ Jobs, Time & Mileage
- ✓ Vendors & Payables
- ✓ Purchases
- ✓ Inventory
- ✓ Employees & Payroll
- ✓ Banking
- ✓ Accountant & Taxes
- ✓ Budgets
- ✓ List
- ✓ Transaction History
- ✓ Transaction Journal
- ✓ Print and Send Forms

Review Reports Submenus

Congratulations! You have reached the "Promised Land!" This is where you are going to see the results of all the entries you've been making. The Reports menu has submenus of various reports to help determine if you're going forward or backward financially. One of the activities you may like to do here is to place a report you frequently use on the Icon Bar. Remember to preview a report to see if your results are correct. One way to spot check your report is to look for errors on the Profit & Loss and the Balance Sheet reports, not the Statement of Cash Flows. **Any where you see an amount with minus (-) is a sign of error, unless it is a sub-account being subtracted from a main account as in Accumulated Depreciation and Truck account or Discount Received on purchase as a subtraction from Cost of Goods Sold or Discount Given on sales as a subtraction from Sales Income.** When you find a minus amount, you have the entry backward and needs to go the other way from income to expense or vice versa.

- Click **Reports menu**

The following activities are found under the Reports menu:

- **Report Center:** One of the best features of the Report Navigator is that it allows you to see all groups in one window, so you can click a report group and see all the reports in that group, instead of going through the Reports menu that would only allow you to see one group at a time.

- **Memorized Reports:** The most frequently used report should be customized and memorized, so you don't have to re-customize that report every time you open it. For example, when you open the Profit and Loss Standard, you may customize the report by selecting a date range to see the result of that date, and when you exit the report you lose all your customization. But if you memorize your report after customization, the settings are saved for future use.

- **Process Multiple Reports:** Normally, you would open a report, review and exit to open another report. Not anymore! QuickBooks has an option that allows you to open all the reports at one time and review them without exiting and coming back. You can also process multiple reports by group instead of opening all the reports individually on your desktop.

- **Company & Financial:** This group has all the reports that are related to the financial status of your business. It includes Profit & Loss—Standard, Detail, YTD Comparison, By Job, By Class, and Unclassified. Income & Expenses—Income Customer Summary, Income by Customer Detail, Expense by Vendor Summary, Expense by Vendor Detail, and Income & Expense Graph. Balance Sheet & Net Worth—Standard, Detail, Prev Yr Comparison, and Net Worth Graph. Cash Flow—Statement of Cash Flow and Cash Flow Forecast.

- **Customers & Receivables:** This group contains reports about your customers and their activities. It includes A/R Aging—Summary, Detail, Account Receivable Graph, Open Invoices, and Collections. Customer Balance—Summary, Detail, Unbilled Costs by Job, and Transaction List by Customer. List—Customer Phone List, Customer Contact List, and Item Price List.

- **Sales:** If you want to narrow down to Customer sales only, come to this group. It includes Sales by Customer—Summary, Detail, Pending Sales, and Sales Graph. Sales by Item—Summary and Detail. Sales by Rep—Summary and Detail.

- **Jobs, Time & Mileage:** The best of the best set of reports. If you can learn how to use and interpret these set of reports, the financial life of your business will never be the same—guaranteed! If you want to zero in on costs and profit to find out how much profit you're getting, how much time you are spending on each job, and how much you are spending on each vehicle, you definitely want to come to this set of reports. It includes Job & Profitability—Job Profitability Summary, Job Profitability Detail, Profit & Loss by Job, Item Profitability, and Unbilled Cost by Job. Job Estimates—Job Estimates vs. Actual Summary, Job Estimates vs. Actuals, Estimates by Job, and Open Purchase order by Job. Time—By Vehicle Summary, By Vehicle Detail, By Job Summary, and By Job Detail. Mileage—By Vehicle Summary, By Vehicle Detail, By Job Summary, and By Job Detail.

- **Vendors & Payables:** When it comes to finding out how much you paid to your vendors and how much you still owe them, this is your destination. Includes A/P Aging—Summary, Detail, and Accounts Payable Graph. Vendor Balances—Vendor Balances Summary, Vendor Balances Detail, Unpaid Bills Detail, and Transaction List by Vendor. 1099—Summary and Detail. Sales Tax—Sales Tax Liability and Sales Tax Revenue Summary. List—Vendor Phone List and Vendor Contact List.

- **Purchases:** When you set up the Purchases Preferences and you bought and paid your vendors for inventories, you will have Purchases reports. They include: Purchases by Vendor Summary, Purchases by Vendor Detail, and Purchases by Item Summary, Purchases by Item Detail, Open Purchase Order, and Open Purchase Orders by Job.

- **Inventory:** Inventory valuation is important to a business, especially a merchandise business. As you buy and sell inventories, reports are generated by QuickBooks. Inventory reports include: Inventory Valuation Summary, Inventory Valuation Detail, Inventory Stock Status by Item, Inventory Stock Status by Vendor, Physical Inventory Worksheet, and Pending Builds.

- **Employees & Payroll:** If you decide to use the QuickPayroll, you will have employee and payroll reports. This set of reports includes Payroll—Payroll Summary, Payroll Item Detail, Payroll Detail Review, Payroll Transaction by Payee, Payroll Transaction Detail, Payroll Liability Balances, Payroll Item Listing, Employee Earnings Summary, and Employee State Taxes Detail. Employee—Employee Contact List, Employee Withholding, and Paid Time Off List.

- **Banking:** The Banking set of reports allows you to open, review, and print banking reports such as deposits and check reports. This set of reports includes Banking—Deposit Detail, Check Detail, Missing Check, Reconciliation Discrepancy, and Previous Reconciliation.

- **Accountant & Taxes:** From time to time, you want to review account balances or transaction activities, this set of reports will give you what you're looking for and then some. It includes Account Activity—Trial Balance, General Ledger, Transaction Detail by Account, Journal, Audit Trail, Voided/Detailed Transactions, Voided/Detailed Transactions History, and Transaction Listing by Date. Listing—Account Listing and Fixed Asset Listing. Income Tax—Preparation, Summary, and Detail.

- **Budgets:** Planning is one of the keys to business success, and budget reports will enable you to see your plans as they relate to your financial goals. It includes Budget—Budget Overview, Budget vs. Actual, Profit & Loss Budget Performance, and Budget vs. Actual Graph.

- **List:** Employee, Customer, and Vendor information are always needed in the daily life of a business manager. Since all the required information is provided in the List windows, this is the one place you will come for contact information of every person without running from one file to another. It includes Customer—Phone List and Contact List. Vendor—Phone List and Contact List. Employee—Contact List. Other Names—Phone List and Contact List. Listing—Account Listing, Item Price List, Item Listing, Payroll Item Listing, Fixed Asset Listing, Term Listing, To Do Notes, and Memorized Transaction Listing.

- **Custom Summary Report:** Most reports you would pull in QuickBooks are pre-set. If you want to customize your own report, this is the window to use. It allows you to set date ranges, include checks (voided or not), and other choices.

- **Custom Transaction Detail Report:** Not only can you customize a summary report, QuickBooks also allows you to customize transactions. You can add as much detail in your report as you like.

- **QuickReport:** This excellent report allows you to quickly review the activity of every account. It is handy and quick, and can be accessed from every account register. The QuickReport button is located at the top of the register.

- **Transaction History:** If you want to see the history or activities of an account, all you have to do is open that account, click on it, and run the Transaction History report and the history will be displayed for you.

- **Transaction Journal:** You are looking to see the debit and credit QuickBooks did on an account, just open the account and run this function. The debit and credit report will be displayed for you.

Review Report Center

If you are looking for the one window where you can see all the financial reports in QuickBooks—the Report Center is definitely the one place to come. If you set up all the Preferences correctly and completely, as soon as you open the Report Center, you would be greeted by 12 report tabs. When you click each tab, it will display the reports available for the tab. It is vital for you to practice by clicking each tab and reviewing what reports are located under each tab; sooner or later you will want to open these reports.

- Click Reports menu
- Click Report Center

Company & Financial: By clicking the Company & Financial tab located at the left of the window, QuickBooks will display the following Report groups

- Profit & Loss
- Income & Expenses
- Balance Sheet & Net Worth
- Cash Flows

Customers & Receivables: By clicking the Customers & Receivables tab, QuickBooks will display the following Report groups:

- A/R Aging
- Customer Balance
- Lists

Sales: By clicking the Sales tab, QuickBooks will display the following Report groups:

- Sales by Customer
- Sales by Item
- Sales by Rep

Job, Time & Mileage: By clicking the Job, Time & Mileage tab, QuickBooks will display the following Report groups

- Job & Profitability
- Job Estimates
- Time
- Mileage

Vendors & Payables: By clicking the Vendors & Payables tab, QuickBooks will display the following Report groups:

- A/P Aging
- Vendor Balances
- 1099
- Sales Tax and List
- Lists

Purchases: By clicking the Purchases tab, QuickBooks will display the following Report groups

- Purchases by Vendor
- Purchases by Item
- Open Purchase Orders

Inventory: By clicking the Inventory tab, QuickBooks will display the following Report groups

- Inventory Valuation
- Inventory Stock Status

Employees & Payroll: By clicking the Employees & Payroll tab, QuickBooks will display the following Report groups:

- Payroll
- Employee

Banking: By clicking the Banking tab, QuickBooks will display the following Report groups

- Banking

Accountant & Taxes: By clicking the Accountant & Taxes tab, QuickBooks will display the following Report groups:

- Account Activities
- Listing
- Income Tax

Budgets: By clicking the Budgets tab, QuickBooks will display the following Report groups:

- Budgets

Lists: By clicking the Lists tab, QuickBooks will display the following Report groups:

- Customer
- Vendor
- Employee
- Other Names
- Listing

Process Multiple Reports

Sometimes, you just want to preview and print one report. All you have to do is go to the Report menu, find the one report, open it and print. However, other times you may want to preview and print a set of reports. Now there is a quicker and easier way to preview and print a set of reports at one time. The Process Multiple Reports tool will allow you to choose a group of reports and print them. The groups are Accountant, Banking, Company, Employees, Register Reports, and Vendors.

Activities:

- Click **Reports menu**
- Click **Process Multiple Reports**
- Select Memorize Reports From: Select **Company**
- Highlight **1/1/2009 under From** (right of window)
- Type **1/1/09**. Press **Tab**. Type **12/31/09**
- Repeat for Profit & Loss and Statement of Cash Flow
- Click **Display**
- Click **X** to close Cash Flow Statement
- Click **X** to close Profit & Loss
- Click **X** to close Balance Sheet

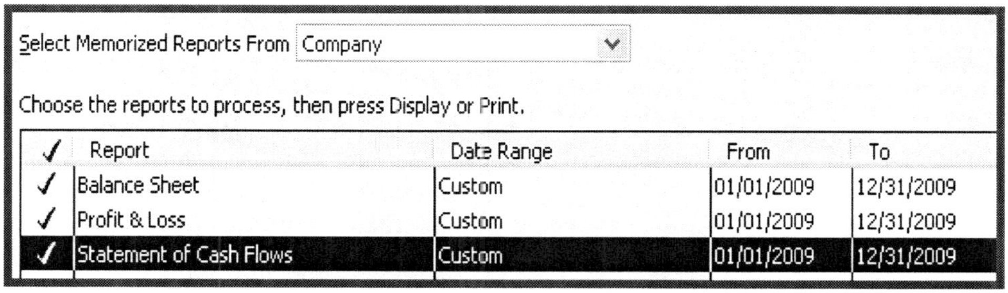

Company & Financial

QuickBooks has several groups of reports; the first group is Company & Financial, with the Profit & Loss as a sub-report. Often you want to see how much income is left after you've paid your bills. The Profit & Loss statement will give you the summary of your income and expenses. The balance on this report will determine how much money you have in your bank account. The more net income, the more cash in your bank account. However, not all net income is in your bank account.

Activities:

- Click **Reports menu**
- Click **Company & Financial**
- Click **Profit & Loss Standard**
- Date: Select **This Fiscal Year**
- From**:** Accept **1/1/09** To: Accept **12/31/09**
- Click **Collapse** (top of window)
- Columns: Select **Quarter**
- **Net Income is 2,033,313.26**
- You may practice with other reports in that section

Quick Company 2009

Profit & Loss

January through December 2009

	Jan - Mar 09	Apr - Jun 09	Jul - Sep 09	Oct - Dec 09	TOTAL
Ordinary Income/Expense					
Income					
Opening Balance Income	1,914,500.00	0.00	0.00	0.00	1,914,500.00
Landscaping Services	394,811.34	0.00	0.00	0.00	394,811.34
Total Income	2,309,311.34	0.00	0.00	0.00	2,309,311.34
Cost of Goods Sold					
Materials	213,700.00	0.00	0.00	0.00	213,700.00
Discount Received	-4,530.00	0.00	0.00	0.00	-4,530.00
Total COGS	209,170.00	0.00	0.00	0.00	209,170.00
Gross Profit	2,100,141.34	0.00	0.00	0.00	2,100,141.34
Expense					
Adjustment to Decr Inventory	1,250.00	0.00	0.00	0.00	1,250.00
Opening Balance Expense	6,500.00	0.00	0.00	0.00	6,500.00
Automobile Expense	384.00	0.00	0.00	0.00	384.00
Depreciation Expense	666.67	0.00	0.00	0.00	666.67
Payroll Expenses	57,568.41	0.00	0.00	0.00	57,568.41
Telephone Expense	459.00	0.00	0.00	0.00	459.00
Total Expense	66,828.08	0.00	0.00	0.00	66,828.08
Net Ordinary Income	2,033,313.26	0.00	0.00	0.00	2,033,313.26
Net Income	**2,033,313.26**	**0.00**	**0.00**	**0.00**	**2,033,313.26**

Income & Expense Graph

A picture, they say, is worth a thousand words. This is especially true with the income and expense graph. QuickBooks has made it interesting and informational by providing a bar graph and a pie chart. The bar graph has two bars—the big one is your income and the small one is your expenses. The pie chart has two pies—the big pie is your income and the small pie is your expenses. A box to the right further breaks down your expenses with payroll the largest expense.

Activities:

- ❖ Click **Reports menu**
- ❖ Click **Company & Financial**
- ❖ Click **Income & Expense Graph**
- ❖ Click **Dates…**(top left of the window)
- ❖ Graph Date: Select **This Year**. Click **OK**

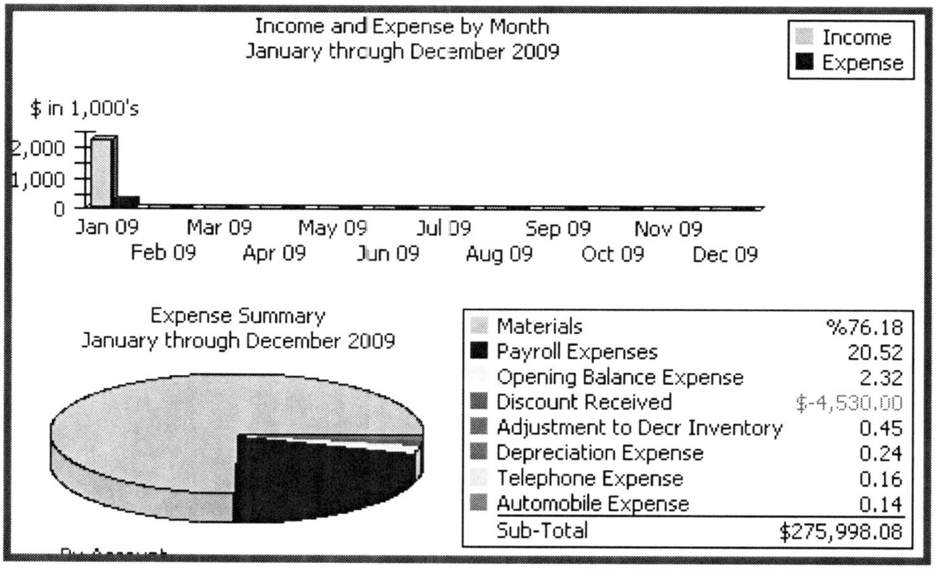

- ❖ Click **View menu**
- ❖ Click **Add "QuickInsight Income & Expense" to Icon Bar**
- ❖ Label: Type **Inc/Exp Graph.** Click **OK** to "Add Window to Icon Bar"
- ❖ **Look! Graph is added to the Icon Bar for future use**
- ❖ **Total Expense is 275,998.08**
- ❖ Click **X** to close Graph window

Customer & Receivables

The second group of reports is the Customers & Receivables. The A/R Aging Summary is the first sub-report under this group. The Balance Sheet report will tell you if you have an Account Receivables balance—that is, how much your customers owe you. The next question is, "Who owes you and how long has it been?" The A/R Aging Summary will tell you exactly how long it has been, such as 30, 60, 90, or 120 days. You're a poor collector if you have anything more than 120 days.

Quick Company 2009

A/R Aging Summary

As of December 31, 2009

	Current	1 - 30	31 - 60	61 - 90	91 - 120	> 120	TOTAL
Jerry Johnson	0.00	0.00	0.00	0.00	0.00	4,040.77	4,040.77
John Allen	0.00	0.00	0.00	0.00	0.00	555,605.48	555,605.48
Tommy Brown	0.00	0.00	0.00	0.00	0.00	459,637.26	459,637.26
US Machines	0.00	0.00	0.00	0.00	0.00	5,556.05	5,556.05
TOTAL	**0.00**	**0.00**	**0.00**	**0.00**	**0.00**	**1,024,839.56**	**1,024,839.56**

Activities:

- Click **Reports menu**
- Click **Customers & Receivables**
- Click **A/R Aging Summary**
- Date: Select **This Fiscal Year**
- Click **Collapse** (top of window)
- Interval (days): Type **30.**
- Through (days past due): Type **120**. Press **Tab**
- You may practice with other reports in that section

Sales

The third group of reports is Sales. The Sales by Customer Summary is the first sub-report under the sales group of reports. If you have several salesmen who service different customers in different regions, one of the most effective ways of arranging your report is Sales by Customer. You want to use the report to find out who your major customer is, and you want to be able to direct future sales to the competitors of your major customer. This is one way to increase sales.

Activities:

- Click **Reports menu**
- Click **Sales**
- Click **Sales by Customer Summary**
- Date: Select **This Fiscal Year**
- Columns (top right): Select **Quarter**
- Click **Collapse**
- You may practice with other reports in that section

Quick Company 2009

Sales by Customer Summary

January through December 2009

	Jan - Mar 09	Apr - Jun 09	Jul - Sep 09	Oct - Dec 09	TOTAL
James Adams	215,346.78	0.00	0.00	0.00	215,346.78
Jerry Johnson	40.77	0.00	0.00	0.00	40.77
John Allen	168,730.48	0.00	0.00	0.00	168,730.48
Tommy Brown	10,637.26	0.00	0.00	0.00	10,637.26
US Machines	56.05	0.00	0.00	0.00	56.05
TOTAL	**394,811.34**	**0.00**	**0.00**	**0.00**	**394,811.34**

Job, Time & Mileage

The fourth group of reports is Job, Time & Mileage. The Job Profitability Summary is the first sub-report in this group. You've discovered you're making money, but, you want to know which job is making you the most money. Some jobs will require you to spend a lot of money and make little in the process. However, other jobs will require only small investments and with lots of profit. The Job Profitability Summary report is the one key report that shows you the job with the most profit.

Activities:

- Click **Reports menu**
- Click **Job, Time & Mileage**
- Click **Job Profitability Summary**

Quick Company 2009

Job Profitability Summary

January through December 2009

	Act. Cost	Act. Revenue	($) Diff.
James Adams	116,968.20	215,346.78	98,378.58
Jerry Johnson	0.00	40.77	40.77
John Allen	101,250.00	168,730.48	67,480.48
Tommy Brown	0.00	10,637.26	10,637.26
US Machines	0.00	56.05	56.05
TOTAL	**218,218.20**	**394,811.34**	**176,593.14**

- Date: Select **This Fiscal Year**
- Click **Collapse** (top of window)
- You may practice with other reports in that section

Vendors & Payables

The fifth group of reports is the Vendors & Payables. The A/P Aging Summary is the first sub-report under this group. If you look at your Balance Sheet statement, and see Account Payable (A/P) with a balance, you want to know how long it has been since you forgot to pay your bill. It is a bad business practice to owe your vendors for more than 120 days. As it shows that your financial health is in bad shape. It also shows that your vendors are poor collectors with poor collection policy.

Activities:

- Click **Reports menu**
- Click **Vendors & Payables**
- Click **A/P Aging Summary**
- Date: Select **This Fiscal Year**
- Interval (days): Type **30**
- Through (days past due): Type **120**. Press **Tab**
- You may practice with other reports in that section

Quick Company 2009

A/P Aging Summary

As of December 31, 2009

	Current	1 - 30	31 - 60	61 - 90	91 - 120	> 120	TOTAL
Electric America	0.00	0.00	0.00	0.00	0.00	1,500.00	1,500.00
TOTAL	**0.00**	**0.00**	**0.00**	**0.00**	**0.00**	**1,500.00**	**1,500.00**

Purchases

The sixth group of reports is Purchases. The Purchases by Vendor Summary is the first sub-report under the purchases group. From time to time, you want to run this report to see your purchases by vendor. You want to know which vendor is receiving the most money from you and what they are selling to you. You want to find out if you're getting any kind of cash discounts for early payments; and if you are using your buying power enough to get price breaks—at least 20% discount.

Activities:

- Click **Reports menu**
- Click **Purchases**
- Click **Purchases by Vendor Summary**
- Date: Select **This Fiscal Year**
- Columns: Select **Quarter**
- You may practice with other reports in that section

Quick Company 2009

Purchases by Vendor Summary

January through December 2009

	Jan - Mar 09	Apr - Jun 09	Jul - Sep 09	Oct - Dec 09	TOTAL
US Supplies	225,000.00	0.00	0.00	0.00	225,000.00
TOTAL	**225,000.00**	**0.00**	**0.00**	**0.00**	**225,000.00**

Inventory

The seventh group of reports is Inventory. The Inventory Valuation Summary is the first sub-report under the Inventory group. If you sell merchandise to customers, this is one of the most significant reports you need to review every month. You want to know which inventory is stagnant and which one is moving fast. From last month to this month, do you still have the same valuation for the same inventory? Valuation should be going down; it is being converted into cash and possibly into profit.

Activities:

- Click **Reports menu**
- Click **Inventory**
- Click **Inventory Valuation Summary**
- Date: Select **This Fiscal Year**
- You may practice with other reports in that section

Quick Company 2009

Inventory Valuation Summary

As of December 31, 2009

	Item D...	On Hand	Avg C...	Asset Value	% of Tot...	Sales...	Retail Val...	% of T...
Inventory								
Fertilizer	Materials	1,000	100.00	100,000.00	42.5%	150.00	150,000.00	42.5%
Flowers	Materials	1,051	50.00	52,550.00	22.4%	75.00	78,825.00	22.4%
Soil	Materials	1,100	75.00	82,500.00	35.1%	112.50	123,750.00	35.1%
Total Invent...		3,151		235,050.00	100.0%		352,575.00	100.0%
TOTAL		**3,151**		**235,050.00**	**100.0%**		**352,575.00**	**100.0%**

Employees & Payroll

As far as the Employees and Payroll menu is concern, the payroll summary is one of the key reports that helps you to understand what is going on in the payroll department. Any time you want to know how much was paid to an employee or how much in total was the payroll expenses, the payroll summary report is absolutely very necessary. Most of the times, you want to run the "This Calendar Year" report to pick up all the activities with the year and this is done by clicking the column box.

Activities:

- Click **Reports menu**
- Click **Employees & Payroll**
- Click **Payroll Summary**
- Dates: Select **This Calendar Year**
- Columns: Select **Year**
- You may practice with other reports in that section

Quick Company 2009

Payroll Summary

January through December 2009

	Hours	Rate	Jan - Dec 09
Employee Wages, Taxes and Adjustments			
Gross Pay			
Salary	80		3,846.15
Hourly	80	50.00	4,000.00
Overtime Hourly	1.06667	75.00	80.00
Commission			15,000.00
Bonus			30,000.00
Total Gross Pay	161.06667		52,926.15
Deductions from Gross Pay			
Dental Insurance			-20.00
Health Insurance			-40.00
Total Deductions from Gross Pay			-60.00
Adjusted Gross Pay	161.06667		52,866.15
Taxes Withheld			
Federal Withholding			-15,881.00
Medicare Employee			-766.56
Social Security Employee			-3,277.70
Total Taxes Withheld			-19,925.26
Net Pay	**161.06667**		**32,940.89**

Banking

From to time you will want to review the previous month's reconciliation reports. The banking report submenu has previous reconciliation reports you can process to see the details of last month's activities. There are three reports options available: summary, detail, and both (summary and detail). You have option to select a report with transactions cleared at the time of reconciliation in pdf. But, it's best to select the second option, transactions cleared plus any changes made to those transactions since the last reconciliation.

Quick Company 2009

Reconciliation Summary

USA Checking, Period Ending 01/31/2009

		Jan 31, 09
Beginning Balance		800,000.00
Cleared Transactions		
Checks and Payments - 7 it...	-250,480.25	
Deposits and Credits - 4 ite...	1,308,563.03	
Total Cleared Transactions	1,058,082.78	
Cleared Balance		**1,858,082.78**
Register Balance as of 01/31/2009		1,858,082.78
Ending Balance		1,858,082.78

Activities:

- Click **Reports menu**
- Click **Banking**
- Click **Previous Reconciliation**
- Account: Select **Checking**
- Type of Report: Click **Summary**
- Click **Transaction cleared plus any changes…**(2nd option)
- Click **Display**
- You may practice with other reports in this section

Accountant & Taxes

When you run the Balance Sheet report, you will see your assets, liabilities, and owner's equity. When you run the Income Statement report, you will see your income, expenses, and net income. The Trial Balance report is a "buy one get two reports." It shows you the balances of both your Balance Sheet and Income Statement. Best of all, it shows your balances in Debit and Credit columns. By looking at the columns, you can tell if you have a problem with an account.

Activities:

- Click **Reports menu**
- Click **Accountant & Taxes**
- Click **Trial Balance**

- Date: Select **This Fiscal Year**
- Scroll to the bottom
- **Total Debit is equal to Total Credit 3,831,032.01**
- You may practice other reports in this section

Quick Company 2009

Trial Balance

As of December 31, 2009

	Dec 31, 09	
	Debit	Credit
Inventory Asset	235,050.00	
Undeposited Funds	0.00	
Truck:Accumulated Depreciation		666.67
Truck:Truck at Cost	40,000.00	
Accounts Payable		1,500.00
Visa Credit Card		524.00
Payroll Liabilities	0.00	
Sales Tax Payable	0.00	
Mortgage Loan		500,000.00
Office Building Loan		50,000.00
Opening Balance Equity		964,500.00
Opening Balance Income		1,914,500.00
Landscaping Services:Materials		320,550.00
Landscaping Services:Labor		48,750.00
Landscaping Services:Subcontractors		6,000.00
Landscaping Services:Misc Income		19,511.34
Materials	213,700.00	
Discount Received		4,530.00
Adjustment to Decr Inventory	1,250.00	
Opening Balance Expense	6,500.00	
Automobile Expense:Fuel	84.00	
Automobile Expense:Repairs & Maint	300.00	
Depreciation Expense	666.67	
Payroll Expenses	57,568.41	
Telephone Expense	459.00	
TOTAL	**3,831,032.01**	**3,831,032.01**

Budgets

Without goals, they say, you would not know when you reach one. It is essential to set financial goals, otherwise, you will not have control over your spending habits and you will not work hard enough to reach your income goals either. The time to set the Profit and Loss Budget for next year is before the end of this year, that way you have a good handle on how you spend your money in promotion, advertising, and other marketing campaigns.

Quick Company 2009

Profit & Loss Budget Performance

January through December 2009

	Jan - Dec 09	Budget	Jan - Dec 09	YTD Budget	Annual Bu...
Ordinary Income/Expense					
Income					
Opening Balance Income	1,914,500.00		1,914,500.00		
Landscaping Services	394,811.34	1,200,000.00	394,811.34	1,200,000.00	1,200,000.00
Total Income	2,309,311.34	1,200,000.00	2,309,311.34	1,200,000.00	1,200,000.00
Cost of Goods Sold					
Cost of Goods Sold	0.00	480,000.00	0.00	480,000.00	480,000.00
Materials	213,700.00		213,700.00		
Discount Received	-4,530.00		-4,530.00		
Total COGS	209,170.00	480,000.00	209,170.00	480,000.00	480,000.00
Gross Profit	2,100,141.34	720,000.00	2,100,141.34	720,000.00	720,000.00
Expense					
Adjustment to Decr Inven...	1,250.00		1,250.00		
Opening Balance Expense	6,500.00		6,500.00		
Automobile Expense	384.00		384.00		
Depreciation Expense	666.67		666.67		
Payroll Expenses	57,568.41		57,568.41		
Telephone Expense	459.00		459.00		
Total Expense	66,828.08		66,828.08		
Net Ordinary Income	2,033,313.26	720,000.00	2,033,313.26	720,000.00	720,000.00
Net Income	**2,033,313.26**	**720,000.00**	**2,033,313.26**	**720,000.00**	**720,000.00**

Activities:

- Click **Reports menu**
- Click **Budgets**
- Click **Profit & Loss Budget Performance**
- Accept **FY 2009—Profit & Loss by Account.** Click **Next**
- Accept **Account by Month.** Click **Next**
- Click **Finish**

- ❖ Dates: Select **This Fiscal Year**
- ❖ Click **Collapse**
- ❖ You may practice with other reports in this section

List

From time to time you want to run a report and review the prices of your items. If you are a business owner, you want your accountant to run this report to make sure the correct prices are reflected on the invoice sent to customers. What if you want to increase prices across the board, as we did in one of the exercise? This is the right time to run the Item List report to see if the price adjustments are what you needed or if additional changes are required to increase or decrease the numbers.

Activities:

- ❖ Click **Reports menu**
- ❖ Click **List**
- ❖ Click **Item Price List**
- ❖ Click **Modify Report….** Click **Header/Footer** tab
- ❖ Uncheck **Subtitle**. Click **OK**
- ❖ You may practice with other reports in this section

Quick Company 2009

Item Price List

Item	Description	Price
Decking	Subcontractor work	610.00
Delivery	Employee work	160.00
Framing	Subcontractor work	460.00
Gardening	Employee work	120.00
Installation	Subcontractor work	310.00
Tree Removal	Employee work	130.00
Trimming	Employee work	110.00
Fertilizer	Materials	150.00
Flowers	Materials	75.00
Soil	Materials	112.50
Holders	Supplies	20.00
Pots	Supplies	45.00
Shrubs	Materials	51.00
Wire	Materials	30.00
Fin Chg	Finance Charges on Overdue...	12.0%

Transaction History

Every transaction has a history, and the history is listed by type, transaction number, date, vendor name, if any, account involved, and the paid amount. To see the detail of that transaction, all you have to do is double click on it; you will be taken to the Write Check window, if the transaction involves a check payment. Now you will be able to see the details of the check. Click X to close the check window, preview, and print the report if you choose to do so.

Quick Company 2009
Transaction History
All Transactions

Type	Num	Date	Name	Account	Paid Am...	Origina...
Bill Pmt -Check	**1003**	**01/02/2009**	**Telephone Ame...**	**USA Checking**	**-3,959.00**	
Bill		01/01/2009	Telephone America	Opening Balance...	3,500.00	3,500.00
TOTAL					3,500.00	3,500.00
Bill	Cell 1...	01/02/2009	Telephone America	Telephone Expen...	459.00	459.00
TOTAL					459.00	459.00
TOTAL					3,959.00	0.00
Unapplied Amount					0.00	

Activities:

- Click **Banking menu**
- Click **Use Register**
- Select Account: Select **USA Checking.** Click **OK**
- Click **on Telephone America check for 3,959.00**
- Click **Reports menu**
- Click **Transaction History**
- You may practice with other history report

Transaction Journal

If you want to see how QuickBooks made a journal entry on a particular account, this is where to come. That is, you want to see what is going on behind the scenes. Not every account's journal entry is displayed by QuickBooks; some are displayed with just the account balance without showing the debit and credit. Transaction Journal function does not work at the major report level; you have to double click on the account in the main report to open the sub-report and then proceed to the journal entry.

Activities:

- Click **Reports menu**
- Click **Company & Financial**
- Click **Profit & Loss Standard**
- Dates (top left of the window): Select **This Fiscal Year**
- Transaction Journal will NOT run in this report
- Double click **Repair/Maint for 300.00**
- Transaction Journal will run in this report
- Click **check number 1006 for 200.00**
- Click **Reports menu.** Click **Transaction Journal**
- This is how QuickBooks does Debit/Credit Journal entries

Quick Company 2009

Transaction Journal

All Transactions

Trans #	Type	Date	Num	Name	Memo	Account	Debit	Credit
56	Check	01/15/2009	1006	America Auto Serv...		USA Checking		250.00
				America Auto Serv...	Repairs	Repairs & Maint	200.00	
				America Auto Serv...	Fuel	Fuel	50.00	
							250.00	250.00
TOTAL							**250.00**	**250.00**

Print Forms

You might like to know there are more report windows other than from the Reports menu. These little-known windows are located in the File menu. Just click the File menu, and then click Print Forms. You will see a list of forms to choose from. The Bill Payment Stub is one of them. When you open the window, the default date range is today; if you want a different range of dates, you have to change the Date box and the Thru box with your choice of dates.

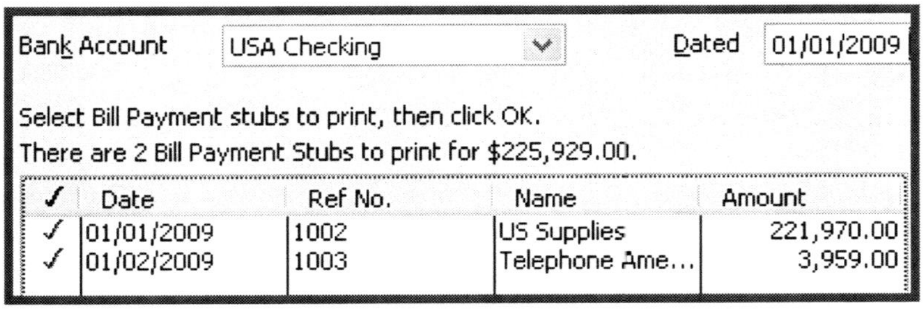

Activities:

- Click **File menu**
- Click **Print Forms**
- Click **Bill Payment Stubs**
- Bank Account: Accept **USA Checking**
- Dated: Type **1/1/09**. Press **Tab**
- Thru: Type **12/31/09.** Press **Tab**
- Accept **Select All** (bottom right of window)
- Click **Preview** (right of window). Click **Zoom In**
- Click **Next Page** (top left) Click **Close or Print** if printer is ready
- Click **X** to close Bill Payment Stubs window

Send Forms

When you were completing estimates, invoices, purchase order, and bills, you learned how to click "To be e-mailed" at the bottom of the document. If you have chosen to e-mail them, the next step is to go to the Send Forms submenu under the File menu. You have option to send only one document or send a selected batch of documents. You must subscribe to this service to use it. Remember to edit at least the first e-mail, so you can see if there are errors that need to be corrected on other documents.

Activities:

- Click **File menu**
- Click **Send Forms**
- Click **Select All** (right of window)
- Click **Edit E-mail** (right of window)
- In the bottom window. Accept **"Thank you for your service."**
- Press **Enter Key 2 times** to create a spaces
- Type **Kelly Johnson.** Press **Enter**
- Type **Director of Finance**. Press **Enter**.
- Type **Quick Company**

- ❖ Click **Check Spelling** (right of window). Click **OK**
- ❖ Click **OK** to close Edit E-mail
- ❖ Click **Close or Send Now** if you subscribed to the email service

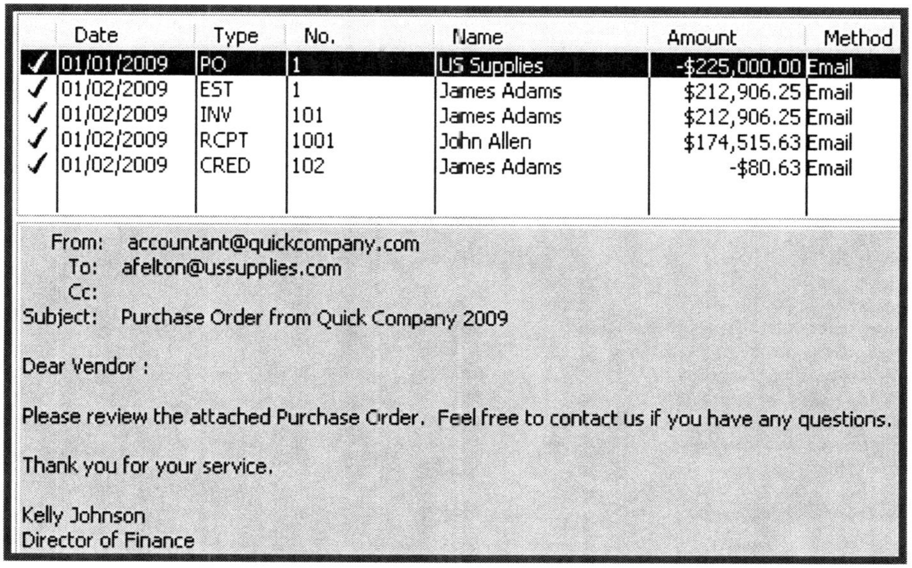

Financial: Profit & Loss

There are no financial activities that affect the Profit & Loss statement in this chapter. At this point you should know the contents of the Profit & Loss statement which includes the total income, cost of goods sold, gross profit, operating expenses which QuickBooks choose to call just expenses and finally the net income which is the bottom line. Also, you need to know at this point that total income minus total expenses equal to net income and that amount is now $2,033,313.26.

Activities:

- ❖ Click **Reports menu**
- ❖ Click **Company & Financial**
- ❖ Click **Profit & Loss Standard**
- ❖ Date: Select **This Fiscal Year**
- ❖ From: Accept **1/1/09.** To: Accept **12/31/09**
- ❖ Click **Collapse**
- ❖ **Net Income is 2,033,313.26**
- ❖ Click **X** to close window

Quick Company 2009
Profit & Loss
January through December 2009

	Jan - Dec 09
Ordinary Income/Expense	
Income	
Opening Balance Income	1,914,500.00
Landscaping Services	394,811.34
Total Income	2,309,311.34
Cost of Goods Sold	
Materials	213,700.00
Discount Received	-4,530.00
Total COGS	209,170.00
Gross Profit	2,100,141.34
Expense	
Adjustment to Decr Inventory	1,250.00
Opening Balance Expense	6,500.00
Automobile Expense	384.00
Depreciation Expense	666.67
Payroll Expenses	57,568.41
Telephone Expense	459.00
Total Expense	66,828.08
Net Ordinary Income	2,033,313.26
Net Income	**2,033,313.26**

Financial: Balance Sheet

Also in there are no financial activities in this section that has any material effects on the Balance Sheet statement. It is important to know though that total assets must equal to total liabilities and owner's equity. The net income in the owner's equity section is the same net income from the Profit and Loss statement. Total current assets plus total fixed asset equals to total assets. Current assets balance is currently $3,488,108.18 and Total Assets is $3,549,837.26.

Activities:

- Click **Reports menu**
- Click **Company & Financial**
- Click **Balance Sheet Standard**
- Date: Select **This Fiscal Year**
- As of: Accept **12/31/09**
- Click **Collapse**
- **Total Assets is 3,549,837.26**
- Click **X** to close window

Quick Company 2009

Balance Sheet

As of December 31, 2009

	Dec 31, 09
ASSETS	
Current Assets	
Checking/Savings	
Petty Cash	100.00
Money Market Account	100,000.00
USA Checking	1,858,082.78
USA Payroll Checking	42,431.59
USA Savings	250,000.00
Total Checking/Savings	2,250,614.37
Accounts Receivable	
Accounts Receivable	1,024,839.56
Total Accounts Receivable	1,024,839.56
Other Current Assets	
Inventory Asset	235,050.00
Total Other Current Assets	235,050.00
Total Current Assets	3,510,503.93
Fixed Assets	
Truck	39,333.33
Total Fixed Assets	39,333.33
TOTAL ASSETS	**3,549,837.26**

Chapter Summary

Good financial reports are the reward for your hard labor. When you were setting up your preferences, creating accounts and item listing, completing customers' and vendors' information, the ultimate goal was to generate complete and accurate report. A report is not satisfactory if it does not give you the right information you are looking for. You were wondering if you have to provide all those information about customers or vendors. No, you don't have to, but if you want a better report, you need to key in some data which are pulled into the report.

What we accomplished:

- Reviewed Reports submenus
- Processed multiple reports
- We ran reports, graphs and forms under the following headings:
- Company & Financial
- Income & Expense Graph
- Customer & Receivables
- Sales
- Job, Time & Mileage
- Vendor & Payables
- Purchases
- Inventory
- Employees & Payroll
- Banking
- Accountant & Taxes
- Budgets
- Item
- Transaction History
- Transaction Journal
- Print Forms
- Send Forms
- Processed financial statements

Additional Financial activities:

- No financial activities were performed in this chapter

$

Chapter 11

Window Menu

Objectives: After ycu've completed the chapter, you will be able to:

- ✓ Describe Window submenus
- ✓ Use the Close All function

Review Window Submenus

Most users do not remember that they can access any opened windows from the Windows menu. Not only that, QuickBooks has made it easy by creating Open Windows box located at the left side of the window. Now, you have two options: either to open windows from the Open Windows box or go through the Window menu and click on the window you would like to open.

- Click **Windows menu**

The following activities are found under the Window menu:

- Close All: Any time you have too many open windows on your QuickBooks Screen, to remove all these open windows, all you have to do is click the Window menu and click Close All, and all open windows will disappear; this is better than clicking X one by one to close each opened window. Be sure you want to close all windows. Some windows will not close automatically, especially the Report window if you change the default settings or customize the report. For example, if the Date setting is "Today," and you change the setting to "This Fiscal Year." When Quickbooks gets to the report with changed default setting, it will prompt you with a "Would you like to memorize this report?" At this point you have the option of clicking either Yes or No. Most of the time you should click No, and this action will release the Close All procedure.

- Tile Vertically: This button will allow you open windows on your desktop vertically. To change Home Page see Cascade paragraph below.

- Tile Horizontally: This function allows you to open windows on your desktop horizontally. To change Home Page see Cascade paragraph below.

- Cascade: Cascading your open windows is also available with Quickbooks. **To change Home Page to normal window. Click Window menu and click Close All. Click Company and Home Page. Drag the right edge to cover the right edge of the computer. Drag the bottom edge to the bottom but leave a small space.**

Close All Windows

Close All is one of the handy tools you should know how to use. If you have a good working knowledge of Microsoft Office products, you should have a good idea of what Close All can do. You need to try it yourself to know exactly what windows will be closed. Close All will not close any Modified Reports, especially, if you have changed the settings on that report. The Close All will process your command until it gets to the Modified Report and it will ask if you want to memorize the report.

Activities:

- Click **Window menu**
- Click **Close All**
- Click **Company menu**
- Click **Home Page**
- Click **Window menu**
- **Look! You have Tile Vertical, Title Horizontal, and Cascade**
- Click **View menu**. Click **One Window**
- Click **Window menu**
- **Look! Tile Vertical, Title Horizontal, and Cascade are gone**
- Click **View menu**. Click **Multiple Window**

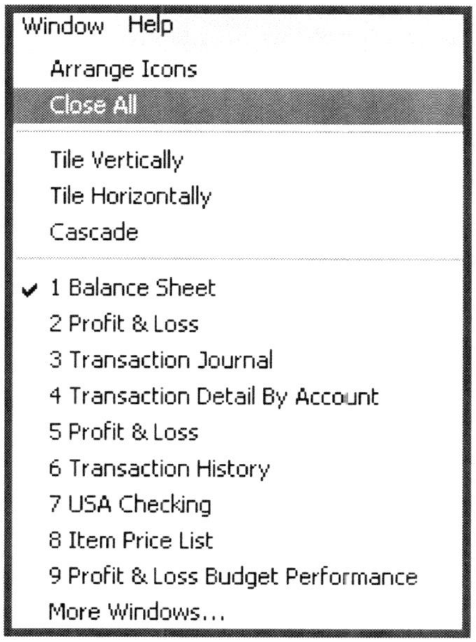

$

Chapter 12

Help Menu

Objectives: After you've completed this chapter, you will be able to:

- ✓ Explain QuickBooks Help submenus
- ✓ Identify the Learning Center Tutorials contents
- ✓ Research with the QuickBooks Help
- ✓ Use the Year-End Guide
- ✓ Process financial reports and compare results

Review QuickBooks Help Submenus

In your spare time, you should test-drive the Help menu and its submenus. You never know when you will run into a problem and you want QuickBooks to give you directions on how to accomplish a task. It is good practice to use Help to find a simple answer—that way, you have an idea of how to use Help to solve complex problems. The procedure of finding answers in QuickBooks Help is easy; you just have to make up a few key words on the subject in question. Remember to click the Related Topics located at the bottom of every suggested answer; this might give additional information you never thought of before.

- Click **Help menu**

The following activities are found under the Help menu:

- **QuickBooks Help:** The Help menu is one of the most powerful windows on your QuickBooks software. I don't know about you, but I want somewhere I can go, day or night, to get an answer when I need one. QuickBooks Help menu is the one help-center you don't have to dial and wait for all the prompts before getting answers. The only advice I'll give you is to get to know how to use the Help submenu windows, you don't know when you would really need it. This book will cover most of the windows, however, occasionally you might want to test a feature and the QuickBooks Help submenu will be there for you 24/7.

- **Learning Center Tutorial:** The first of the windows that shows up after you've create a new file is the QuickBooks Learning Center. It is annoying to allow the learning window to keep popping up every time you open a file. The first task is to disable the window from opening up by clicking the "Show this window at startup" box located at the bottom left of the window. You click the box to remove the checkmark already in the box. You can test-drive any of the Learning Center windows anytime you want additional insight on how the software works.

- **Year-End Guide:** At the end of the year, you must visit this window to learn what information is necessary to close the year on a sound footing. The checklists in this window are a good start to making sure you are on track to covering the Year-End activities such as, reconciling accounts, accruals, corrections, closing books, and adjusting Retained Earnings, etc.

Review Learning Center Tutorials

The QuickBooks Learning Center has the tabs and links on how to successfully operate your QuickBooks software. In your spare time, I highly recommend you test drive some of these links and learn how to perform some of the activities. But remember some may seem redundant and too easy after using this book. Most of the information on the QuickBooks Learning Center is covered in this book. You will need to turn on your computer speaker to be able to listen to the audio transcript, and turn it off any time by clicking the X at the top right corner of the Learning Center.

- Click Help menu
- Click Learning Center Tutorials

Click and review the following video links found under the QuickBooks Learning Center:

Accept Overview & Setup Tab (left of the window):
- QuickBooks overview
- Overview QuickBooks accounts
- Adding and using QuickBooks accounts
- Items (products & services you sell)
- Customers
- Vendors
- Reports

Click Customer & Sales (left of window):
- Introducing the Customer Center
- Prepare an estimate
- Create an invoice
- Generate a sales receipt
- Create a statement
- Enter and deposit customer payments
- Customize sales forms
- Track upfront deposits and returns
- Time and billing

Click Vendors & Expenses (left of the window):

- Introducing Vendor Center
- Write checks and enter expenses
- Enter bills
- Pay bills
- Track and pay sales tax

Click Inventory (left of the window):

- Overview
- Set up
- Buying and selling inventory
- Using reports to manage inventory

Click Payroll (left of the window):

- Payroll overview
- Information needed to set up payroll
- Paying employees
- Paying taxes and liabilities
- Filing taxes and forms
- After-the-fact payroll for accountants

Click Under What's New (left of the window):

- Upgrade from QuickBooks 2005 or earlier?
- What's new in QuickBooks 2009
- Additional training resources

QuickBooks Help

QuickBooks Help is an invaluable submenu. It's always handy when you run into a problem you know how to tackle. Most people don't even remember they have a database of helpful steps that came with their software. It's easy to use, just type the first few letters that relate to your topics, and Help will bring up the closest options for you to select. If you find it, scroll down the left window to see if you can find the main title and continue to look at the subtitle. Click on the word and click Display.

Activities:

- Click **Help menu**
- Click **QuickBooks Help**
- Click **Search tab** (top right of window)
- In the white box. Type **account numbers**. Press **Enter**
- Click **Add account numbers to your account**
- Read the step as displayed in the lower box
- Click **Print** (top of lower window)
- Click **Cancel or Print** if printer is ready
- Click **X** to close QuickBooks Help window

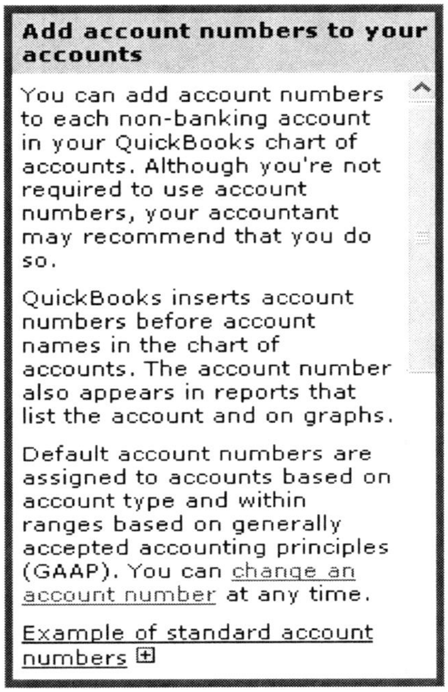

Year-End Guide

The end of the year is one of the most significant periods of your QuickBooks life. You have various tasks that must be performed at the end of the year. You've heard so many times from accountants, "We are closing end of the year books." To help you go through this period successfully, QuickBooks has assembled the tasks it thinks you need to accomplish. It helps you to make sure no stones are left unturned. As you go through the list, you will check off the ones you've completed.

Activities:

- Click **Help menu**
- Click **Year-End Guide**
- Click on the phrase **Reconcile all bank and credit card accounts**

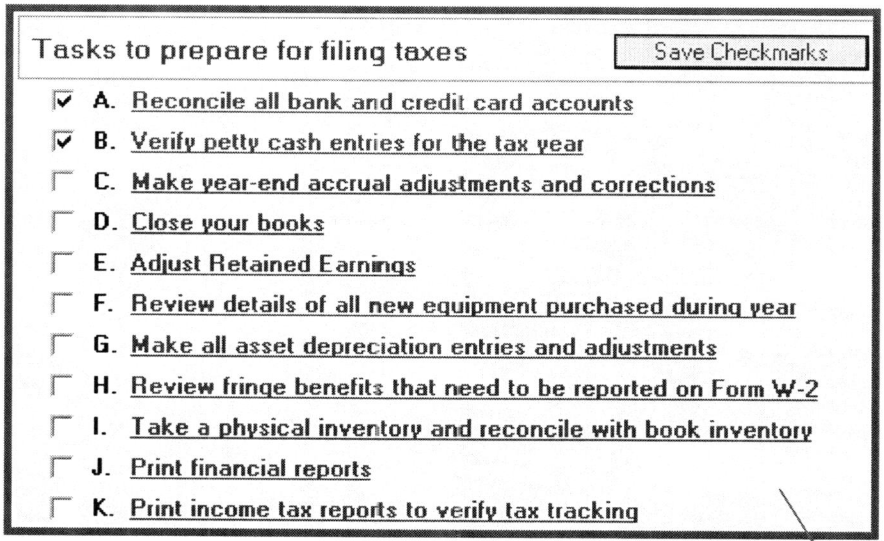

When you've completed a task you checkmark the box and click the Save Checkmarks button.

- Read the explanation in the QuickBooks Help window
- Click on the phrase **Verify petty cash entries**
- Read the explanation in the QuickBooks Help window
- Click **X** to close Help window (right of window)
- **In the Year-End window. Scroll to the bottom**
- Click **Pay payroll liabilities**
- Read explanation in the QuickBooks Help window
- Click **X** to close QuickBooks Help
- Click **X** to close Year-End window

Financial Results: Profit & Loss

Congratulations! This is the final Profit and Loss statement is this book. There are no changes from chapter nine reports; there are no transactions. Don't forget to set goals of what your financial statements would look like at the end of the Year. You should print and analyze your Profit & Loss statement every month, to see if you are meeting your goals. If you're not meeting your Profit & Loss goals, be sure to meet with a competent accountant, who can tell you exactly what to do to reach your goals.

Activities:

- Click **Reports menu**
- Click **Company & Financial**
- Click **Profit & Loss Standard**
- Date: Select **This Fiscal Year**
- From: Accept **1/1/09.** To: Accept **12/31/09**
- Click **Collapse**
- **Total Net Income is 2,033,313.26**
- Click **X** to close window

Quick Company 2009
Profit & Loss
January through December 2009

	Jan - Dec 09
Ordinary Income/Expense	
Income	
Opening Balance Income	1,914,500.00
Landscaping Services	394,811.34
Total Income	2,309,311.34
Cost of Goods Sold	
Materials	213,700.00
Discount Received	-4,530.00
Total COGS	209,170.00
Gross Profit	2,100,141.34
Expense	
Adjustment to Decr Inventory	1,250.00
Opening Balance Expense	6,500.00
Automobile Expense	384.00
Depreciation Expense	666.67
Payroll Expenses	57,568.41
Telephone Expense	459.00
Total Expense	66,828.08
Net Ordinary Income	2,033,313.26
Net Income	**2,033,313.26**

Financial Results: Balance Sheet

There are no activities from chapter nine reports. You must print the Balance Sheet statement every month to see if you're meeting your Balance Sheet goals. It is important to know that cash flow is the "life blood" of a business; without it, the life of your business is limited. The major reason many businesses fail is poor cash management. They are collecting less from Customers and paying more to Vendors. Numbers don't lie; always listen—they're telling you the truth!

Activities:

- Click **Reports menu**
- Click **Company & Financial**
- Click **Balance Sheet Standard**
- Date: Select **This Fiscal Year**
- As of: Accept **12/31/09**
- Click **Collapse**
- **Total Assets is 3,549,837.26**
- Click **X** to close window

Quick Company 2009
Balance Sheet
As of December 31, 2009

	Dec 31, 09
ASSETS	
Current Assets	
Checking/Savings	
Petty Cash	100.00
Money Market Account	100,000.00
USA Checking	1,858,082.78
USA Payroll Checking	42,431.59
USA Savings	250,000.00
Total Checking/Savings	2,250,614.37
Accounts Receivable	
Accounts Receivable	1,024,839.56
Total Accounts Receivable	1,024,839.56
Other Current Assets	
Inventory Asset	235,050.00
Total Other Current Assets	235,050.00
Total Current Assets	3,510,503.93
Fixed Assets	
Truck	39,333.33
Total Fixed Assets	39,333.33
TOTAL ASSETS	**3,549,837.26**

Chapter Summary

In this section, we worked with two chapters at the—the Windows and QuickBooks Help menus. There are not much to the Windows menu than to remember you're your QuickBooks window is crowded with open windows, it is time to clear them all out with a click of a button. That is using the Close All function. In the QuickBooks Help chapter we looked at the Help function. It is also essential to remember the Learning tutorial which is always handy should you need additional information. We practiced how to use the New Business Checklist and Year-End Guide.

What we accomplished:

- **In the Window menu, we**:
- Reviewed the window submenus
- Practiced close all function
- **In the QuickBooks Help menu, we**:
- Reviewed the QuickBooks Help submenus
- Reviewed the Learning Center Tutorials contents
- Researched with the QuickBooks Help
- Practiced Year-End Guide
- Processed financial statements

Additional Financial activities:

- No financial activities were performed in this chapter

Index

A

A/P Aging, 309
A/R & sales graphs, 156
A/R Aging, 309
Access Finance Charge, 160
Account Activities, 310
Accountant & Taxes, 320
Accountant's Copy, 25
Accounting, 54
Accounts Payable Graph, 224
Accounts Receivable Graph, 191
Accumulated Depreciation, 88
Add Credit Card Processing, 158
Add Job, 160
Add Window to Icon Bar, 73
Adding and using QuickBooks accounts, 336
Adjust Quality/Value on Hand, 199
Adjust Quantity, 128
Adjust Tax, 73
Admin, 131
Administrative, 109
Advanced Find, 41, 52
Advanced Services Administration, 125
Alerts Manager, 127
Annual Salary, 238
Assess Finance Charges, 158
Asset, 119
Assets and Assets, 148
Assets and Equity, 147
Assets and Expenses, 148
Assets and Income, 148
Assets and Liabilities, 148
Automobile Expenses, 119

B

Back Up, 27
Balance Sheet, 309
Bank, 87
Bank Debit Card, 114
Bank Reconciliation, 287
Bank Statement, 285
Banking, 304, 307, 319
Banking menu, 270, 324
Bills, Items & Inventory, 55
Bonus, 239, 246, 256
Budget, 307
Budgets, 138, 304, 310, 322
Business Structures, 77
Business Taxes, 78
Business Truck, 106
Buying and selling inventory, 337

C

Calculator, 41
Cascade, 332
Cash Flow, 309
Change Account Color, 44
Change Item Price, 156, 159
Chapter Summary, 22
Chart of Accounts, 14, 42, 83, 127, 128, 183, 279
Check, 52
Check Register, 129
Checking Preferences, 56
Class List, 84
Class List:, 84
Click Banking Menu, 291
Click Reconcile, 291
Close All, 331, 332
Close Company, 25
Commission, 239, 256
Commission & Bonus, 239
Company & Financial, 20, 34, 304, 306, 311
Company Information, 129, 130
Company menu, 33, 129
Company Preferences, 66
Compensation, 240
Construction, 112
Contract, 113
Control Panel, 13
Convert Quicken into QuickBooks, 23
Copy, 42
Copy Check, 44
Copy Last Sheet, 253
Corporation, 77
Cost of Goods Sold, 93, 101
Create a statement, 336
Create an invoice, 336
Create Bank Accounts, 16
Create Credit Memo/Refunds, 160
Create Credit Memo/Refunds:, 158
Create Credit Memos/Refunds, 156
Create Estimates, 157, 160

Create Invoice, 157, 160
Create Liability Account, 17
Create New Check, 47
Create New Company, 15
Create Purchase Order, 201, 203
Create Sales Receipts, 128
Create Statements, 158, 160
Credit Card, 89
Credit Card Account, 89
Custom Summary Report, 308
Custom Transaction Detail Report., 308
Customer, 310
Customer & Job tab, 159
Customer & Receivable, 314
Customer & Receivables, 304, 306
Customer & Vendor Profile, 114
Customer & Vendor Profile Lists, 82, 84
Customer Balance on PDF, 193
Customer Center, 29, 157, 161
customer center contents, 156
Customer Information, 160
customer jobs, 156
Customer Type List, 111
Customers, 14, 18, 19, 29, 125, 128, 156, 157, 159, 161, 172, 174, 176, 177, 178, 179, 181, 182, 185, 186, 187, 194, 195, 226, 228, 290, 309, 314, 336, 341
Customers menu, 190
Customers Menu, 156
Customers submenus, 156
Customize Columns, 160, 234
Customize Icon Bar, 72, 73
Customize sales forms, 336
Cut, 42

D

Deduction, 242
Delete a check, 41
Delete Bill w/o Payment, 221
Delete Bill with Payment, 222, 223
Delete Check, 43, 53
Delete Company, 35
Delete Employee, 234
Dental Insurance, 242, 244
Deposit Payments, 183
Depreciate Your Assets, 126
Depreciation, 150
Designing Financial Report, 98
Desktop, 27
Duplicate checks, 292
Duplicate Checks, 296

E

Edit, 73
Edit Account, 88
Edit Admin's Passwords, 134
Edit Check, 43
Edit Check Register, 274
Edit Customer, 159
Edit Customer: Job, 160
Edit Employee, 234
Edit menu, 42, 47, 48, 49, 51, 59, 74
Edit menu., 190
Edit Notes, 159, 202, 234
Edit User's Password, 132
Edit Vendor, 202, 203
EFT Electronic Funds Transfer, 114
Employee, 111, 310
Employee Center, 232
Employee Default, 234
Employee Setup, 231
Employees, 307
Employees & Payroll, 304, 318
Employees menu, 235, 256
Employees tab, 234
Employer Identification Number, 78
Employment Tax Record Keeping, 80
Employment Taxes, 79
End Balance, 291
Enter and deposit customer payments, 336
Enter Bill for Received Inventory, 210
Enter Bill for Received Items, 203
Enter Bill from Received Items, 201
Enter bills, 337
Enter Bills, 128, 203
Enter Credit Card, 270
Enter Credit Card Changes, 267
Enter Credit Card Charges, 129, 203
Enter Inventory for Received Bill, 199
Enter Office Bill, 199
Enter Opening Balance, 87
Enter Sales Receipts, 157, 160
Enter Statement Changes, 160
Enter Statement Charges, 157
Enter Time, 128, 158, 232, 234
Enter Vehicle Mileage, 124, 127
Equity, 89, 119
Equity Accounts, 89
Error of Commission, 294
Error of Commission:, 292
Error of Multiple Mistakes, 292, 295
Error of Omission, 292, 294
Error of Transposition, 292, 295
Estimates, 128, 171

Excel, 159
Excise Tax, 79
Exit, 27
Exit main window, 10
Exit sub window, 10
Expense, 119
Export, 31
Export IIF Files, 31
Export Reports to Excel, 35

F

Fate's Pay Stubs, 258
Federal, 243
Federal Unemployment, 243
Federal Unemployment., 260
Federal Withholding, 260
File menu, 27, 29, 31, 32, 33
Filter By, 202
Finance Charge Preferences, 58
finance charges, 156
Finance Charges, 179
Financial Services., 112
Find, 45, 52, 160, 203, 234
Fixed Asset Item List, 106
Flat View, 160
Floppy, 13
Fuel, 119

G

General, 59
General Journal Entry, 286
General Preferences, 59
Generate a sales receipt, 336
Go To Register, 273
Go To Transfer, 44

H

Health Insurance, 242, 244
Helpful Hints, 4
Hierarchical View, 160
Home Page, 33, 125
Hourly Wages., 237

I

Icon Bar, 72
IIF Files, 32
Import, 32
Import IIF Files, 32
Income, 119
Income & Expense Graph, 313
Income & Expenses, 309
Income Accounts, 90
Income Sub accounts, 91
Income Tax, 78, 310
Installation, 113
Installation Tips, 12
Insurance, 112, 119, 241
Integrated App & Service Connection, 59
Integrated Applications, 60
Interest Earned, 291
Introducing the Customer Center, 336
Introducing Vendor Center, 337
Inventory, 307, 318
Inventory Accounts, 92
Inventory Activities, 201
Inventory Adjustment, 219
Inventory Asset, 100, 101, 150
Inventory Items, 100
Inventory Part, 100
Inventory Supplies, 150
Inventory Valuation, 310
Inventory with Bill, 208
Inventory without Bill, 209
Invoices, 128, 173
Item List, 31, 83, 101, 159, 201
Items, 336
Items & Services, 128

J

Jerry's Pay Stubs, 259
Job & Mileage Reimbursement, 240
Job & Profitability, 309
Job Estimates, 309
Job Expense: Materials, 102
Job Expenses, 93, 94
Job, Time & Mileage, 315
Jobs, 306
Jobs & Estimates, 61
Jobs, Time & Mileage, 304

L

Labor Items, 103
Learn About Payroll, 234
Learning Center, 335
Learning Center Tutorial, 335
Liability, 119
Limited Liability Company, 77
List, 308, 323
Listing, 310
Lists, 309

Lists menu, 31, 33, 42, 49, 111, 114
Lists to IIF Files, 31
Loan Calculator, 282
Loan Manager, 266, 268
Loan Manager-Account, 280
Loan Manager-Lender, 281
Loan Manager-Loan, 283
Local backup, 27

M

Make Customer: Job Inactive, 160
Make Deposit, 266
Make Deposit:, 268
Make Deposits, 156, 160
Make Entry, 46
Make General Journal Entries, 127
Make Vendor Inactive, 203
Manage Payroll Items, 233, 259, 260
Marketing Tools, 128
Markup Income, 91
Materials, 100
Maximize main window, 10
Maximize QuickBooks, 34
Maximize sub window, 10
Measure Profitability, 126
Medicare, 243
Memorize Check, 48, 49
Memorize Check:, 43
Memorized Reports, 304, 305
Memorized Transaction List, 115
Memorized Transaction List:, 84
Menu bar, 9
Merging Accounts, 96
Merging Main Accounts, 98
Merging Sub accounts, 97
Mileage, 309
Mileage Reimbursement, 240
Minimize Calculator, 51
Minimize main window, 9
Minimize sub window, 10
Money Market Account, 87
Month-End Journal Entries, 149
Mortgage Interest Expense, 281
Multiple Reports, 311

N

Navigating Register, 11
Navigation Tips, 5
New Check, 43, 47
New Company, 29
New Construction, 113
New Customer, 29, 30, 159
new customers, 156
New Employee, 233, 234
New Transaction, 159, 202
New Vendor, 19, 202, 203
Non Inventory Part, 101
Non Profit Tax Exempt, 107
Non Taxable Sales, 65
Non-inventory Accounts, 94
Non-inventory Items, 101
Non-Taxable Labor, 108
Notepad, 44

O

One/Multiple Windows, 72
Online Banking, 268
Open a company file, 30
Open Company, 23, 30
Open or Restore, 28
Open or Restore Company, 24, 30, 31
Open Previous Company, 24, 32
Open Purchase Orders, 310
Open Register, 74
Open Window List, 9, 72
Opening Balance Expense, 91
Order Checks & Envelopes, 267
Other Expense, 119
Other Expenses Accounts, 95
Other Income, 119
Other Names List, 84, 109, 268
Other Names List:, 84
Overhead, 109
Overtime, 236
Overtime Hourly, 237, 246
Overview QuickBooks accounts, 336
Owners Contribution, 90
Owners Distribution, 90
Owners Draw, 90
Owners Equity, 90
Owners Retained Earnings, 89

P

Paid Time Off Report, 234
Partnership, 77
Paste, 43
Pay bills, 337
Pay Bills, 128, 200, 203
Pay Employees, 256
Pay Inventory Bill, 199
Pay Jerry Jordan, 255
Pay Office Bill, 199

Pay Operating Expense Bill, 213
Pay Payroll Liabilities, 260
Pay Sales Tax, 199
Paying employees, 337
Payment Method List, 113, 114
Payments, 182
Payroll, 150, 232, 310
Payroll & Employee Preference, 62
Payroll & Employee Preferences, 231
Payroll and Compensation Info, 246
Payroll Expense, 237, 238, 239
Payroll Forms, 233
Payroll Item List, 84
Payroll Liabilities., 242
Payroll overview, 337
Payroll Summary, 234
Payroll tab, 234
Payroll Transaction Detail, 234
Payroll w/o Subscription, 235
Planning & Budgeting, 126
Preferences, 45, 59, 60, 61
Prepaid Expenses, 150, 151
Prepare an estimate, 336
Prepare Letters with Envelopes, 127
Price Level List, 84, 106
Print, 26, 129, 159, 181, 184, 201, 202, 204, 218, 220, 221, 233, 267, 271, 272, 274, 276, 278, 279, 304, 312, 325, 326
Print Batch Checks, 272
Print Form, 26
Print Pay Stubs, 257
Print Setup, 26
Print Single Checks, 271
Process Multiple Reports, 304
Profit & Loss, 34, 309
Profit & Loss Standard, 34, 116
Purchase Order, 207
Purchase Orders, 128
Purchases, 307, 317
Purchases by Item, 310
Purchases by Vendor, 310

Q

Quick Company, 14
QuickBooks Help, 334
QuickBooks overview, 336
QuickBooks Window Parts, 8
QuickReport, 160, 202, 234, 304, 308

R

Receive Inventory, 128
Receive Inventory with Bill, 199
Receive Inventory without Bill, 199
Receive Item and Enter Bill, 201
Receive Items, 201, 203
Receive Items & Enter Bill, 203
Receive payments, 156
Receive Payments, 128, 158, 160, 190
Reconcile, 129, 268
Reconcile Bank Statements, 266
Reconciliation Process, 291
Record, 46, 48
Record Credit Card Charges, 266
Record Deposits, 129
Record Keeping, 79
Recurring Monthly Bills, 116
Refresh, 160, 203, 234
Refunds & Credits, 128
Register QuickReport, 266
Register Report, 266
Related Reimburse, 240
Reminders, 63, 126, 140
Remove Closing Date, 136
Repairs & Maint, 112
Repairs & Maintenance, 119
Report Center, 305
Reports, 336
Reports & Graphs, 64, 304
Reports menu, 34, 191, 195
Re-sort List, 160
Restore, 27
Revert, 42
Review Banking Submenus, 267
Review Company Journal Entries, 124
Review Company Menu, 125
Review Edit Menu, 41
Review Edit Submenus, 42
Review Help Menu, 334
Review Lists Submenus, 83
Review QuickBooks Learning Center, 334
Review Vendor Submenus, 200
Review View Submenus, 71
Review Window Menu, 331

S

S Corporation, 77
Salary, 238, 256
Sale Rep List, 111
Sales, 304, 306, 314
Sales & Customers, 61
Sales by Customer, 309
Sales by Item, 309
Sales by Rep, 309

Sales Graph, 192
Sales Receipt, 174
Sales Rep List, 110
Sales Tax, 65, 199, 200, 309
Sales Tax Code List, 107
Sales Tax Item, 65
Sales Tax Preferences, 64
Save as PDF, 26, 34
Save Copy or Backup, 25, 27
Save PDF, 23
Save Report as PDF, 34
Scientific, 51
Search, 44
Self-Employment Tax, 78
Send Forms, 26, 326
Service Charge, 291
Set Closing Date, 135
Set Closing Date:, 126, 127
Set Up Password, 131
Set Up Users & Passwords, 125
Shipping, 26
Show Estimates, 160
Show Full Customer List only, 160
Show Full Customer List Only, 203
Sick Hourly, 237, 238
Sick Pay, 237
Sick Salary, 238
Simple, 52
Simple Find, 41, 51
Social Security, 243
Sole Proprietorship, 29, 77
Sort Register, 276
Split Entry, 277
Splits, 277
Standard, 51
Starting a business, 77
Statement Charges, 128
Statement Date, 291
Statements, 128
Subcontractors, 94, 105, 112
Subcontractors Items, 104
SUI (Company Paid, 243
Summary, 152
Supplies, 102
Switch to Multi-user Mode, 25

T

Taskbar, 9
Tax Forms, 220
Tax Guidelines, 76
Tax: 1099, 66
Taxable Sales, 65
Taxes, 243
Templates, 84
This Fiscal Year, 35, 116
Tile Horizontally, 332
Tile Vertically, 332
Time, 309
Time & Expenses, 66
Time Tracking, 156, 252
Title bar, 9
To Do List, 124, 126
Tool bar or Icon Bar, 9
Total Assets, 38
Track and pay sales tax, 337
Track reimbursed, 66
Transaction, 159
Transaction History, 44, 304, 308
Transaction Journal, 304, 308
Transaction tab, 202, 234
Transfer from Checking, 109
Transfer from Payroll., 109
Transfer from Petty Cash, 109
Transfer Funds, 266, 268
Transfer to Checking, 109
Transfer to Payroll., 109
Transfer to Petty Cash., 109
Truck, 88
Truck Accounts, 87
TX-Unemployment, 244

U

Uncategorized Expense, 91
Uncategorized Income, 91
Undeposited Funds, 278
Undo, 42
US Treasury, 260
USA Checking, 74
Use, 160, 203, 234
Use Calculator, 44, 50, 51
Use Notepad, 49
Use Register, 44, 46, 73, 74, 160, 266, 267
Use Weekly Timesheet, 185, 252
Using reports to manage inventory, 337
Utilities, 25, 31, 32, 33, 112

V

Vacation Pay, 237
Vacation Salary, 238, 239
Vehicle Mileage, 142
Vendor, 310
Vendor Balance on PDF, 225
Vendor Balances, 309

Vendor Center, 200
Vendor Information, 203
Vendor tab, 202
Vendors, 14, 19, 66, 125, 128, 157, 200, 202, 203, 207, 208, 209, 210, 211, 212, 213, 214, 215, 216, 217, 219, 220, 226, 281, 304, 306, 309, 311, 316, 336, 337, 341
Vendors & Payables, 224, 316
Verify Data, 33
View, 51
View menu, 72, 73, 74
View Menu, 71
Visa, 114
Void a check, 41
Void Check, 43, 48

W

Wages, 152
Warn about duplicate, 61
Weekly Timesheet, 184
Word, 159
Write checks, 337
Write Checks, 129, 203, 266, 267
Wrong Journal entry, 292

Y

Year-End Guide, 335

Using QuickBooks Payroll with High Speed College Edition

This is one of the best books on how to use the QuickBooks Payroll software in the market today. In *Using QuickBooks Payroll with High Speed*, Emmanuel Ike, gives students practical steps on how to run a complete payroll cycle.

SOW Publishing

Please visit our website www.sowpublishing.com to see some of the books we published or in the process of being published. If you want catalog, price list, or information for classroom purchases, please e-mail us, sales@sowpublishing.com.

Our products include:

1. Using Quicken with High Speed
2. Using QuickBooks with High Speed Small Business
3. Using QuickBooks with High Speed College Edition
4. Using QuickBooks with High Speed School Edition
5. Using QuickBooks Payroll with High Speed College Edition
6. Using QuickBooks Payroll with High Speed School Edition
7. Using Excel With High Speed College Edition
8. Using Word With High Speed College Edition
9. How to repair your credit report

Printed in the United States
216828BV00003B/3/P